For Dick and Mary D.

with my gratitude and admiration.

Marty

YALE SERIES IN ECONOMIC HISTORY

The Fiscal System
of Renaissance France

BY MARTIN WOLFE

NEW HAVEN AND LONDON

YALE UNIVERSITY PRESS

1972

Published with assistance from
the Mary Cady Tew Memorial Fund.

Copyright © 1972 by Yale University.
All rights reserved. This book may not be
reproduced, in whole or in part, in any form
(except by reviewers for the public press),
without written permission from the publishers.
Library of Congress catalog card number: 72-75213
International standard book number: 0-300-01487-2

Designed by Sally Sullivan
and set in Linotype Electra type.
Printed in the United States of America by
Vail-Ballou Press, Inc., Binghamton, N.Y.

Published in Great Britain, Europe, and Africa by
Yale University Press, Ltd., London.
Distributed in Canada by McGill-Queen's University
Press, Montreal; in Latin America by Kaiman & Polon,
Inc., New York City; in Australasia and Southeast
Asia by John Wiley & Sons Australasia Pty. Ltd.,
Sydney; in India by UBS Publishers' Distributors Pvt.,
Ltd., Delhi; in Japan by John Weatherhill, Inc., Tokyo.

For Dorothy

Preface

One of my purposes in writing this book was to organize into a useful survey the appallingly large body of information and interpretation we possess on the fiscal system of Renaissance France. My hope was to make the book as self-contained as possible; this explains the brief passages on political affairs. It also explains the sketch of medieval taxation in the introductory chapter.

A problem faced by all writers on institutional history is that description of institutions often gets in the way of historical narrative, and vice versa. I tried to cope with this by placing the main descriptive materials in appendixes. My aim in chapters 2–8 is to give as clear an account as possible of the nature and significance of every important change in this complex set of institutions over the entire span of the fifteenth and sixteenth centuries. The appendixes are aimed at showing how the fiscal machine worked rather than how and why it changed. Appendixes A–F deal with the fiscal officials, and appendixes G–K with the main revenues.

I hope the appendixes will be read as well as referred to. They serve as more than a presentation of supplementary materials. Readers who are interested in French fiscal affairs in this era mainly for purposes of comparison with the Middle Ages or with the Old Régime—or with another country—may find the appendixes the more useful portion of this book.

A word on sources. On administrative matters I favored Renaissance treatises over modern ones, since modern writers often demonstrate an insufficient understanding of the more complex features of Renaissance fiscal procedure, whereas many Renaissance works (especially those of the later sixteenth century) were publications by experts trying to explain to their own contemporaries the workings of the fiscal machine. There are references in my study to documents in the manuscripts department of the Bibliothèque Nationale and at the Archives Nationales; but I consulted only those manuscripts needed to help me understand some obscure points. I spent a great deal of time with the royal edicts available at the Bibliothèque Nationale, the "Actes Royaux" catalogued by Albert Isnard. Whenever the edict in question is to be found adequately presented in Isambert or Fontanon, collections available in many libraries outside France, I cite these collections. Where the edict was located only in a collection published during the Renaissance, I cite the collection by the name of its publisher, since the editor rarely is given. Edicts cited without other reference were, for the most part, published separately during the Renaissance and can be located under the given date in Isnard.

Where necessary, dates in this study have been changed so as to count the new year from January 1 rather than from Easter (the calendar shift took place in France in 1564).

A brief discussion of the monetary system is given in appendix F along with the explanation of _billonage_. I have used _livre_ throughout the text to denote _livre tournois_. By the fifteenth century the _livre parisis_, an essentially local monetary unit reckoned as 1.25 _livres tournois_, had disappeared almost completely from government accounts.

This book is dedicated to my wife Dorothy, who, I hope, will remember the fun and the scholarly satisfactions it involved as well as the dreary hours of transcribing, typing, revising, and arguing over style and organization.

M. W.

Philadelphia
May 1971

Contents

1

Medieval and Renaissance
Fiscal Systems—A Perspective

Somewhere along the road from the first German barbarian invasions of the Roman empire to the anarchy of the ninth century there was a wide and deep break in tax history. We are not at all sure just when this break came. The uncertainty is a facet of the famous "Pirenne thesis" controversy, the problem of assigning a date to the end of Roman institutions and attitudes. It is clear, however, that during the sixth and seventh centuries the decay of cities and the increasing autonomy of great landlords were making it increasingly difficult for the Germanic kings to maintain the intricate Roman fiscal systems they had taken over. By the eighth century, government under the Frankish rulers was being paid for not by a centralized tax system but by a vast network of estates. Revenues—in goods and services rather than in money—were being collected from thousands of *villae* comprising the royal *fiscus,* the territories owned by the kings as landlords, not as heads of state.

There is an obvious cleavage, therefore, between Roman and early medieval tax history. The contrasts between the fiscal systems of the Dark Ages and the High Middle Ages, and those between medieval and early modern times, though significant, are less striking. A tax collector of Gaul in the fourth century A.D., suddenly propelled four centuries forward, would have had to seek other means of employment. On the other hand, if a manorial steward employed by Hugh Capet (987–996) had been transported by time machine to the days of Saint Louis (1226–70), he would probably have found little trouble continuing in the same profession. Can we say the same of an additional three-century jump, that is, from the days of Saint Louis to those of Francis I (1515–47)? One of the purposes of this introductory chapter is to demonstrate that this is not the case.

Some scholars profess an inability to see important qualitative differences between medieval and Renaissance government in general, and fiscal affairs in particular. Thus G. R. Elton says, "There was no 'new monarchy' round about 1500: only, for the moment, more favourable conditions for the old policies of kings. The monarchies of Francis I and Henry VIII differed in very few essentials from those of Philip IV and Edward I. . . ." Joseph Schumpeter claims that "until the bureaucracies had conquered the fiscal stronghold of the Estates, the growing Leviathan had to be fed on old sources of revenue," a picturesque statement that gives a seriously distorted impression; and Herbert Heaton falls into this trap when he says, "To meet the growing military and civilian expenditures, the national governments of the sixteenth century still relied largely on the revenue system of a feudal state." Even Gustave Dupont-Ferrier, who was a specialist in fiscal history and should have known better, agrees that "with old materials, the crown cleverly constructed a new financial organism." [1]

The terms of our problem can be stated quite simply. Were differences between medieval and Renaissance taxation slight enough to allow us to disregard them, or at least to claim that the fiscal organization appears essentially the same over this entire span? Or were there indeed changes, but changes that should be thought of as modifications, so that while the fiscal system did evolve, its main features at the beginning are still manifestly visible at the end of this span? Or did the era produce an abrupt, sweeping alteration in the ways of paying for government, as during the French Revolution? Or, finally, were the changes, while perhaps not revolutionary, still important enough to predicate a discontinuity—that is, a set of institutions and attitudes so different from those of a prior period that the new situation could not have come about through the accretion of small changes or "mere evolution"? [2] This last position, I feel, is the correct one.

1. G. R. Elton, *Reformation Europe 1517–1559* (London, 1963), p. 299; Joseph Schumpeter, *History of Economic Analysis* (New York, 1954), p. 201; Herbert Heaton, *Economic History of Europe*, rev. ed. (New York, 1948), p. 226; Gustave Dupont-Ferrier, *Etudes sur les institutions financières de la France à la fin du moyen âge*, 1 : 59. Cf. Joseph Reese Strayer, *On the Medieval Origins of the Modern State* (Princeton, 1970), pp. 91–92: "Neither administrative gimmicks nor military power explain the success of the sixteenth-century state. Intelligent use of existing resources and increased cooperation between rulers and subjects were the essential ingredients of the 'New Monarchies.' "

2. This definition is essentially the same as that of Alexander Gerschenkron, *Continuity in History and Other Essays* (Cambridge, Mass., 1968), pp. 33–35,

Paradoxically, one reason the dimensions of the contrast between medieval and Renaissance taxation are difficult to perceive is the enormous amount of high-caliber scholarship devoted to the earlier era. It is not merely that the main features of medieval taxation have been thoroughly discussed; even relatively slight scraps of medieval records have been transcribed and evaluated with the expertise only graduates of the Paris Ecole des Chartes can provide. Volumes of fragmentary medieval tax accounts have been published at the expense of the French government. Foreign scholars, too, have contributed to the large library of great works on small facets of French medieval taxation. To put it mildly, this effort has not been matched by studies on Renaissance taxation—perhaps because Renaissance scholars everywhere seem to favor cultural over institutional history. Despite the fact that our records of Renaissance taxation are more voluminous than those for any comparably long era during the Middle Ages, recent monographs on Renaissance taxation have been scanty. Our knowledge of medieval taxation, therefore, is much more advanced.

This outpouring of works on medieval taxation has been part of a great flowering of all phases of medieval scholarship since World War I. As a result of their deepening understanding of their period, medievalists have found it easy to overturn older notions. During the nineteenth and early twentieth centuries, scholars imagined there had actually been a "Renaissance," a rebirth of practically everything worthwhile; and they coupled this notion with absurd misconceptions regarding the supposed stagnation of medieval life. Today we know that during the Middle Ages remarkable progress was being made in science, business affairs, technology, art and architecture, and some branches of government. We also realize that several aspects of medieval life were extended with little change into the sixteenth century and later.

Unfortunately—as is often the case with revisionist efforts—the pendulum has swung too far in the other direction. The revisionists have raised a widespread attack against the older idea that Renaissance government can be characterized as a "new monarchy." Thanks to

---

where he discusses "kinks" in the rates of growth in industrial output. My definition depends, of course, on acceptance of historical periods as valid objects of comparative study. For a good discussion of this problem, see Robert C. Stalnaker, "Events, Periods, and Institutions in Historians' Language," *History and Theory* 6, no. 2 (1967).

their derisive rejection of the older belief that there was a fundamental
change in the functions and powers of kingship during the late fifteenth
and sixteenth centuries, we no longer accept the naïve view that kings
during the Renaissance wiped the slate clean and drew a new picture
entitled "modern absolutism." But this should not allow us to toss
aside the "new monarchy" concept altogether. In particular, to argue
that fiscal affairs changed only slightly during the Renaissance would
be to commit an error of the same proportion as to maintain that the
Renaissance fiscal system was entirely new.

At this point it would be satisfying to be able to turn to the methods
of comparative history and to select an appropriate technique for comparing the fiscal system of the Middle Ages to that of the sixteenth
century. Unfortunately, "the methods of comparative history" is only
an empty phrase; and an appropriate comparative methodology, if
one ever appears, is not likely to be available in the near future. We
must rely, therefore, on informal, commonsense confrontations of the
main characteristics involved. We can begin by sketching the features
of fiscal affairs during the reign of Saint Louis, paying particular attention to categories such as the nature of the revenues, constitutional
relations (that is, the tax power of the ruler), and fiscal administration.
Then we can compare these characteristics to certain features of the
reign of Francis I. Finally we shall have to take account of the many
important changes in taxing during the late Middle Ages (that is, the
fourteenth century), to see whether our conclusions would be different
if we were to base our comparison, say, on the 1350s rather than the
1250s.

The most striking feature of royal revenues in the days of Saint
Louis is their antiquity.[3] Almost all of them had been used since the
eleventh century, and some of them were much older. Several were
actually shards of the Carolingian fiscal system; most, however, seem to
have been created during the Dark Ages to support the hundreds of

3. For general accounts of fiscal history during the High Middle Ages, see Ferdi-
nand Lot and Robert Fawtier, *Histoire des institutions françaises au moyen âge*;
Joseph Reese Strayer, *The Administration of Normandy under Saint Louis*;
J.-J. Clamageran, *Histoire de l'impôt en France*, vol. 1; Lot and Fawtier, *Le
premier budget de la monarchie française*; and Bryce D. Lyon and A. E. Verhulst,
Medieval Finance: A Comparison of Financial Institutions in Northwestern Europe.

warrior landlords controlling France, the seigneurs.[4] We can only guess when or where such revenues first appeared. When the first scraps of records after the Dark Ages allow us to form some picture of the fiscal process, we see a surprisingly large number of these revenues diffused throughout the seigneuries of France. Whereas their value, of course, depended on the size and wealth of the various domains, the nature of the revenues was about the same whether they were accruing to a relatively petty seigneur, to a count or duke in charge of a feudal principality, or to Saint Louis himself.

These conglomerations of more or less petty revenues included only a few items we would regard as taxation in the sense of regular, obligatory contributions by the French for the expenses of royal government, as well as for the king's personal and household needs. Most of them, rather, seem more like rents, fees, fines, or licenses.

I use the plural term *domaines* throughout this study to show I mean all these older patrimonial and prerogative revenues, the fees and dues (whether from lands held directly by the king or those of his vassals), as well as the rents and income from the sale of produce. These quasi-proprietarial revenues, plus seigneurial taxes such as *tailles* and tolls, were called *domaines* or *ordinaires* during the late Middle Ages and early Renaissance to distinguish them from the newer *impositions* or *extraordinaires*. In the English language there is no convenient term for this bundle of older revenues, since "domains" in English refers to territories. "Ordinary revenues" cannot be used to translate *ordinaires*, since the terms *ordinaires* and *extraordinaires* underwent fundamental transformations during the Renaissance, as we shall see.

Among the king's most important seigneurial-style revenues was the *champart*, a rent in the form of a share of the crops. Although the burden of the champart declined during the Middle Ages, it was still worth between a twentieth and a sixth of the crop in various parts of the royal domain during the Renaissance.[5] Another fee, the *cens*, was paid by free peasants on manorial tenures and by burghers on town lots and buildings; but its value had been fixed in money terms and

---

4. Carl Stephenson, "The Origin and Nature of the Taille," in his *Medieval Institutions*, pp. 99–103.

5. Roger Doucet, *Les institutions de la France au XVIe siècle*, 2 : 476–77.

therefore had shrunk with the decline in the purchasing power of money during the High Middle Ages. By the mid-thirteenth century, the cens was really a quitrent, more valuable as proof of the lord's right to extract inheritance fees and other dues than for the money it brought in by itself.[6] Free peasants who held *censives*, for example, had to pay *relief*—often a whole year's income—when these lands passed to an heir. And when a censive was sold outside a tenant's family, another substantial fine was exacted: *lods et ventes*, worth between 3 and 12 percent of the holding's total value. If the tenancy involved in a sale was a noble fief rather than a censive, the overlord could exact a *quint*, presumably one-fifth the purchase price.

A relatively important group of village revenues was the *banalités*, fees on those economic functions which were monopolized by the king as seigneur. All grain, for example, had to be turned into flour at the lord's mills; all grapes had to be pressed at his presses; all bread had to be baked in the seigneurial ovens; all iron tools had to be made and repaired at the lord's forge.

Another set of seigneurial dues was that drawn from men classed as serfs. Serfs paid *chevage*, a small poll tax; *formariage*, a fine for marrying out of the king's domains; and *mainmorte*, a cruel fee exacted when a serf died without a son on the manor, in which case the steward appropriated what he regarded as the most valuable tools, animals, or other property of the serf's family. On the other hand, free peasants and serfs alike paid regular labor dues ("week work") and had other working obligations during harvests or emergencies such as war time.

Royal justice also brought the king profits from court costs and fines from wrongdoers. In addition, every contract entered into by subjects of a ruler had to bear the lord's seal; when the notary affixed this seal he also collected a fee. These "incidents of justice and of the seal" could be only a few pence each; but they were collected often and were jealously guarded by royal magistrates.

The medieval local taille requires a word of explanation, since it is a quite different affair from the taille with which most of us are familiar: the taille of the Renaissance and the Old Régime. Originally, the seigneurial taille had been a harsh and arbitrary levy, the chief device

6. *The Cambridge Economic History of Europe*, 1 : 329; William M. Newman, *Le domaine royal sous les premiers Capétiens* (Paris, 1937), p. 6 and n. 1.

by which the lords forced their subjects (both townsmen and peasants) to meet that part of their expenses not covered by regular rents and dues.[7] Even in the High Middle Ages, therefore, the taille had more of the flavor of a tax than did other seigneurial revenues. The word itself, it should be noted, does not mean a particular kind of tax but rather a method of taxing, that is, affixing each man's portion (taille) of the lump sum needed. The rise of towns after the tenth century meant that more peasants became involved in market activities, so that they could pay some taxes in cash. With cash in their purses, village leaders learned how to haggle for a lower and less arbitrary taille. Eventually, where one found villages still suffering under arbitrary tallaging they were almost always village of serfs.[8] Many towns and even whole districts of villages compacted for ending the taille by agreeing to pay an annual fixed sum, an arrangement known as *taille abonnée*.[9]

A quite different category of royal revenue was that derived from commerce. At fairs, the king received exhibitors' fees (*stallage*) from traveling merchants, plus several lucrative license fees, including those for money changers servicing the fairs. In towns, the king's agents collected entry duties (*tonlieux, barrages, coutumes*). On the highways, especially at fords, bridges, and points of exit from the royal domain, the king collected tolls and export duties. And in his royal mints, the king exacted a few pennies in the pound as his *seignorage*, a term from seigneurial times still in use today.

A small amount of money came to the king from nobles and prelates in the royal domain and from the king's vassals. Some dues that a seigneur could exact from his subjects, a king could take from his vassals: an example is the *droit de gîte*, the obligation of hospitality, which could cost a vassal dear if his king liked to travel often and with a large retinue. Fiefs could escheat to the king when a vassal's family died out. The king could add the fief to his own holdings or bestow it

---

7. Clamageran, *L'impôt*, 1 : 201.

8. Paying arbitrary tailles, however, was not in itself regarded as proof of servile status, as was the payment of *formariage, chevage,* or *mainmorte*. Marc Bloch, *Rois et serfs* (Paris, 1920), p. 26.

9. In some portions of the royal domain the taille disappeared completely by the time of the Hundred Years' War. Guy Fourquin, *Le domaine royal en Gâtinais d'après la prisée de 1332* (Paris, 1963), p. 52.

on another vassal; in the latter case, such a grantee would be expected to reciprocate with a large monetary gift. When a fief was up for sale the king had the right to substitute himself as purchaser. This right was known as *retrait féodale*. It would be exercised when the king reckoned that income from the fief was especially valuable.

Another of the king's revenues was based on his right to call out all vassals and tenants for military service. The king "raised the host" by proclaiming the *ban et arrière-ban;* that is, he issued a call for all who could serve as warriors, his direct vassals as well as their own vassals (who were the suzerain's rear [*arrière*] vassals), plus the king's noble and more important nonnoble tenants from the royal domain. These warriors had to appear at a specified time and place with the number of knights and fighting men appropriate to each vassal's or tenant's station.

Because warfare was becoming a more specialized affair during the High Middle Ages, the king had to use professional soldiers, as well as the often untrustworthy "feudal host." He employed permanent household guards, and on occasion he hired mercenaries on a month-to-month basis. He also tried to assure himself of dependable soldiers by supporting poorer nobles on his domains; some of these were given land fiefs, others were paid with money fiefs.[10] Therefore, the king often preferred money rather than personal service from those subject to the ban et arrière-ban. Such payments were especially urged from rear-vassals unless they had the reputation of being great warriors. Now the earlier rather vague obligations of vassals and tenants were replaced by a careful spelling out of their military obligations. Towns and even villages were required to pay *aide de l'ost.*

Some petty and irregular income also came to the king from the church. Several cathedral towns and monasteries were under the king's direct protection, often as the result of a quarrel between the religious establishment and the local lord. When the king became the military protector of a bishopric or abbacy, he often obtained a fraction of its revenues—for example, half the tailles in the villages it controlled. More important was the prerogative known as *régale*, the prince's right to all the revenues of any "vacant" religious establishment, that is, one without a properly nominated and confirmed prelate. This often repre-

10. Bryce D. Lyon, *From Fief to Indenture,* pp. 198 ff., 270, and passim.

sented a valuable windfall, since many ecclesiastical bodies were wealthy; and some kings (though not the uprighteous Saint Louis) on occasion scandalized public opinion by contriving to keep positions open as long as possible.

Finally there is a miscellaneous group of petty revenues which, like the *régale*, can be thought of as windfalls: the king's rights over shipwrecks, treasure troves, strays, the goods of deceased foreigners (*aubaine*), and the property of illegitimates dying without legal heirs (*bâtardise*). The Jews, also, were a source of income from licenses to function as merchants and usurers, from fines for permission to live in the royal domain, and of course from the repeated seizure—until 1394, when they were finally expelled—of their goods and their claims over debtors.

One of the most revealing insights into the nature of the medieval fiscal system is the famous dictum requiring the king to "live of his own" (*vivre du sien*). Men of the thirteenth century were strongly of the opinion that the king should *not* tax, that he should limit himself —except during emergencies—to his traditional, patrimonial, and prerogative revenues of the sort just discussed.

Strange as it may seem to us, this attitude included the belief that income from the domaines should be sufficient not only for the king's personal and household needs but also for the expenses of government. If the king's expenses proved higher than his income, he was expected first to resort to expedients such as mortgaging his lands and pawning his jewels. Only then could he come to his subjects and his vassals for aid. Even when a king made a reasonable-sounding appeal for a subsidy he was likely to be met by much grumbling among persons who wondered why he had not been providential enough to amass a war chest during relatively good times. And he was not allowed simply to appropriate other men's property; he was expected, rather, to consult them and to obtain their assent by giving them adequate reasons, since —in the words of another medieval dictum—"that which affects all should be consented to by all." In some cases, it is true, help was supposed to be forthcoming without much question: for example, in situations calling for feudal aid, when the king knighted a son, married off a daughter, went on a crusade, or was captured in battle. Otherwise, even if the king's need arose out of a great undertaking for the benefit of France as a whole, his appeal might well be rejected by some of his vassals and towns, or he might have to resort to hard bargaining and many compromises. That the king should "live of his own" was an important constitutional concern for thirteenth-century France, and not an empty formula. Taxing in the modern sense—and in the manner by which most revenues were raised during the Renaissance—was regarded in the thirteenth century as a quite exceptional affair, one that had to be ringed about with many restrictions.

Since government during the thirteenth century was becoming a much more costly affair, these limitations on royal tax power frequently placed the king in a desperate position. France's merchants and craftsmen were growing richer and her peasant population was increasing rapidly; but the domaines revenues were not flexible enough for the king to use them in obtaining a proportional share of this rising national wealth. If France had possessed a national parliament capable of frequent convocations, she would have had a mechanism for meeting the king's increasing need for aid. But France's first Estates-General, the first convocation of prelates, nobles, and burghers comparable to England's already well-established Parliament, had to wait until 1302; and, in fact, a national assembly did not really become important in royal fiscal affairs until the 1330s. It was not until the end of the thirteenth century that France experienced what we would call national imposts, in spite of an obvious need for them—at least from the king's point of view.

The first timid steps toward national taxation were the clerical tenths (*décimes*), also called "crusader tithes." Such taxes seem to have been collected twice during the previous century, on the occasion of the Second and Third Crusades (1147 and 1188). What little we know of the levy in 1188 indicates that it fell on nobles and townsmen as well as clerics, except of course those who took the cross and went off to fight in the Holy Lands. However, by the reign of Saint Louis, the tenths fell mainly on clerical benefices.[11] These levies were subject to

---

11. On the early tenths, see Lot and Fawtier, *Histoire*, 1 : 102, 107; Achille Luchaire, *Manuel des institutions françaises: période des Capétiens directs* (Paris, 1892), pp. 579, 581; Clamageran, *L'impôt*, 1 : 279, 288; and Georges Picot, *Histoire des Etats Généraux*, 1 : 132.

papal approval and to at least formal consent by assemblies of French prelates; and the church insisted on maintaining the posture that such levies were free, voluntary grants or *dons gratuits*, a term that in the Renaissance came to be used interchangeably with *décimes*. Saint Louis was able to obtain many grants of tenths; and other kings cajoled the church into granting tenths for reasons that had little to do with the good of the faith, let alone with crusades. When the government desperately needed additional money the clergy might be persuaded to vote double or even triple tenths; and in 1284 Philip III managed to have himself awarded four.[12]

A point-by-point comparison of royal revenues and tax power in the mid-thirteenth and the mid-sixteenth centuries demonstrates that what stands out is not the similarities but the differences. Under Francis I, more than nine-tenths of the royal income came not from the domaines but from sources clearly recognizable as taxes. Clerical tenths, too, became annual affairs and can be viewed as taxes in all but the most formal sense. Emergency expenditures were met by issuing royal bonds, by squeezing the vast horde of fiscal officials, and by selling additional venal offices, as well as by large-scale borrowing from Italian merchant-bankers and others attached to the rapidly developing money market at Lyons. Coinage and coin debasement were virtually eliminated as sources of revenue.

Francis I was able to impose heavy and diverse national taxes without the consent of the taxed, and he could increase the burden of individual revenues without popular consent. This tax power was monopolized; that is, the French nobility, except in a few fiefs, had lost its power to tax—though seigneurs still collected their traditional revenues. In the days of Saint Louis, the king's traditional resources (plus his ability to request subsidies) were looked on as imposing tight boundaries on the scope of his actions, whereas in the Renaissance the king's attitude seemed to be that the fiscal system must respond satisfactorily to whatever demands were placed on it—by dynastic, military, or political needs. And these are only the more obvious points of contrast, as one can see in chapter 3 and appendixes G–K.

12. Clamageran, *L'impôt*, 1 : 288.

The fact that the thirteenth-century French monarchy managed not only to keep on its feet but also to extend its domain, therefore, had little to do with the nature of its revenues or the strength of its tax power. This is even more true for the caliber of its fiscal administration. Until well into the High Middle Ages, royal fiscal affairs were still carried on in the spirit of estate management, that is, stewardship in the seigneurial tradition. In fact, the key revenue agents were still the stewards and castellans of the king's manors and castles. These were the men who had primary responsibility for managing the king's properties and for amassing the small amounts of surplus cash that could be used for provincial affairs or shipped to the king. It is true that manorial revenues during these years were managed on a more businesslike basis.[13] Most of the more important local revenues were "farmed out" to enterprisers, who received the right to collect the domaines in return for lump sum payments. Amounts in excess of this sum became the revenue farmers' profits; and, if they collected less than the amounts paid, it was their loss—not the king's.

It is true, also, that beginning in the twelfth century there was an improvement in middle-echelon management. At the district level, for areas about the size of a diocese—and for some purposes in the towns —the king now employed provosts (*prévôts*) to act as combination sheriffs and overseers of the revenues. In the towns, and on the main river routes and highways, the king maintained "masters of ports and passages" for his tolls; and revenues from royal wood, game, and other rights in the forests now were given over to the care of royal wardens. In the provinces and more important districts, Saint Louis was able to look to the powerful bailiffs (*baillis*) and seneschals for financial management, as well as for supervising the royal military forces and keeping the king's peace. Bailiffs checked up on the proper granting of revenue farms at the local and district levels and at times took on the job of awarding the more valuable contracts themselves. Certain important, nonrecurring revenues such as *franc-fief*, feudal aid, and emergency subsidies were controlled directly by the bailiffs rather than being farmed out or left in the hands of the provosts. Bailiffs were especially vigilant concerning the king's rights in the rapidly growing towns. They often

13. Lyon and Verhulst, *Medieval Finance*, pp. 49–52; Joseph Strayer, *The Royal Domain in the Bailliage of Rouen* (Princeton, 1936).

intervened in municipal government in the name of the king; thus an interesting development in self-government, which had been visible during the twelfth century, now faltered and disappeared. The cities of medieval France had less control over their internal affairs than those of other major countries of Western Europe.

The most salient feature of thirteenth-century fiscal administration was its lack of specialization. While collecting the king's revenues was, of course, an important part of the duties of these stewards, provosts, bailiffs, and wardens, it was far from being their only function. Almost all of them played additional roles in justice, military affairs, and general administration. Therefore the term "revenue official" applies to them only in a limited sense.

We can also characterize this system as decentralized in its very essence. The work of the royal officials—or rather that part of their work which was applied to revenue administration—was sharply bounded by local jurisdictions, local outlooks, and even local loyalties. Away from the king's court there were no regular officials entirely committed to protection of the king's monetary rights; all that Saint Louis could do (and this was a daring innovation) was to send out itinerant inspectors from time to time who, among their other duties, could investigate charges of graft, mismanagement, or wrongful appropriation made against revenue collectors. It was easy for the king's nobles, especially those in distant territories, to appropriate a share of the king's revenues. Vassals outside the royal domain, of course, possessed almost completely independent fiscal systems of their own, and were involved with the fiscal problems of the king only when questions of subsidies, coinage rights, or clerical tenths were raised. Even bailiffs inside the royal domain were notorious for using the revenue system for themselves and their families more than for the crown.

In spite of the king's need for more efficient central revenue agencies, medieval fiscal management had only a small and indistinct place at court. Here again, as at the local and provincial levels, control over revenues was tightly enmeshed with other functions. For various reasons, the chamberlain and the chancellor were also responsible for some control over expenditures and some responsibility for receipts—but there was no court official even remotely comparable to a finance minister. Indeed, there were no specialized upper-echelon fiscal officials whatsoever. The king, therefore, could have had only the haziest notion of the potential value of his revenues. While we know of a few lists of anticipated receipts as far back as 1202–03, they are a far cry from modern budgets or even the Renaissance *états généraux* [14] (see appendix D). For his household needs, as well as for military affairs, the king maintained money boxes and several clerks to take charge of them; such arrangements could hardly be called "treasuries." In fact, when the king needed really effective protection for his money, he deposited it with the Knights Templar, an order of warrior monks who combined banking with their religious interests. Because of their many "temples" in France, they were also able to provide the king with his only effective means for paying his creditors in distant parts of the country.

Under Saint Louis the fiscal system was not a pivotal, nor even a distinct, branch of government. In a sense it was submerged in the feudal relations between king and nobility and in certain features of manorial management. During the late Middle Ages, on the other hand, the fiscal aspects of government were not only exceedingly important in their own right, but often they appeared on the very center of the national stage. Repeatedly, they figured in crises of enormous proportions. Examples are the famous confrontation between Philip the Fair and Boniface VIII over the king's power to tax the church; the attempt by the Estates-General during the early 1350s to use the purse strings in order to shift the balance of power away from the king; the shock caused by new taxes and new officials needed to cope with the ransom for King John the Good (captured at the battle of Poitiers, 1356); the tax rebellions of 1382–83, including the uprising of the Paris *maillotins*; and the struggles over control of the royal revenues among the regents and grandees during the long unhappy reign of Charles VI (1380–1422), which culminated in outright civil war during the last phases of the Hundred Years' War.

Since the Valois monarchy did not collapse under the weight of these crises and emerged from the Hundred Years' War stronger than ever, one could guess that the government must somehow have found

14. Lot and Fawtier, *Le premier budget*; Robert Fawtier, ed., *Comptes du Trésor*, pp. v–lxiv.

enough additional revenues to cope with its fearsome combinations of enemies. In fact, the late Middle Ages witnessed a score of fundamental innovations in the areas of tax structure, tax power, and tax administration.[15] Such a contrast in the pace of change is sufficient in itself to mark off this era in fiscal history from that of the High Middle Ages. But should we regard the fiscal history of the late Middle Ages as bringing medieval tax history to a close? Or should it be thought of as the beginnings of Renaissance tax history? Here a confident answer is not easy to give. My own view is that for all its enduring innovations, the fourteenth century still shows so many contrasts with the Renaissance that it deserves to be regarded as a separate era in fiscal history.

This can be demonstrated in the area of fiscal administration by observing the shifts in the relative importance of the *trésoriers de France*. These were France's first high-level, specialized fiscal officials. They represent an innovation made by Philip the Fair, who needed a new treasury after he despoiled and suppressed the Knights Templar (1307–12). Philip could have solved this problem by enlarging the functions of his household treasury, the Chambre aux deniers, which guarded funds destined for the kitchen, the stables, the hunting establishment, and many petty expenditures such as gifts for foreign dignitaries. Instead he created a new and superior treasury, known simply as the Trésor.[16]

In charge of the Trésor were the *trésoriers*—two, three, or four of them at various times during the fourteenth century. The trésoriers were supervisory officials, not cashiers or accountants; the actual job of receiving cash and paying it out was handled by a *changeur du Trésor* and a group of clerks. The trésoriers operated out of Paris, but France's regions were divided into areas of special responsibility for

15. For general accounts of fiscal history during the late Middle Ages, see Maurice Rey, *Le domaine du roi et les finances extraordinaires sous Charles VI, 1388–1413*, and his *Les finances royales sous Charles VI: les causes du déficit, 1388–1413*; Joseph Reese Strayer and Charles H. Taylor, *Studies in Early French Taxation; The Cambridge Economic History of Europe*, 3 : 299–340, 472–92; John B. Henneman, Jr., "Financing the Hundred Years' War: Royal Taxation in France in 1340," *Speculum* 42, no. 2 (1967), "The Black Death and Royal Taxation in France, 1347–1351," *Speculum* 43, no. 3 (1968); and A. Vuity, *L'origine et l'établissement de l'impôt sous les trois premiers Valois (1328–1380)*.

16. L. L. Borrelli de Serres, *Recherches sur divers services publics du XIIIe au XVIIe siècle*, 3 : 88–89.

each of them. One usually traveled with the king, and they all had access to the king's ear, since they were, by right, members of the royal council.

While at first they functioned mainly to supervise receipts and expenditures, the trésoriers gradually came to have authority over the sources of such receipts, particularly the domaines. By the fifteenth century they could issue orders concerning the domaines to bailiffs and seneschals. They worked with other high officials to provide the crown with a sort of subcouncil for the direction of all royal revenues. But Francis I stripped the trésoriers of their high advisory powers. They were then forced out of central government and, after many changes in their functions, they were reduced to the level of provincial supervisors. As we shall see in chapter 3, the reforms of Francis I constitute a decisive break in the history of fiscal administration.

Another improvement in fiscal administration during the late Middle Ages was the gradual elaboration of a network of fiscal courts (see appendix C). First came the Chambre des comptes. In a sense this fiscal court can trace its origins back to the High Middle Ages, when the royal council provided itself with clerks and lawyers for the special task of examining the records of those who were spending the king's money. As royal finances became more complex, and the amount of paper work (and parchment work!) increased, experts in finance and accounting were attached to the royal council when it sat to formulate royal policy. Eventually, these special meetings of the council came to be regarded as a more or less regular subcouncil. Around 1320, the fiscal clerks and lawyers, plus some magistrates and accountants, were made independent of the royal council and given their own set of chambers. Almost immediately, it appears, the Chambre des comptes assumed supreme control over all fiscal accounts—all the records submitted by royal agents everywhere—including those from officials such as the provosts who were not limited to fiscal activities.

The two other main fiscal courts, the Cour des aides (to oversee the imposts) and the Cour du Trésor (a more or less parallel organization for the domaines) both began to function about a century later. Around 1400, groups of upper-echelon tax officials occasionally began to function as justices rather than full-time administrators.[17] After some hesi-

17. Dupont-Ferrier, *Etudes*, 2 : 258–63.

tation by the king, and some periods in which hostility to the new and burdensome tax system forced these courts out of action, they began to function regularly in the 1420s and 1430s.

Of all the branches of fiscal administration, the fiscal courts remained the most stable in their general operations and purposes from the end of the late Middle Ages through the Renaissance. The main changes that occur during the late fifteenth and sixteenth centuries are the provision for branch courts for the provinces and a considerable decline in the importance of fiscal judicial procedure considered as a whole.

The officials for supervising the new national imposts, the *élus* (at the district level) and the upper-echelon *généraux des finances*, were an even more significant innovation of late medieval administration. Their appearance represents a victory for the king over the Estates-General in a long, complicated struggle for control over the imposts.

The first attempt—apart from clerical tenths—to saddle France with national imposts was made by Philip the Fair, who had begun to experiment with excises in the 1290s. This attempt had proved a disastrous failure, and Philip switched to various forms of direct taxes. He finally settled on the *fouage* (hearth tax).

In spite of the bitter resistance they touched off, the imposts were levied occasionally during the "feudal reaction" (ca. 1315–45) that followed Philip the Fair's strong reign. Another national tax first appeared in this period: the royal levies on salt, the *gabelles*.[18] For the most part, these levies were made with the consent of a national Estates-General or that of provincial Estates. Various combinations of the new excise, salt, and hearth taxes were voted to the king during the late 1340s and the 1350s, when the nation was fearful and vulnerable following the stunning defeats at Crécy and Poitiers.

Several remarkable conditions were tacked on to a grant of salt and excise taxes by an Estates-General to John the Good in 1355.[19]

18. Jules Viard, "Un chapitre d'histoire administrative: les resources extraordinaires de la royauté sous Philip VI de Valois," *Revue des Questions Historiques* 44 (1888): 188–91.

19. Picot, *Etats Généraux*, 1 : 38, 134; ord. of Paris, Dec. 28, 1355, in E. J. Laurière et al., *Ordonnances des roys de France de la troisième race* (hereafter cited as ORD), 3 : 1925; and see ORD, 4 : 172, for March 12, 1356, esp. the preamble.

Among these was one requiring the king to permit the election of *généraux surintendants* from among the delegates; they would observe the collection of the revenues and the uses to which the money was put. In other words, the Estates-General wanted assurances the money would go to the soldiers and not be wasted in the manner for which the king was famous. In addition to such high-level fiscal management, the Estates-General also controlled local collections through agents (often deputies themselves) called *élus*, one in each of the north and central bailiwicks (*bailliages*).

For a few years after 1356, while King John was a prisoner of the English, the Estates-General voted little, complained much, and— under the leadership of Etienne Marcel—actually seized control of Paris and went into rebellion. Soon after the rebellion was crushed, salt and excise taxes were reimposed. This was done without consulting an Estates-General. The government held that the huge ransom demanded for John the Good (3 million gold écus) should be met with a feudal aid rather than an impost, and that this sort of an aid did not require popular consent.[20]

The royal order imposing the new taxes retained the élus of 1355–56 —but for an entirely different purpose. Astonishingly, they were now all king's men. They were appointed by the royal council, paid rather good wages, and entrusted with the responsibility of auctioning off the excises to tax farmers, in addition to supervising the collection of funds. The généraux surintendants also changed dramatically from agents of the people to agents of the crown.[21] Now called "généraux conseillers sur le fait des aides" in royal ordinances, they were to parallel for the new imposts the type of supervisory work the trésoriers were performing for the old domaines. Toward the end of the fourteenth century the new fiscal hierarchy was provided with new revenue districts: the *élections* —a name that carried over the mockery of popular control into the Renaissance—and the *recette générale* or *généralité*.

20. Ransom payments were stopped after about 1.7 million écus had been paid—half of that promised. See Dorothy M. Broome, *The Ransom of John II, King of France, 1360–1370*, p. xxiv.

21. Dupont-Ferrier, *Études*, 1 : 73–75. And see the valuable description of the new "extraordinary" system in the edict of Feb. 1379, as discussed by Alfred Coville, *Les Cabochiens et l'ordonnance de 1413*, p. 208.

There is no doubt, therefore, that by the end of the fourteenth century, fiscal administration was larger, more articulated, and better able to cope with emergencies than during the mid-thirteenth century. Furthermore, lines of responsibility, scales of wages, standardized procedures, and punishment for malfeasance were being laid down (especially for officials involved in collecting imposts), and many of these rules continued with little change into the Renaissance.[22]

But in other respects, fiscal administration in the mid-sixteenth century was a vastly different affair. Unlike the passive treasury of Charles V, Francis I's treasury (now called the *Epargne*) had a significant role in centralizing receipts and expediting payments. By the 1540s, furthermore, local and provincial auditing had sharply reduced the powers of the Renaissance Chambre des comptes. Offices in every facet of the fiscal system became venal during the Renaissance—including those in the fiscal judiciary. Under Francis I, a most important function of fiscal office was to provide the government with emergency funds; the king not only sold vacant offices but also created hundreds of new, redundant, and even useless ones for the sale price they brought. Another sharp contrast between fourteenth- and sixteenth-century administration is that during the latter period the officials who handled the imposts greatly outnumbered those concerned with collecting the domaines and with managing the money affairs of the royal household. Fiscal officialdom during the Renaissance was beginning to look less like a body of royal servants and agents and more like a national bureaucracy.

The types of taxes used in the late Middle Ages, it is true, do not seem strikingly different from those used during the Renaissance. The royal imposts, while not yet collected each and every year during the earlier era, were levied virtually each time fighting flared up. This is certainly the case for the excise and salt taxes, which often were collected even in years of truce during the later part of the Hundred Years' War. The direct taxes were collected not as alternatives to indirect levies (as during the days of Philip the Fair) but often in addition to them. And during the 1360s and 1370s a new set of national taxes

22. See, e.g., the letters-patent of Jan. 14, 1401, in ORD, 8 : 409–20; and Oct. 20, 1409, in ORD, 9 : 468–78.

was added to the fisc: the royal export duties or *traites*. In other words, if we were simply to list the names of the imposts to be found around 1370 and then to compare this to a similar list from around 1540, we would see only a few changes—and these would be in the form of additional taxes laid down during the later era, not the cancellation of older levies.

On the other hand, when one compares the total structure of revenues during the two eras, some fundamental differences do appear. In the late Middle Ages, for example, revenue from debasement of the coinage was still one of the crown's most important sources of funds— and it was employed often, in spite of the bitter hostility it aroused. Revenue from loans, furthermore, was still a relatively haphazard affair during the late Middle Ages, and it fluctuated wildly from one year to another, depending as it did on desperate improvisation rather than on established procedures in regular money markets. And a glaring contrast can be found in the proportions between domaines and impost revenues. For the years at the end of the fourteenth century, imposts were only bringing in (to judge from the fragmentary records available) about 10 to 30 percent of the net receipts.[23] The relative value of the imposts during the reign of Francis I, on the other hand, amounted to some 95 percent or more of the total.

The sharpest contrast between the fiscal systems, however, comes from neither the structure of revenues nor the characteristics of administration, but rather from the nature of the king's tax power. Here the role of national and provincial parliaments was so different that this factor alone might seem enough to dispel the idea that in fiscal affairs the Renaissance was only a continuation of the late Middle Ages.

The century from about 1330 to about 1430 was the golden age in the development of French representative institutions before 1789. It has been said that at this time there was, if anything, too much representation in France; the wide variety in the types of assemblies and the large number of such institutions may actually have weakened the

23. Rey, *Le domaine du roi*, pp. 81–99. Net receipts, here, are funds recorded as available to the Trésor. The relative value of the imposts to total gross revenues (all funds due the king) may have been higher than that for the domaines. Estimates for the imposts can be found in Rey, *Le domaine du roi*, pp. 261–62.

chances for a strong national Estates-General.[24] Most of the territories
that had been consolidated into feudal principalities had their own
provincial Estates and retained them after being absorbed into the
royal domain. Some provinces, in fact, had three-order Estates for several of their separate districts in addition to one general convocation
for the whole province; an all-province Estates, in this case, was likely
to be called an Estates-General.[25] The Ile de France, as such, had no
provincial Estates, but some districts in north France (Vermandois,
Orléanais, Touraine) had their own Estates, at least for parts of this
era. In addition, the king called up single-order assemblies for large and
small territories (the nobles of lower Auvergne, the prelates of the Ile
de France). For a time after 1350 there were bailiwick assemblies in
north and central France.

   Another confusing matter concerned the section of France where
Provençal rather than French was the main language (Languedoc,
Quercy, Rouergue, Dauphiné—the "langue d'oc" lands); at times they
had their own regional Estates-General, partly for reasons of particu-
larist jealousies, partly because of the expense and danger for men of
south France when they had to journey to an assembly point in the
north or center. This Midi assembly was matched by an Estates-General
for the northern, central, and western districts (the "langue d'oïl"
lands, where the word for "yes" was *oui* rather than *oc*).

   Because of the complexity in France's representative institutions,
the king developed an unfortunate tendency to appeal directly to
town, local, and provincial assemblies rather than bringing his case
first to an Estates-General. The harm resulting from reliance on the
lesser assemblies, of course, was that in such piecemeal negotiations
each province dug in its heels only when its own tax burden was at
issue. If everyone's attention had been focused on the Estates-General,
there might have developed a national consensus regarding the country's rights when the king wished to increase the tax burden.

   The role of assemblies in the development of royal tax power hinged

24. P. S. Lewis, "The Failure of the French Medieval Estates," *Past and
Present,* no. 23 (1962).
25. For the situation in the province of Languedoc see Paul Dognon, *Les institutions politiques et administratives du pays de Languedoc du XIIIe siècle aux
Guerres de Religion,* pp. 195–269.

on certain events during and just after the reign of Charles V, "the Wise" (1364–80). Once he was firmly on the throne, Charles V relegated the Estates-General to a minor position. National assemblies during the later 1360s were called only to approve certain royal decisions; and no such assemblies were allowed to meet during the entire decade of the 1370s. Meanwhile, the king continued to collect imposts authorized by the Estates-General for the ransom of John the Good— long past the time when John died and the ransom payments themselves stopped.

Year after year, to the end of Charles V's reign, the hearth, salt, and excise taxes continued to be levied. By what authority? What of the promises given in the 1350s that the new taxes would be temporary? [26] Was it not true that at the Estates-General of 1367 the king had vowed he would abolish the excises as soon as possible? What of the charges, so often raised, that much of the money from national taxes was going not for war and defense but for gifts to courtiers and to princes of the blood royal, for the costly upkeep of the royal household, to build new castles, or to fill the king's many treasure chests? These were problems that increasingly caught the conscience of the king.

In September 1380 Charles V, who had been ailing much of his life, began a pitiful, drawn-out struggle with death. The dauphin, the future Charles VI, was not quite twelve years old. A council of regency established the queen and the duke of Burgandy as guardians of the future king and the duke of Anjou as regent of the country. Even before the king was dead, these three—with two other princes of the blood, the dukes of Bourbon and Berry—set to quarreling over their respective powers and privileges. Sad and frightened concerning the future of his country, the dying king may have been even more afraid of what was in store for his immortal soul. Surrounding his deathbed with monks and officials, he begged forgiveness of all his subjects for any harm he might have caused them. More to the point, he gave orders on several matters calculated to protect his son and ease his conscience. The most important of these orders concerned the hearth taxes.

26. See the ord. of Paris, Dec. 28, 1355, "Et se il plaisoit à Dieu que . . . nosdictes guerres fussent finies dedans un an, lesdittes aides cesseroient du tout. . . ." In F. A. Isambert et al., eds., *Recueil général des anciennes lois françaises*, 4 : 771–95.

The king knew the hearth taxes were deeply resented, and that this resentment had figured in several revolts in the towns of the Midi during 1378 and 1379. Perhaps he felt that his unpopular brothers would have to make some grand gesture in order to keep the country calm while the future Charles VI remained a minor, and that they would never do this unless he forced their hand.[27] In any case, he called for a royal edict to be drawn up canceling the hearth taxes forthwith.

Whatever the king's motives for this deathbed renunciation, in the eyes of the people of France it demonstrated that their government recognized that unauthorized collecting of hearth taxes was a crime. The dead king's abolition of hearth taxes (together with his supposed remarks regretting the excises) was announced in every corner of the land; and in many major cities this announcement ignited resentment that had been smoldering for many years.

In November 1380 an Estates-General was called to Paris. The regents had probably already determined to give up the excises as well as the hearth taxes in order to calm the country.[28] In any case, they had to move quickly. A serious uprising in Paris seemed to herald a general revolt. Under the threats of the Paris mob, the government announced it would cancel salt taxes, excises, and in fact *all* royal revenues except tariffs and income from the domaines.[29]

It is true that the salt and excise taxes were reimposed on the country in 1383; and in 1384 the royal direct tax was reimposed too, though in the form of a taille rather than a hearth tax. But there were many additional years during the turbulent last stages of the Hundred Years' War when one or more of these imposts was not levied.[30] This was the case for the tailles during the entire period 1412–23; and after 1418 the royal excises were not imposed on the country again until 1428. During these years the national and provincial Estates once again became an indispensable aid to the king in collecting whatever national subsidies were allowed him.

27. Harry A. Miskimin, "The Last Act of Charles V: The Economic Background of the Revolts of 1382," *Speculum* 38, no. 3 (1963).
28. L. Mirot, *Les insurrections urbaines au début du règne de Charles VI, 1380–1383*, p. 34.
29. Ord. of Nov. 16, 1380, in Isambert, 6 : 542–44.
30. For the tailles see Rey, *Le domaine du roi*, pp. 324–57, 390–404.

These dramatic breaks in the continuity of the king's right to levy imposts at his own discretion show that this sort of power was not as yet firmly in his grasp. It was the great reforms of the 1430s and 1440s that finally gave the king "absolute" power over the imposts. Therefore these reforms should not be regarded as continuing trends of the late Middle Ages. We should think of the early Renaissance, rather, as the time when it was decided down which of two "tracks" France would go—that leading to an English-style relationship of shared responsibility over national taxes between crown and parliament, or the one leading to Renaissance "absolutism." Not until then does it become clear that at the same time the English were preparing to teach the world some lessons concerning "the power of the purse strings," the French were participating in the formulation of another sort of fiscal lesson: "Whatever must be done can be financed."

2

Charles VII Seizes
"Absolutist" Tax Powers

First stage: before 1428

The special excitement of this period of French tax history is that decisions were taken and procedures consolidated that were to mold the country's life for another three hundred years. The changes wrought by Charles VII (1422–61) in French taxation constitute one of the decisive steps in the history of Western civilization. The pattern was set in France, and this sort of royal tax power became the model for other countries. Historians are anxious to know, therefore, just what were the circumstances surrounding these changes. But royal edicts, the main source of our information, of course step warily around the issue of consent to taxes, since the king and his council were not eager to call any more attention to this matter than necessary. Our other sparse records do not tell us what the deputies in the critical Estates-General of 1436 or 1439 had in mind when tax matters were being decided.

Another block to our clear understanding lies in the well-entrenched misconceptions still appearing in our texts. The two most harmful clichés are that the Estates-General deliberately surrendered its rights over the chief imposts and that this was done in order to give the king a standing army to end the wars with England.[1] There was a tremendous jump forward in royal tax power—of this we may be sure. But the way it was accomplished was much more complex.

The French people, during the 1420s, were in a desperate situation. Wild bands of intermittently employed soldiers scoured the land for

1. A recent example is Norman Zacour, *An Introduction to Medieval Institutions* (New York, 1969), p. 132. He says, "when in 1438 the estates-general allowed the establishment of a standing army and granted the king the permanent collection of the *taille* without having to refer back to the estates, the way was clear for the continued development of royal absolutism in France."

supplies and plunder. Civil wars and political confusion throttled commerce and caused a serious drop in food production. The bigger cities were wracked by plagues. The bloody quarrels of Burgundians and Armagnacs had been halted only briefly by France's defeat by the English at the Battle of Agincourt (1415). In Paris, Charles VI, under the thumb of Burgundy, watched his country crumble. He died in 1422, after agreeing to accept the king of England as his heir (Treaty of Troyes, 1420). South of the Loire and east of English-controlled Bordeaux, the dauphin Charles (more or less backed by Armagnac nobles and several important towns) was recognized as Charles VII. Fearful and indecisive, the "king of Bourges," as he was called derisively by the Burgundians, wrung his hands, sent complaining missives to foreign courts, and let his towns and nobles fight their own battles.

The king's desperate political position, just as much as his need for revenues, explains the unprecedentedly large number of national, regional, and local assemblies he called up. These assemblies were a device by which the king could show himself to his people, to flatter them by seeking their counsel; they were also a means by which the French could signal their fealty to the Valois dynasty. There was more real cooperation between the king and the nation's representatives than ever before or, for that matter, ever again until 1789.

Thanks in part to these assemblies, Charles VII was remarkably successful in getting revenues from the harassed and devastated provinces under his control. Even before his father died, an Estates-General at Clermont, convoked by him as rightful dauphin of France, had voted him special levies of 800,000 livres.[2] The Estates-General of the "langue d'oïl" provinces called to Bourges in January 1423 actually voted him a subsidy of a million livres, an enormous sum for the times.[3] In March 1424 the Estates-General at Selles voted him another million livres; so did the "langue d'oïl" Estates at Poitiers and Riom in 1425; and there were other large grants by other assemblies in 1426 and

2. This was in 1421. Between 1418 and 1421, when he was the head of the Armagnac faction south of the Loire, the future Charles VII had relied on provincial Estates only.

3. This figure sometimes is given as a million francs. But the franc d'or was not struck any longer, and had become a sort of money of account equivalent to the livre tournois.

1428. The available figures indicate Charles was voted more than a million livres annually in the 1420s and slightly more in the early 1430s.[4]

Obviously the smaller provincial and local assemblies, as well as the Estates-General, were extremely important to the crown in obtaining consent to tax. A grant by a national assembly was mainly *en principe*, as the modern French would say; often it was vague on important details such as the type of taxes to be raised and the proportion for various sections of the country. Thus there had to be a second round of negotiations with provincial and local assemblies and town councils. If relatively rich and undamaged municipalities like Lyons complied, others almost always begged for, or insisted on, reductions.[5] In outlying provinces, especially the principal fiefs, agreement on tax levies had to be reached by promising the barons a large fraction of the tax returns.

Many times in the 1420s and 1430s, therefore, the king went directly to local assemblies without obtaining prior grants from the Estates-General.[6] The constitutional significance of such procedures is that it never became a fixed part of French tradition for the king to get a prior grant from national assemblies before proceeding to collect national taxes.

Second stage: 1428–35

The main taxes on commerce, the *aides*, had not been collected since 1418.[7] In that year John the Fearless, duke of Burgundy, had surrendered the aides in the part of France he controlled in order to stir up some enthusiasm for himself as a possible king of a united France among the citizens of Paris and the main towns of the north. (He still collected such aides, though, in his own Burgundian lands.) This move was so

---

4. Lot and Fawtier, *Histoire*, 2 : 271–72.

5. Even Lyons sometimes forced reductions or managed to change the type of tax requested. Louis Caillet, *Etude sur les relations de la commune de Lyon, avec Charles VII et Louis XI*, pp. 36 ff., 69.

6. J. Russell Major, *Representative Institutions in Renaissance France, 1421–1559*, p. 39.

7. The word *aides* is used in this study to signify excises as distinct from "aid" in the sense of "subsidy" or feudal aid.

exceedingly popular that Charles VII had to do the same for towns still loyal to the house of Valois.[8]

The gabelles were still being collected by Charles VII, but only to the extent that agents in charge of them were able to function.[9] There is evidence that the French, even in these rough and demoralized times, were ashamed of the financial embarrassments suffered by their king. We have a colorful story, possibly apocryphal, concerning the lack of royal credit. It seems a shoemaker brought a new pair of shoes for the king to his chateau at Bourges. He laced them on the royal feet, where they were duly admired by those present. Then, learning he would have to wait for his money, the shoemaker tore open the laces, pulled off the shoes, and departed with them. Another such story concerns a gift of linen cloth by townspeople near Bourges to the royal mother-in-law; they had learned she did not have a sufficient supply of underwear.

It is easy to understand, therefore, why repeated debasements of the coinage by Charles VII did not produce violent public reactions such as those against Philip IV or Charles VI. Calling in the coins and re-issuing them with less gold and silver content, in fact, was one of the king's main sources of revenue during these frantic years. Even the gold coins, relatively sacrosanct up to now, were debased 25 percent between 1420 and 1430.[10] Charles VII worked his mints as hard as he could; in dozens of tiny towns loyal to the "king of Bourges," mints that had rarely been used more than once every few years now steadily turned out masses of ugly, poorly struck, debased coins.

The year 1428 was a time of terrible danger to the Valois dynasty. In that year the English gathered their strength for an assault to the south; as a preliminary step, they laid siege to the city of Orléans, the last important stronghold north of the Loire still loyal to Charles VII. Fortunately, Charles had already called an Estates-General to meet at Chinon. Possibly as a consequence of the new and exceedingly visible

8. Charles VI—or rather his wife—had done the same (January 1418) for the Paris region, as had Henry V for Normandy. Antoine Thomas, *Les états provinciaux de la France centrale sous Charles VII*, 1 : 26–27, 69–70, suggests that the king had also abandoned direct taxes; but this is doubtful.

9. See Isambert, 8 : 593.

10. Jean Lafaurie, *Les monnaies des rois de France: Hugues Capet à Louis XII*, pp. 97–100.

threat, this assembly was well attended by deputies from almost every area outside of Anglo-Burgundian control, even from far-off and independently minded Dauphiné. They were deliberating at the very time (October) that the English set up camp around Orléans.

This was the grim state of affairs when Joan of Arc began her mission against France's enemies, raised the siege of Orléans, bullied the king into journeying to Rheims for a proper coronation (1429), and so electrified the French that the piecemeal English domain in France soon cracked and tottered. Though Joan was to be martyred in 1431, the French situation continued to improve; a few years later Burgundy was induced to drop its English alliance and to recognize Charles VII as king.

The action of the assembly at Chinon in 1428 was to have a most significant effect on French tax history. The delegates there voted the king 500,000 livres, to be raised, in part, in the form of aides; in addition, he was granted a special tenth from the clergy.[11] In itself a national grant of aides was nothing new; in spite of the fact that the king had renounced this form of taxation, the Estates-General at Selles (August 1423) and that at Poitiers (1425) had voted for some indirect taxes.[12] But on these earlier occasions, though the king had succeeded in getting assemblies to vote aides, local authorities had refused to concur, insisting on levying direct taxes (tailles or hearth taxes).

In 1428, however, the funds voted were raised as taxes on commerce. So far as we know, this marks the first time the king of France had received large revenues in the form of indirect taxes since 1418. Apparently emboldened by the favorable turn in military events, Charles proceeded, in the following two years, to collect the aides without even obtaining additional votes in the Estates-General; instead, he went directly to the provinces and towns, or sometimes even ordered royal commissioners to collect the aides solely on his own authority.

There is no doubt, therefore, that one of the greatest services of the Maid of Orléans to the house of Valois was to create circumstances

11. Clamageran, *L'impôt*, 1 : 475, says the amount was 400,000 francs. Cf. Caillet, *Lyon*, p. 67.

12. Major, *Representative Institutions*, pp. 27–28.

that enabled the government to reimpose indirect national taxes on France. To his everlasting disgrace, the king showed no great inclination to use some of this money to ransom Joan after her capture.

National aides were voted in 1431, 1433, and 1434, though each time some towns and provinces managed to get the government to accept tailles instead. In early 1435 the king split the Estates-General of the "langues d'oïl" areas into two sections, the eastern provinces meeting at Issoudun, the western at Poitiers. The Poitiers assembly of 1435, we know, specifically consented to allow the king aides for four years. Once again, and probably for the last time, many regions obtained a conversion of aides to tailles.

Meanwhile, the number of armed brigands had increased greatly, since many French and Burgundian soldiers were being dismissed. Both France and Burgundy were so poor and desolate that there was little for the soldiers to go home to. More and more of them, consequently, "went on the road" in bands (thus, *routiers* in contemporary speech). Peasants fled before these pillaging "flayers" (*écorcheurs*). The écorcheurs lived a riotous life with little danger, since there were few regular troops that could threaten them. No province escaped—not even Burgundy itself.[13] Fields and vineyards were ruined for lack of peasants, and some large towns were all but depopulated. A few routier captains were in effective control of areas so large that they had whole bands of tribute collectors, a military parody of a fiscal bureaucracy.

Third stage: 1436–39

In the year 1437 the last struggles of the Hundred Years' War were proceeding so well for the French that the king finally was able to venture a trip to Paris. The English, who a decade earlier had held all the north and west of France, were being driven from their remaining footholds. Thus a battered, exhausted, but—at long last—more or less united country wearily organized its forces for the last campaigns. Infuriated by the écorcheurs, sick of the senseless struggles for power among the great nobles, the French were not in a mood to resist the king's demands for what he claimed he needed to end the war.

13. Ferdinand Lot, *L'art militaire et les armées au moyen âge*, 2 vols. (Paris, 1946), 2 : 62–69.

In February 1436 an Estates-General of the "langue d'oïl" provinces had been called to Poitiers, primarily to ratify the concessions made to Philip the Good, duke of Burgundy. The Estates next turned to an examination of the king's financial position. A combination of gratitude for the peace with Burgundy and recognition of the king's expenses in connection with it led the Estates to vote for the collection of aides for a period of three years. Essentially, this was only a reaffirmation of the aides voted the previous year by the assembly meeting at Poitiers. But because of the new strength of the king this grant turned out to be one of the most important steps in the history of French taxation.

Immediately, the government issued an ordinance on the aides which both laid down the basis of the taxes and clarified the nature of the machinery for collecting them; this same ordinance, in fact, contained so many rules and regulations on levying aides that it amounted to a consolidation of all former edicts on aides from the days of King John the Good when aides first were imposed on the nation (1355–56).[14] The taxes themselves were to be on both wholesale and retail transactions. All the retail sales of "provisions and merchandise" (probably intended to mean mainly meat, textiles, and ironware)—except small sales (under five sous) of items grown or made by the peasants selling them—were taxed at one sou per livre of the sale price, or 5 percent. Wine and "minor beverages" (beer and cider) sold at retail paid thirty deniers per livre; and, most importantly, beverages sold at wholesale paid one sou per livre.

As each area in the north and center of France was recovered from the English, Charles simply imposed on it the whole mechanism of the royal aides. This meant new tax burdens for the reconquered lands, since the English had not imposed aides widely; but the loyalty of the recovered areas, or perhaps their relief at the removal of Burgundy from the struggle, made the task an easy one for the government. In May 1436 a small regional assembly in Paris confirmed the king's right to impose aides in that city, in addition to giving him the right to levy taxes in Champagne and other lands recovered from the English.

The provinces of the Midi now obtained a concession regarding the aides that probably was of some importance in the retention of pro-

14. ORD, 13 : 211–15.

vincial Estates in southern France. Back in the 1420s, the Languedoc, Dauphiné, and Rouergue Estates, meeting at times as a combined assembly of the *pays de langue d'oc* and at times as separate provincial Estates, unquestionably had possessed the right to vote hearth taxes and other national imposts. In the early 1430s, partly as a result of the national enthusiasm kindled by Joan of Arc, these Estates voted taxes rather generously; and some of these later grants were for aides, that is, for indirect taxes.[15] But resistance to the aides seems to have been particularly strong in this part of the country. A meeting of the "langue d'oc" Estates at Béziers in 1437 gave the king aides for three years, a grant similar to that of the central and northern provinces. But in 1439 the Midi provinces petitioned the king to collect no more aides. After years of wrangling, in 1443 Languedoc and Dauphiné were given the right to buy off the aides with annual lump sum payments to be known as the *équivalent* (see appendix H) and to be raised in whatever form deemed appropriate by the provincial Estates themselves.[16] As the years went on, it became easier for the government to let matters drift than to dispense with the équivalent, since this would have meant adding another branch to the tax machine and depriving some difficult-to-manage provinces of some well-entrenched liberties. The provincial Estates in the south, therefore, were left with an important fiscal function; and by so serving the crown they helped to preserve their precious local assemblies.

Today we can see the great constitutional significance of all these developments in 1435 and 1436 concerning indirect taxes. Contemporaries, however, must be excused for not realizing that the king and his council were well on the way to treating aides—and the whole machinery for collecting them—as a sort of domaines property, comparable to the gabelles. Not that the king, now or later, ever made an official proclamation to this effect. At first, as far as the country was concerned, the only difference was that the aides had been voted for three years instead of one. Unfortunately for consent to taxation, the wording of the 1436 vote of taxes was not very specific on what was to

15. Clamageran, *L'impôt*, 1 : 477.
16. The government also allowed a few south-central provinces to pay an *équivalent*, particularly La Marche, Limousin, and Périgord. Thomas, *Les états provinciaux*, 1 : 132–33.

happen at the end of the three-year period.[17] There are some indications that crown tax officers and judges tried to claim, after 1439, that the Poitiers grant of 1436 meant that the deputies intended to let the king have the aides indefinitely. The royal ordinance of 1436 on the aides, though *not* the grant by the Estates-General on which the ordinance supposedly was based, does contain the phrase that aides must be farmed out "each and every year," which is, at least, open to the interpretation that a grant of more than three years was intended. More probably, however, most of the deputies at Poitiers simply assumed that if the king wanted the aides to continue he would, as a matter of course, convoke another Estates-General and make another request.

If this is the case, it was a grave error. Never again at an Estates-General, either of the whole nation or of the "langue d'oïl" provinces, were the people asked to vote aides. The government continued to levy these taxes on its own authority, year after year.[18]

THE ACQUISITION OF TAX POWER OVER THE TAILLES

The ordinance of November 1439

The fiscal events beginning with the year 1439 rightly occupy an important place in even elementary histories. The textbook cliché concerning this crucial development can be expressed as follows: In 1439 the French finally realized that internal order and national defense required that the king be given a standing army and that the army would have to be supported by permanent taxes. The assembly at Orléans in that year surrendered the ancient right of consent to national taxes and voted the king the power to impose tailles at will. This amounted to a kind of institutional suicide, since it allowed the king to ignore the Estates-General and thus laid the foundation for later royal absolutism.[19]

17. Caillet, *Lyon*, pp. 82–83.
18. Aides accounted for about a quarter of royal revenues toward the end of this reign; according to Commynes this amounted to 500,000 livres out of 1.9 millions. See Alfred Spont, "La taille en Languedoc, de 1450 à 1515," *Annales du Midi* 2 (1890) : 366–69.
19. The cliché is based on Picot, *Etats Généraux*, still the only general work on this subject. Writing in the declining years of the Second Empire, Picot was anxious to demonstrate that participation in government by the people had a long and honorable past. See his preface, pp. xiv–xvi. I have found this cliché

Another reason often advanced to explain why the deputies were willing to surrender control over the tailles is that the king in return proclaimed the end of the right of seigneurs to raise local tailles, just as he proclaimed the end of their right to maintain private armies.[20]

Did the ordinance of November 1439 in fact give the king the right to collect tailles each year? A careful examination of the ordinance itself,[21] together with a consideration of the state of affairs in 1439, indicates that it did nothing of the kind. Yet soon afterward the king was claiming (rather vaguely) just such a right.[22] Nowhere in the ordinance itself, however, is it stipulated that further consent to tailles, or any tax, is *not* required. Nowhere does it state that in the years following 1439 the king may collect tailles to the amount of 100,000 livres (the sum granted in 1439) or any other amount. Article 41, in fact, specifically states that national tailles in the past had always been levied "du consentement des trois Estats"; and there is no indication that either the king or the Estates-General planned to desert this tradition. Neither the ordinance of November 1439 nor the general situation at that time contains an indication that the vote of tailles that year was in any way different from many similar grants in previous years.[23]

That there was as yet no question of eradicating the power of the Estates-General over national tailles is suggested by the fact that the king made preparations to hold another Estates-General the following year, in 1440. We know that a large number of deputies actually assembled at Bourges for this purpose; but just at that moment a poorly organized revolt, the "Praguerie," broke out against the king, led by a few impor-

---

in recent American texts by Zacour (quoted above, n. 1); Easton; Brinton, Christopher, and Wolff; Strayer and Munro; and Wallace Ferguson. Advanced works, too, use the same mistaken ideas.

20. Picot, *Etats Généraux*, 1 : 327–30. This prohibition refers to tailles on free men; a seigneur's serfs might still be tallaged, according to local custom and rights.

21. Isambert, 9 : 57–71; see also ORD, 13 : 306–13, esp. items 36–44. It is difficult to understand why P. Imbart de la Tour in his *Les origines de la Réforme*, 2d ed., 3 vols. (Melun, 1946–48), 1 : 49n., says the ord. affirms "the royalty's right to levy the taille."

22. This claim appears, for example, in ordinances exempting certain groups from tailles to be imposed in succeeding years. See the ordinances of Sarry-lès-Châlons, June 19, 1445, and Bourges, Nov. 1447, in ORD, 13 : 428–30, 521–22; see also ORD, 16 : xxii.

23. Lot and Fawtier, *Histoire*, 2 : 264.

tant nobles with the assistance of the king's own son, the future Louis XI. (The name of the revolt was a reference to the Hussite wars centering in Prague which had ended a few years previously.) Either the turmoil of revolt made it impossible for the king to call the meeting to order, or he was intimidated by the rebels' threats to appeal to the Estates against the king.[24] In any case, after being forced to linger on at Bourges for months, the deputies finally were sent home. As it turned out, the 1439 Estates-General at Orléans proved to be the last in the reign of Charles VII.

For the next four or five years we know almost nothing about the development of royal tax power, except that obviously it was growing stronger and spreading over a larger territory. The necessity for ransoming the duke of Orléans in 1441 for 200,000 écus is supposed to have caused a heavy though temporary increase in tailles, and the extraction of many forced loans.[25] The war with the English went on, as bitter as ever; the Praguerie had to be suppressed and its leaders placated with pensions; and a few campaigns by royal troops were unleashed against the worst of the *écorcheurs*. All this took a great deal of money. The king continued to collect the tailles for the most part on his own authority. On several occasions, however, requests for approval of tailles were made to provincial assemblies in the domain lands; but even this local and scattered consent to tailles ended in 1451. That year is the last for which we have any record that Charles VII asked consent to tailles of *any* representative body, national, regional, or local, in the north or central provinces.[26]

The military reforms of 1445

Another misconception we often encounter is that the reforms of the year 1439 gave France both royal tailles and a regularly paid professional army.[27] The fact is that while the changes in the nature of the tailles in

24. Picot's interpretation of the "Praguerie" is that it was a reaction by nobles to the provision in an ordinance of 1439 removing from most lords the right to put tailles on their own free peasants. *Etats Généraux*, 1 : 337.

25. Clamageran, *L'impôt*, 2 : 3 ff.

26. Later, Normandy managed to obtain pro forma rights of consent to the tailles.

27. Thus René Gonnard, *Histoire des doctrines économiques*, 2 vols. (Paris, 1921), 1 : 99, has Charles VII instituting "permanent armies and taxes." See

1439 did suggest the need for basic military reforms, these reforms were not completed until six years later, in 1445. The armies that Charles VII had at his disposal in 1440 and 1441 may have been better paid, but they were essentially the same mixture of part-time and full-time soldiers as those before 1439.

As far as we know, the French deputies at Orléans in 1439 did *not* request a regularly paid professional army along the lines of later reforms or of any other description.[28] The military provisions of the 1439 ordinance (in the first thirty-five articles) were negative rather than positive; they were aimed primarily at ending baronial armies in France. Neither then nor at any other time did representatives of the French people formally demand of Charles VII the sort of military reforms he then established. The initiative here again seems to have been taken entirely by the government.

The main provision of the great military reforms of 1445, according to the ordinance published May 26 of that year, was to establish a standard form of organization for twenty regular companies of heavy cavalry.[29] The make-up of each lance (six mounted men) was prescribed; each company was to be based in a specific garrison town; military discipline was to be maintained strictly. In return, each lance was guaranteed pay of thirty livres per month.[30] This meant that France was committed to pay the core of its army the huge sum of 720,000 livres annually, at least in years when the *compagnies d'ordonnance* were up to full strength.[31]

The reforms of the military did not stop with giving France a new

---

also C. Soule, "Le rôle des Etats Généraux et des Assemblées de Notables dans le vote de l'impôt," in *Etudes sur l'histoire des assemblées des états*, p. 97.

28. "Regularly paid professional army" seems better than "permanent standing army," a term one often sees applied to the compagnies d'ordonnance, since part of these troops were not "standing" in peacetime, when garrisons were allowed to fall below full strength.

29. It is not clear whether there were five companies of 100 lances each for the "langue d'oc" lands plus fifteen for the rest of the country, or if the total figure was fifteen; most historians, however, accept the figure of 2,000 lances. Cf. Pierre Clément, *Jacques Coeur et Charles VII*, 2 vols. (Paris, 1863), 1 : 123.

30. Sometimes given as 31 livres.

31. Two thousand lances multiplied by 30 livres and by twelve months. Until around 1451 some of the funds were supplied, not directly from the royal treasury, but by provincial Estates and other local authorities.

professional cavalry. Another less successful effort was made at the same time to improve the quality of the French infantry by creating a corps of *francs archers*—infantrymen who were supposed to be trained in the use of bows or crossbows. These "free archers" were allowed to live at home in peacetime, but it was necessary for them to drill regularly and to be ready for active service at a moment's notice; in return, they were accorded a most important privilege—exemption from paying tailles (hence "free").[32] They were also supposed to receive four francs a month each when on active duty. But these troops proved to be a disappointment; they were too slow to assemble and too apt to run when the fighting took a bad turn. The future basis of the French infantry was not to be these native troops but the famed Swiss pikemen.[33]

While the compagnies d'ordonnance and the francs archers were organizational innovations, the main change in the style of fighting was the increase in the number of cannon employed. The newer, better counselors for the king grasped the importance of this weapon. Gaspard and Jean Bureau, particularly, busied themselves with bringing in foreign artillery experts. Not only did they use the king's increased fiscal resources to buy more cannon, they produced improved pieces, which were much more mobile, more accurate, and safer for the crews that handled them. Jacques Coeur, the king's famous financier, also used his first-rate brains and his first-rate credit to buy up these expensive weapons by the hundreds and to train a large number of competent artillerists.

The truce with the English ended in 1449, and the military situation that had existed before 1439 was now about to be reversed. The first campaigns of the resumed wars were against the harassed English garrisons in Normandy. The massed cannon attacks of the French crushed those English forces that dared venture into battle, making it easy for the reformed French cavalry to sweep the field. France had a series of victories just as amazingly complete as were the defeats of Crécy and Poitiers one hundred years previously. Normandy, which had been an English province since 1415, was retaken in less than a year, during the

32. We know, however, that some of the men were chosen from groups so poor they paid no tailles in any case. Caillet, *Lyon*, pp. 154–56.
33. Sir Charles Oman, "The Art of War in the Fifteenth Century," *The Cambridge Medieval History*, 8 vols. (Cambridge, 1911–36), 8 : 658–59.

campaigns of 1451. Two years later the English and their Gascon allies around Bordeaux finally were forced to surrender. Though no peace treaty was signed, in effect the Hundred Years' War was over.

From two tailles to one

All these military reforms and campaigns took an enormous amount of money. Unfortunately, we have almost no information as to what sums actually were expended by the government for its new armies, or how these expenses were related to changes in the tailles. We know that in the spring of 1452, just at the time the new compagnies d'ordonnance were becoming established in their garrison towns, the government was collecting what contemporaries referred to as an additional (and concurrent) taille, called "the soldiers' taille" (*la taille des gens de guerre*).[34] In the absence of details regarding the precise burden of this new tax, we can only imagine that it was based on the pay of the military companies: a total of 720,000 livres annually. We know, also, that the older "aid for war needs" collected since 1439 was sometimes referred to as "the king's taille," but we do not know its amount.

As we have seen, the deputies at Orléans in 1439 meant for "the king's taille" to be a small amount—about 100,000 livres. The burden of the older taille certainly increased between 1439 and 1445. The mechanism of this increase, as we shall see, was not the consent of the Estates-General (for none were held after 1439) but a combination of royal fiat and bargaining with the more important towns and with provincial Estates where they still existed. Spont shows that around 1445 the "aid for war needs" carried in royal accounts amounted to some 300,000 livres for the "langue d'oïl" areas and 120,000 for the "langue d'oc" lands; these two sums together give us about 420,000 livres raised by the older taille for the whole kingdom. If we assume that none of the revenues from the older taille went to pay the salaries of the new compagnies d'ordonnance, we can add the 720,000 livres of the new "soldiers' taille," giving us a grand total of about 1.14 million livres. This is very close to the 1.2 millions regarded by many persons in the late fifteenth

---

34. An edict of 1452 called it "les tailles ordonnées pour le vivre & entretenement des gens de guerre." See Pierre Charpentier, ed., *Recueil des ordonnances* . . . , p. 19.

century as the "normal" level for the tailles during all the later reign of Charles VII.[35]

The same sources, however, tell us that from 1451 to 1452, when the war with England was virtually over, there was a reduction in the level of the tailles which was effected by the king's canceling the older taille (the "aid for war needs") and levying only the newer taille. Henceforth, and for the remainder of the reign of Charles VII, France's taille was limited to the "soldiers' taille," although the French were soon referring to the new taille as the "king's taille," or simply as *the* taille. Modern historians, too, agree that Charles VII reduced the tailles in the period 1451–52, and that this cut was accomplished by canceling the older taille.[36]

It is important, however, to dispel any impression that the state was collecting *less* in tailles, for the country as a whole, after 1451. Indeed, it does not seem reasonable that the king would have cut the tailles in 1451 or 1452, even though great victories were being won in Guyenne and in Normandy. The royal armies were still maintained at their peak level—necessarily so, since there was no peace treaty or even a truce in 1452. On the contrary, in that year the army had to be deployed to crush an English invasion of the Bordelais which was combined with an uprising in that district. In fact, there was no formal peace treaty even in 1453, the date customarily accepted as the end of the Hundred Years' War.

There is no question that parts of the country were granted lower total tailles; we know this is the case for Auvergne [37] and for Languedoc.[38] The reason for this reduction, however, was not decreased costs (because of lower military expenses) so much as higher revenues. Two additional provinces now had to pay the royal taille—Guyenne and Normandy. The rest of the country benefited because the same burden of total tailles was spread out.[39] We know the taille was an *impôt de répartition* (see appendix G); so that this sort of adjustment (keeping

35. Lot and Fawtier, *Histoire*, 2 : 270; Spont, "La taille en Languedoc," pp. 493–96.
36. Thomas, *Les états provinciaux*, 1 : 164–65.
37. Ibid., p. 165.
38. Spont, "La taille en Languedoc," p. 496.
39. In 1463 Normandy alone paid 300,000 livres in tailles. René Gandilhon, *La politique économique de Louis XI*, p. 282.

the total the same while changing the amounts paid per unit) certainly
was in keeping with the nature of the tax. Later in the Renaissance,
Normandy and Guyenne together accounted for between a quarter and
a third of all the French tailles; this fraction is just about the same as
the reported decline in this tax enjoyed by at least some of the French
provinces in 1451–52. In any case, after 1452 the taille was a single tax,
and until the advent of Louis XI it remained fixed for the country at
the level of just about 1.2 million livres.[40]

WAS THERE CONSENT TO TAXES AFTER 1439?

The revisionist position

There is no broad consensus about the significance of the tax reforms
of Charles VII. At one extreme is what I have called the textbook cliché,
a point of view summed up in Clamageran's dictum that the year 1439
marks the end of the Middle Ages and the beginnings of modern history.[41] At the other extreme are writers who deny any special significance
to the era 1435–53; one of them is Charles Petit-Dutaillis, in his old
but admirable work in the Lavisse series.[42] Petit-Dutaillis, whose general
opinion of Charles VII is low, believes that this weak, guilt-ridden person was incapable of pushing through any important break with tradition. For Petit-Dutaillis, and for others, the tax reforms in this era are
just another link in a long evolutionary line of increasing royal power
that continues from the Middle Ages.

An entirely different approach can be found in J. Russell Major's
series of studies on representative institutions in Renaissance France.[43]
Major argues that the year 1439, and in fact the whole era 1435–53,
did not end the need for the king to obtain consent to taxes. In spite of

40. According to Petit-Dutaillis, in Lavisse 4² : 255 n. 3, there was a slight
decline in the last year of the reign of Charles VII to 1.06 million livres.

41. Clamageran, *L'impôt*, 1 : 497.

42. Petit-Dutaillis, in Lavisse 4² : 20, 259.

43. In addition to Major's *Representative Institutions*, his other works of
special interest for this topic are *The Deputies to the Estates General in Renais-
sance France*; "The French Monarchy as Seen through the Estates-General,"
Studies in the Renaissance 9 (1962); and "French Representative Assemblies:
Research Opportunities and Research Published," in *Studies in Medieval and
Renaissance History*, vol. 1.

the temporary decline of the national Estates-General, the king was still obliged to obtain consent to taxes from local and provincial bodies and from powerful lords. Major's aim is to show that the whole Renaissance era was thoroughly representative and decentralized in its political institutions, even more so than the Middle Ages. It is only in the seventeenth century, he states, that Old Régime France really becomes the well-organized, centralized, "absolute" government some people think they see in the late fifteenth and the sixteenth centuries.

In taking up the question of taxes, Major underlines the fact that even the national Estates-General of the 1420s and 1430s had been only "large preparatory assemblies" [44] which, by granting the king a levy, served to make it more likely that towns and provinces would follow suit. The abandonment of the Estates-General by Charles VII, therefore, constituted no startling change in the ability of the French to control the nature, the burden, or the management of their taxes. The king continued to go to local representative bodies; the main change was that the government now avoided preliminary grants *en principe* from an Estates-General. Since the time, expense, and danger of long trips to an Estates-General were regarded by the French themselves as a thorough nuisance, the fact that the king no longer called them up was really in accord with the national will, rather than thwarting it.

How much provincial tax power?

A long list of provincial assemblies, appearing at one time or another during the Renaissance, is easy to compile; and some of these assemblies, it is true, did have substantial rights to participate in the formulation of local fiscal policy and in the management of the local fiscal system.[45] The very length of this list does not end all argument, however. Surely the problem has to be phrased more precisely. *How much* consent to taxes (or other forms of popular control over the fiscal machine) was there in *how large a fraction* of Renaissance France? With many provincial Estates vanishing from the picture during the fifteenth century, is tax power in the remaining provinces possessing Estates the rule or

44. Major, *Representative Institutions*, p. 26.
45. Major gives this list in his "French Representative Assemblies," pp. 189–215.

the exception? In other words, we need some "quantification" of the problem. We need to determine not only the exact nature of the traditional privileges of each province in tax matters, but also how frequently these power were exercised. Evidence showing any sort of assembly at any one time in a certain region does not allow us to regard this area as a "consent region," since such evidence may be simply the exception to the "no-consent" rule. We need also to weigh contrary evidence; that is, cases in which "absolute" fiscal decisions by the king were made in provinces in which Estates were supposed to have "consent" and other tax powers.

The first point to establish is that after 1450 the provinces of more than half the territory of France, *for most of the Renaissance*, did not possess provincial Estates. After 1444–45, about the time of the military reforms, a "constitutional" division of the realm in tax matters seems to have been undertaken by the state. Certain provinces, especially those of the older royal domain, were consulted less and less frequently. The outlying provinces, however, where the Estates were important or where there were no royal élus in charge of fiscal administration, were still given some voice in the levying of tailles and aides. The provincial Estates of the north and center, such as those of Champagne, Poitou, the Orléanais, La Marche, Limousin, and Auvergne, which had served the crown in many ways, were allowed to disappear by the simple expedient of not calling them up.[46] The year 1451 is the last on record in which the north and central provinces (apart from Normandy and, later, Brittany) were asked to give their consent to a levy of tailles. After that time, provincial assemblies in these districts vanished, for the most part, except for brief resurrections (of a few) on one or two occasions, as during the Wars of Religion.

By the end of the reign of Charles VII, only Normandy, Languedoc, Dauphiné, and a few south and central counties enjoyed more or less regular provincial Estates. It is obvious that the king now regarded provincial Estates as a special privilege rather than as the rule for his subjects. This is vividly illustrated by events in the Bordelais-Gascony territory. When the English were decisively defeated there in 1451, the nobles and burghers reluctantly came to terms with the king, recognizing his au-

46. For Auvergne and its neighbors see Thomas, *Les états provinciaux*, 1 : 165–74.

thority and accepting French justices, military governors, and other officials in return for certain concessions, among which was the promise that the king would respect the privileges of the Estates of Guyenne. Included in this promise were the Bordeaux-Bazas-Agen lands of the Garonne basin; the districts of Périgord, Rouergue, and Quercy just to the east; and the lands south of the Garonne we think of vaguely as Gascony—chiefly Armagnac and the Landes, including several tiny territories such as Comminges and Condomois. These lands, with strong traditions of autonomy and well-established local or provincial assemblies, had sometimes met together as the "Estates-General of Guyenne." In 1452, however, an English invasion force landed near Bordeaux and was welcomed enthusiastically by many of the inhabitants, who helped drive out their French rulers from virtually all the Bordelais. But the French compagnies d'ordonnance and artillerists made short work of the English and their French supporters; Bordeaux was taken and sacked and deprived of its privileges, including the right to have provincial Estates.[47] Royal tax collectors swarmed into the Bordelais, which thereafter had its tailles imposed and collected by royal agents.

Périgord, Rouergue, and Quercy were allowed to keep their provincial Estates, as were the smaller Gascon lands; the Estates of Armagnac, however, vanished at some time during the 1450s.[48] There was a brief revival of the "Estates-General of Guyenne" under a brother of Louis XI who was made duke of the territory; these Estates-General began to function again just before the beginning of the Wars of Religion. But Bordeaux and its hinterland never again became a *pays d'états*. And Périgord, even though it had an assembly, also had its tax affairs controlled by élus and counted for tax purposes as an *élection*. A few of the town councils in the Guyenne-Gascony lands (particularly Agen) seem to have been remarkably successful in forcing tax concessions from royal officers. However, except during the Wars of Religion, southwest France had little more control over the granting and administration of taxes than did the north and center. The only exceptions

47. Robert Boutruche, *La crise d'une société: seigneurs et paysans du Bordelais pendant la Guerre de Cent ans* (Paris, 1947), 399–424.
48. Major, *Representative Institutions*, pp. 44–45. During the Wars of Religion, assemblies in these districts became more important. But Sully forced all the counties of south and west Guyenne to become pays d'élections, and their Estates vanished.

are Quercy, Rouergue, and one or two other tiny and thinly populated lands.[49]

As early as the mid-fifteenth century, therefore, a "constitutional" distinction was evident between *pays d'états* and *pays d'élections*.[50] In later reigns additional provinces—Burgundy, Provence, and Brittany— were added to the realm, and to make the transition easier these provinces were allowed to keep their Estates. The Nivernais, just west of Burgundy, managed to establish a fairly important provincial assembly in the later sixteenth century. On the other hand, the Estates in the lands of the Bourbon family, the Bourbonnais and the Beaujolais (where Estates had never been particularly strong), were annulled by Francis I after the treason trial of the Constable of Bourbon (1524–25). Artois, in the northeast of France, had very active Estates, but this region was lost in 1529 to the Hapsburgs.[51] During the Wars of Religion some provincial Estates were reconstituted in areas where they had not functioned for many years; this is true, for example, for the Estates of Auvergne. But this late blooming was pinched off by Henry IV at the close of these wars.

Normandy, Provence, Dauphiné, Languedoc, Brittany, and Burgundy —almost two-fifths of the area of the country—were left as provinces with regularly convoked Estates having significant tax powers during most of the Renaissance.[52] If Agenais, Quercy, and Rouergue are added, the figures change by only a few percentage points.

49. For the complicated territorial structure of "greater Guyenne" see Louis Desgraves, "La formation territoriale de la généralité de Guyenne," *Annales du Midi* 62 (July 1950).

50. The phrase *pays d'états* is rare in the fifteenth century; it is fairly common in the sixteenth century and therefore is not, as some think, a concept limited to the Old Régime.

51. Later in the sixteenth century the duke of Lorraine, a vassal of the Holy Roman Emperor with several fiefs in France, was confirmed in his right to convoke Estates in these fiefs (edict of Paris, Aug. 8, 1575). Apart from la Marche, however, these fiefs were effectively outside the royal tax system of France. So were the Béarn-Navarre lands of the Bourbons (until 1589) which also convoked Estates. On Navarre, see André Vandenbossche, "Les états pyrénéens et l'impôt," in *Etudes sur l'histoire des assemblées des états*, pp. 157–68.

52. To obtain this figure, I did nothing more sophisticated than placing a fine grid over a map of France, counting the squares in and out of these six provinces, plus Quercy, Rouergue, and the Agenais. Major gives the impression that Estates

An analysis of the extent of consent to taxes, ideally, should take into consideration other than provincial assemblies: town councils, convocations or local representatives of single orders, and the "general" (three orders) assemblies of segments of provinces known to modern scholars as *états particuliers*. Many assemblies were called for special purposes. Often, a number of "Notables"—high officials, prelates, great nobles, and princes of the blood—might be summoned to meet with the royal council to give advice. The king might call together the nobles of a particular region not possessing Estates, such as the Touraine-Anjou area; or he might summon representatives of several town councils to deliberate together; and, of course, the clergy continued to meet as an order in both diocesan and large-area assemblies. But the same problems on which these special assemblies advised the king might just as well have been fixed by royal fiat. Such special purpose convocations (apart from those of the clergy) had no permanency, few settled traditions, and little institutional coherency.

Obviously, the impulse to work out problems by consultation between royal agents and representatives of the French was far from dead after 1453. So far as these special assemblies are concerned, the only generalization that seems possible is that during the Renaissance they diminished the tax power of the crown only to a limited extent. We can say the same for bailiwick assemblies electing delegates to Estates-General; these assemblies had nothing to do with taxes.[53]

The most interesting problem involving the tax power of groups other than provincial Estates is that of the town councils. Some towns, because of their great wealth, became exceedingly important in fiscal affairs whenever the state had to raise forced loans or other emergency levies. Before 1451, in areas with no provincial assemblies, it was important for the king to demonstrate that the heavy increases in tailles had popular consent; thus some town councils were asked for their approval. But with the establishment of the "king's taille" the practice of asking

---

met through the Renaissance in two-thirds of France; see his "The Crown and the Aristocracy in Renaissance France," *American Historical Review* 69 (April 1964): 643, and "The French Monarchy," p. 124.

53. Gustave Dupont-Ferrier, *Les officiers des bailliages et sénéchausées et les institutions monarchiques locales en France à la fin du moyen âge*, pp. 812–13.

assent to tailles by towns as such was stopped. Of course French towns still could petition the royal council directly for redress of fiscal grievances, just as could any group (or important individual) in the realm. And the end of "consent" privileges for the towns did not mean that they lost all fiscal privileges. Many of them enjoyed complete exemption (*franchise*) from the "ordinary" or nonemergency tailles. But none of them had the right actually to contest the burden of taxes, except through the usual respectful petitions. Even Louis XI, who is supposed to have favored his townsmen, saddled them unmercifully with forced loans when he needed money and paid little attention to the anguished protests they raised. In summary we can say that towns, like the special assemblies, did not abridge the tax power of the crown.[54]

More important were the dozen or so états particuliers within Languedoc or on the fringes of Burgundy (sometimes called *pays adjacents*). These included the territories of Charolais, Mâconnais, Auxerrois, and Auxois near Burgundy, and lands which were enclaves in Languedoc, such as the territories around Albi and Castres. All of these had assemblies fairly regularly for most of the Renaissance,[55] and they enjoyed a remarkable recovery during the Wars of Religion. Yet none of them had the right to "consent" to tailles (even in the formal sense possessed by the Norman Estates); neither did they control the diocesan or parish *assiette* of the tailles. They seem to have had some privileges over indirect taxes, however, and several of them managed to "make a composition" with the king to avoid paying the more objectionable aides. They also seem to have been allowed some leeway in dickering over the burden of forced loans and other emergency grants—a privilege they shared with the larger provincial Estates.

In perspective, the modest privileges and restricted responsibilities of

54. For a contrary view see Major, *Representative Institutions*, p. 48. Major refers to a possibility that in Auvergne, for example, assemblies of several towns may have taken over some of the functions of an Estates. "French Representative Assemblies," p. 195.

55. It is instructive, in reading about such assemblies, to learn that "regular" or "periodical" does not mean "annual"; the Estates of Burgundy, for example, usually met only once every three years. J.-L. Gay, "Fiscalité royale et Etats Généraux de Bourgogne, 1477–1589," in *Etudes sur l'histoire des assemblées des états*, pp. 179–210. It is true, however, that at times Burgundy and other provincial Estates authorized committees for the Estates which operated between sessions.

all these local and specialized assemblies in the fiscal system cannot support the revisionist argument. As a group they do not signify the retention of tax power by the peoples' representatives, but rather the great jump forward in the tax power of the crown.

What was negotiable after 1453?

The fact that a province possessed an Estates did not carry it out of the sphere of royal tax power. In the two-fifths of the country so privileged, royal tax power was reduced, it is true—but not by very much. This should especially be underlined in the case of Normandy. This province possessed an Estates which met regularly through most of the Renaissance and which did go through the motions of voting consent to tailles. But such acts were only formalities, allowed by the crown as a gesture to Normandy's heavy tax burden and her medieval charters of privilege. Almost from the time Normandy was recovered by Charles VII from the English, the burden of its taxes was fixed by the royal council, and the council gave the Norman Estates little chance to disapprove or bargain.[56] Even in provinces with well-established "consent" traditions, full-fledged debates on taxation, such as we would expect in meetings of modern assemblies, seldom were permitted. Concessions had to be hammered out by negotiations with the government. In some of the remaining fiefs the right to assemble the Estates was supposed to be in the hands of the barons; but even some of these Estates were increasingly falling under the thumb of the king.[57] The main function of provincial Estates, it would appear, was to meet in order to learn what was expected of them in the way of additional help to the king.

The ability of provincial Estates to protect their lands from new or heavier taxes was severely limited. It was only in the matter of tailles and forced loans that all the Estates had at least some rights. Languedoc and Brittany, which were important salt-producing areas, did have additional

---

56. Henri Prentout, *Les états provinciaux de Normandie,* 1 : 147–59. See also R. Villers, "Le rôle financier des états de Normandie," in *Etudes sur l'histoire des assemblées des états,* p. 127. Early in the Renaissance, however, the Norman Estates were able to resist a surtax on the tailles on a few occasions.

57. This was the case for the viscounty of Turenne, for example. On the other hand, the Estates of Béarn-Navarre were truly responsible to their feudal lord until 1589.

rights to protect themselves against the gabelles.[58] Languedoc also had the right to pay an équivalent as a substitute for aides, and to negotiate over the level of this tax, or at least a portion of it. But even Languedoc was part and parcel of the royal tax system. When the king decided to establish additional venal offices, these were planted willy-nilly in Toulouse as well as in Paris. When the king raised the taxes on wine, the increase was paid—without any recourse or right to protest—by the burghers of Rouen and Dijon, as well as those of Orléans.

This is not to say that the tax privileges of the pays d'états were negligible or that they were not esteemed by the people of these provinces. But to state without extensive qualifications that "consent to taxes" existed in such provinces gives a seriously distorted picture. We should never imagine that the pays d'états had as much tax power as did even the lowliest principality of the Holy Roman Empire or the states in the United States today.

As Jean Hennequin, Renaissance author of one of the best books on taxes, put it, "The Normandy [and other] Estates are nothing but vestiges and traces of the former rights of such provinces. For it has become fixed that what used to be granted has become the kings' patrimonial and hereditary right, without distinction as to peace and war time." [59]

Perhaps more important than control over the burden of taxation for the people of the pays d'états was their right to control certain portions of the provincial tax apparatus. These rights varied from province to province and changed during the course of the Renaissance. But they did mark off some of the pays d'états from the rest of the country. The foremost of such rights was over the *répartition* of the taille, that is, the allocation of the total taille among the subordinate districts. Since one of the greatest grievances during the Renaissance was not so much the total burden of the taille as the fact that wealthier and more populous districts often bore a disproportionately light burden, the right of repartition was an important one. Only Languedoc, Burgundy, and Provence had this right all through the Renaissance. Dauphiné possessed it

58. Provence, also, successfully resisted, on one occasion, the crown's attempt to increase the burden of the salt taxes there. Not so Burgundy: see Gay, "Fiscalité royale," pp. 190–92.

59. Jean Hennequin, *Le guidon général des finances* . . . , p. 191.

in the fifteenth century, but it was allowed to lapse, and it fell into the hands of royal officials. Normandy, also, had possessed this right in the fifteenth century; but Louis XI took it away, leaving the Normans with only the right to make counterproposals on repartition to the royal commissioners.[60] Until 1451 the provincial Estates of Auvergne, and to a lesser extent those of the Limousin and La Marche, had some rights concerning repartition. But after that time the king's agents handled this task themselves.[61] In all the other pays d'états the allocation of the total taille inside the provinces was handled by royal commissioners without consulting the Estates. The weak Estates of Quercy and Rouergue, for example, had nothing to say about this important matter.[62]

Some tax officials in the pays d'états, also, were appointed by, and responsible to, the Estates of the provinces rather than the crown. This was the case for those officials connected with taxes (usually local tolls) set aside to pay the *affaires du pays*—upkeep of important bridges and roads, repairs of key fortifications, and payment of some law enforcement officials of the province. The collecting and paying officials in such cases were presumably more tender in their treatment of local taxpayers than officials who were royal agents. Languedoc and Burgundy, furthermore, had the right to appoint and pay most of the lower-echelon officials who handled the direct taxes; Languedoc lost this right in 1572, however.[63]

The existence of even a relatively weak provincial Estates did permit the possibility, at least, of obtaining concessions by negotiating with royal commissioners, or by sending delegates directly to the royal council armed with arguments—and with bribes. Such a privilege was especially valuable when the government was in financial trouble and had to appeal for quick grants in the form of loans, outright gifts, or perhaps a grant of provisions to troops on the move.

But "consent to taxes," even for the most active of the provincial

60. Later in the Renaissance, apparently, the Norman Estates possessed the right of repartition in some years but not in others. In the 1570s they surrendered it definitively to the crown, apparently of their own volition. Jean Vannier, *Essai sur le bureau des finances de la généralité de Rouen*, pp. 93–95.

61. Thomas, *Les états provinciaux*, 1 : 88–100.

62. Spont, "La taille en Languedoc," p. 371.

63. Gaston Zeller, *Les institutions de la France au XVIe siècle*, p. 64; see also Clamageran, *L'impôt*, 2 : 22–23, esp. for Normandy.

Estates, never carried with it the right to *refuse* the customary taille
(or any tax) or even to negotiate concerning this; it was only on the
question of increases in the rates and in surtaxes (*crues*) that they
could negotiate. In Languedoc, for example, which had the privilege of
voting some of its taxes, the Estates were not allowed to withhold such
a vote until their grievances had been discussed; Francis I made this
specific in 1538.[64] In other words, "parliamentary initiative" was min-
imal. When the grievances of a province reached scandal proportions,
of course, the royal council had to listen to official representatives of
provincial opinion, a privilege not extended to provinces without
Estates.

French tradition, public opinion, and even the specific promises of
the crown certainly demanded that as soon as the crisis of 1439 was over
—about the time of the truce of 1444—the king should have stopped
collecting aides and tailles; but he did not.[65] The same factors certainly
called for the king to convoke the national Estates-General again when
another emergency came along; for example, when fighting broke out
again in 1449; but he did not. And this was *his* choice, even though it
is probably true that many Frenchmen, as LaBarre scornfully comments, were relieved they would not have to bear the "great expenses,
exertions, and inconveniences" of travel to assembly points. The king
certainly could have preserved the provincial assemblies of the north
and central provinces if he had so wished.

To sum up: the reign of Charles VII saw a basic change in the
method of imposing and fixing the level of national tailles and aides. In
the 1420s either the king with his council had sent out royal commissioners to ask provincial representatives to undertake fair shares of
the emergency expenses, or the king had requested a subsidy from a
national Estates-General, after which some further bargaining with
local authorities was often necessary. After 1453 there was no question
that the tailles and aides would be raised each year; for all but a few
provinces the level of the tailles was decided arbitrarily and in advance

64. Paul Dognon, *Les institutions . . . de Languedoc*, pp. 574–75; see also
Doucet, *Les institutions*, 1 : 349–50; Spont, "La taille en Languedoc," pp. 484–85,
493–94.

65. René-Laurent La Barre, *Formulaire des esleuz*, p. 79, put it this way:
Charles VII was given these taxes "tant & si long temps, que la guerre dureoit
qu'il avoit à l'Angloys: laquelle cesserait, devoit aussi cesser ladite levée."

by the government; and repartition among the provinces was fixed by the king at the same time. For about three-fifths of the country, a commission was sent directly to the royal *élus*, spelling out what sums had to be raised in each province and in each élection or diocese.[66] Elus and commissioners, in all but a few provinces, then proceeded to levy the taxes on the authority of the king, not on the joint authority of the king and Estates.[67]

Before Charles VII seized tax power, Estates-General or other assemblies had, on occasion, refused to pay taxes.[68] Previously, it was the tax grant itself that was negotiable; afterward, it was something much less —and for only two-fifths of the realm.

De facto "absolutism" only

The burden of taxes, in contrast to tax power, did not change during this decay of representative institutions. Keeping the tailles stable at a low level must have pleased the commoners who had to pay them. At the same time the ordinance of 1439 formally ended the right of nobles to raise tailles on free men in their districts. The same rule applied to the few main towns still controlled by noble vassals. Thus people could tell themselves that if the king was squeezing them, at least he was preventing his vassals from applying similar pressure. The nobles, of course, received a specific guarantee of exemption from royal tailles; the more trustworthy military captains were assured of regular employment in the compagnies d'ordonnance; the famous Pragmatic Sanction of Bourges (1438) relieved the French clergy of some of its payments to Rome. There was a bit of something for almost everybody in the settlements arranged by Charles VII, a situation that may have made it more bearable to see how feeble the country's representative institutions were becoming.

The right to impose taxes without consent was never conveyed to the monarchy or, for that matter, specifically claimed by the monarchy

---

66. Charles VII quickly moved élus into provinces where they had not functioned previously. Thomas, *Les états provinciaux*, 1 : 167–69.

67. The actual work of collecting the cash could still be carried on by the agents of some towns. For Lyons, see Caillet, *Lyon*, 263–66.

68. Thomas, *Les états provinciaux*, 1 : 70–72.

during the Renaissance. In the sixteenth century and even later, it was still possible for many observers to imagine that the French people possessed the right to grant taxes. The wording of royal tax edicts, especially the preambles, often gives the impression that the king had obtained the consent, or at least the advice, of his council and perhaps of the "Notables" of France.[69] Here and there, even after 1453, some scattered fig leaves remained to cover the nakedness of "tax absolutism." It still was perfectly possible for a town council, a powerful noble, or even the curé of an impoverished village to petition for some tax relief. But these were only shreds and patches of the sort of consent to taxes the English possessed, or the sort the French might have obtained if their constitutional development had followed another path.

AFTER THE DEATH OF CHARLES VII

Louis XI

The period of about seventy years between the fiscal reforms of Charles VII and those of Francis I is full of colorful events, generally, but it is not particularly significant in French tax history. We might think that the "universal spider," Louis XI (1461–83), left his imprint here; but this is not the case. Although Louis XI is famous for his high-handed use of the fiscal system, he changed it hardly at all. Indeed, with the potent fiscal tools developed by Charles VII, there was little need for Louis XI to make basic tax changes.

Ironically, one of the demands raised by the future Louis XI during the Praguerie of 1440 (in which he had been involved) was that the monarchy revise taxes drastically and cut away a major portion of the tax burden. Before his accession and for a very short while afterward Louis promised sweeping tax reforms and even made more specific commitments to some towns and provinces. He went so far as to promise the townspeople of Rheims, where the coronation ceremony took place, that *all* their "extraordinary" taxes would be abolished.

69. See La Barre, *Formulaire*, pp. 76–77, 360. Thus the edict of Fontainebleau, Nov. 10, 1602, speaks of taxes (of March 1597) as having been "accorded" to the king by the "three orders" (really, a Notables) of Rouen.

After waiting in vain for some tax relief, the exasperated people of Rheims organized a revolt and drove out the royal tax officials.[70] This was more than Louis XI had bargained for; the Rheims revolt was crushed, the ringleaders ferociously punished, and the tax system relentlessly clamped on again.

The uproar that resulted from this brutal reversal of policy and promises induced Louis to try a bold tax reform in a few selected provinces. In Languedoc, Normandy, and some of the other pays d'états, he allowed the provincial Estates to redeem all the "extraordinary" taxes (tailles, aides, and gabelles) in return for a lump sum annual payment, an *abonnement annuel*. Motivation for this reform was clear: the king would be relieved of the expenses of a tax bureaucracy, since the people of the provinces themselves were to handle the collection of this single tax; in addition, the hatred that always marked the relations between royal tax officials and the people would be avoided.[71] Louis had been told his treasury would lose nothing by such an exchange. But the would-be reformers were too optimistic. After only two years Louis realized he was suffering a serious decline in revenues from these provinces, and he promptly returned to the system of Charles VII.

By 1465 it was obvious that all Louis's promises concerning tax reforms were coming to nothing. Widespread disappointment and anger encouraged the grandees of France to stage an uprising in order to recover the power and independence they had enjoyed before the reforms of Charles VII—an uprising embellished by the name "War for the Public Weal." Louis suffered some grave defeats and had to make some humiliating concessions to break up this alliance of nobles, including giving Normandy as an appanage to his brother Charles of France who had taken the field against him.

Hardly had the dust of the "War for the Public Weal" settled than Louis decided to renege on the promises wrung from him. This was the occasion for calling the only Estates-General of his reign, assembled at Tours in 1468. Louis wanted a propaganda advantage by allowing the delegates to declare that they would never agree to permitting the alienation of an important province like Normandy. In these political

---

70. According to the letters-patent of December 1461 (Isambert, 10 : 422), only lower-class elements were involved.

71. Spont, "La taille en Languedoc," p. 501.

maneuvers, the king was enthusiastically supported by the deputies, who had no desire to see a reconstitution of a powerful feudal nobility with its incessant civil wars.

When fiscal affairs were brought up at Tours, however, the govern- ment experienced a few bad moments; vivid protests were raised con- cerning Louis's failure to abolish extraordinary taxes. But the crown's agents demonstrated they had no intention of asking this Estates- General for additional money. In the end, Louis was able to stave off all demands for important fiscal reforms. He even managed to obtain an authorization from the deputies to the effect that in case of another rebellion by nobles, the king should "without awaiting an additional assembly or convocation of Estates—since these are not easily brought together—do all that the maintenance of justice requires. . . ." [72] This phrase "all that the maintenance of justice requires" (*[il puisse faire] tout ce que ordre de justice le porte*) later was interpreted as an invita- tion to the king by the Estates to proceed to raise the revenues he needed without calling up another national assembly.[73]

Louis XI increased the tax burden on the French ruthlessly. In the last years of his reign taxes were approximately three times as heavy as at the beginning, a serious matter for a country just beginning to re- cover from the devastation of the Hundred Years' War.[74] Not that Louis was given to lavishing money on high living for himself or for his court. He worked hard at the business of being king, and he liked his work. He gave good wages and rich gifts to the middle-class mer- chants he favored as his chief administrators and advisors. For himself, he cherished only two expensive indulgences, his dogs and other pets and the large donations he made to various religious establishments. He dressed in plain, even mean clothes, and he hated pomp and dis- play. Life at his court was notoriously dull and unrewarding. Renais- sance writers, therefore, found him an easy mark for sarcastic com- ments on how mercilessly he raised taxes even though he was a "prince

72. Picot, *Etats Généraux*, 1 : 342.
73. Petit-Dutaillis, "Louis XI," *Cambridge Medieval History*, 8 : 295–96; Cla- mageran, *L'impôt*, 2 : 45–46.
74. From a total of about 1.8 million livres in 1461 to about 4.7 millions in 1483, according to Gandilhon, *Louis XI*, pp. 295–97; other sources suggest that maximum total taxes in this reign reached almost 6 millions.

to be pitied." [75] When it came to gifts and pensions for the great nobles, however, Louis XI was generous enough. His personal preference for living like a bourgeois and surrounding himself with middle-class counselors does not mean he cut off the flow of favors from the public treasury to the aristocrats, or that he reduced their fiscal exemptions and other financial privileges. As a class, the nobility fared very well under the fiscal régime of Louis XI. The chief vassals received large annual pensions—from 10,000 to 12,000 livres each.[76]

A major share of the money that Louis XI squeezed out of his subjects went to pay for his famous wars with Burgundy. Luckily for France, Duke Charles the Rash of Burgundy was killed in an unimportant fracas with some Swiss troops near Nancy (January 1477), and he did not leave a male heir. As a result, Louis XI was able to add Burgundy, Nevers, and portions of Flanders and Picardy to the French domains. The threat from the eastern frontier was gone—at least for a few generations. But the Burgundian wars were far from being the only serious financial strain on Louis's treasury. The expenses for the "War for the Public Weal" and for the recovery of Normandy from the duke of Berry were very high.[77] Furthermore, Louis was a "machiavellian before Machiavelli"; he was very free with French funds for the purpose of bribing influential persons attached to foreign courts, including Philippe de Commynes and several others serving the duke of Burgundy. A great deal of money went in the form of subsidies to the duke of Brittany and the king of England in attempts, not always successful, to keep them neutral during the fight with Burgundy.

Louis XI was even more lavish when it came to supporting his armed forces. He built up the French cavalry considerably; and, most important of all, he began the policy, thereafter a standard practice for French kings, of employing Swiss infantry mercenaries regularly. Partly because the Swiss were also enemies of Burgundy, partly because the French infantry was rather ineffectual, Louis paid over an annual subsidy, in peacetime as well as during wars, to several Swiss cantons. This allowed him to draw on several thousand excellent

75. E.g., La Barre, *Formulaire*, pp. 79–80.
76. Petit-Dutaillis, "Louis XI," p. 292.
77. For Normandy, see Clamageran, *L'impôt*, 2 : 26.

Swiss pikemen when needed; of course, during campaigns these mercenaries had to be paid additional amounts directly. Sums assigned to army
paymasters tripled during Louis's reign—from about 900,000 livres per
year to about 2.7 million livres.[78]

The two main sources of increased French revenues during this reign
were the much heavier tailles, borne mostly by the peasants, and a very
large number of forced loans and "gifts" from the cities.[79] The style of
Louis's fiscal policies was established right at the beginning of his
reign, in 1463, when he determined to buy back from Burgundy several
cities on the Somme, as he had the right to do according to the Treaty
of Arras (1435). For this, Louis had to raise 400,000 gold écus; when
his treasury could turn up only half that sum Louis raised the rest by
a heavy *crue* on the tailles, a stern imposition of forced loans on several
towns, and the appropriation (temporarily) of funds held in escrow by
French tribunals.[80]

There were a few other rather minor but interesting fiscal expedients
Louis employed. In 1470 he forced all commoners who owned considerable estates to accept titles of nobility, for which they had to pay.
He also increased the number of venal positions in the bureaucracy,
probably not so much for the money they brought the treasury as for
the opportunity to grant his favorites who took these posts attractive
positions with high wages.

What impressed his contemporaries even more than the type of expedients employed was the manner in which Louis imposed them. He
was prone to fly into a rage at any sign of resistance to his fiscal measures.[81] While his father had often employed negotiations with towns
or provinces which would not or could not pay, Louis took anything
less than immediate compliance as a personal affront. He almost always backed up his tax collectors and fiscal courts against taxpayers.
As a result, tax officials took such advantage of their privileged position
that hatred of them reached explosive proportions by the time Louis XI
died.

78. Petit-Dutaillis, in Lavisse 4² : 405.
79. Additional revenues were obtained when the counties of Provence, Bar, and
Maine were added to the domain in 1480–81; the lords of these lands died without leaving proper heirs.
80. Gandilhon, *Louis XI*, p. 344.
81. Petit-Dutaillis, in Lavisse 4² : 406.

Louis XI and the towns

One of the most famous aspects of Louis XI's economic policies was his concern for improving French trade and industry. Perhaps because he possessed rather bourgeois tastes himself and liked to associate with merchants, or because he understood that better trade would speed French recovery, he issued many decrees in favor of the wealthier middle classes. He promoted the development of a French silk industry; he worked hard to build up the fairs at Lyons at the expense of a nearby rival, Geneva; he encouraged long-distance trade and what turned out to be a vain search for important gold and silver mines; he even toyed with the idea of lowering internal tolls. On the whole, such policies were rather successful and deserve some of the credit for the prosperity of France in the 1470s—more than it had seen for many, many decades.[82]

Some historians have seen Louis's concern for the French bourgeoisie as signaling a desire to free the towns from all direct taxes. Clamageran, for example, believes that the king deliberately extended taille-exemptions already enjoyed by some so-called *bonnes villes* until almost all of them paid only indirect taxes. Clamageran sees this development, a policy of depending on the towns to pay aides and the villages to pay tailles, as reflecting a class distinction. He finds that in the eyes of contemporaries, by the end of Louis's reign, the tailles were thought of as peasants' taxes, marking an important change from the days when tailles were borne by all except clergy, nobles, and officers of the crown.[83]

Louis XI's inclination toward limiting towns to indirect taxes and peasants to direct taxes is a most interesting but unfortunately rather obscure development. There seems no questioning the fact that there was a real movement toward such a separation; but there are many bits of conflicting evidence: that is, examples of peasants paying aides and burghers paying tailles. Furthemore, it is impossible to discover if this

82. On Louis XI's attitude toward promoting economic growth, see Gaston Zeller, "Louis XI, la noblesse et la marchandise," *Annales: Economies, Sociétés, Civilisations* 1, no. 4 (1946); see also Gandilhon, *Louis XI*, pp. 295–96.

83. Clamageran, *L'impôt*, 2 : 69. Many historians have borrowed this concept from Clamageran.

sort of tax incidence was truly a deliberate crown policy, or if the increased number of exemptions from tailles was an unplanned development (see appendix G).

Exemption from the tailles did not give French cities any greater independence. Louis XI, in spite of his high regard for townsmen, steadily increased his pressure on towns to force them to submit to control by crown officials in all their affairs.[84] It is true, however, that Louis sometimes called together assemblies made up of representatives of his *bonnes villes* when he had to raise a forced loan, or when he wanted to get the burghers' views on other economic matters such as tolls, tariffs, and the state of the currency.[85] But such assemblies were expedients that signal Louis's suppleness in dealing with potential resistance rather than his support for "representative" participation by towns in his affairs. For the most part, when he decided to demand loans or "gifts" from the towns he did so without any pretense of consultation. When he had pushed a town's debt beyond its ability to meet the interest payments he would bestow an octroi on it. These octrois were usually tolls or small levies on sales or on the movement of goods into or near a town. Receipts from octrois went into the towns' treasuries. But such octrois were limited to a specific number of years, and could not be altered in any way without the crown's permission.

Given Louis's fiscal policies, it was inevitable that the relative importance of the aides and gabelles would diminish as time went on. In the last years of his reign, when the tailles were bringing in close to 4 million livres a year, the aides and gabelles together were worth only 655,000 livres.[86] At times Louis is known to have turned over the whole revenue of a town's gabelles to the town government; and he was rather free with grants of salt tax revenues to religious establishments as well as to towns.

Though they paid relatively light taxes, the richer townsmen did bear an important part of the fiscal burden. Louis treated them as a sort of reservoir of wealth to which he could turn when the need arose. In an emergency, after the fiscal experts in his council decided how much was needed, the élus, commissioners, and other officials would

84. Henri Sée, *Louis XI et les villes*, esp. pp. 40–42.
85. Major, *Representative Institutions*, pp. 52–53.
86. Petit-Dutaillis, in Lavisse 4² : 406 n. 1.

simply present the individual town governments with a bill for their respective portions. Henri Sée, in his study of Louis XI and his relations with the towns, concludes that these forced loans cost more than the tailles from which they were exempt. The rates of the tailles, at least, were fairly steady from year to year, even though in the long run they kept increasing; whereas the arbitrary power of the crown to impose forced loans might milk a town dry one year and leave it relatively untouched the next.[87]

Charles VIII and Louis XII

Immediately after the death of Louis XI, resentment against his oppressive rule boiled over and produced a situation which seemed to bring France to the verge of an important change in the French constitution and in royal tax power. The heir to the throne, Charles VIII (1483–98) was only a young boy, and a regency had been composed of some great nobles and Charles's older sister, Anne de Beaujeu, and her husband. Another Praguerie or War for the Public Weal seemed just around the corner, for the French nobility was more restless and dissatisfied than ever. The regency council was the scene of a hot struggle by various cliques maneuvering for power and privilege. Finally the council agreed to follow French tradition by calling an Estates-General at Tours (1484) to obtain national approval for the regency government and to hear and satisfy the many grievances of all classes and provinces.

Even before the Estates-General assembled, the Beaujeus promised an important cut in the tax burden. But the deputies, once at Tours, showed they were not satisfied by this. They demanded dismissal of many of the mercenary soldier companies, reduction of the pensions granted to favorites, removal of many of the most notoriously unfair tax officials, and cancellation of the alienation of crown lands made by Louis XI, so that there might be an increase in "ordinary" revenues. The regency quickly complied with most of these demands, but remained vague and noncommittal regarding the further demand that all future "extraordinary" taxes should wait upon prior consent from an Estates-General. Some deputies also demanded that in provinces with

87. Sée, *Louis XI et les villes*, pp. 126–29.

Estates the entire network of royal tax officials be abandoned. But the government was able to point to the failure of the *abonnement annuel* experiment in Normandy and Languedoc (1462) as proof that local agencies could not cope with the job of raising all the taxes.[88] Several important voices were raised to proclaim the principle of consent to taxes.[89] There was even a tendency to go further, and to demand some general control over the government by popular representatives in the name of the sovereignty of the people.[90]

Certainly one of the most powerful factors behind the resentment expressed by so many deputies was the great increase in taxes under Louis XI, especially the tailles. With some of the deputies proclaiming they would refuse to vote any tailles whatsoever, the regency was in a decidedly difficult position. In answer to requests by the government that they vote a taille, the deputies of the Third Estate presented a moving portrayal of the plight of the peasants, harassed unbearably by the collectors of tailles and gabelles.[91] When representatives of the regency pointed out that the royal administration would collapse without funds, the deputies insisted they be given the right to go over all of the accounts, so as to verify the allowable government expenses. The regency complied, after some hesitation; but the accounts presented to the deputies were such palpable frauds, with exaggerated expenses and minimized incomes, that another impasse was reached.[92]

Finally some deputies proposed that the Estates-General grant the king the same amount of tailles collected during the reign of Charles VII, or about 1.2 million livres. The chancellor demurred, pointing out that the value of money had fallen so low that it would require 1.5 million livres to equal in purchasing power the tailles collected prior to the reign of Louis XI. A compromise was worked out whereby some of the more recent royal tolls and tariffs would be revoked; in return the deputies would assent to a levy of 1.2 million livres in tailles, plus 300,000 livres extra for the current year only, as a gift for the new

88. Clamageran, *L'impôt*, 2 : 25, 76.
89. Possibly one of these was Philippe de Commynes. See the comments on Commynes's memoirs in Ewart Lewis, *Medieval Political Ideas*, esp. 1 : 137–39.
90. Major, *Representative Institutions*, pp. 87–89.
91. Picot, *Etats Généraux*, 2 : 69–72.
92. Clamageran, *L'impôt*, 2 : 60–61, 67–68; Picot, *Etats Généraux*, 2 : 73–74.

rule (*don de joyeux avènement*). Most importantly, the deputies insisted on another convocation of the Estates-General in two years to consider again the matter of "extraordinary" taxes.

Therefore, while the Estates-General did not succeed in satisfying all its grievances concerning taxes, it did win a significant victory in reducing the tailles to less than one-third the level collected during the last years of Louis XI. Before long, however, it was apparent that any power the Estates-General had possessed in 1484 to force the king to convoke an Estates-General in order to collect future tailles was irretrievably lost. The Beaujeus ignored demands that another Estates-General be called in 1486, although that had been part of the agreement at Tours. The *don* of 300,000 livres that had been voted supposedly for one year only was collected again the very next year; and in fact the rate of the taille was increased gradually to about 2.5 million livres by the end of the reign.

The French, however, seemed to grow less concerned with taxes as the fifteenth century drew to a close. The country's prosperity was growing steadily, and the tailles and other taxes were maintained at a quite moderate level, compared to the days of Louis XI. Exciting political events, furthermore, now occupied the nobles' attention. In 1488 the last duke of Brittany died, leaving only a daughter, Anne de Bretagne, as his heir. The Beaujeus moved vigorously to break up a marriage between Anne and the Hapsburg ruler, and in 1491 the French invaded Brittany and forced that province to accept Charles VIII as Anne's husband; the first step had been taken toward French absorption of this vital province. The year 1494 saw the beginning of the Wars of Italy—the opening of an entirely new phase in the relations between France and the rest of Europe. For the French, these campaigns were not too serious a financial burden, since for ten years or so much of the expense was borne by the Italian provinces through which the armies marched.

Louis XII, *père du peuple*

Louis XII (1498–1515) won resounding acclaim for his restraint in tax matters, and in fact behaved so thoroughly in accord with the ideals of fiscal righteousness that he established an important legend.[93] Louis is supposed to have announced at the beginning of his reign that he would limit taxes to the minimum needed for the defense of the realm; and apparently he kept his word as long as he could. When he mounted the throne he freed crown officials and pensionnaires from their traditional obligation to give a "gift for the joyous accession." Louis kept down the level of the tailles—with the exception of a few years—almost to the end of his reign, and even lowered it on occasion. Around 1500, the tailles cost the French only about 2.3 million livres annually compared to the 3.9 million collected under Louis XI. In one famous incident, Louis XII actually ordered his agents to stop a surtax they were already in the process of collecting when the reason for the increase, a revolt against the French in Genoa, petered out.[94] When hard pressed for funds Louis preferred to alienate portions of the domaines revenues or to rely on loans and forced loans rather than to impose heavier taxes.

Louis underlined his attitude by ostentatiously avoiding excessive luxury expenditure in his own household and gifts to courtiers. He managed to cut the annual total of gifts and pensions from over 500,000 livres annually around 1500 to less than half of that by 1510 (though in 1513 and 1514 this type of expense went up again).[95] "Le roi roturier" (the commoner king), the legend goes, was the epithet given him by disappointed courtiers. To this the king is supposed to have made the dignified reply: "I much prefer to make the dandies laugh at my miserliness than to make the people weep at my open-handedness." His reward, in history, is the title "Père du peuple." Another of his achievements that endeared him to commentators on taxes in later, less happy eras was a great improvement in the revenues from the domaines. Increases in the size of the royal domain, and a much improved administration, allowed Louis XII to almost triple domaines income to a total of 231,000 livres annually, or about 6.5 percent of total revenues—by far the greatest proportion of this category of royal

93. La Barre, *Formulaire*, pp. 96–97, claims Louis XII virtually limited his revenues to those coming "de son Domaine, et signament de son patrimoine"—a wild exaggeration.

94. Antoine Bailly, *Histoire financière de la France*, 2 vols. (Paris, 1830), 1 : 206.

95. Spont, "La taille en Languedoc," p. 510.

income during the Renaissance.[96] Louis XII certainly showed he was attempting, at least, to "live of his own."

We now know that up to a point it was relatively easy for Louis XII to please the taxpayers because for many years his wars in Italy more than paid for themselves through plunder. At the very end of his reign, when he was in great difficulties, the taxes went up; but the legend and the attitude which nourished it persisted.[97]

ROYAL BORROWING DURING THE EARLY RENAISSANCE:
THE FISCAL SPONGE

During the worst periods of the Hundred Years' War, such as when it became necessary to ransom John the Good, and during the Armagnac-Burgundian civil war in the first years of the fifteenth century, the government borrowed large sums of money from merchant-bankers. We have seen that this was also the case during the time of the "king of Bourges" before the 1430s—but this early borrowing was done reluctantly. The great reforms of Charles VII are also significant in that they allowed the king to put the bankers back in their place.

Certain royal officials, such as the famous Jacques Coeur, functioned as borrowing agents for the king, searching out capital. But even Coeur was stripped of his wealth and position—in a fearsomely cruel and autocratic manner. This signalized the French king's confidence in his tax revenues—as did, perhaps even more, the fact that Coeur was not replaced by a comparable financial agent.[98] Louis XI continued this policy of avoiding the services of professional lenders.[99]

While the great Italian merchant-bankers were doing a thriving business lending to other rulers, in early Renaissance France they were called on mainly when kings led their forces across the Alps during

96. Imbart de la Tour, *Les origines de la Réforme*, 1 : 188–97; Spont, "La taille en Languedoc," p. 369.
97. The cahiers presented to the Estates-General of 1576 recount the legend, as do the arguments at the even more critical Estates-General of 1588. Clamageran, *L'impôt*, 2 : 224; and Nicholas Rolland du Plessis, *Remonstrances . . . sur les desordres et misères de ce royaume* (Paris, 1588), p. 117.
98. Accounts of Jacques Coeur are legion. There is a good survey by A. R. My-ers, "The Rise and Fall of Jacques Coeur," *History Today* 16, nos. 7 and 8 (1966).
99. Gandilhon, *Louis XI*, pp. 344–48.

the Wars of Italy. Until the 1540s, as we shall see in chapter 4, the kings of France got along rather well without foreign or French merchant-bankers. The proportion of borrowing to total revenues was small enough so that in most years interest-bearing debts could be repaid fairly easily out of taxes; and effectively there was no French royal long-term debt at all.

The king's ability to handle many of his emergency expenses without recourse to professional money lenders helps explain why there were relatively few great French capitalists during this era. Another reason is that the business techniques of the French were surprisingly backward. They had not learned, for example, to form partnerships easily or to accept funds for deposit. They did loan out small sums, but usually only in return for annuities on income from real estate.

Whatever the reasons, the kings of France seemed to shun loans from professional money lenders. Instead they used expedients such as pledging crown jewels, squeezing cash from officials and courtiers, or forcing loans on towns. When the king, for example, forced loans on his "good towns," they were hardly in as favorable a position to refuse him as was, say, an agent of the Medici. And for most forced loans the king paid no interest, at least officially, though he might make other concessions to coat the pill. Furthermore, when the king borrowed from his ever-increasing body of officials he also paid no interest, though the lenders sometimes were compensated with disguised interest in the form of higher salaries or other payments. It is helpful to think of such expedients as "inside" credit resources and to distinguish them from loan resources outside the direct control of the king.

Italian merchant-bankers in France, of course, were often subject to pressure to loan the king money when they would have preferred not to; but the degree of compulsion here was much less, since foreign merchants, at the worst, could write off their losses and leave the country. Those who granted "outside" loans were primarily motivated by profit opportunities; those caught up in the web of "inside" credit, on the other hand, counted themselves lucky if they emerged without severe losses. When the French king had to borrow, therefore, he could consider two sets of credit resources, each with different advantages and disadvantages.

One of the more important forms of "inside" credit was the king's ability to squeeze large sums of money from his corps of fiscal officers. To men of the Renaissance, this was a highly justified device. They were quite convinced that tax collectors and their associates normally used their strategic positions to build personal fortunes that were rightfully the king's. Whether or not fiscal officials were corrupt, they did act as a mechanism to soak up some of the country's cash both because they held so much of it in their keeping and because they themselves tended to be wealthy.

In every edict, tract, and manual that discusses the general qualifications of tax officials, the first criterion mentioned is that they be *solvables & capables*; this apparently is more important than being *bonnes, loyales, & lettrez*. Ostensibly, rich men were required because poor men were more likely to gouge the taxpayers and cheat the crown. But it is apparent from the way the system operated that a very important reason fiscal officials had to be rich is that they had to lend money to the crown.

There were many ways of squeezing this fiscal sponge. The simplest was *anticipations*, or overdrafts. When tax income fell too low (as during a crop failure) or expenses went too high (as during the movement of an exceptionally large number of troops through a district), tax officials were asked to advance needed funds out of their own purses.[100] In return, the lending official would be given a warrant specifying from which of next year's tax receipts he was to be repaid, and how much. At other times the official was granted an increase in salary to repay him for the overdraft.

This point is worth stressing because many of us have had our ideas on this matter shaped by Richard Ehrenberg's famous *Capital and Finance in the Age of the Renaissance* (London, 1928), the classic work on public finance during this era. Ehrenberg gives the impression that the French government was completely dependent on capitalists for loans.[101] But the fiscal sponge—that is, the large amounts of cash moving through the French tax machine—explains how, especially be-

100. Rey, *Le domaine du roi*, p. 276.

101. Even Ehrenberg admits the huge payments for the ransom of Francis I's sons were handled without tapping the capital markets (see *Capital and Finance*, pp. 289–300); see also Michel François, *Le cardinal François de Tournon*, pp. 80–83.

fore the 1540s, the king was able to get along with only small and relatively infrequent help from "outside" credit. In the late Middle Ages, we must recognize, France began to go along a fiscal-financial track of her own.[102] Because of the particularly lucrative and "absolutist" tax structure in France the government found itself possessed of a mechanism which could provide almost enough quasi loans, forced loans, and other sums to handle emergencies.

102. E. B. Fryde and M. M. Fryde, "Public Credit, with Special Reference to North-Western Europe," *Cambridge Economic History of Europe*, 3 : 484, locate the beginnings of this divergence in the late fourteenth century.

3

A More Tractable Tax System:
The Reforms of Francis I

Jacques de Beaune, sire of Semblançay

Political history is conveniently marked off by reigns, revolutions, wars, and treaties. But in the slow, complex changes that make up most of the material of institutional history, it is often difficult to find good dividing points. However, this cannot be said about the 1520s in French fiscal history, when some basic changes were dramatized by the execution of the person most closely identified with the old system. This unfortunate man was Jacques de Beaune, sire of Semblançay, one of the *gens des finances* during the later years of the reign of Louis XII and, for eight years, under Francis I. His disgrace and death mark the end of the revenue system of Charles VII (just as the decline and fall of another, more famous, royal financier, Jacques Coeur, marked its beginning). The career of Jacques Coeur is a familiar story; but, except to specialists in French history, Semblançay remains an unknown figure. And yet the events that brought Semblançay to the gibbet are part and parcel of the decision to institute the fiscal reforms of the 1520s. Therefore his story is worth telling in some detail.

Semblançay, born around 1458 (the precise date is unknown), came from the same background as Jacques Coeur. His family had included successful merchants of Tours, specializing in the cloth trade. Young Jacques established himself in Brittany, where he obtained an office in the still autonomous financial system of that duchy. He is supposed to have accomplished some diplomatic missions for the duchess of Brittany after her marriage to Louis XII, king of France. And he may have had some influence in reconciling Queen Anne to her enemy, Louise of Savoy, the mother of Prince Francis of Angoulême (Francis was next in line to succeed Louis XII when it became apparent the king and Anne would not have a male heir).

In 1495, possibly as a reward for his diplomatic services, de Beaune was given one of the top positions in the royal administrative system —the generalship of Languedoc's finances. He quickly put together one of the kingdom's great fortunes and became as indispensable to the king as he had been to Anne of Brittany. As de Beaune's importance increased, the king heaped gifts, additional offices, and honors upon him. In 1498 he was given a patent of nobility, and in 1515—the year of the accession of Francis I—he obtained the title "Sire de Semblançay," which went along with one of his recently acquired estates.

In 1509 Semblançay advanced to the generalship of Languedoïl, the highest paying post in the whole financial system. After this time he is referred to as *surintendant général des finances* in some works of the period. But this was flattery; it certainly did not mean he had the powers of the *surintendant des finances* of the later Renaissance. Among the gens des finances in Semblançay's time, the one who held the generalship of Languedoïl enjoyed precedence; but he was only the first among equals. Those who believe Semblançay exercised the authority of a Sully or a Colbert have been misled.

Before the reforms of Francis I, the king employed all four *généraux des finances* (in charge of the "extraordinary" taxes) as well as the four *trésoriers de France* (in charge of the "ordinary" taxes) as a subcouncil of finance. These gens des finances had the obligation of consulting together on matters of high policy. On such occasions they functioned as a unit—a *collège*, to use a contemporary term. Most importantly, they had primary responsibility for producing the national preliminary budget, the *état général de prévision*. They were also the chiefs of all the middle- and lower-echelon fiscal officials apart from those of the fiscal courts.

The généraux had another duty of pressing concern to the king: they saw that cash was available at all times for the government. This last point is vital, since France had such a decentralized system of payments. The généraux had to be able to move money about the country quickly, which meant they had to know which of the collectors had supplies of cash and which officials could be tapped for emergency loans. When the king needed cash in a hurry, or when fighting troops were too far from their regular paymasters, the généraux had to locate funds and scrape them together. During the Wars of Italy, between 1495 and 1520, the généraux performed prodigies for the king. But later, when the fighting became extremely costly, the gens-des-finances system broke down and was discarded.

Francis I strove constantly to add to the glory he won in 1515 at the battle of Marignano, when he defeated the vaunted Swiss infantry and went on to conquer Milan. He even attempted to get himself elected Holy Roman Emperor by tendering magnificent bribes to several of the Electors—who took his money and then voted for Charles of Hapsburg instead. Francis I is also famous for his magnificent state reception for Henry VIII of England on the Field of the Cloth of Gold (June 1520), a series of entertainments reputed to have cost the French some 200,000 livres.[1] As the level of royal expenditures soared, Semblançay's services became invaluable. By 1518 he was recognized officially as the foremost officer of the royal fiscal system.[2]

The crisis of 1521–22

Semblançay's role in government finance became even more important after 1520. The French were harried out of Milan by Charles V; and the struggle was broadened to additional fronts in Flanders, the Lowlands, Burgundy, and Navarre. Semblançay's talent for talking Italian and French merchants into parting with their money was never more necessary. Begging letters came to him from the king and the queen mother, Louise of Savoy, who acted as regent while her son was off on campaigns.[3] Exerting himself to the utmost, Semblançay managed to raise 364,000 livres in the autumn of 1521 alone; for the two years

1. Roger Doucet, L'état des finances de 1523, p. 6.
2. Arthur de Boislisle, "Semblançay et la surintendance des finances," Annuaire-Bulletin de la Société de l'Histoire de France 18 (1881). He believes that Semblançay was officially surintendant; but Doucet finds he had only the functions not the title. Etude sur le gouvernement de François Ier dans ses rapports avec le Parlement de Paris, 1 : 186–87.
3. Alfred Spont, Semblançay (?–1527): la Bourgeoisie financière au début du XVIe siècle, p. 180; and De Boislisle, "Semblançay," pp. 236–37.

of crisis, 1521 and 1522, Semblançay's borrowing and other measures raised almost 2 million livres for his king.[4]

But it was not enough. The royal council had to authorize the most desperate expedients to pay the French gendarmerie and the Swiss and German mercenaries whom Francis was collecting for another campaign to recover Milan. Large portions of royal lands were sold, dozens of noble titles and new royal offices were sold, and the taille was raised by one surtax after another. All the gens des finances were sent out to scour towns for municipal and private loans.[5] The king, at Semblançay's suggestion, issued an edict allowing royal agents to appropriate church vessels of precious metal; a great scandal resulted when they seized the gilt and silver screen erected by Louis XI around the tomb of St. Martin of Tours.[6] Semblançay tried to warn the queen mother that he was near the end of his resources: "People run from me," he wrote; "their purses stay closed."

It was in these desperate months that Semblançay made a serious mistake. As private banker to the queen mother he had been given 160,000 livres of her personal money for safe keeping; about 53,000 livres had been spent on the queen's account, so that 107,000 livres remained owing to her. Semblançay also had been entrusted with a special fund of 600,000 livres, money paid to Francis I by Charles V (out of the revenues of Naples) as part of the general settlement following the successful French campaign of 1515–16. At first this sum was supposed to constitute a reserve for emergencies; that is, Semblançay did not have specific permission to use it on his own authority. In any case, Louise had come to regard this additional hoard of cash, also, as her personal wealth—apparently at some point the king had promised it to her.[7]

Constantly bombarded by demands to pay the soldiers, Semblançay interpreted letters from the queen mother, directing him to "use every means," as sufficient authority to send these private funds off to the army paymasters. Had not the king, in August 1521, also urged him, "Do not trouble yourself about anything, for I will guarantee you

4. Doucet, François Ier, 1 : 188.
5. Doucet, L'état des finances de 1523, pp. 6–7.
6. Spont, Semblançay, pp. 189–90.
7. Doucet, François Ier, 1 : 189.

against all eventualities"?[8] Semblançay later claimed—with much justice, it would seem—that the king and the queen mother had given him at least implicit permission to use any and all of their funds.

The queen mother felt otherwise, to put it mildly. Louise of Savoy was an inordinately greedy woman who had used her position at court to build up a great fortune in land and money.[9] She was hardly the sort of person who could forgive Semblançay for spending her private wealth and, what was possibly worse, for revealing her as not willing to donate every penny to the cause of national glory.

In the spring of 1522 a large French army under Lautrec, a general whose chief recommendation was that he was the brother of Madame de Châteaubriant (the king's mistress), was approaching Milan, committed to recovering the city. The signs were good—Hapsburg forces in Lombardy were relatively small, and there were plenty of pro-French elements inside Milan. But Lautrec was so poorly and so fitfully provided with cash that his Swiss mercenaries, the core of his army, were becoming undependable. Finally, in April 1522, the Swiss captains announced they could no longer keep their troops together; but for the sake of their honor, they stated, they would make one frontal attack on the imperial troops at Bicocca, a few miles from Milan. Lautrec pleaded with them to wait only a few more days, but they rebuffed him; there was nothing he could do but join in the attack, which was poorly conceived and resulted in a disastrous slaughter of the French and especially the Swiss. The surviving Swiss immediately packed up and went home, and the French were forced to break off the campaign. The crowning irony is that army paymasters truly had been on their way to Lautrec, but they had been provided with a guard insufficient to get them through Hapsburg-controlled country. The money bags had been only a few days' march from the Swiss all the while.[10]

After the disaster at Bicocca, Lautrec came back to the French court to make his excuses. He accused Semblançay of holding back the troops' pay and therefore of being the chief cause of France's shame.

8. Ibid.

9. For details on French revenues allotted to Louise of Savoy these years, see Doucet, L'état des finances de 1523, pp. 32 n. 3, 41, 68 n. 4.

10. This interpretation of the location of the army's pay is from Ernest Lavisse and Alfred Rambaud, eds., Histoire générale du IVe siècle à nos jours, 12 vols., 2d ed. (Paris, n.d.), 4 : 98.

Semblançay and his fellow financiers, however, were able to show the money had been sent. But the story of Semblançay's supposed treachery spread widely, since he was a handy scapegoat for absolving the court and French chivalry of their failure.[11]

About this time the généraux and trésoriers were putting together a revised estimate for fiscal 1521. It showed that despite increased taxes, alienations of domain lands, and other expedients, expenses had outrun income by the enormous total of 3.56 million livres. Such a deficit was the equivalent of an entire year's revenue in this era. Royal finances were in such terrible disorder that the état de prévision for 1523 showed an anticipated deficit of about 2.8 million livres; even after emergency tax increases were thrown into the breach, the deficit for 1523 was at least 815,000 livres, and probably much more.[12] The king was furious and made some ominous remarks about how all his fiscal agents were cheating him. Semblançay, however, was retained in his official position; in fact, the king was still pressing him to arrange for more loans from the Lyons merchants. Poor Semblançay, now quite old and tired, and apprehensive about the steadily mounting recriminations against his colleagues and himself, would have liked nothing better than to retire. But such a way out was not to be permitted.

The fall of Semblançay

In March 1523 the royal council created a new type of fiscal official, the trésorier de l'Epargne, and transferred to this person some of the powers of the généraux des finances. The first alterations in the fiscal

11. Guillaume du Bellay, one of Francis I's military commanders in later years and the author of a famous book of memoirs, claimed Semblançay held back 400,000 écus from the soldiers on the pretext the money had been requisitioned from him by Louise. Spont, Semblançay, p. 188; and Sir Charles Oman, A History of the Art of War in the Sixteenth Century (New York, [1937]), pp. 177 ff., 184n. Other Renaissance writers besides du Bellay accuse Semblançay and other gens des finances; Jean Bourgoin, in his Le pressoir des esponges du roy, p. 10, blames Semblançay and his fellows for the defeat at Pavia, the imprisonment of the king, and "autres accidents sinistres." Similar interpretations are still found in modern works.

12. Doucet, L'état des finances de 1523, pp. 12, 20. See also Georges Jacqueton, "Le Trésor de l'Epargne sous François Ier (1523-1547)," Revue Historique 55 (1894) : 26, who estimates the total accumulated deficit at the end of 1523 at about 4 million livres.

system of Charles VII were already taking place. At the same time, Semblançay's salaries were stopped, and it was apparent that he was disgraced, although he was allowed to retain some of his honors (and the king was still harassing him with demands that he raise more money). We know that 173,000 livres in loans were obtained by Semblançay in 1523, even after the process of his disgrace was well under way.[13] Semblançay was ordered to have his accounts cleared by an investigating commission, which had already undertaken the job of checking the books of some of his colleagues.[14]

Many of the details of the Semblançay episode, from this point on, remain very obscure; certainly it is difficult to understand why the king insisted on such ferocious punishment. But it seems clear that after 1523 Francis and his mother probably did believe, as Louise wrote in her journal, that they had been "continuously robbed" by the gens des finances since the first year of the reign.[15] Contrasting the opulence of the "gens" with his monetary embarrassments, it was easy for Francis to believe that the situation would improve once he seized their ill-gotten gains. Ignorant as the king was concerning the details of his loosely organized fiscal system, it was easy for the chancellor, Antoine Duprat (who was Semblançay's implacable enemy), to convince him that he could recover millions of livres that belonged to the crown if he punished some of the fiscal officials and threw a scare into the others.[16]

13. Doucet, *L'état des finances de 1523*, p. 21.

14. This commission had been established in January 1523 under the control of Duprat.

15. Jacqueton, "Le Trésor de l'Epargne," pp. 3–4. The statement she made of how she and her son had been "continuously robbed" by the gens des finances since 1515 must have made a great impression; it is quoted and referred to in tracts, treatises, and even edicts. See also Spont, *Semblançay*, p. 208. Louise's journal is in C. B. Petitot et al., *Collection complète des mémoires relatifs à l'histoire de France*, ser. 1, 52 vols. (Paris, 1819–26), 16 : 399. See also Henri Hauser, "Le 'journal' de Louise de Savoie," *Revue Historique* 86 (1904) : 281, 286. The statement also appears, quite unexpectedly, in a treatise on fiscal reform written just about the time of the 1523 reforms; see University of Pennsylvania MS. Fr. 18, and see the transcription and translation in Martin Wolfe and Norman Zacour, "The Growing Pains of French Finance, 1522–1523," *Library Chronicle* 22 (1956) : 62–63, 81.

16. Chancellor Duprat had additional grievances against the "gens"; he accused them of being unwilling to provide sufficient funds for the campaigns of 1524–25 and 1527. Michel François, *Le Cardinal François de Tournon*, pp. 59–60.

Semblançay, on the other hand, beyond a doubt believed that he had not only acted within the law but that he had used his experience and talents to pull France out of one financial scrape after another. Certainly he had received letters from the king and Louise that begged him for more money and thanked him effusively for past financial feats.[17] Quite courageously, though perhaps foolishly, he challenged the competence of the commission set up early in 1523 to verify his accounts. He used the formality of arguing that he was not a *comptable* —an official who received cash and therefore kept books—but rather an *ordonnateur*, a supervisor; insofar as he had accounts, they were his own personal books, representing work he had done as the king's agent.

Louise of Savoy, irritated by Semblançay's presumptuousness, had him brought before the special investigating commission in March 1524. She gave notice that all persons who would not submit to this commission would be jailed for lese majesty. Semblançay then came forward with the required information, but he insisted on presenting accounts drawn up according to his own interpretation of the facts.

What particularly vexed Semblançay was the queen mother's insistence that he had injured her by amalgamating her affairs with those of the crown. In other words, Louise wanted the 707,000 livres Semblançay had spent in 1521 to be regarded as his personal debt to her, while Semblançay naturally insisted it be deducted from the huge amounts he was owed by the king, much of which he had borrowed from French and foreign merchant-bankers. One of the principal pieces of evidence Semblançay produced was a royal warrant for the huge sum of 1,574,000 livres for money raised in 1521 and 1522; this included the 707,000 livres belonging to Louise. The warrant was a rather vaguely worded acknowledgment of the total debt of the crown to Semblançay. In form it was an order to comptables to pay Semblançay the specified amounts; of course, large sums of money were simply not available in *généralité* treasuries these hectic years. Semblançay seems to have demanded the warrant in order to reassure his own creditors, especially the foreign merchant-bankers in Lyons.[18] He was afraid that if he man-

17. De Boislisle, "Semblançay," p. 234.
18. The warrant itself is listed in the *Catalogue des actes de François Ier*, vol. 5, no. 17461. See Doucet, *François Ier*, 1 : 196 ff.; Spont, *Semblançay*, p. 179; and Doucet, *L'état des finances de 1523*, p. 7.

aged to pay back Louise first he never would recover the rest of the money.

The fiscal commission forced Semblançay to draw up separate reckonings for Francis and Louise and ruled that Semblançay could not cancel his debt to the queen mother with the credits he held against the king. But the same commission, to the amazement of the king, verified the correctness of every item Semblançay said he had borrowed to meet royal expenses: 911,000 livres for 1521, and 322,000 more for loans raised since then.[19] (This judgment was given in January 1525.) If the king had actually made good on his promises, Semblançay would have been able to pay Louise and have 526,000 livres left over—money which, he assured the commission, he needed immediately to pay back the merchants who had trusted him with their funds.

This was the state of Semblançay's affairs during the sad years 1525–26, in which France suffered an even more disastrous military adventure. The battle of Pavia (November 1525) not only annihilated another French army but also made Francis I a prisoner of his Hapsburg enemies. For two years, therefore, Louise and Duprat were too busy holding the country together and preparing to resist invasion to do much about Semblançay, who was now trying to placate his creditors, anxious about their loans to him, as well they might be; a financier out of favor was a financier who could not pay. Semblançay and his family still had considerable real property—estates, town houses, furniture—and his creditors now began proceedings to attach them. But Duprat and the queen mother were in a better position to get revenge and repayment. Later in 1526, with the king safely home from captivity after signing away all that Charles V wanted, Duprat began accumulating evidence for a criminal trial for Semblançay. The government now possessed damaging evidence provided by Jean Prévost, a high tax official himself, who apparently had made a deal with Duprat in an effort to save his own neck.[20] Suddenly, in January 1527, Semblançay was seized and thrown into the Bastille.

No less than twenty-five counts were raised against him at the trial. The main charges were that he had had no authority to spend Louise

---

19. De Boislisle, "Semblançay," p. 250.
20. We know that in this crisis Jean Prévost enjoyed the protection of Louise of Savoy.

of Savoy's money; that he had profited mightily on money collected as revenues and loaned to Italian bankers at interest; that he had forged statements of loans to the king; and that he had lied to the king about his own obligations to his creditors. Semblançay's defense was that he had padded his statements of loans to bankers in order to defend himself against the crown's insistent demands for further loans.[21]

Most of the remaining charges involved technical irregularities regarding Semblançay's methods; but he was able to refute them easily or to show that the king knew that emergencies called for unusual methods. For example, Semblançay was blamed for substituting his own credit for the king's so that loans could be made to him personally; this did confuse the legal situation, but it was exactly what the king had begged him to do, and the judges must have known this perfectly well.[22] Another important charge was that some of the money he had raised and turned over to the paymasters was not in cash but in *décharges* (pay warrants); paymasters who needed so-called *espèces sonnantes* ("ringing coins," that is, hard cash), had to realize these décharges at a serious discount. The implication was that Semblançay had made great profits in secret arrangements with the collectors and others called on to cash these décharges. But this is the sort of practice that had been going on among the gens des finances since the mid-fifteenth century. Insofar as Semblançay was guilty of such charges (and the records of the trial show this is far from proved), it was the system that stood condemned, not the man; but the man was to pay with his life.

Far from broken in spirit, Semblançay continued to deny the substance of the charges against him while making eloquent but dignified appeals for mercy. These were useless; he was condemned August 9, 1527, and hanged three days later. His noble title was stripped away in order to deny him a more dignified death by beheading.

With rather cruel haste, another commission was set up to liquidate

21. Henry Lemonnier, *Les guerres d'Italie: La France sous Charles VIII, Louis XII, et François Ier*, p. 233.

22. Semblançay was also charged with accepting a bribe of 13,000 livres from Cardinal Wolsey; this turned out to be a loan to Semblançay from Wolsey, carried out with authorization by the crown and used for royal purposes. Doucet, *François Ier*, 2 : 225 ff.

his property. This new group, known after the building where it met as the Tour quarrée commission, fixed the order in which Semblançay's creditors were to be paid. Louise was allowed to strip his houses of furniture and tapestries. The king was paid the 300,000 livres adjudged him by the trial commission as "restitution"—of what, was not specified. Semblançay's widow and heirs, maintaining the polite fiction that it was the judges and not the king who had been at fault, brought suit to clear Semblançay's name and to set aside the judgment ordering his remaining property sold. For this they were punished for contumacy so severely that it was borne home to all that the king would not be thwarted, whatever the justice of the situation.

The Tour quarrée commission also undertook the task of extracting as much money as possible from Semblançay's former colleagues. Victims of the same hatreds, jealousies, and misunderstandings that had tainted Semblançay, more than a score of important fiscal officials suffered punishments ranging from death to the loss of their jobs and salaries plus heavy fines. In theory, some of these fines amounted to several hundred thousand livres, though apparently only a small fraction was actually recovered for the crown.[23] This special judicial commission, apparently still meeting in its "square tower," continued into the 1530s.

THE TRÉSORIER DE L'EPARGNE

Toward a centralized treasury

It was easy for Francis I to vilify the old fiscal system and to execute one of its heads. It would have been much harder to have created a new and better system. But he certainly tried. The reign of Francis I is characterized by a surprisingly large number of changes in the fiscal system, strung out over a period of twenty-five years (1523–47).[24] Almost all these changes concern the higher levels of fiscal administra-

23. Ibid., pp. 241–42. Another of the gens des finances, Jean de Poncher, a close associate of Semblançay, was hanged.

24. Some idea of the great number of these changes can be obtained by leafing through the huge list of titles of fiscal edicts in the eight volumes of titles of ordinances, *Catalogue des actes de François Ier.*

tion, rather than the structure of taxes or constitutional matters of tax power, as during the fifteenth century.[25]

Some of these reforms can be dismissed as fumbling, some as cynical gestures; some certainly hurt more than they helped. On the whole, however, they represent an interesting and ambitious attempt to grapple with a most exasperating fiscal problem: the country is rich and taxes are rising; why, then, cannot the tax system provide satisfactory amounts of revenue?

Disregarding for the moment all but the most essential of these changes, we can see that there are really two groups of reforms having as their pivots the edicts of December 1523 and December 1542. The first set of reforms replaced the gens des finances with a new directorate, more responsive to the royal will and more able to provide ready cash. The second group, which continued into the reign of Henry II, was aimed at developing a more effective provincial control over lower-echelon élection officials; this effort finally produced the framework of the généralité of the Old Régime.

The reform of March 1523

The royal edict of St. Germain-en-Laye, March 18, 1523, marks the beginning of the end of the gens des finances fiscal system. On that date the order went out to create a new official, the "trésorier de l'Epargne et receveur général des parties casuelles et inopinées des finances." The term *Epargne* was chosen to show that this new treasurer was to have different functions from those of the *changeur du Trésor.* The main function of the new trésorier de l'Epargne was to build a war chest large enough to allow Francis I to throw his forces into the field as the situation required, without being baffled by the creaky machinery of his fiscal system.

The source of this war chest was to be "all casual and unexpected funds"; that is, those windfall revenues that could not be anticipated in regular budgets—fines, feudal dues, expropriations and escheats, the clerical tenths, forced or voluntary loans, proceeds from the alienation of royal domaines, and, most importantly, sales of venal offices. There

25. One important financial reform not concerned with fiscal administration, however, did appear in this reign: the first royal bonds, *rentes sur l'Hôtel de Ville.*

had been individual collectors for many of these revenues previously; now they were to be all "levied and held in one hand only" and earmarked for the military. Philibert Babou, who formerly had been trésorier for Languedoïl (as Louise of Savoy's personal finance agent, he had worked for Semblançay's downfall), was chosen to be the first trésorier de l'Epargne.[26]

The reform of March 1523 stands in French Renaissance tax history as a great success. It certainly was acclaimed as such by the government, which probably was anxious to show how right it had been in its decision to attack the gens des finances. In the preamble to the even more important fiscal reform of December 1523, the king expressed himself as being delighted with the March edict; he gave it credit for having saved his subjects from another surtax on tailles or some other exasperating expedient.[27]

The reform of December 1523

The next step in this series of reforms—and the key step—was the edict of Blois, December 28, 1523.[28] The trésorier de l'Epargne was given a completely different role. The government was ready to try centralizing *all* the country's revenues in the same office. Therefore the trésorier de l'Epargne was to have his powers vastly augmented. He was to receive the net revenues of both the "ordinaries" (the domaines), and the "extraordinaries" (the tailles, aides, gabelles, and traites). Apart from authorized local expenses, all French revenues were now to be shipped to a central treasury.[29] And, even more daring, all payments except those regularly carried in national or élection budgets would also be made from the Epargne.

To appreciate the sweeping changes attempted by this reform we have only to list their main effects.

Centralized collections. Funds from all sources, once certain speci-

26. Babou fought at Pavia alongside the king and was also taken captive. Later, he was made bishop of Angoulême.
27. See Isambert, 12 : 223.
28. Ibid., 222–28.
29. Jacqueton, "Le Trésor de l'Epargne," 55 : 9–10, refers to a preliminary edict in which the tailles were transferred to the Epargne three months before the other "extraordinaries" (September 1523)

fied payments and all local expenses were deducted, were to be sent to a centralized treasury.[30] In essence this reduced the former généralité-level treasuries and the bailiwick treasuries for domaines revenues to way stations between local collection agencies and the central treasury. Even the changeur du Trésor, formerly in charge of all the surpluses (*restes*) of the domaines, now was directed to turn them over to the Epargne. The *receveurs généraux* in territories not in the généralités (the *recettes générales* of Guyenne, Brittany, Burgundy, Dauphiné, and Provence) now were to transport their funds to Paris promptly.

Centralized payments. All the main expenditures, except those customarily made at the local level, were now to be made from the central office rather than at the provincial or district level. The system of using revenues where they were raised as informal treasuries was to be abandoned. But the door was not closed completely on the older style of payment. The trésorier de l'Epargne was given the right to authorize payments from généralité or élection tax collectors, provided he employed a warrant signed by the king or one of the financial secretaries.

Gens des finances demoted. The main function of the généraux des finances and the trésoriers de France—that of locating funds for emergency payments and moving money to where it was needed—was eliminated. And in fact the gens des finances were reduced to the status of middle-echelon supervisors.

Unified revenues. The new centralized treasury canceled the traditional distinction between the "extraordinaries" and the "ordinaries," since both types of revenue were now under the control of one official, the trésorier de l'Epargne.

The Parties casuelles and the new "extraordinaries"

Almost at once the king retreated a step from his decision to centralize all funds. In June 1524 the *casuelles*—the fines, tenths, escheats, and sales of venal offices for which the Epargne had first been created in March 1523—were put under the care of a second new official, the *receveur général des finances extraordinaires et des Parties casuelles*, who, like the trésorier de l'Epargne, was to answer directly to the king.

30. In the December 1523 ordinance this central depository was to be located in the château of Blois; in other words, it was to follow the court. The reforms of 1532 changed this, fixing the treasury of the Epargne at the Louvre.

But the Epargne greatly overshadowed the new *casuelles* treasury. The sums of money handled by Parties casuelles were small. They fluctuated wildly (as would be expected of this sort of income) from a low of 170,000 livres to a high of more than 1.5 millions during the 1520s, out of about 5 millions in total revenues. Funds remaining after expenditures in the Parties casuelles treasury, furthermore, were ordered to be shipped to the Epargne at the end of each year.[31]

After 1523 we see a tendency to use the label "ordinary revenues" not only for domaines but also for tailles, gabelles, traites, and aides—all the "regular" revenues. The term *extraordinaires* now is applied to the *inopinées*, those revenues that could not be predicted or determined at the beginning of a fiscal year. The old concept died hard, however, and we still find these terms used in their pre-1523 meanings in royal edicts and in some of the treatises on taxes.[32] For example, the *Vestige des finances* (a sort of question-and-answer training manual published shortly after these reforms and continuing to appear without change all through the sixteenth century) retains the old meanings.[33]

The aims of the Epargne system

As is the case with many great and lasting institutional reforms, the creation of the centralized Epargne was only partly planned in advance. There is evidence that the breakdown of the fiscal system came before the discussion of general fiscal reform.[34] The reforms themselves, however, are not really as "empirical and at times contradictory" as

31. Jacqueton, "Le Trésor de l'Epargne," 55 : 20, 21–24.

32. La Barre, writing in 1622, still uses the old meanings; see *Formulaire*, pp. 72–73. Some older histories seem to show that their writers were ignorant of this basic reform. See, e.g., J. Caillet, *De l'administration en France sous le ministère du cardinal de Richelieu* (Paris, 1857), who uses the terms in their pre-1523 sense even when speaking of the early seventeenth century; see also Lucien Romier, *Lettres et chevauchées du bureau des finances de Caen*, pp. xvi, xvii.

33. Jacqueton, *Documents*, pp. xxviii–xxix, 205–42. The *Vestige* was never published separately, but regularly appeared as an appendix to *Le Thrésor du nouveau stille et prothocolle de la Chancellerie de France*; I have found it in the edition of 1599. On the first new use of the term *extraordinaire* in 1523 see Wolfe and Zacour, "Growing Pains," pp. 58–63.

34. These discussions may even have involved Louise of Savoy herself; see Wolfe and Zacour, "Growing Pains," Introduction and p. 81; see also Zeller, *Institutions*, p. 284.

they are characterized by Roger Doucet; [35] and it is an error to regard them as mainly an expression of royal wrath against the gens des finances. The changes between March and December 1523 do indeed show that the government was feeling its way. But the very scope of the complex reforms demonstrates that there was more to them than the king's urge to obtain vengeance. The retention of basic features of the new system in later years, and the many attempts to improve it, suggest that while its originators may not have had the whole program in mind from the very beginning, it was found encouraging, if not entirely satisfactory, once the framework was set up.

Forcing all revenues to come to two central treasuries theoretically gave the king the ability to put his hands on a larger proportion of the country's tax revenues whenever such action was necessary, resulting in less reliance on expedients and on borrowing.[36] It was also supposed to show the king what his cash situation was at any one time, a simple matter now that there were only two central treasuries rather than 110 or so scattered about the country.

One of the more admirable features of these reforms is the attempt to reduce as far as possible the method of authorizing payments through décharges. These were warrants for expenditures not included in the regular budgets, such as emergency payments and royal gifts. Bills for these expenditures, when presented for payment, had usually been met not with money but with décharges authorizing a specified local treasurer to release (*décharger*) the sum required. If a creditor of the crown was lucky or influential, he was assigned payment on a treasurer in his own neighborhood, one who had sufficient cash to honor the décharge and was willing to do so. Anything less than this fortunate combination of circumstances involved the creditor in a maddening expenditure of time and effort. All too often, he ended by accepting less than the sum to which he was entitled. Most unfortunate were those who had been instructed to collect from poor and distant treasuries. In such cases, the most practical thing to do was to discount the décharge by presenting it to a nearby, superior fiscal official who could arrange to collect its full face value—at a substantial profit for

35. Doucet, *François Ier*, 1 : 290; see also Doucet, *L'état des finances de 1523*, p. 29.
36. Ord. of Dec. 28, 1523, in Isambert, 12 : 223.

himself. Now this category of payments was given to the Epargne with the expectation that this sort of graft would be ended.

Another feature of the reforms was that they were supposed to permit a significantly greater degree of secrecy in royal affairs. Formerly, when most emergency payments were made at the généralité or even the district level, a whole chain of middle- and lower-echelon *comptables* necessarily had to learn who were the king's creditors; they might also gain knowledge of troop movements and fortifications. Now knowledge of royal payments was available to only a few clerks in the Epargne office.[37]

The reformers did not intend that every sou collected in France be sent immediately to the Epargne; some payments were still to be made locally. The edicts and treatises are clear on this point. District and provincial collectors were to hold back enough funds to pay "pensions and charity, wages of our officials, costs of justice, repairs [to town walls and fortresses] and other ordinary and traditional charges, which will remain in the hands of the *receveurs particuliers*, for the latter to pay out in the accustomed manner." [38] As previously, the direct collection costs of tailles and other imposts were to be deducted before local collectors turned the money over to généralité collectors, who in turn deducted their own wages and costs from receipts before turning over their collections to the trésorier de l'Epargne. The wages of provincial branches of the Chambre des comptes and the Cour des aides, and money going to half-pay soldiers on limited garrison duty (*mortes-payes*), were also deducted.

The Epargne in operation

The plan for centralizing payments required a much more extensive movement of cash through the country. In the system of Charles VII, expenditures not provided for in an état had required (in the best of circumstances) a double set of orders, one from the crown (warrants) and one from the gens des finances, the only officials who could be

37. This sort of secrecy was one of the prime advantages urged by the reform proposal in University of Pennsylvania MS. Fr. 18, referred to in n. 16 above; see Wolfe and Zacour, "Growing Pains," p. 65.

38. Isambert, 12 : 223; see also Antoine Fontanon, ed., *Les édicts et ordonnances des rois de France . . . ,* 2 : 619.

expected to know where an adequate supply of surplus revenues could be found. In the new system, all funds not needed for regular local expenses were to be sent to the Epargne, where all "extraordinary" payments would be made.[39] The trésorier de l'Epargne was to report each week to the royal council on the state of cash holdings.

In the old system, district and provincial comptables first had to inform their superiors of the *restes* in their treasuries; then a double set of shipping orders would come down, one to be retained by the comptables and one to be sent along with the money. In the new system, all that was needed for the money to start on its way was for provincial collectors to give direct receipts (*simples quittances*) for whatever cash they received. Shipments of cash from généralité and bailiwick collectors, likewise, now required only *simples quittances* from the trésorier de l'Epargne in Paris. Gathering in the funds would now be much less encumbered with red tape.

The offices of trésorier de France and général des finances were not abolished. Sixteenth-century France was just as reluctant to cancel part of its government apparatus as is its modern counterpart. But there was a practical reason, also, for keeping these offices: they were all venal; to abolish them would have required the return of the purchase price. Instead of canceling the offices, therefore, the king simply reduced the powers of the officials. In their new capacity, they were to assist the movement of cash from local to généralité comptables. They were to make the rounds of their districts at least twice a year, stirring up those comptables whose shipments of cash were not in line with estimations. They were also directed to take oaths from local collectors as to whether they were retaining any cash revenues, and to send these depositions on to the Epargne.[40] But they were not to have a hand in formulating the national provisional budget; they were no longer members of the royal council; they did not sit as a *collège* to advise the king; and it seemed as though their future was highly uncertain.[41]

39. Jacqueton, "Le Trésor de l'Epargne," 55 : 14–15. In a few carefully defined cases, however, the Epargne was permitted to turn over décharges rather than cash.

40. Isambert, 12 : 226.

41. The ord. of Rouen, Feb. 7, 1532, however, continued the obligation of trésoriers and généraux to formulate local budgets. This obligation was confirmed April 12, 1547; see Isambert, 12 : 11.

The old popular term *gens des finances,* however, did not die out. We find it even in official proclamations, as in the fiscal edict of September 1549.[42] Now, the term was used more vaguely, meaning high-level fiscal officials in general.

The government announced it was greatly pleased with the fiscal reforms. The edict of July 9, 1524, which established a separate *trésorier des Parties casuelles,* claims that in spite of heavy expenses, the new centralization of funds had spared the king the need for "retrenchment and recoil" of wages and pensions, "and furthermore, we have acquitted ourselves of many debts which we had assumed in the past, which is an almost incredible development." But did the Epargne system really work as well as the reformers hoped? [43]

The reality of the later 1520s is sadly distant from the high claims of 1524. We know that in the year 1528 only about one-fourth the payments effected by the Epargne were cash payments. The rest, unfortunately, were orders to pay on généralité or district treasuries, in other words, décharges.

Apart from the technical difficulties inherent in this ambitious reversal of practices, the 1523–24 reforms overestimated the rate at which cash could reach the Epargne. Transporting a mule train between Lyons and Paris, for example, took three weeks or more. Often, the cash in the hands of local comptables was simply too small to justify the cost of shipping it over a great distance; in such cases collectors were ordered to hold their funds. Revenues were not flowing back to the Epargne quickly enough.[44] Rather than wait, the government authorized its army paymasters and others who needed money urgently to apply to the local treasury nearest them.

This should not be interpreted as meaning that the reforms were utter failures. A large fraction of payments were actually made in cash and from the Epargne. Therefore, at least some of the evil traffic in décharges was canceled. And whether in cash or in warrants, all the payments were authorized through one official rather than a dozen. The element of control over expenditures was much better. Rather than

42. Ibid., 13 : 105.
43. Answering this question is the main task Georges Jacqueton sets himself in "Le Trésor de l'Epargne."
44. Jacqueton, "Le Trésor de l'Epargne," 56 : 22–23.

calling for a consensus among the gens des finances, the government addressed itself to one man only, the trésorier de l'Epargne.

The new system also provided better and faster knowledge about the total cash available. The trésorier de l'Epargne enabled the king "to see or have shown in our council the funds and situation of our finances, at any time that it pleases us." As the man required to "administer the entire accounts for the receipt and expenditure of all our finances," he was in a position to know.[45]

There were other minor benefits from the reforms. The services of généralité auditors were no longer needed since fewer payments were being made at that level. Because of the greater simplicity in authorizing shipments, and the abandonment of records of transfer authorizations (*écrous*), the paper work of the fiscal system was less complex. But the king was far from satisfied; he hoped that further administrative changes would bring still better results.

THE EFFORT TO BUILD WAR CHEST RESERVES

The fiscal reforms of February 1532

One of the reasons the king was impelled to try out new administrative arrangements was that every few years brought a new military crisis, so that the scale of expenditures seemed to rise in a never-ending spiral. Francis I repudiated the peace treaty signed after the disaster at Pavia and organized his troops to resume fighting almost immediately. In 1527 the French unleashed another major effort to recover Lombardy. The war broadened to other parts of Italy, Provence, and the northeast borders of France. These campaigns, which ended with the Peace of Cambrai in 1529, brought France little, other than temporary control over Genoa and parts of Flanders; both soon had to be surrendered.

The peace terms required Francis I to make a huge cash payment. The king also had to ransom his sons, left in Spain as hostages. The ransom was set at 2 million écus (4 million livres); this was such a huge amount that the first payment, 1.2 millions, required a thirty-two mule pack-train to carry it to Spain.[46] The pension granted to Henry VIII of

45. Letters-patent of Romorantin, April 30, 1545.
46. Bailly, *Histoire financière de la France*, 1 : 222–23.

England in 1527 to win his alliance, furthermore, had to be continued. And of course the Swiss cantons continued to receive their annual grants in peace as in war.

It was only too clear that Francis I needed cash on a huge scale. He was determined to get it not through a vast credit operation, as did the Hapsburgs, but mainly through his tax system. An always-available war chest, a concept already developed during the reforms of the 1520s, was his answer.

The focus of the reform edict of 1532, therefore, was the relation between the tax machine and the war chests. The edict of Rouen of February 7 fixed the Epargne money chests in the treasure rooms of the Louvre palace instead of allowing them to follow the court. Two additional money chests, furthermore, were authorized by this edict for war reserves only; that is, they were set apart from the other money chests of the Epargne.

There were ritual precautions to insure that once cash came into a war chest it would remain there. Though they appear naïve to us, they were regarded by the government as a highly useful device for protecting reserves. The money chests, first of all, were provided with special grilled slots so that coins could be dropped in but not removed without unlocking. A special committee, headed by the august personnages of the first and second *présidents* of the ancient and "sovereign" Chambre des comptes, was present when cash was deposited or withdrawn. Also assisting were two special auditors, one to record incoming cash, and one outgoing cash.

The actual opening of the chests involved even more important officials. Each chest had four different locks and keys: the king had one; Montmorency, the king's favorite, had the second; Biron, the finance expert in the royal council, possessed the third; and the fourth was in the hands of chancellor Duprat. And of course there always had to be a detail of soldiers on hand to guard the money once it was removed. It must have been a crowded scene in the treasure room when the king decided to open his money chests. But these elaborate precautions were regarded as worthwhile in order to impress on everyone the seriousness of depleting reserves without good cause.[47]

Many interesting items were earmarked for the chests, though too

47. Jacqueton, "Le Trésor de l'Epargne," 56 : 17.

often the exigencies of war whipped away the funds before they could be moved to Paris. Whenever possible, Francis I put the "extraordinary" levies on the church into war chests. Fines and *compositions* from guilty or too-suddenly rich fiscal officials also found their way there. When the fabulously wealthy Duprat died (1535), his heirs were persuaded to give a "loan" to the king that was channeled into the war chests.[48] Also entered here was the dowry of Catherine de Medici, now married to young prince Henry; she brought with her the sum of 292,500 livres.[49] Another source of cash was the remainder left in the regular chests of the Epargne at the end of each year.

The fiscal reform of 1532 in no sense abandoned the Epargne system of centralized collections and disbursements. On the contrary, the efforts begun in 1523 to direct royal revenues to "one sole hand" were accelerated. Beginning in 1527, in fact, the king established a new agent in each généralité and each recette générale, the *commis à l'exercise*, whose job was to expedite collection of the chief imposts and speed them to the Epargne. The *commis à l'exercise* were royal agents rather than venal officials and therefore presumably more responsive to the king's will. The previous middle-echelon généralité collectors, the receveurs généraux, now were regarded as superfluous, and they were dismissed.

The 1532 edict of Rouen, supplemented by additional royal orders in 1533, broadened the commis à l'exercise to three-man committees and gave them the significant additional task of collecting domaines as well as imposts. The change reduced the *receveurs ordinaires* of the domaines to the rank of lower-echelon collection officials. The changeur du Trésor was left with little to do, since the commis à l'exercise now supervised the transfer of funds directly from local collection officials to the Epargne.

The commis à l'exercise were to send all funds to the Louvre without delay; they were not to keep them "in their hands nor in their houses nor anywhere else" for more than a week or two, no matter what the excuse. All collectors of revenue were ordered not to wait for directions from above, but to ship along their collections promptly, on the authority of

---

48. Clamageran (*L'impôt*, 2 : 106), regards this incident as an outright seizure of Duprat's wealth.
49. Jacqueton, "Le Trésor de l'Epargne," 56 : 18–19.

nothing but the *quittance* they would receive from the next higher official.

The failure of the war chest reserve system

In the latter part of the sixteenth century, during the less happy era of the Wars of Religion, Jean Bodin and several other writers commented on the wise fiscal policies of Francis I. They praised his ability to amass great stocks of funds for his war needs and thus spare his subjects the shock of constantly repeated emergency levies. Later rulers, particularly Henry IV (after 1602), also tried to establish war chests in anticipation of projected campaigns. According to commentators on taxation, such as the anonymous author of the *Traitté des finances de France* (1580), a reserve was one of the pillars of fiscal policy: "Public finance can be reduced to three points, to wit: to use it to amass revenues by honest means; to use [these revenues] properly; and to save up some to put them aside against need." Charles de Figon, writing in 1579, comments regretfully that in the good old days there used to be money chests in the Louvre, but now money has to be paid out so quickly it is spent on the spot where it is received. Another facet of the Renaissance's admiration for Francis I's fiscal policy was the large fund he was supposed to have left for his heir; La Barre, writing in 1622, placed this sum at 1.7 million écus.[50]

But we know that even the war chests of Francis I were only partially successful, and then only for brief periods. In 1535, for example, just before the opening of an especially costly campaign, official records suggest there should have been almost 5 million livres in the chests; contemporary writings, however, make it clear the king could not have had more than about 1.7 million livres at that time.[51]

Francis I seems to have felt that he needed a reserve of 3 millions at least. All too often, the drain of the Hapsburg wars was so heavy that the

50. The *Traitté des finances de France* is reprinted in *Archives curieuses de l'histoire de France*, 1st ser., 9 : 343; Charles de Figon, *Discours des estats et offices* . . . , p. 42ʳ; La Barre, *Formulaire*, p. 412. See also Paul Cauwès, "Les commencements du crédit public en France," *Revue d'Economie Politique* 9 (1895) : 826.

51. Jacqueton, "Le Trésor de l'Epargne," 56 : 19–20.

war chests were emptied long before the year's campaign was well begun. The king had no choice but to resort to irritating emergency levies, loans, and other expedients. During these periods the centralized Epargne system of collection and payment had to go by the board, and the government paid through orders on généralité and even district collectors. The war chest committee, with its complex rituals and separate locks and keys, was canceled in 1537. The enormously expensive campaigns of 1536 and 1537, costing about 5 millions each year, had kept the chests empty for so long they became rather pointless. They were released to the trésorier de l'Epargne to use along with his regular collection chests.

The king, at least until 1542, never lost faith in the utility of administrative improvements. His optimism was buoyed up by the system's ability, given a few months of peace, to hoard an impressive amount of money. Between 1532 and 1535, for example, the great majority of Epargne payments, perhaps as much as eleven-twelfths, were effected in cash.[52] In times of stress, rather than deplete his treasury completely, the king tried to rebuff demands of creditors, kept back officials' salaries and favorites' pensions, and even borrowed money from Lyons bankers at ruinously high interest rates. On occasion, attempts were made to maintain war chests by concentrating tax collections in the first quarter of a year and holding off as many regular and extraordinary payments as possible until the last quarter; but the tides of war could not be offset by such calendaring. As late as 1546 the king's official position was that the only reason he could not get his reforms to work well was that officials were neglecting "to urge on the payment of our funds."[53]

Additional auditors were posted for généralité collectors, and additional penalities for malfeasance were imposed. On June 8, 1532, a royal edict laid out in brutal terms the punishment to be applied to all fiscal officials thwarting the royal will, "of whatever estate, quality, or condition they may be, if they are found to have falsified warrants, receipts, accounts, or muster roles, they will be hung up and strangled."[54] But these threats went on year after year. Indeed, given the possibilities of

52. Ibid., pp. 14–17. This so encouraged the king that in 1525 he instituted a second war chest, to be supplied from the casuelles.
53. Ord. of St. Germain-en-Laye, March 1, 1546, in Isambert, 12 : 907.
54. Isambert, 12 : 362, 364.

social control available to the crown, it is doubtful they could have accomplished much.

ROYAL BORROWING UNDER FRANCIS I

Among his many innovations in public finance, Francis I is given credit for originating the *rentes sur l'Hôtel de Ville de Paris*, an important new form of royal credit. As we shall see, however, one of the most interesting aspects of this new credit device is how sparingly the king used it.

Public opinion had long resisted the idea that when the king borrowed from merchant-bankers, he had to pay their usual interest rates or give them equivalent favors. In France the king tried to maintain the fiction that while he might have to pay interest when borrowing from foreigners, his "good and loyal officials and subjects" would loan him their money free of charge. The government denounced usury in many edicts, some surprisingly late in the sixteenth century.[55] Usury was still defined as the charging of *any* interest for the mere loan of money, even if the rates were reasonable and the money borrowed was employed in a profit-making enterprise. Jean Bodin said that when the country was in danger, it was a Frenchman's "pious duty" to come forward with his money. A man as knowledgeable as Bodin, writing as late as 1576, was so passionately opposed to all forms of usury that he demanded the state refrain from borrowing at interest altogether, no matter how reasonable the rate.[56] For merchants, who more and more needed credit to handle the growing volume of long-distance trade, interest had to be camouflaged (rather unsubtly and deceiving no one) as payment for the expense and trouble of effecting an exchange for foreign coins.

When the king borrowed from his subjects, therefore, whether or not they were in the business of lending money, they ran the danger of being condemned for the sin of usury by law as well as by public opinion. They also ran the practical danger of having the king decide there was no need to repay either interest or principal, because the loan itself had been a sinful act. The hypocrisy that resulted can be demonstrated by the interest payments for a great series of royal loans, the *Grand*

55. See the letters-patent of Paris, July 1, 1565; see also the edicts of Paris, Jan. 20, 1567, Aug. 1576, and Oct. 6, 1576.
56. Cauwès, "Les commencements du crédit public," pp. 848–49.

Parti (1555–59), which were called "free gifts" in the ordinance announcing them.[57]

The rentes on the Hôtel de Ville of Paris narrowly skirted the problem of royal usury.[58] As their name suggests, these rentes were supposed to be obligations not on the king but on the municipality of Paris. And money to support the rentes was to come not so much from the personal income of the king as from a particular group of royal taxes which were under the control of "City Hall," the provost of merchants and the magistrates who directed the town government.[59] Local taxes on meat, fish, and wine, plus some of the town gabelles, were earmarked for the rentes. These taxes were chosen because they were regarded as the most dependable sources of royal revenue in the city. Since the administration of the interest payments was in the hands of town officials, who came from the same bourgeois background as the wealthy people who would be making the loans, a clever arrangement of mutual trust was created. Rentes, at least at first, were rather popular. Interest payments on this sort of bond were set at the quite moderate rate of the *denier douze* (the "twelfth penny," or 8⅓ percent).

The first rentes on the Hôtel de Ville of Paris were initiated at the time that the gens des finances were being downgraded (1522); possibly this device had as one of its aims to demonstrate that such high financial officials were not indispensable. The person who had the most to do with proposing the rentes was the chancellor, Antoine Duprat (who, as we have seen, was an enemy of Semblançay).

It has often been claimed that the rentes were the beginnings of a French "public debt." [60] It would seem this is claiming too much. We can define a public debt as one which is regarded as a charge on each and

57. See Roger Doucet, "Le Grand Parti de Lyon au XVIe siècle," *Revue Historique* 171, no. 3 (1933) : 493, and 172, no. 1 (1933), cited hereafter as "Grand Parti, 1" and "Grand Parti, 2."

58. Bernard Schnapper, *Les rentes au XVIe siècle*, pp. 42 and passim, believes the 1522 rentes were acceptable because they were regarded as a variation of the late medieval *rente à prix d'argent*, which—unlike the earlier *rent de bail à héritage*—was based on the presumed money income of the borrower rather than on real estate.

59. The initiating ord. is dated Sept. 2, 1522.

60: E.g., Henri Sée, *Histoire économique de la France*, 2 vols. (Paris, 1939), 1 : 88; Lemonnier, in Lavisse 5¹ : 241; and Cauwès, "Les commencements du crédit public."

every citizen of the state. The rentes, however, were still regarded as the personal debt of the king to the Paris townsmen. The town government had interposed itself between the king and the lenders, so that the guarantee of the burghers' own government was substituted for the obviously less dependable guarantee of the crown.[61] It was only in the advanced city-states of Italy that loans could be made on the "full faith and credit" of the government.

In some works, one gets the impression that the rentes on the Hôtel de Ville were a powerful aid to French public finance, that after 1522 "public credit" was regularly drawn upon by the French government.[62] Paul Cauwès sees in the issuing of rentes in 1522 "a new era" in financial history.[63] But this is seriously exaggerated. Francis I did not like this form of credit and he used it sparingly. The first issue was for only 200,000 livres. The next issue was not floated until 1536 (one year after the death of chancellor Duprat), for the relatively paltry sum of 100,000 livres. Two more issues of rentes were sold in this reign (1537 and 1543). The total sum for the reign of Francis I was 725,000 livres; this is only slightly more than one year's return from the gabelles.[64]

THE BEGINNING OF THE GÉNÉRALITÉ

The edict of Cognac, December 1542

The year 1542 marks yet another pivot in the fiscal history of the reign of Francis I. This change coincided with the beginnings of another and even more costly conflict with the Hapsburgs. In his last years as king, from 1542 to 1547, Francis I was rather worn out and distraught and had less time for financial affairs. But the edict of Cognac brought about a fiscal reform of the greatest importance.

During the era of Charles VII and up to 1542, there had been four

61. Schnapper, Les rentes, pp. 152–53.
62. E.g., in Earl J. Hamilton, "Origin and Growth of the National Debt in Western Europe," American Economic Review Papers and Proceedings (May 1947).
63. Cauwès, "Les commencements du crédit public," p. 101.
64. These totals are based on Schnapper, Les rentes, pp. 172–73. Clamageran, L'impôt, 2 : 28, 147 (apparently following Véron de Forbonnais, Recherches et considérations sur les finances de France . . .), reports the total for Francis I, as only 75,000 livres.

very large généralités for the older royal domain: Languedoïl, Normandy, Languedoc, and Outre-Seine-et-Yonne. In addition there had
been recettes générales for Guyenne, Dauphiné, Provence, Burgundy,
and Brittany.[65] Now the limits of the généralités were to be changed and
new, smaller généralités established; this reform set the basis for généralités as the Old Régime was to know them.[66]

The edict of Cognac split up the four older généralités as follows:
Languedoïl was divided into four units (one of which absorbed Brittany), Normandy into two, Outer-Seine-et-Yonne into three, and
Languedoc into three.[67] The new twelve units were called, at first,
recettes générales. Added to the five previous recettes générales (five,
rather than four, since Brittany was soon given its own recette générale
again), the new system made up seventeen recettes générales in all.
The treasuries and offices of these new fiscal districts were established
at Rouen (East Normandy), Caen (West Normandy), Paris, Amiens
(Picardy), Châlons (Champagne), Tours (Touraine-Maine), Bourges
(Berry), Poitiers (Poitou-Anjou), Issoire—later shifted to Riom—
(Auvergne-Beaujolais), Lyons (Lyonnais-Forez), Agen—later changed
to Bordeaux—(Guyenne), Montpellier (East Languedoc), Toulouse
(West Languedoc), Dijon (Burgundy), Grenoble (Dauphiné), Aix
(Provence), and—when Brittany obtained its own center again—
Nantes. Later rulers added Moulins (Bourbonnais-Nevers), Soissons
(Valois–North Champagne), Orléans, and Limoges, making a total of
twenty-one districts for the period of this study. Gradually, beginning
soon after 1542, the term recette générale was abandoned in favor of
généralité.

In charge of each of the new recettes générales was a receveur général. But he was decidedly a more important official than others with the
same title before 1532, who had been replaced by the commis à l'exercise. The new receveur général—an officier and not a commis—took
over the main responsibility for prying cash out of the hands of local
comptables. He was a supervisor, rather than a passive collector of funds.

65. See Dupont-Ferrier, Etudes, 1 : 57–58. Sometimes Guyenne counted as a
fifth généralité; see Wolfe and Zacour, "Growing Pains," p. 73.
66. Isambert, 12:805–06.
67. But cf. Zeller, Institutions, p. 285, who believes that each of the four old
généralités was split into four units.

He was obviously an upper-echelon administrator; as a mark of his status, his salary was set at the top bracket—1,200 livres.[68]

The edict of Cognac authorized the receveur général to collect all regular revenues, those from the domaines in addition to the imposts. This meant a final fusion of what used to be considered "ordinary" and "extraordinary" revenues. There was no longer a need for a special cofferer for the domaines; thus the post of changeur du Trésor disappeared. The receveur général also was directed to collect many of the casuelles, including the clerical tenths, and forced loans and other levies on towns.

The post of receveur général des Parties casuelles, still in existence, was reduced to handling receipts from venal offices. This was a job of increasing significance, however, since the sale of offices was rapidly increasing (see chapter 4). In the 1520s the head of the casuelles had been administratively equal to the trésorier de l'Epargne; now he became only a specialized receveur général. In January 1544, the Parties casuelles was directed to turn over all its funds remaining at the end of a quarter to the Epargne rather than maintaining them in a separate chest. The Parties casuelles was also directed to pay out of its current receipts on orders from the Epargne, the same as all receveurs généraux. The trésor de l'Epargne was now truly "the great purse and common receptacle of revenues where they merge and end up." [69]

Fiscal administration during the last years of Francis I

After 1542, without abandoning the ideal of a centralized treasury, the king gave up the attempt to effect all or most of his expenditures in cash and from Paris. The seventeen treasuries of the recettes générales (the new généralités) now were visualized as branches of the Epargne. They were empowered to make regular local payments, such as officials' salaries, pensions, and charities—but not automatically—on the basis of inclusion of such items in their budgets. These payments had to be authorized by warrants from the Paris Epargne. The attempt to pay most "extraordinary" obligations out of the Epargne reserves was modi-

68. Ord. of Cognac, Dec. 7, 1542; this is a separate ord. from the edict of the same date establishing the new recettes générales.
69. La Barre, *Formulaire*, p. 79.

fied but not dropped; all such unforeseeable payments that could not be met from Paris were to be paid by the généralités, also on order from the trésorier de l'Epargne.[70]

The breakdown of the war chest reserve system meant an increase in the importance of the trésorier de l'Epargne. He was not only the direct chief of all the receveurs généraux, but he was also in charge of determining where emergency funds could be located. To some extent, therefore, he was given part of the authority that had been possessed by the old gens des finances before 1523. But the Epargne was not allowed to tap local, that is élection or bailiwick collectors; its operations were limited to the généralités. And there was no question of the trésorier de l'Epargne moving up to the policy level where the gens had functioned. He was still very much the technical agent of the royal council, though a more important one than previously. Particular recognition was given to the new status of the trésorier de l'Epargne in 1545, when it was ruled his office was not to be a venal one. In other words, the king was determined not to let this agent develop any property rights in his position by purchasing it.[71]

After 1542, the means to fill war chests—on the occasions when funds could be found for this purpose—were a travesty on the war reserve concept as it had developed in 1532. In fact, the main funds placed in these chests were obtained by borrowing from French and foreign merchant-bankers and other wealthy persons. Instead of borrowing only when needed, Francis I hoarded some of these funds in his war chests. Meanwhile, the heavy interest rates on this money—often as high as 16 percent—had to be paid even though the money was lying idle.

The great bulk of emergency payments were not made by the Epargne directly, but on orders by the Epargne in the form of *mandements portant quittance* ("warrants acceptable as receipt") directed to the receveurs généraux. Of course the Epargne still received the surplus funds from the généralités.[72] In addition to casuelles and clerical tenths, the receveurs généraux gathered up the domaines and impost revenues collected by élection and bailiwick officials.[73] The généralités were

70. Several edicts these years deal with this problem; see, e.g., that of Fontainebleau, April 7, 1546.
71. Letters-patent of Romorantin, April 30, 1545.
72. Ord. of Fontainebleau, April 7, 1546.
73. Letters-patent of Evreux, April 1, 1544.

obviously becoming the main unit for fiscal administration. As a result, the anachronistic trésoriers de France and généraux des finances were directed to take up permanent residence in the chief cities of the généralités and leave Paris forthwith if they did not wish to lose all their wages.[74]

The long-enduring attractiveness of the war chest concept is demonstrated by the fact that in the first months of the reign of Henry II (1547–59) the king made a gesture toward returning to it. A decree was published directing that all funds except casuelles be shipped again from the treasuries of the généralités to the Louvre. The decree explained that the abandonment of the war chest system had been caused by recent wars, during which it had been necessary "to gather and distribute [royal] funds so precipitously that it was not possible for [the government] to continue this system." But now that peace had returned, the system of the 1530s was to be reimposed. Payments were once again channeled through the Epargne, except emergency payments, which might be made from a généralité. The war chests were to be re-created from the money shipped to the Louvre; this money was to be handled according to the same protective regulations as during the reign of Francis I.[75] But this law was only a statement of good intentions. War with the Hapsburgs soon resumed. During the reign of Henry II, as during the last years of his father's reign, the généralité treasuries, on order from the Epargne, continued to effect the great majority of royal payments in France.

TAX "ABSOLUTISM" AND FRANCIS I

One of the best-known aphorisms concerning royal power in France, tirelessly repeated in modern accounts, is supposed to have come from Emperor Maximilian I himself. "The man who sits on the throne of the Holy Roman Empire is a king of kings; the king of the Spaniards is a king of men who know how to assert their rights; but the king of the French is a king of beasts, for in whatsoever he commands or desires he is instantly obeyed, as man is by beasts." Whether or not Maximilian actually said this, contemporary writings provide many examples of the

74. Cf. Wolfe and Zacour, "Growing Pains," p. 68.
75. Decree of St. Germain-en-Laye, May 1547, in Isambert, 13 : 4–15.

belief that Francis I was indeed a "king of beasts" so far as taxes were concerned.[76]

Until recently, the manner in which Francis I used his tax system, and the supposedly heavy burden of taxes he laid on the French, were taken by scholars as part of the proof of his absolutism. By "absolutism" here historians usually mean the great increase in the constitutional powers of the king as compared to the fifteenth century. In particular, this refers to the greater centralization of government, the absence of checks on the crown, and the weakening of the complex of medieval privileges for classes, provinces, guilds, and other groups. The more narrow, local loyalties of such groups were replaced by the loyalty of individual Frenchmen for their sovereign. "The king no longer counts his vassals; there remain only his subjects." [77]

Today, however, scholars are much less sure about the "absolutism" of Francis I, and whether his era does truly signalize a transition from medieval kingship to modern monarchy. They argue that he was just as sensitive to tradition and just as responsive to the laws of the land as his medieval predecessors. The French army and bureaucracy were too small and too poorly organized for the king to rule in any way other than through the support and cooperation of his subjects. He was, therefore, a "constitutional" ruler, not an Arabian Nights tyrant who governed according to whim. "Absolutism" comes only with the Old Régime in the seventeenth century.[78]

It is tempting to paraphrase W. K. Hancock on imperialism and to say that absolutism is no word for scholars. Obviously it was hardly possible for Francis I to "tax at will," a phrase we still see in too many recent works. Henri Hauser's dictum that in this era the king "was practically able to set taxes at any figure he chose" is simply nonsense.[79] Increasing the burden of taxation was a complex matter: the govern-

76. Eugenio Albèri, ed., *Le relazioni degli ambasciatori veneti* . . . , 1st ser., 4 : 32.

77. Lavisse and Rambaud, *Histoire générale*, 4 : 139.

78. These views are best summarized in Major's "The French Monarchy as Seen through the Estates General," pp. 113–25.

79. "The European Financial Crisis of 1559," *Journal of Economic and Business History* 2 (1929–30) : 245. Francis I, when asked by the emperor Charles V what were the annual royal revenues, is supposed to have replied, "Whatever I wish." Albèri, *Relazioni*, 1st ser., 4 : 196. Picot, *Etats Généraux*, 5 : 200, repeats this boast and gives the impression it reflected the real situation.

ment had to take into account myriads of rights, exemptions, and traditions. For new taxes, new cadres had to be formed and trained. Public opinion was a potent impediment to bizarre fiscality. The peasant masses and the lower-class urban groups lived near the level of subsistence. And the nation's stock of specie was only slightly responsive to the will of even an absolute monarch.[80]

Available evidence certainly contradicts the widespread notion that Francis I tyrannically burdened his subjects with vastly heavier taxes. Increases in revenues during this reign are not particularly awesome. Total revenues rose from just under 5 million livres in 1515 [81] to over 9 millions the year before Francis died, in 1546.[82] These estimates do not include the causelles—items such as sales of offices, fines, alienation of domaines, and the clerical tenths, which were considerable at times— and other greater or lesser "extraordinary" items such as the special levies on the rich burghers. Though very welcome when they came in, these items could not change the total picture greatly. We can say, therefore, that annual royal revenues just about doubled during this reign.

This increase took place over a period of thirty-two years. The annual rate works out to something less than 2.2 percent—hardly a crushing addition to a tax burden. For the country as a whole, furthermore, the real burden of the tax increase must have been lightened by the moderately rising price trend toward the end of the reign. This price trend, at least before 1547, stimulated the French economy more than it hurt. Also, French prosperity was helped by opportunities for French artisans and merchants in even wealthier Spain. Another consideration was the increase in the French population at this time, which should have reduced the per capita burden of the taxes even further.

The structure of French taxes did not change significantly. The tailles, as we would expect, rose most in absolute terms: from about 2.4 million livres at the beginning of the reign to some 5.3 millions at its close. The rate of the gabelles in north and central France tripled: a *muid* of salt

80. On the scarcity of specie in the land see Roger Doucet, "La richesse en France au XVIe siècle," *Huitième Congrès International des Sciences Historiques* (Zurich, 1938). See also François, *Tournon*, p. 80 ff.

81. Spont, "La taille en Languedoc," p. 369; for 1514, 4.3 million livres for regular taxes and .6 millions for emergency levies.

82. Clamageran, *L'impôt*, 2 : 130–31.

was taxed 45 livres after 1537. But for the whole country the value of gabelles was only around 700,000 livres in 1547, compared to less than 400,000 in the early part of the reign. Although we have almost no dependable information on the aides and other indirect taxes, we are told they rose from about 1.2 millions to 2.15 millions—again, just about a doubling.[83] Revenues from the domaines, on the other hand, did not rise at all. Many seigneuries escheated to the crown or were seized; but the king gave them away almost as quickly as he took them in. Tolls, chancery rights, feudal dues, and other domaines brought in about 400,000 livres at the end of the reign, almost exactly the same as in 1523 and, as a matter of fact, the same as the previous century.

Our judgment, then, has to be that Francis I did not substantially change either the burden or the structure of French taxes. He added only one important tax in his long reign: the "pay for 20,000 foot soldiers" (see chapter 4). There were a few minor new revenues in this reign: the *insinuation* of 1539 (a copy of an Italian charge on registering deeds), and a lottery in the same year, supposedly farmed out for 2,000 livres.

One change in tax power that attracted a good deal of attention from contemporaries was the king's ability to exact clerical tenths more easily from the church. This was one of the consequences of the famous Concordat of Bologna (1516) which took from local chapters of clerics the right to nominate prelates of the Gallican church and transferred it to the king. Soon assemblies of prelates could be selected which found it hard to deny the king as many clerical tenths as he needed. A tenth, these years, was stereotyped at about 100,000 écus; but it was "given" two, three, and finally four times a year—and, on exception, even more often. Meanwhile, the pope's right to consent to such levies, even formally, vanished. However, both the tendency toward multiple tenths and the weakening of papal authority over them were well established before Francis I.

Apart from tenths, Francis I did not force any striking change in the constitutional situation regarding taxation. However, we should take care not to be misled by developments in constitutional theory. There is no doubt that several very important political commentators—though

83. Ibid., pp. 112, 125, 130.

certainly not all of them—became apologists for tax "absolutism." Writers such as Chasseneuz, Budé, and Grassaille insisted that in tax matters, as in all state affairs, the king was above human law and group privileges; he was subject only to divine and natural law.[84] This development does indeed mark a change from the tenor of constitutional thought during the fifteenth century. But the *real* legal-institutional relationships in the era 1515–47 were, on the whole, about where Charles VII had left them in the 1450s. Francis I certainly never dared to take a cue from such apologists for "absolutism" and claim the power to levy imposts at will.

The ability of Francis I to reshape the upper echelons of his fiscal bureaucracy, as a feature of his "absolutism," has escaped the attention of modern scholars and is worth examining. Such administrative changes could be accomplished by simply issuing the necessary edicts bestowing powers on the new officials. In some ways such exercise of royal power was even more "absolutist" than imposing higher or new taxes; certainly the imposition of new cadres of tax officials, new chains of command, and new fiscal districts represents a sharper and more deliberate break with the past than does an increase in the tax burden. In other European countries, changes in institutions as "sticky" as the fiscal bureaucracy were much more rare.

But this is a complex issue. We would not expect a "king of beasts" to have devoted so much of his effort to repeated administrative reforms of the fiscal bureaucracy. Such changes, after all, had as their goal improvements in revenues *without* great increases in the rate of taxes, suggesting a keen regard for the possibly adverse reactions of the king's subjects. Most of the years during Francis I's reign were troubled by serious fiscal deficits. To cope with these (since administrative reforms were not enough), he had to fall back on expedients such as increased sale of venal offices. A truly "absolutist" prince, we should imagine, would have cleared away all obstacles to higher revenues at one fell swoop.

There is some substance to the charge that Francis I's "absolutism" is revealed by his handling of venal offices. Of course the sale of offices was not his invention. A few royal household and administrative posts

84. Wm. F. Church, *Constitutional Thought in Sixteenth Century France*, pp. 36–37 and passim.

had been sold in the late Middle Ages.[85] These sales, however, should be viewed as royal favors to deserving burghers or to the second sons of lesser nobles. Until the late fifteenth century, venality could be described as reciprocity rather than a deliberate sale of offices in a regular market; that is, the king graciously bestowed offices on loyal subjects, and his new officials gave the king a token of their appreciation. But during the fifteenth century, the sale of venal offices increasingly became the rule in the fiscal system. By the time of Louis XII, most of the upper- and middle-echelon fiscal posts were venal—more because the French were anxious to purchase offices than because the crown promoted the practice.[86]

Francis I added new dimensions to venality. All the fiscal offices still not venal were made venal. More perturbing was the fact that many of the offices of the magistrates in both the sovereign and the lower courts —those attached to the fiscal system and other courts—were now sold. It was Francis I who made the sale of royal offices the concern of a specific bureau, the Parties casuelles. Most shocking of all is the manner in which the king invented and sold off useless and redundant offices (*supernuméraires*) as a type of levy on the whole body of officials. The most famous example of this device was his addition of twenty *conseillers* to the already more than adequate number of lawyers attached to the Parlement of Paris. The bitter protests raised by the judges had little effect; what counted for the king was the 120,000 livres (6,000 for each position) he meant to have.

Ironically, it was Parlement itself that had to implement this expedient by registering on its books the royal letters-patent that authorized the sale of the new offices. The king placed the matter before Parlement on a "put up or shut up" basis—if they would raise the 120,000 livres among themselves, he would cancel the proposal; if not, he would force them by instituting a *lit de justice*. Parlement dropped its opposition and

---

85. Françoise Autrand, "Offices et officiers royaux en France sous Charles VI," *Revue Historique* 242 (Oct.–Dec. 1969) : 319–24; Roland Mousnier, *La vénalité des offices sous Henry IV et Louis XIII*, pp. 2–3. Some great French barons also sold offices in their own establishments, but some did not: see L. Despois, *Histoire de l'autorité royale dans le comté de Nivernais*, p. 278.

86. For the fifteenth century's *archomanie* (craze for offices) see Dupont-Ferrier, *Études*, 1 : 75, 193, and passim.

accepted the new officials.[87] In the same manner Francis I increased the number of judges and officials in other sovereign courts. The Parlement of Bordeaux, for example, numbered twenty-nine officials in 1515; however, in 1547 there were sixty-six.[88]

In summary, we should regard the tax system and the tax policies of Francis I as only slightly more "absolutist" than that of the later fifteenth century. On balance the public finances of his reign show a modification of the system of Charles VII, not a significantly different tax system. We have been told that although monarchs such as Charles VII and Louis XI did much to pave the way for the "absolute" monarchs of the Renaissance, these earlier kings really belong to the Middle Ages rather than modern times.[89] A careful study of tax history does not support this view. So far as taxation is concerned, it makes more sense to see the whole period from Charles VII to Henry IV as one large but cohesive epoch in the history of French taxation.

87. Doucet, *François Ier*, 1 : 149 ff.
88. Mousnier, *Vénalité*, p. 27.
89. Lemonnier, in Lavisse 5¹ : 237, says of the 1523 fiscal reforms: "C'en est fini de la monarchie féodale, réduite à son domaine et se faisant *aider* exceptionellement par ses vassaux."

4

The Changing Balance of
Taxes, Loans, and Expedients

An age of financial crisis begins

The French king, in the mid-sixteenth century, enjoyed revenues that were the envy of monarchs in other lands. Nevertheless, French commentators on fiscal affairs during the 1550s and 1560s tell a sad tale of financial woe: the royal jewels are in pawn, the king's lands are being sold at hardship prices, court nobles and rich merchants are being beggared by the king's incessant demands for loans, cathedrals are being forced to sell their holy treasures, the poor are being squeezed beyond endurance, the soldiers and officials have not been paid—and still the king's debts rise!

Debts incurred by the Hapsburg rulers of Spain and the Holy Roman empire are a standard feature of Renaissance history; so is the extent to which the Tudor kings of England borrowed from abroad. The Valois kings, on the other hand—until the reign of Henry II—borrowed relatively little, and the role of credit and of lenders in France was correspondingly less. Pressures generated during the late Renaissance, however, forced a basic change in the relations between taxation and credit. This changing composition of the elements of public finance was the most important feature of fiscal history in the era between Francis I and the Wars of Religion.

The main reason for the growing importance of loans and of fiscal stratagems was that Henry II refused to abandon his claims to Milan and Naples; he pushed hard against his northeast frontier, and bid for the support of Protestant princes in Germany against Emperor Charles V. Each campaign became more costly than the previous one. After the Spanish harquebus had demonstrated its superiority over the pike in the earlier

Wars of Italy, a higher proportion of foot soldiers had to be supplied with the new firearms. The new techniques of building fortifications out in the field, rather than relying on walled towns, made frontal assaults more costly in money as well as in blood. Cannon were becoming such an important feature of campaigns that they proved to be the key factor in several victories for the French. But they were fearfully expensive—in fact, a separate account, *l'extraordinaire de l'artillerie*, was established for royal expenditure records.

The court of Henry II was also a serious financial drain. The splendor of the court outshone everything that even Francis I, supposedly a spendthrift monarch, had done. More and more was being spent on lavish entertainment, costly clothes, and jewels for members of the royal family. The court was also becoming a vital source of funds for an increasing number of nobles. Gifts of money or of royal lands, life-time pensions, and the higher-paying royal offices—already plentiful in the reign of Francis I—now became a serious concern to the nation. Moralists and political reformers saw in this "impertinent giving" a key symptom of social degeneration; but to the nobles who received it, this largesse became increasingly important as their own living expenses rose and their way of life became more sumptuous.

Another problem for the royal treasury was that the "price revolution" of the sixteenth century was seriously reducing the purchasing power of money. After rising slowly during the 1530s and 1540s, French prices climbed more sharply in the 1550s, tapered off in the 1560s, and rose most steeply in the 1570s. In the Paris area, the same good quality wheat that sold for about 3.2 livres a *setier* (about twelve bushels) in 1547, sold for 16 to 18 livres in 1574.[1]

This does not mean, of course, that government expenditures increased fivefold for every item purchased between 1547 and 1574. The price of wheat itself fluctuated, often violently, so that in the very next year (1575), after the death of Charles IX, a setier of wheat could be bought for only 8 or 9 livres. The figures for wheat are relatively reliable, but they give no assurance that they reflect the general trend in the costs of government and of the royal household, since other prices—for

1. Henri Hauser, *Recherches et documents sur l'histoire des prix en France de 1500 à 1800*, pp. 107–08; Micheline Baulant and Jean Meuvret, *Prix des céréales extraits de la mercuriale de Paris*, 1 : 342 and passim.

manufactures and for services—rose much less rapidly.[2] Unfortunately, the national états available do not give the sort of information needed to show the proportions for each type of expenditure. Detailed spending accounts, for the most part, have disappeared. But the records show that the greatest portion of royal expenditures went for wages, salaries, and pensions. A somewhat smaller amount was paid for interest on royal debts, an even smaller proportion went for manufactured commodities, and relatively little was spent on foodstuffs.

The average cost of royal purchases, therefore, rose considerably less than the fivefold rise in wheat prices. But even if the real purchasing power of one livre of royal revenues fell by only 50 percent, the purchasing power of royal revenues fell much more than total tax income rose. The regular taxes climbed only from about 9 million livres annually at the death of Francis I to 12 millions at the advent of Henry III.

This combination of rising costs and heavier expenditures compelled the treasury to look to emergency surtaxes and other expedients. These "extraordinary" (in the post-1523 sense) levies brought in close to 3 million livres each year during the 1550s.[3] But the annual volume of royal borrowing was even greater.

The Lyons capital market

France's best chance for developing a financial center capable of lending large sums to the king lay with Lyons.[4] A moderately important commercial and craft center during the Middle Ages, Lyons had become one of the great cities of France shortly after the Hundred Years' War. In the 1460s political turmoil in Florence had forced some wealthy Tuscan merchants out of Italy, and they took up residence in Lyons. They had been welcomed enthusiastically by Louis XI, who gave them important privileges, including the right to practice banking. Lyons quickly became part of the international credit network by which merchant-bankers expedited commodity transactions and capital trans-

2. Nef, "Prices and Industrial Capitalism in France and England," pp. 258–61.
3. Clamageran, *L'impôt,* 2 : 196–97.
4. In the later sixteenth century an additional important money market developed in Rouen. At that time, when there were two major money markets in France, there were nine in Italy and six in Spain. Henri Lapeyre, *Une famille de marchands, les Ruiz,* p. 290.

fers. Soon scores of able and ambitious mercantile families either moved to Lyons or established agencies in the town; the Medici, Frescobaldi, Bonvisi, and Capponi families had branches there.

The "Tuscan" colony of Lyons (there were also some Lombards, and many persons from other Italian regions) brought in increasing amounts of capital for the growing money market. The textile, printing, paper, and other industries of the town responded to this stimulus, and the importance of the commodity fair at Lyons increased. But the credit fairs, called "Lyons settlements," soon accounted for an even larger volume of business than the sales of commodities.

In the 1540s it seemed as though Lyons was on its way toward outstripping the great financial centers of Antwerp and Genoa. A few Spanish, Portuguese, and Flemish merchants also set up agencies in Lyons. Even bankers from the rich towns of south and west Germany established themselves in Lyons. Like the Italians, they worked at importing and exporting as well as at banking operations. The increasing wealth and sophistication of the Lyons money market, therefore, and the manner in which it was tied to international finance, represented an enormous opportunity for the French monarch.

During the reign of Francis I, the king's most noteworthy response to this opportunity had been to give Cardinal de Tournon, governor of the Lyonnais and one of the king's most valued advisors, an extraordinary commission (1536) to raise money there for the government virtually in any manner he saw fit.[5] The king's instructions had allowed Tournon to alienate crown revenues, to negotiate voluntary loans or impose forced ones, and in general to exploit the entire royal, municipal, and international financial resources of Lyons so as to support the royal armies then fighting in Italy.

Tournon and the later loan expediters negotiated with Lyons merchant-bankers either as individual concerns or as a consortium (*parti*). Often the king's agents were able to arrange repayment by assignments against royal or municipal taxes. The lucrative *douane de Lyon* (see appendix J) was a favorite instrument for such repayments. The king's agents could also tap the short-term money market—the capital generated by

5. Much of the following, for the period before the Grand Parti (1555), is based on Roger Doucet, *Finances municipales et crédit public à Lyon au XVIe siècle,* esp. pp. 10–52.

commodity and credit transactions every three months at the Lyons fairs. A major objection to fair loans, however, was that they cost up to 16 percent interest, since lenders could charge 4 percent for three months, that is, from fair to fair.[6]

When the pace of royal borrowing increased during the late 1540s and the 1550s, the city government of Lyons was forced to cooperate more closely with the royal loan agents. The city was required to lend its own funds to the crown or even to borrow in its own name from richer merchants in order to meet the king's need for credit. Often the king's agents used force or threats of force; on at least one occasion some town magistrates actually were jailed until the *consulat* gave in. Pressure was also brought to bear on the foreign merchant-bankers in Lyons; they were threatened with punitive taxes or even with expulsion if they did not cooperate.

The royal pressure for funds resulted in a violent scramble to shift the burden of the loans and their repayment on somebody else's shoulders. Naturally the consulat argued that these burdens made it necessary for the government to allow the town a larger number of municipal taxes; the king usually agreed. Some of the new sources of town revenues were lucrative, and for a while it seemed as though the pace of increased town revenues would keep up with the rising town debt. But as royal loans continued to pile up, the townspeople and foreign merchants began to resist the imposition of still more taxes. Soon Lyons could no longer prevent its municipal debt from climbing. Funds raised for crown loans had to be turned over quickly and in full. The arrangements made for their repayment sometimes dragged on for several years, and they rarely were paid back in full.

No doubt the king would have been willing enough to let Lyons increase local taxes by any means in order to liquidate its debt. But various groups in the town had different views. The artisans and the lower classes often reacted violently when a decision was made to increase local excises, a tax burden that directly affected their cost of living. Citizen-merchants, on the other hand, favored excises falling on all residents, while the lower- and middle-class groups preferred forced loans and capital levies on the town's wealthiest families. The town councilors

6. Henri Hauser, "The European Financial Crisis of 1559," *Journal of Economic and Business History* 2 (1929–30): 246.

were caught in the middle of the controversy; they favored citizen-merchants (as opposed to foreigners and the lower classes), but they also had to take into account the threats of social unrest.[7] The foreign bankers fought vigorously against increases in tolls and tariffs imposed on the Lyons district; since most of them were merchants themselves they wanted to be able to compete on equal terms with French and foreign merchants not based in Lyons.

The Grand Parti and the crisis of 1557–58

In 1555 Lyons was at the height of her Renaissance fortunes. The city became the scene for an attempt to consolidate royal loans and improve royal credit. This experiment was the famous *Grand Parti*.

We do not know enough about the operations of the Grand Parti or about the nature of the terrible crisis that followed to give a definitive assessment of its place in the history of French public finance.[8] What we do know suggests that in its time it was rather limited in scope and significance—in spite of its importance for modern scholars wanting to learn more about the development of Renaissance capital markets and royal borrowing practices. The episode certainly does not justify the attitude found in some studies that public finance under Henry II was rotten to the core. The Grand Parti, as such, did not plunge France into the financial difficulties the country experienced during the reigns of Charles IX and Henry III. The rising costs of government, the "price revolution," the accidental death of Henry II, the fact that Francis II and Charles IX came to the throne so young, and the Wars of Religion —these were more direct causes of financial woes.

For the merchant-bankers, the Grand Parti marked a significant change in the method of repayment. Previously, they had loaned money to the crown under a variety of terms—for longer or shorter periods, and at greater or lesser interest rates. They were now offered, in exchange for these old and somewhat risky claims, a new, attractive, consolidated,

7. Doucet, *Lyon*, pp. 22–24.
8. Both royal and town records of Grand Parti transactions have disappeared. Doucet's impressive *Revue Historique* study on this affair (see above, chap. 3, n. 57) seems much more thorough and convincing than Hauser's "Financial Crisis," which is based on Richard Ehrenberg, *Capital and Finance in the Age of the Renaissance* (London, 1928).

and medium-term loan. They received payments of 5 percent quarterly, paid at the regular meeting times of the four Lyons fairs. This 5 percent was supposed to include interest of 4 percent on the unpaid balance. The 1 percent amortization rate of the first payment, of course, would increase as the unpaid balance diminished, canceling the debt in slightly more than ten years.[9] Previous royal loans had contained various amortization arrangements; but this was the first large-scale loan in which the government, in effect, made a guarantee of a specific and ample amortization rate. Rentes, of course, could be eliminated through repurchase by the government. But for rentes there was no guarantee that the principal sum ever would be repaid—making them, potentially, perpetual annuities.

The first loans of the Grand Parti were a great success. This was an era when the silver mines of the New World were pouring their yield through Spain into Europe. Capital markets, therefore, were exceptionally "easy." Even in Lyons, bankers on occasion were lending out money at only 2 percent per fair period.[10] Furthermore, the political future of the Hapsburgs seemed so doubtful (Charles V, totally discouraged, had announced his intention of abdicating) that Swiss, German, and some Italian bankers who usually entrusted their investments to Antwerp or Genoa now preferred to send their money to the relatively safer haven of Lyons. Also in its favor was the Grand Parti's seemingly effective plan for obtaining cash to pay interest and amortization. According to the key operative ordinances in 1555, the Grand Parti payments were to come from the most certain (*les plus clairs*) revenues under the control of the receveurs généraux of Lyons, Toulouse, and Montpellier.

In any case, the Grand Parti was accepted so enthusiastically when it was first put into operation in 1555 (for a total of about 3.4 million livres) that the government was able to raise additional money in the same manner that year and again in 1556.[11] Many creditors who had

9. That is, in 41 "fairs" (quarters). Doucet shows ("Grand Parti, 1," pp. 492–98 and 498 n. 2) that when Ehrenberg states that the Grand Parti could not possibly have resulted in complete amortization plus regular 4 percent interest, he makes the mistake of computing interest on the total loan rather than the unpaid balance. Doucet also cites one writer who shows that contemporaries in 1557 understood that at the announced rates the debt would be amortized in about ten years.

10. Doucet, *Lyon*, p. 45.

11. Doucet, "Grand Parti, 1," p. 500.

loaned the king money in other ways were encouraged to transfer their old claims against the city of Lyons into new Grand Parti obligations. Thus in 1555 the first participants in the Grand Parti were allowed to transfer their old Lyons town rentes into shares in the new scheme, to an amount not to exceed one-third their new subscriptions; there were similar exchanges later of other old loans. All in all, by the time the Grand Parti ran into its first crisis in 1557, the state had obtained a total of about 9,658,000 livres.[12]

A proper perspective on the Grand Parti certainly should include some notion of its relative importance compared to other royal "outside" borrowing (from professional or, at least, voluntary lenders) in this period. At the time the Grand Parti was raising some 9.7 million livres, Henry II borrowed 3.1 millions in new rentes; it is true, however, that most issues of these rentes appear to have been forced on the Parisians and therefore were not really "outside" loans. In addition we know of dozens of short-term loans in Lyons and elsewhere, made in 1555 (only a few months after the Grand Parti was launched) and running to 1558; these were completely personal matters between the king and the great merchant-bankers. Indeed, perhaps the greatest of the king's creditors during this period, the Strasbourg bankers Minkel and Obrecht, refused to become involved in the Grand Parti, preferring to obtain the king's personal guarantee.[13]

Loans at least equal to those of the Grand Parti came to Henry II from the pope and other Italian rulers and from merchant-bankers besides those of Lyons. Many of these Italian loans were organized by a single agent, Albizzo (or Albisse) Del Bene. Del Bene, who actually started operations in 1550 just before the Wars of Siena began, was one of the most energetic and successful Florentines stationed at Lyons. The hub of his private affairs probably was his operations as an agent of the Guadagni, a great house of Tuscan bankers. He also functioned in the 1530s and 1540s as a tax farmer of the French gabelles and of some of

12. According to Doucet ("Grand Parti, 1," pp. 496–97, 502) this money came largely from professional bankers, as did most royal loans before 1555, and not from vast numbers of middle- and upper-class Frenchmen, as Ehrenberg and others believe. See Hauser's somewhat unconvincing reply to Doucet on this point: "Le crise de 1557–1559 et le bouleversement des fortunes," in *Mélanges offerts à M. Abel Lefranc.*

13. Doucet, "Grand Parti, 1," p. 505. Other foreign bankers, however—Italians and even Marranos of Istanbul—did participate.

the import tariffs at Lyons. Apparently he was an energetic supporter of the Valois "mission" in Italy; he may even have volunteered to act as the king's agent. The king gave him the grandiloquent title of "Surintendant général des finances françaises en Italie," and he also was authorized to seek loans in Germany and elsewhere. If funds for repaying loans were not available from the Epargne, it was Del Bene's right to obtain cash from the *trésorier de l'extraordinaire des guerres* in Piedmont (the French stronghold in Italy). This army paymaster in turn got his funds from Lyons or sometimes all the way from Poitiers.[14] The king's debts in Italy often had to be settled with cash rather than with offsetting credit, since loans by Italians to Frenchmen far overbalanced French financial claims against Italy (mostly drafts to pay for French commodity exports). Shipping cash over long distances was an irritating and expensive way to settle royal debts. There are records of one shipment of 125,000 livres for which the cartage and security expenses alone came to 6,750 livres, or 5.4 percent.[15]

Del Bene's total borrowing in Italy for Henry II (covering the years 1551–57) that are a matter of record amount to about 8,026,000 livres—more than four-fifths as much as the Grand Parti. There is reason to suspect that much more was borrowed by Del Bene, but the records either have disappeared or were deliberately kept secret.[16] There were additional loans organized by Del Bene in 1558—the year in which the Grand Parti scheme began to collapse.

The shattering defeat of a large French army at St. Quentin in north France (August 1557) first caused the Lyons bankers to lose their confidence in the Grand Parti loans. A wave of nervousness had shaken the financiers a short time before, when news came of the famous "bankruptcy" (really, an onerous debt consolidation) of Philip II of Spain.[17] For a while the bankers of Lyons allowed themselves to be encouraged

14. Michel François, "Albisse Del Bene, surintendant général des finances françaises en Italie," *Bibliothèque de l'Ecole des Chartes* 94 (1933) : 337–60.

15. François, *Tournon*, pp. 344–45.

16. François, *Tournon*, p. 360.

17. The collapse of the Grand Parti was, in fact, only one of a large number of apparently connected financial crises upsetting much of western Europe. One eminent scholar believes a severe crop failure, necessitating large silver movements, was to blame. Astrid Friis, "An Inquiry into the Relations between Economic and Financial Factors in the Sixteenth and Seventeenth Centuries," *Scandinavian Economic History Review* 1, no. 2 (1953).

by peace negotiations between the Valois and Hapsburg rulers (culminating in the most welcome peace of Cateau-Cambrésis, April 1559). They actually loaned the French king several million additional livres, loans which either were incorporated into the Grand Parti or were associated with it by virtue of similar conditions. The total of all unpaid Grand Parti and associated loans rose to about 12 million livres. But then Henry II was killed accidentally during the tournament held to celebrate peace; and the future of France looked so dark that Grand Parti creditors began to despair—with good reason, as it turned out.

Though interest payments on Grand Parti loans were cut down in 1558 and stopped completely in 1559, there was no official decree of bankruptcy; neither was there a sincere attempt by the king to consolidate and refloat this loan. The government stated only that interest payments were suspended and that the trésorier de l'Epargne, rather than the receveur général of the Lyonnais, would now handle all matters involving the Grand Parti. But all the complicated interest and amortization arrangements were stopped, and the revenues of the Midi provinces that had been earmarked for this account were directed into the royal treasury. For years thereafter the king put off his creditors in the most outrageous fashion, either rebuffing their efforts or accepting repayment plans "in principle," while instructing the trésorier de l'Epargne not to pay out anything on this account. Grand Parti creditors tried applying pressure as a group, but soon the consortium broke up, each banking house trying to salvage what it could from the wreck.

Incredibly, the situation remained suspended in this distressing state for about three decades, during which, little by little, parts of the royal obligations were grudgingly paid off. But the final liquidation was not effected until the advent of Sully, chief minister of Henry IV. Sully displayed little patience with those who insisted on full back-interest payments. In fact he insisted on paying no current interest at all, and he cut the amount of back interest outstanding to virtually nothing.

Forced loans and "soldes" after 1559

It was a serious loss to French public finance that the long-term amalgamated type of loan represented by the Grand Parti was not developed into a regular tool of fiscal policy. Certainly the crisis of 1557–

58 shook the bankers' confidence; but they could have been coaxed back (as were other bankers after similar "bankruptcies" in Spain) with appropriate guarantees and concessions.

It seems to have been at least partly because of the government's wishes in the matter that royal "outside" borrowing after 1559 returned to the pattern of borrowing before 1555—that is, primarily short term "personal" loans. Catherine de Medici seemed to prefer personal loans because they could be kept secret. She clung to personal negotiations in her tightrope maneuvers among the French factions struggling for power. These negotiations often were accompanied by large-scale bribery. Therefore Catherine favored loans that would not show up in national or local budgets, which were documents that had to be handled by many fiscal bureaucrats. Such a policy was not only an aspect of Catherine's fine Italian hand, it also was a quite understandable reaction to the enormous outpouring of public indignation that came when the government was forced to reveal the huge size of its debts at the time of the Estates-General of 1560.

Catherine had maintained favorable relations with several Italian states, and she now put these connections to good financial use. Her personal borrowing agent in Italy, Davido Sardini, is supposed to have collected about 2.6 million livres for her in the years 1573–74 alone—at an enormous profit for himself.[18] Catherine was able to arrange loans from Venice, the Grand Duchy of Tuscany, the papacy, and even from Switzerland, reversing the trend for capital to move from France to Switzerland. Later these states, especially Tuscany, were to experience years of frustration in attempting to persuade Catherine to pay off her loans; she tended to regard these loans as subventions by her allies in the common war against Calvinism.[19]

France's borrowing policy after 1559 seems to have been dominated not so much by an attempt to improve credit techniques as by a vigorous effort to cut down the proportion of "outside" loans and to employ more "inside" credit (from the "fiscal sponge" and other expedients) while expanding the tax base. The Guises, ruling as regents for young Francis

18. A Vührer, *Histoire de la dette publique en France*, 2 vols. (Paris, 1886), 1 : 32.

19. Eletta Palandri, *Les négotiations politiques et religieuses entre la Toscane et la France* . . . (Brussels, 1908), pp. 109–10; see also Doucet, *L'état des finances de 1567*, p. 11; and N. M. Sutherland, *The French Secretaries of State in the Age of Catherine de Medici*, pp. 130–31.

II, and later Catherine herself, forced the church to permit regular and heavy taxing of its wealth as well as to guarantee interest payments on additional royal rentes; in fact, rentes were used much more extensively than under Francis I or even Henry II. Francis I had sold only 725,000 livres of rentes, and Henry II sold 6.8 millions. However, during the reigns of Francis II (1559–60) and Charles IX (1560–74) approximately 25.9 million livres in rentes were issued. Rentes on city governments other than Paris appeared in Rouen, Provins, Rennes, Marseilles, and perhaps other cities. And when the usual aides, octrois, and clerical levies were not enough to support interest payments, the gabelles and even the tailles were thrown into the breach.[20] The early issues of rentes can be thought of as "outside" credit; but by the 1570s they were largely another form of forced loans.

Resistance against the later rentes developed to such a point that at times the king ordered those Parisians who had previously loaned money to the government to absorb the new issues, on the grounds that their previous loans proved they were rich enough.[21] In 1576 the king threatened to take control of the administration of the rentes from the Paris city government and give it to two *controleurs généraux de rentes*; this project was dropped after the Parisians "donated" a suitable sum to the royal treasury.[22]

Forced loans in the form of rentes were not the only fiscal expedient visited on the cities of France during the later Renaissance. On one occasion Henry II ordered the Parisians to bring all their silver plate to the mint as a forced loan;[23] and Charles IX seized the goods and money held in escrow by notaries pending court decisions.[24] But the

20. The budget for 1574, transcribed by Philip Dur, "Constitutional Rights and Taxation in the Reign of Henry III" (Ph.D. diss., Harvard, 1941), p. 222, shows 250,000 livres from rentes "sur la maison de la Ville de Rouen." The government refused to float rentes in Lyons. Doucet, *Lyon*, pp. 43–44.

21. Edict of Blois, Feb. 1563. There had been parallel measures in the days of Henry II. See Cauwès, "Crédit public," pp. 835–36, 852, 860; and Doucet, *Lyon*, p. 53. See also Jean Combes's significant reference to those who were constrained to pay as being on the "roole des emprunts." *Traicté de tailles & autres charges, & subsides . . .* , p. 119.

22. Edict of Paris, April 1576.

23. Edict of Paris, Feb. 1553. See also James W. Thompson, *The Wars of Religion in France, 1559–1576*, p. 86. The following year all vessels of gold and silver were ordered brought in and exchanged for rentes. Cauwès, "Crédit public," p. 862. By Feb. 1555 precious metal plate had brought in 300,000 livres.

24. Doucet, *L'état des finances de 1567*, pp. 7–8.

most important fiscal expedient by far, apart from venality and forced loans, was the *soldes pour les gens de pied*. It was first tried during the reign of Francis I and established, after some experimenting, as the *solde de 50,000 hommes de pied* in 1543.[25] Comparable levies were declared in 1553, 1555, 1575, 1582, and 1588; it is likely they were raised other years as well. The soldes were recognized as substitutes for tailles on the major "free" towns.[26] They were heavy burdens; the quota for the *prévôté* of Paris alone for 1543 and 1553 was 180,000 livres, and the national levy for 1577 seems to have been 1.2 million livres.[27]

Unlike the soldes, forced loans on towns were, in principle, to be repaid; in fact many of them were. At least interest payments on forced loans seem to have been met with some degree of responsibility. Whether or not interest was paid, forced loans certainly were regarded as burdens by contemporaries; La Barre, for example, thought the main difference between such loans and tailles was that the former were "taken solely from the rich and well-off," while tailles were borne by "the strong carrying the weak." [28]

More than a dozen forced loans on all the chief cities of France are recorded for the period 1547–84; and many others, we know, were raised from single towns or provinces. Some forced loans were for enormous amounts. Lyons's quota for the forced loan of January 1558 was 96,000 livres, to be raised by peremptory levies of 50 to 1,000 écus each on the town's richest burghers.[29] The forced loans of 1558 brought in 4.6 million livres from all France. The total for 1575 was 3 millions, with one million from Paris alone.[30] Later the same year, Paris had to provide additional loans on two occasions. Thus in these years forced loans and other emergency levies on the towns were bringing in almost as much revenue as the tailles.[31]

With the advantage of hindsight, it is obvious that the staggering

25. The first attempt was in 1538, *la solde de 20,000 hommes de pied*. See the edict of St. Germain-en-Laye, May 3, 1543, "pour la soulde des gens de pied appelez vulgairement soldats" ; and see Combes, *Traicté*, pp. 115–16.

26. See Zeller, *Institutions*, p. 259, who claims that in 1555 soldes were placed on villages, too, becoming "another taille."

27. Letters-patent of Blois, Feb. 17, 1577.

28. La Barre, *Formulaire*, p. 139.

29. Doucet, *Lyon*, p. 57.

30. Clamageran, *L'impôt*, 2 : 140–41, 190–91.

31. Doucet, *Lyon*, p. 53.

expenses of the Wars of Religion doomed in advance the government's efforts to muddle through with "inside" credit plus an abundance of expedients and occasional emergency "outside" loans. Such an attempt may have made sense during the reign of Francis I; but after 1562 it was entirely inappropriate. Some initiative from the king was needed to provide a better method for tapping the growing capital resources of French merchants and bankers. But no financial reforms were undertaken, and a credit vacuum appeared.

The opportunity was ripe for a new breed of moneylenders, prepared to profit from the state's embarrassment. These new lenders were called *partisans* (those who formed a *parti*, or association) or *traitants* (those who made a *traité* with the crown). While there was no clear separation between the two terms, *partisans* usually referred to enterprisers who extended rather large loans to the king in return for taking over all the income from certain revenues (rather than receiving a fixed sum as an assignment to be paid out of certain revenues). The term *traitants* referred, rather vaguely, to those who were able to suggest new taxes or opportunities for increasing the rates of old taxes or enlarging the number of venal offices. In return for all the receipts arising from these new revenues, the traitants would loan funds to the king; the size of the loan was presumably set so that interest and amortization would be equal to the new revenues. But such operations carried too many opportunities for scandalously high profits—or, at least, such was the opinion of French taxpayers, who were convinced that traitants and partisans were one of the chief reasons they were taxed so grievously while the king's debts continued to rise.[32]

The popular outcry against partisans and traitants was particularly loud against foreigners. While the French, in their popular assemblies, were demanding that foreign financiers be thrown out of the country, the king was protecting them, exempting them from royal imposts, and granting them lucrative posts in the fiscal administration. In 1586 the king tried to encourage more foreign financiers to invest in the royal

---

32. See, e.g., the complaint of Bishop d'Epinac of Lyons at the Estates-General of 1576, stating that excessive rates of interest, made in "parties desraisonnables avec quelques estrangiers & autres," are bound to continue; the traitants will never allow the king to release himself from such debts, "puis que vostre pauvreté seroit leur richesse." Pierre d'Epinac, *Harangue prononcée devant le roy . . .* , pp. 99–100.

debt by definitively abolishing the *droit d'aubaine*, an old prerogative of the king by which he obtained all the property of foreigners dying in his realm.[33] The problem of popular feeling against the foreign financiers, "a race always cursed and always irreplaceable" (Henri Sée), remained unresolved all through the Renaissance. Nicolas Froumenteau pictures them "with France's blood on their hands"; and the famous early mercantilist, Barthélemy de Laffemas, in a bitter tirade, accuses them of "building palaces with our money," and of having a hand in "maliciously concocting" all the newer taxes of France. "Let us," he urges, "show them the road that leads back to their country."[34]

The partisans and traitants became so important they were allowed to pick and choose which revenues among the aides, octrois, tariffs, and tolls they preferred as guarantees and assignments. As time went on they managed to divert into their own purses a large portion of the royal indirect taxes, which in turn seriously limited royal tax revenues, thus making it even more imperative for the king to borrow. The outcome was the construction of the "General Farms" of the Old Régime; they were associations of financiers who managed all the royal taxes on commerce in return for loans to the state.

NEW FISCAL BURDENS ON THE CLERGY

The Estates-General of Orléans and Pontoise-Poissy

The death of Henry II brought to France crises of regency, religion, and revenues; it is hard to say which was the most serious. As usual, fierce resentment over other grievances made fiscal injustices seem intolerable. The French were in no mood to accept, under the fifteen-year-old Francis II or the nine-year-old Charles IX, the sort of irritating fiscal expedients they had suffered under Henry II. They demanded fiscal reforms; and the regents—the Guises and (later) the queen mother, Catherine de Medici—hastened to comply. The main result of these efforts, accomplished just before and during the Estates-General of

33. Edict of Paris, May 1586.
34. Froumenteau, *Le secret des finances de France* . . . , introduction; Laffemas, *Les trésors et richesses pour mettre l'estat en splendeur* . . . (Paris, 1598), pp. 36–37.

1560–61, was to shift a greater and a more regular share of the tax burden to the clergy. The church was forced to sell part of its wealth to support new issues of rentes. On the eve of the Wars of Religion France added an important feature to her fiscal structure.

The short, unhappy reign of Francis II (July 1559–December 1560) was not formally a regency, since the young king, according to tradition, had attained his majority at age fourteen. Francis II was completely in the hands of his wife, Mary, Queen of Scots. Mary, in turn, carried out the orders of her uncles, the Guises. The Guises worked hard to cut expenses; they dismissed additional officials and troops, cut down pensions, were stingy with gifts to nobles, and instituted proceedings to recover parts of the royal domaines that had been given away or sold at unreasonably low prices.[35] They sent the favorites of Henry II packing, including the Constable de Montmorency and the redoubtable Diane de Poitiers. For a short time the Guises were able to reduce court costs considerably. By December 1560, when the Estates-General at Orléans opened, the government could claim it had cut royal court and household expenses by more than two million livres annually compared to the days of Henry II.[36] All these admirably vigorous attempts to improve the health of the royal treasury earned the Guises the undying hatred of the noble captains and courtiers who wanted more money from the court and who had become accustomed to getting it.

However, these savings could not begin to bridge the financial gap. In south and west France many districts were turning into Huguenot strongholds, and the reformed faith was gaining many adherents among the burghers of Caen, Rouen, Tours, Bourges, and other important north and central cities. Much more serious, in the eyes of the court, was the fact that increasing numbers of nobles were now declaring for Protestantism. The Guises redoubled their persecutions of Huguenots, and hundreds of martyrs gave witness to the mettle of the new faith. As tension mounted, more signs of popular religious violence appeared—assas-

---

35. On the attempt to cut down venal offices, see the royal decl. of Villers-Cotterets, dated September, and that dated Sept. 4, 1559, and the edict of Romorantin, May 1560, in Fontanon, 2 : 582. Royal hunting expense reductions alone are supposed to have saved 100,000 écus. Michel Devèze, *La vie de la forêt française au XVIe siècle*, 2 : 149.

36. Clamageran, *L'impôt*, 2 : 171.

sinations of priests and Huguenot ministers, desecration of holy images, and smashing of stained glass windows. It was in this atmosphere of financial and religious crisis that the government decided to call a full Estates-General—the first since 1484—to advise the crown on dealing with its problems.

The sections devoted to finances in the addresses by Chancellor l'Hospital to the Estates-General came as a shock. He called for an increase in royal taxes on salt, heavier tailles, a rise in the rates on wines, and other new burdens. He referred to the many years of repeated and costly warfare in the reign of Henry II, and revealed that all the aides and gabelles, as well as a good portion of the tailles, were completely alienated to royal creditors, thus bringing in no cash at all. It was then that official confirmation came of the rumor that the royal debts were in the order of 43 million livres. These gigantic debts of the king, suddenly, were supposed to become the problem of the country.[37]

For the moment, however, the delegates not only rejected the responsibility for these debts but also refused even to discuss most of the chancellor's proposals for higher revenues, offering the usual weak excuse that they had not been authorized by their constituents to advance such grants.[38] They demanded to be dismissed; and the government let them go, though not without a stern warning from l'Hospital and a detailed analysis of how much money they must be prepared to vote the king when they returned as properly authorized delegates. He now warned the clergy, specifically, that they must return later in the year prepared to buy back from royal creditors all the alienated gabelles, aides, and domaines. He then made the astonishing promise that if this were accomplished the state would reduce its main taxes to the level under Louis XII.

The second meeting of the Estates-General was set for May 1561; as it turned out, however, they were not actually convoked until August. They met in two separate bodies—the nobles and commoners at Pontoise, and a special session of the clergy at Poissy. The decision to have some of the clerics meet separately was made so that there could be a formal confrontation between Catholic and Huguenot theologians in order to discuss the possible bases for uniting French Christianity once

37. Picot, *Etats Généraux*, 2 : 198, 366–73.
38. An attempt was made to head off some of the complaints of the delegates by promulgating a sweeping reform ordinance, Jan. 31, 1561. Isambert, 14 : 63–98.

again. This assembly, so important for Renaissance religious history, is known as "the colloquy of Poissy." [39]

At Pontoise, the delegates of the Second and Third Estates presented the crown's spokesmen with spirited demands for reforms in fiscal administration and for a drastic reduction in the tax load. Along with these negative reactions to the king's demands for more money, however, there were definite hints, in the sessions of both Second and Third Estates, that the delegates at Pontoise would welcome a decision to extract more money from the church. In part, this move was a sort of repayment for Catherine's policy of religious moderation, and it was supported by both moderates and Huguenots. In part, however, it was tied to the general hostility against the church. The Council of Trent and the controversy it stirred had been the occasion for violent attacks against the clergy's personal, moral, and educational standards; reform of the church was a problem that was on everyone's mind. The French clergy were decidedly on the defensive. The great wealth of the Gallican church loomed as at least a partial answer to the state's financial crisis.

The "contract" of Poissy, 1561

Occasional taxing of clerical wealth by the crown was nothing new. In a sense it went as far back as the "crusader tithes" of the High Middle Ages; every king since Philip the Fair had obtained some sort of financial support from the clergy. From the time of the Concordat of 1516, Francis I had taken clerical tenths from the church regularly—often two, three, and even four times a year, especially toward the end of his reign. But, in theory, clerical payments to the crown were still regarded as emergency devices. They had always been granted subject to several well-defined conditions.

It is hard to tell from accounts of the Estates-General of 1561 just what were the main factors behind the bold new plan to force larger, annual, and obligatory payments from the church. Certainly, in part, it came from the Huguenot attacks on Catholicism; the most audacious demands for stripping the church of its wealth seem to have been raised by the Huguenot mayor of Autun, Jean Bretaigne.[40] It may have been

---

39. It soon broke up, however, having accomplished none of its objectives. Mariéjol, in Lavisse 6¹ : 47–51.

40. Clamageran, *L'impôt*, 2 : 176, 181.

promoted by the court and its councilors who were using the shift in public opinion against the church to bail the government out of its terrible financial straits. On the other hand, some accounts show Guise and Montmorency (and other Catholic grandees) exceedingly anxious to raise funds from the church, not so much for paying off the king's debts or for lightening the tax burden on the commoners but for financing a large army, which under their leadership could exterminate the Huguenot heresy.[41] Finally, there does appear in this confused picture a genuine feeling on the part of the moderate Catholic majority that the time had come to move away from the traditional exemption of the church from regular fiscal support of the crown. Probably all these factors did enter into the decisions at Pontoise and Poissy that forced the church to the unprecedented step of assuming responsibility for a significant portion of royal revenues over a long period of years—as it turned out, permanently.

There is an intriguing similarity between the demands raised at Pontoise to strip the church of part of its wealth and the debates of 1789 that led to the famous *assignats*. In 1561, as in 1789, many delegates argued that the church was wealthy far beyond what was needed for its proper functioning and that the state easily could appropriate much of this wealth without damage to French society. Jean Bretaigne went so far as to assert that if the government sold all the income-producing real estate owned by the church and deposited the money with private bankers, the resulting income from interest alone would be more than adequate to pay for the upkeep of the clerics and the maintenance of their buildings and services. Other commoners suggested that the king should have the right to tax the income of each benefice annually by a ratio of its income; they even drew up estimates of such rates. One plan called for a tax of 20 percent on benefices with a gross income under 500 livres annually and up to 75 percent for those worth about 12,000 livres annually.[42] The official *cahier* of the Third Estate at Pontoise proposed that an exact survey be made of the entire extent of clerical wealth and income. This aroused consternation among the clerics at Poissy, who retreated behind their traditional freedom from such inquisitorial tactics and announced that they would refuse to comply. Even the nobles at Pontoise (many of whom were Huguenots) went along with

41. Thompson, *Wars of Religion*, pp. 98–101.
42. Clamageran, *L'impôt*, 2 : 181–83.

the suggestions that at least part of the royal debts should be paid off by the church.

After the theological "colloquy" at Poissy collapsed and the Calvinists left, the French prelates remained in session as the representatives of the First Estate. It was now the clergy's task to consider the precedent-shattering demands for royal levies on church wealth that were being raised by the Second and Third Estates at Pontoise. The arrangement that resulted (October 21, 1561) is called the "contract" of Poissy; however, its terms were violated so severely and so repeatedly by the king that it was indeed a grotesquely one-sided contract.[43]

The 1561 contract included two important guarantees of financial support by the church. First, the clergy undertook to pay the royal treasury a subsidy of 1.6 million livres per year for six years (1562–67). The money was to be drawn from the income of church farmlands, especially its vineyards.[44] This first annual subsidy was supposed to go in part for the crown's obligations to Grand Parti creditors; but practically nothing was spent on this account. The subsidy also was supposed to allow the king to buy back part of his alienated gabelles, aides, crown lands, and other domaines revenues. Next, the church agreed that when this special subsidy ended, it would pay the king a further 1.3 million per year for ten more years. It was calculated that this second subsidy would allow the king to repurchase 7.56 million livres in rentes on the Hôtel de Ville of Paris (and to meet annual interest charges); these rentes were supposed to represent the remainder of the crown's alienated domaines, aides, and gabelles. In theory, these sums would have been large enough to perform this financial prodigy, since the total would about equal the value of all the rentes of Paris floated during the reigns of Henry II and Francis II.[45] Therefore, the church proposed to provide the crown with revenues totaling 22.6 million livres over a period of sixteen years.

This enormously bitter pill was sweetened to some extent. The king

---

43. The most detailed general account of the "contract" and its confusing later history is found in Louis Serbat, *Les assemblées du clergé de France: origines, organisation, développement, 1561–1615*, part 1.

44. Thompson, *Wars of Religion*, pp. 108–09. This figure should be compared to the annual average of about 805,000 livres in tenths under Francis I. Since 1546 the king had been demanding four tenths a year, that is, around 1.3 million livres.

45. Cauwès, "Crédit public," pp. 836–37. See also Doucet, *L'état des finances de 1567*, p. 24 and n. 2.

promised that there would be no other burden placed on the church for the sixteen years the contract was to run. The clergy requested, quite unrealistically, that the king prevent his finances from becoming so critical again; in response, l'Hospital replied, rather vaguely, that "the king would attend to it." [46]

Other concessions obtained by the church at Poissy were of greater significance for future church-state relations. The king did refrain from following the lead of the more radical deputies who wanted to force through an assessment of church wealth; in general the clergy were to be allowed to handle their own payments to the treasury without embarrassing interference from royal officials. And ecclesiastical courts, rather than royal courts, were to be the final arbiters of disputes arising from repartition of payments to be made under the contract.[47] Most important, the ecclesiastical assembly of France was given the right to distribute the burden of contract payments among the dioceses and monasteries of France, which meant not only that the clergy had formal permission to meet, but also that they fulfilled a real administrative function when they did.[48]

The pope, too—since the clergy of France insisted that he give formal consent to the contract—was able to obtain an important concession. In return for his consent, the French clergy promised that they would refrain from supporting antipapal elements at the Council of Trent and that they would not allow the national assembly of the Gallican church to weaken further the authority of the pope in France.

The concession that seems to have meant the most to the French clergy in 1561 may appear trivial to us—namely, formal recognition by the king that payments under the contract were "free gifts" of the church and not taxes. Even later, in the 1560s and 1570s, when the king was repeatedly violating promises made at the time of the contract and forcing more money out of the clergy, the church persisted in applying

46. Jules Viguier, *Les contrats et la consolidation des décimes à la fin du XVIe siècle* (Paris, 1906), p. 86.

47. Hennequin, *Guidon*, p. 221. The previous year, however, it had been ruled that collectors of tenths did have to answer to the Chambre des comptes. Ord. of Châteaudun, June 15, 1560.

48. Combes, *Traicté*, pp. 126–27, states that "contract" payments were distributed according to "la pancharte ancienne," i.e., the repartition of tenths taken by Francis beginning in 1516. The church had the right to modify the assessment in its details. See also the letters-patent of St. Maur-des-Fossés, June 29, 1566.

this face-saving device. Such persistence was maintained more stead-fastly when it became apparent that the king would have liked formal recognition of the fact that he was taxing the church.[49] The fiction of clerical "gifts" was maintained throughout the remaining decades of the Renaissance and into the era of the Old Régime. This tactic was used to keep the national and diocesan assemblies of the church functioning long after the death of the Estates-General in 1614.

The later history of the contract of Poissy was a bitter lesson in royal promises. In 1567, when the first subsidy of 1.6 million livres annually was to stop, the king brazenly tried to force the church to continue these payments while at the same time paying out its second subsidy of 1.3 millions per year for ten more years.[50] But the church bought off this astonishing demand by turning over a lump sum (700,000 livres) in order to induce the king to keep his word.[51]

In addition to these payments from income and sales of its lands, the church had to suffer other occasional "gifts" and appropriations. There-fore it is difficult to estimate precisely how much the clergy contributed to royal revenues. An additional church burden, the *taxe sur les clochers* —a levy on church income based on the number of belfries (*clochers*) in a parish—was first used in March 1552. It was set at 20 livres per clocher and brought in the large sum of 3 million livres. It was levied on several additional occasions during the Wars of Religion, in 1568, 1574, 1587, 1588, and 1593. For these later levies, however, clerical wealth was so reduced and the country in such turmoil that, although the rate per clocher went up to 31 livres 10 sous, the total amount real-ized was only a fraction of the anticipated sum.[52]

A Venetian ambassador, writing in 1569, reports the church had paid the king more than 12 million écus since the advent of Charles IX (1560), or an average of 4 million livres annually—not including the forced sale of church lands.[53] All the evidence suggests that the church

---

49. See, e.g., Combes, *Traicté*, p. 126.
50. Clamageran, *L'impôt*, 2 : 192.
51. Viguier, *Décimes*, pp. 112–14. See also Doucet, *L'état des finances de 1567*, pp. 12–13.
52. Dur, "Constitutional Rights," p. 219, shows a sum of 376,000 livres for this levy in a budget for 1574. See also Viguier, *Décimes*, p. 45; and Doucet, *Institutions*, 2 : 844.
53. Albèri, *Relazioni*, ser. 1, 4 : 197.

was contributing at this time roughly one-third of all the money coming to the French treasury.

Forced alienations of church property

In 1561, as we have seen, the Estates-General at Pontoise urged the government to sell some of the church's huge property holdings in addition to taxing the church more heavily. Two years later, during the first War of Religion, Catherine de Medici—after overcoming a good deal of hysterical resistance—succeeded in forcing through an "alienation of *temporel*," a sale in favor of the crown of farmlands, vineyards, and rented buildings from which the church derived income.[54] This was a startling violation of traditional relations between church and state that had limited the church's fiscal burden to clerical tenths and occasional "free gifts." Therefore France did participate, at least to a limited extent, in the seizure of church lands and their sale to burghers and nobles during the Reformation, a process not limited to Protestant countries. In this sharp break with the past, the government was supported by an assortment of moderate and radical ("zealot") Catholic opinion—groups that felt either that the sale of church lands was a good thing in itself, or that the church had to bear its fair share of the fiscal burden, or that nothing should stand in the way of gathering sufficient strength to crush heresy.

In the 1563 appropriation of church *temporel*, the basis for deciding each religious community's share of the levy was the *département* of church wealth created in 1516 for the tenths. Enough property was to be sold to give the government 100,000 écus *de rente* annually, an operation which, capitalized at the *denier douze* cost the church nominally 1.2 million écus. The real cost, claimed defenders of the church, was much more, since some lands and revenues were sold at scandalously low prices. The government was rather ruthless in this operation; the only mitigating principle was that no single group was to be deprived of more than one-quarter of its sources of income.[55]

54. See the letters-patent of Chartres, Jan. 1562; the edict of Paris, Nov. 1562; letters-patent of Blois, Feb. 1563; edict of St. Germain-en-Laye, May 1563; and the ord. of Paris, May 20, 1563.
55. Ord. of Paris, May 20, 1563.

The government, of course, wanted the principal sums at once; it was not at all interested in waiting for the annual income. Therefore it floated new rentes on the basis of the forced alienation, using the organization set up in 1522 to handle rentes on the Hôtel de Ville of Paris. Those who purchased these rentes were allowed to pay up to half the price in old rentes or other forms of royal indebtedness; the remainder had to be in hard cash.[56]

Without the Wars of Religion as an excuse for this new kind of levy, the pope undoubtedly would not have tolerated it. Even so, papal consent did not arrive in time and had to be obtained retroactively. His consent carried with it the proviso that any lands or buildings that had to be sold could be repurchased—which in effect allowed church groups to buy back the rentes constituted on their property.[57] As might be expected, those who had bought church revenues cheaply were persuaded to part with them only with great difficulty. Negotiations on this point dragged on for years (partly because some church communities refused to pay their allotted part of repurchase prices) before a final settlement was reached.

The government, with the grudging assistance of papal agents and Frence prelates, exerted itself to publicize the sales of temporel by posting announcements listing details of the particular church properties up for sale throughout the country. Excluded were the religious buildings themselves, such as places of worship and charity, as well as the lands on which they stood including the property needed to support village curés. The items that were least damaging to an abbacy or cathedral chapter were to be auctioned first. If no buyer was found in three weeks, the whole benefice could be seized and its entire income appropriated. On the other hand, if a diocese were wealthy enough to meet its assessment out of ready cash, nothing had to be sold. Those areas that were very poor and could find no buyers for their properties had the king's permission to alienate their tithes or to sell off the tall timber in their forests. Only Catholics could buy clerical properties.[58]

56. Letters-patent of Blois, Feb. 1563.
57. Royal decl. of Paris, Jan. 1564. There was a time limit of one year on such repurchases.
58. *Mémoires & instructions, suivant lesquelles les commissaires . . . procéderont à l'adiudication des choses mises & exposées en vente . . .* (Paris, 1577). See also the letters-patent of Paris, July 5, 1576 and Feb. 10, 1580.

In 1568 and again in 1569, Charles IX found it necessary to impose this sort of capital levy on the Gallican church. Henry III used the expedient three times: in 1574, 1576, and 1586–87. The appropriation of 1568 was a simple capital levy paid "once and for all" rather than an actual sale of church property for the support of additional rentes. In other alienations, also, a good deal of temporel—in at least some of the dioceses— was kept off the market by offering the king a straightforward subsidy or by approving the creation of new venal offices for collecting various payments from the church.[59] The First Estate in the Estates-General of 1576 and again in 1588 issued blistering attacks against these expedients; but public sentiment was still dominanted by resentment against the supposedly unreasonable wealth of the church, and the clerics received little sympathy from nobles and burghers. The pope, anxious to support the war against the Calvinists, often sided with the king against the French church in this matter. Roger Doucet estimates that sales of temporel, from the inception of this device in 1561 until its end in 1587, brought the king a grand total of about twenty million livres.[60]

Both the alienations and the Poissy contract left a bitter heritage of poorly funded royal rentes. The more the government of Henry III sank into debt, the more it became apparent that the king was trying to foist the burden of the continuing interest on these bonds onto the church. What of the government's promise that these extraordinary clerical payments would be used to repurchase the alienated royal aides, gabelles, and domaines, the income from which could then be used to maintain the rentes? The government answered, in effect, that the Wars of Religion had replaced the need to keep its word by a far greater need. Naturally, the church took the position that its obligations under the contract had ended in 1577 and that, once the principal sum of its forced alienations was paid, the obligation to meet interest payments fell on the Epargne. Nevertheless, in 1579 the church did respond to the government's all too obvious financial distress by agreeing to continue clerical subventions of 1.3 million livres annually for another ten years. As soon

59. Ivan Cloulas, "Les aliénations du temporel ecclésiastique sous Charles IX et Henri III (1563–1587)," *Revue d'Histoire de l'Eglise de France* (1958), and "Un aspect original des relations fiscales entre la royauté et le clergé de France au XVIe siècle," *Revue d'Histoire Ecclésiastique* 4 (1960).

60. Doucet, *Institutions*, 2 : 842; see also his *L'état des finances de 1567*, pp. 11–12, 24n, 2, 24n. 4.

as these payments arrived at the Epargne, however, the government used them to float additional rentes rather than to pay the interest on the old ones. The burghers of Paris and of other cities who had more or less willingly purchased the older rentes were left holding the bag. When the municipal officials of Paris made agitated representations to the king, they often received in return only a promise to put more pressure on the church, since the king's excise and salt taxes still were alienated and funds to pay interest could not be found in the royal revenues. In the later 1580s, Parisians became furious over the manner in which the king continued to fob off their claims. This heated controversy over the rentes and their relation to church payments played a small but significant part in the king's loss of control over Paris in 1588.

VENALITY: THE WORST EXPEDIENT

"All-out venality"

During the 1550s and 1560s, critics of government in France began to make increasingly wrathful attacks against the king's sponsorship of venality. (Venality during the early Renaissance is discussed in chapter 3.) During the Wars of Religion, opposition to venality mounted to a furious crescendo. Publicists and jurists attacked it in hundreds of tracts and treatises. Town councils complained they were being ruined by the increasingly heavy burden of local offices visited on them by the king. Meetings of provincial and national Estates voted bitter resolutions denouncing venality. Bodin made it the object of his special scorn in both the *Method* and the *Republic*. Bodin said in 1566 that everyone knows tyrants "fill up the fisc from their injuries and murders. . . . [They] think up new offices and honors, and offer these for a price, that they may have many bound to them. They appoint thieves and criminals for public office, and for the collection of revenue, so that they sap the peoples' resources and blood." [61] Pierre d'Epinac, in 1576, charged that "it is only too well known and obvious, that in making a judge they neither examine the breadth of his knowledge nor the integrity of his life; nor do they point up his long experience nor his respect of age and

61. *Method for the Easy Comprehension of History*, trans. Beatrice Reynolds, pp. 219–20.

virtue; all they want to know is whether his écus are full-weight."[62]
No one stood up to defend "all-out venality" (*vénalité au bout*).
Even the kings admitted it interfered with good administration and justice; they vowed, time after time, to cancel or mitigate the practice. The
great reform edict of Orléans (1561) declared that the king would
abolish venality and affirmed that "offices are holy and sacred affairs."
Meanwhile, in the midst of all these fulminations against it, venality
increased in scope and importance at a fearful rate.

Unfortunately for the reformers, the king was using venal offices as
one of his main means for coping with the recurring fiscal crises. Venality
was becoming one of the most important sources of royal income. For
obvious reasons, the exact amounts of the receipts from sale of offices were
kept secret; and they remain unknown today. Roland Mousnier, our
great authority on venality, gives a Venetian ambassador's estimate that
offices during the later years of Francis I brought some 900,000 livres per
year; but our knowledge of fiscal affairs in the 1540s makes it apparent
this was hyperbole.[63] Between the time of the Estates-General of Orléans
(1560) and 1576 the collector for offices at the Parties casuelles was
supposed to be receiving about 1.25 million livres per year. This amounts
to between 10 and 15 percent of annual royal revenues. By 1581 so many
new offices were being sold that, according to a budget of the era, the
huge sum of 3.5 million écus was realized, supposedly one-third of all
revenues for that year.[64] This vast an amount is hard to credit. In spite
of such obvious exaggeration, and in spite of the fact that we have only
bits and pieces of evidence, everything suggests that the value of venal
offices to the crown increased during the reign of Francis I and rose
much more rapidly during several periods of the later Renaissance.[65]

62. *Harangue*, p. 74. See also François Grimaudet, *Remonstrance . . . aux
estatz d'Anjou . . .*, pp. C3ʳ–C4ʳ, in which he accuses judges of maintaining "a
shop, in which they sell at retail, that which they have bought at wholesale."
    63. Mousnier, *Vénalité*, p. 50. See also Albèri, *Relazioni*, ser. 1, 4 : 253–54; this
is for 1546, and the ambassador implies it is an average for an unspecified number
of years. See also Zeller, *Institutions*, p. 141.
    64. Clamageran, *L'impôt*, 2 : 196, quoting the contemporary journal of Guil-
laume de Taix. The budget for 1574, transcribed by Dur, "Constitutional Rights,"
pp. 219–21, shows 1,367,000 livres for sales of new offices, 680,000 livres for confirmations of *résignations*, and 84,000 livres for *survivances*.
    65. See Mousnier, "Les offices de la famille normande d'Ambreville," *Revue
Historique* 183 (1938) : 10–27.

It is possible that no records at all—at least none comparable to the formal accounts of the Chambre des comptes—were kept by the Parties casuelles.[66] We know that some of these revenues, those for offices created to gratify favorites, or those in provinces with great lords or powerful governors, went in whole or in part into purses other than the king's. Interest in the sale of offices was high, of course, and contemporaries often recorded rumors about the going price of certain posts. Thus Pierre de l'Estoile, who kept a journal during this era, tells us that in 1584 the office of *conseiller* in the Parlement of Paris was valued at 7,000 écus, *maître des requêts* at 9,000 or 10,000 écus, and so on.[67]

The rule of the "alternative"

In 1554 an additional method was found for selling fiscal offices. The edict of Paris, October 1554, at one stroke doubled almost all France's fiscal officials who kept books and handled cash (*officiers comptables*);[68] incredibly, there were now two people for each of these posts. The *alternatif* official received the same base salary each year and, eventually, all the other fees, fines, and expenses as the *ancien* official. The two officials alternated, one serving in odd, the other in even years.[69]

Surely this action, taken without referring to any representative body in France, has to be counted among the most "absolutist" ever. An enormous number of additional officials were placed on the royal payrolls (which means on the backs of the taxpayers) with no attempt to show where the extra money would come from.

It is difficult to estimate precisely how much of an additional burden

66. Doucet, *L'état des finances de 1567*, p. 12.

67. *Registre-Journal*, vol. 1, part 1, p. 175. J.-P. Charmeil, *Les trésoriers de France à l'époque de la Fronde*, p. 33, has located prices for trésoriers from 16,500 to 28,000 livres, various years, 1557–86.

68. Edict of Paris, Oct. 1554, in Isambert, 13 : 406–10. Some steps in this direction had been taken for some officials of the Chambre des comptes of Paris (edict of Fontainebleau, Feb. 1552), for collectors of aides and tailles (edict of Villers-Cotterets, Oct. 1553), and for many military paymasters (edict of Fontainebleau, Dec. 1553). In 1554 the king doubled the number of offices in parlement, each officeholder serving six months of the year (thus, *parlement semestre*); but the device was abandoned in 1558.

69. Ed. Meynial, "Etudes sur l'histoire financière du XVIe siècle," *Nouvelle Revue Historique de Droit Français et Etranger* 44 (1920) : 490–91.

the *règle de l'alternatif* represented; the original ordinance lists eighty-eight specific offices, from exalted officials such as the treasurer of the Parties casuelles down to the collectors of fines in all sovereign courts. In addition, there are entire general categories of officials mentioned in the edict, such as all the assistants to the treasurer of the *prévôt de l'hôtel*, all the collectors of special assessments for the army, and generally "all our other *officiers comptables* of whatever kind and rank, if they be [truly] *comptables*, that is, having control and administration over the funds of our realm, and of our royal household, no matter how great or small [these funds] be. . . ." A few comptables were specifically exempted from the rule, notably the collectors of domaines revenues. But the collectors of all élections (about ninety) and généralités (sixteen), plus the *grenetiers* and other salt tax officials (possibly one hundred) were included. Many other offices were soon added to the *alternatif* list, making a total of about 310.[70] If the average annual salary for these offices was 750 livres, the royal budget would have been drained by an additional 232,500 livres each year. There also would have been a decline in other revenues since these offices carried important fiscal exemptions. For the crown, selling these positions at the rate of the "twelfth penny" would have brought in about 2.79 million livres (12 $\times$ 750 livres $\times$ 310 officials).

The règle de l'alternatif had a long and turbulent history after 1554. Henry II changed his mind and suppressed the *alternatifs grenetiers* the very next year, though the *anciens grenetiers* had to bear the heavy expense of buying back the newer offices, "because our affairs be so hard pressed."[71] The alternatif was also canceled for certain military paymasters in 1557.[72] Knowing that the forthcoming Estates-General in 1560 probably would raise a furious outcry against the alternatif, the government of the Guises under Francis II canceled the practice outright, with some exceptions.[73]

Beginning in 1568, however, Charles IX found it necessary not only to reinstate the alternatif but also to extend it to officials other than

70. Later the same month (edict of Paris, Oct. 1554) even the high ranking office of trésorier de l'Epargne became "alternative."

71. Edict of St. Germain-en-Laye, Sept. 1555.

72. Ord. of St. Germain-en-Laye, Dec. 1557.

73. Edict of Villers-Cotterets, Sept. 1559, and letters-patent of Blois, Jan. 2 and 9, 1560.

officiers comptables, such as various types of auditors (1568); the receveur général of the Parties casuelles (1568); all comptables (1570); and élection comptrollers (1574).[74] Once again an Estates-General (Blois, 1576) managed to force at least some mitigation of the practice.[75] Eventually, Henry III had to reestablish all the previous alternatif offices; he even extended the practice to several additional posts. By 1579 positions in the royal household, as well as other venal offices other than fiscal officials, were alternatif.[76]

In the original edict of 1554, and in the confirming and supplementary edicts following it, one can find elaborate justification for the alternatif. The main argument was that cash in the revenue system was not moving satisfactorily toward the Epargne, partly because comptables were not vigorous enough in their duties, and partly because it was "far from easy and almost impossible" for them to perform all their accounting functions and exert adequate pressure on the taxpayers at the same time. It was notorious, for example, that collectors of tailles often could not clear their books for two or even three years. Thus the alternatif was justifiable both as a threat and as an opportunity. In his "off" year a comptable would be given an opportunity to concentrate on collecting revenues owed but not paid. The threat was that if the money was not collected, the *reliqua* delivered to the Epargne, and the account cleared, the official was to be deprived of his office without compensation for his purchase price.

A *deluge of new offices* [77]

To put "all-out venality" in proper perspective we have to realize that, especially after 1562, France did require more administering. Lawlessness

74. Edicts of La Roquette-lez-Paris, Aug. 1568, and Lyons, Oct. 1574.
75. Ord. of Paris, May 1579, in Isambert, 14 : 435–36.
76. For additional offices made *alternatif* see the edicts of Paris, March 23, 1583; St. Maur-des-Fossés, Sept. 1582; and Avignon, Jan. 1575.
77. Doucet, *Institutions*, 1 : 412–13 and n., regards the task of counting up the number of offices in Renaissance France as hopeless. There exist *états des offices* for various years; but they are fragmentary and otherwise misleading. For a very rough estimate of the magnitudes involved, I counted all the types of offices I have seen mentioned in edicts and treatises for the era of Sully, and multiplied these by the number of offices for each district. For the upper and middle echelons, the result is about 5,400 officials. For the lower echelons (local receivers,

and disaffection unleashed by the Wars of Religion undoubtedly was one of the reasons the government found it necessary to create additional judges, overseers, and forest wardens.[78] But most of the venality edicts were obviously for only one purpose: to feed the treasury. Dozens of them were frankly "bursal"; they admitted that there was no other way available to obtain funds (*faire finance*). Other edicts created offices for functions that seem quite redundant or useless or entirely inappropriate for royal administration. Thus all the money changers of the realm were forced to become royal officials.[79] All persons who sold fish, "fresh, dried, and salted" in the cities, towns, and ports of the realm had to take the oath of office and purchase the post from the crown.[80] And all the smaller salt distribution agencies (*chambres à sel*) were upgraded to *greniers* so that they could have their full complement of eight officials per grenier.[81] The edict of Paris, March 1586, created new paymasters whose sole duty was to pay the wages of minor court officials and others who did nothing for the government but collect *épices* ("gifts") for magistrates at civil trials.[82] This last edict announced (surely one of the lamest excuses ever used by a king for picking his subjects' pockets) that everyone knew how confusing it was for officials to have multiple tasks and how "profitable and useful" it was for each officer to handle one duty "without becoming ensnarled in a diversity of functions."

During the worst periods of "all-out venality," offices were created in veritable wholesale lots—that is, blanketing all towns, parishes, bailiwicks, élections, or other divisions of the country with new, alternative,

---

auditors, and inspectors, plus the numerous clerks, ushers, and scribes) there may have been around 5,600. This estimate of roughly 11,000 officials does not include the part-time (and probably overlapping) offices prescribed for the country parishes —the local tax gatherers, assessors, and constables ordered "for each and every parish." There were about 32,000 parishes in France at the end of the sixteenth century (Doucet, *Institutions*, 1 : 28), or possibly 31,000 country parishes. Taking the minimum number (one) consistent with believing there were *any* such officials in the country parishes, we arrive at the huge total of 42,000 officials at all levels. This is the largest estimate I have seen for any period of the Renaissance; but I believe it is a conservative one.

78. See the edict of Blois, June 15, 1583, which complains of the "faulte & confusion des Estats qui corrumpt toute police."

79. Edict of Anet, Aug. 1555, in Isambert, 13 : 456–58.

80. Edict of Paris, Jan. 1583, in Isambert, 14 : 520–26.

81. Edict of Paris, Nov. 1576.

82. Edicts of Paris, July 1581, and March 1586. Literally, *épices* means "spices."

or additional officials. Henry II created a *surintendant des deniers communs* for each généralité; this royal official had authority to examine the fiscal records of each municipality, and in reality he worked to further weaken municipal self-rule.[83] In 1554 and 1555 the king announced he would create the identical number of forest officials in each bailiwick and seneschalcy—with no regard as to whether these districts were rich or poor in forests.[84] Wholesale creation of offices became more important later in the reign of Charles IX; he authorized four additional constables and four additional royal notaries for every bailiwick.[85] Dozens of these groups of new offices were foisted on the country. Some acts brought into being hundreds of new offices; one act ordered five additional gabelles constables in each city and town in the country, and another decreed an additional collector for tailles in each and every parish.[86]

The French were well aware of the fact that though venality could be found in other countries, theirs was the only large state in Europe where this practice was so pervasive and so important in government.[87] The greatest contrast, of course, was just across the Channel. In England offices could be sold by ministers who (often correctly) considered themselves underpaid; but such practices were regarded as corrupt and punishable according to the laws of the land. There were thousands of venal offices, too, sold in Rome. But venality in Rome was not functionally the same as venality in France. Purchasers of papal positions were "in effect shareholders in the papal debt. The purchase price of their offices was their invested capital; the salary of their office was their interest, at an average rate of 11 percent." [88] However, venal offices in France, for the most part, carried real governmental duties with them; the monetary return from officeholding was thought of as salary as well as interest.

---

83. Edict of Fontainebleau, June 1555, in Isambert, 13 : 448–52.
84. Devèze, *Forêt française*, 2 : 140–48.
85. Edict of Paris, Jan. 1573.
86. Edict of Paris, Oct. 1581.
87. Montaigne declared that there were more officials in France than all the rest of Christendom. Quoted in Gustave Fagniez, *L'économie sociale de la France sous Henri IV, 1589–1610* (Paris, 1897), p. 333.
88. Peter Partner, "The 'Budget' of the Roman Church in the Renaissance period," in E. F. Jacob, ed., *Italian Renaissance Studies* (London, 1960), p. 258.

All contemporary critics agreed that from the point of view of efficiency there were too many officials in France. Sir Robert Dallington counted up all the tax officials in a single élection (at the end of the sixteenth century); he found there were no less than ten lower-echelon receveurs and auditors alone, plus all their servants, clerks, and subalternes. "If then there be thus many in one Election onely," he said, "ye may iudge the infinite number in all France, vpon which they lye, as thicke as the grasse hoppers in Aegypt." [89]

89. The View of Fraunce . . . , p. P3.

5

The Role of the Fiscal System
in Prolonging the Wars of Religion

THE TAX STRUCTURE IS ATTACKED

The fiscal system as a factor in the wars

Some of the most memorable pages in historical literature have been written about the chief personnages and events of the Wars of Religion. But because of its complexity this era as a whole is treated in a discouragingly superficial manner. Many historians limit themselves to a narration of all the eight wars and all the settlements. They have avoided analyzing the potentially important problems of this era, apart from the well-chewed-over question of whether the wars were essentially religious or political.

Our knowledge of public finance in this era is decidedly skimpier than for the earlier Renaissance or even the high and late Middle Ages. Political scientists know that the great debates over taxation, and the role these debates played in the development of divine right monarchy concepts, are important in the history of political thought. Economic historians know that the "price revolution" of this era stimulated Jean Bodin and others to theorize about money and taxes. But apart from this, little use has been made of the tax history of the Wars of Religion. And yet it seems obvious that the tax history of the Wars of Religion has a great deal to offer to the overall interpretation of that era.

There was indeed an important connection between the debate over royal tax power and the actual struggles of the Wars of Religion. The arguments of the jurists gave shape and slogans to the quite justified grievances of the French concerning taxes in the reigns of the last Valois kings; thus theory, working through public opinion, contributed to the virulence of the wars by giving the factions a propaganda leverage against the government and against each other. The manifestos of the

Catholic League after 1584, for example, give an important place to tax injustices.

But the impact of developments in finance on these wars was even more direct. From the beginning, and increasingly after 1584, the revenue system itself became one of the chief prizes in the fighting. It was because of the tax system—its wealth and its local treasuries—that military victories and political-religious settlements (up to those of 1594–98) seemed to matter so little.

Because France was rich, and because her royal revenues had developed into such a large and complex organization, there was an enormous amount of cash circulating through her fiscal system. But now this fiscal wealth became a source of danger, since it was a tremendously desirable object of prey—and such an easy one. Here was a province or a city caught up in the passions of religious struggle; there were its revenues, locally administered and locally collected. Here was a noble man-at-arms, or a mercenary captain, willing to extend his protection for a consideration; the only obstacle was a weak, loathsome, and distant king. The money to finance the transformation from grandee to princeling was virtually there for the taking.

The favorites and the fisc

Before the outbreak of war the contrast between the huge sums of money going to the crown and the growing need for money by French aristocrats was most painful. The pressure on Renaissance nobles to live lavishly was increasing just when seigneurial income was buying less and less; it was at this time that the "price revolution" was beginning to hurt.[1] Many nobles were especially irritated about money, since when "peace broke out" in 1559 (the settlement of Cateau-Cambrésis with the

---

1. See the anonymous (Huguenot) nobleman's complaint that "the dearness of cattle since three years past has increased by half." *Discours pour la subvention des affairs du roy* . . . , (1564), p. 18. It is interesting how seldom the government used the "price revolution" these years to justify higher expenditures. The first official reference to this connection that I have found before the great monetary reform of 1577 is the edict of Paris, Nov. 1576, which explains the king is raising officials' salaries "attendu la cherté du temps." Dur, in "Constitutional Rights," p. 271, has an entry of 200,000 livres in a budget of 1580 for "La chambre aux deniers du Roy à loccasion de la cherté du temps."

Hapsburgs), the warrior aristocracy was deprived of an important source of income. Anxiously they descended on the court, waylaying the king's favorites, begging offices, lands, pensions, and immediate payment of their back wages. The king had himself partly to blame. There had been two generations of the most open-handed liberality for these actions to feed on. Even more than Francis I, Henry II was in the habit of dispensing millions of livres each year in gifts and pensions. When his favorites were captured in battle, he assumed the expenses of ransom. If one of his favorite's daughters had the prospect of contracting an advantageous marriage, the dowry often came from the royal Epargne. If a valuable estate escheated to the crown, it was often regarded as another opportunity to make a grand gesture in favor of some courtier. In 1547, Henry granted Diane de Poitiers a sort of coronation present of the sale of offices during that year, a kindness that is reputed to have brought her 100,000 écus and the hatred of all the nobles who were thus deprived of compensation for offices that might have been theirs to bestow.[2] In 1554 the duke of Guise was given all the income derived from one of the more lucrative internal tariffs, the *traite d'Anjou*.[3]

It was notorious that important tax officials were joining the game of favorites and fisc. The trick required the officials to filtch a portion of the royal revenues they handled and then to bribe a courtier to petition the king for pardon; favorites who obtained such pardon were given a portion of the sum.[4] It came to be widely known that the rate of royal gift giving was running far beyond the value of the domaines, the traditional source for such expenses, and that the king now was willing to give away large portions of the gabelles, the traites, and even the chief aides. The anonymous Huguenot author of the *Discours pour la subvention des affairs du roy*, obviously a member of the lesser nobility, called for a return to *liberalité honneste*, that is, to give pensions and favors only to those well-deserving individuals who had worked for their king and country. He castigated the king for ruining the land in order to gratify "the dainty and excessive greed of certain courtiers," and he

2. Albèri, *Relazioni*, ser. 1, 4 : 61.
3. See Fontanon, 2 : 164. The king also helped his favorites construct new châteaux—where they could entertain the whole court—by giving them portions of royal forest revenues. See Devèze, *Forêt française* 2 : 165–66.
4. See the complaints in item 6 of the ord. of St. Germain-en-Laye, Dec. 1557, Bibliothèque Nationale F46815 (12).

demanded that all gifts and pensions for women be revoked; he said that it was a cruel injustice that such women, after "having enjoyed some of the ruler's person, also enjoy some of the people's purse." [5]

The tragic death of Henry II in 1559 brought to the throne Francis II, who was ill even before he became king; he was to live for less than a year and a half more. The Guises quickly replaced as many of the royal councilors and household officials as possible with their own men, and worked hard to curb the influence of other noble families that challenged their position: the Bourbons and Châtillons, several of whom were Huguenots, and the Montmorencies, headed by Constable de Montmorency, the great favorite of Francis I and Henry II.

While Henry II had been alive, Catherine de Medici remained entirely in the background. But when Francis II died (December 1560), Catherine stepped forward as the sole regent for her ten-year-old son, Charles IX. She adroitly bypassed the Guises in her bid for power; the Guises thereupon angrily left court, adding another disaffected faction to the threatening situation. Catherine had to concentrate all her energy on preventing the violent jealousies among noble families and the tensions between the religious faiths from breaking out into open war.

Pressure for a greater flow of royal favors immediately increased. The scent of cash revenues brought begging nobles to court. Catherine's policy depended on her ability to play off one faction against another in order to keep the peace and to prevent the rivals from joining forces and pushing the weak Valois off the throne. One of the chief tools of this famous "seesaw" policy was gifts from the royal revenues. This policy was self-defeating, however, and the situation quickly became dangerous. Each special mark of favor to a great family or faction chief only increased the resentment and cupidity of others. The day was past when the crown could really satisfy the barons by buying them off. In 1560, when the Guises had been regents, legend has it that François de Guise—who was working hard to cut down expenditures—became so enraged at the constant pleas for largesse that he swore he would hang the next man who asked for a pension. But by the mid-1560s Catherine was hardly in a position to be so righteous. [6]

5. *Discours pour la subvention*, pp. 12, 17, 21.
6. See the later edict of Metz, March 30, 1569, enjoining the Epargne treasurer to pay out gifts and pensions promptly, including those not in the budgets and not

The great majority of the lesser nobles, out of principle or because they did not have the energy or the good luck to break into the inner circles, had to see the flow of royal gifts pass them by. The irritating contrast between their "poor but honest" situation and that of the favorites may help to explain why so many of this class were attracted to Calvinism or to some faction chief. The lower-class merchants and artisans, the first supporters of the Calvinist faith, now were joined by men who had more effective means of making known their disgust with "Sodom," as the Huguenots called the court.

Francis I, referring to his revenues, boasted that France was a meadow he could mow when he wished.[7] After 1562 that meadow was almost as lush as ever, the cowherds exploiting it were fat and sleek, and the main fence-mender was only an Italian widow. Men everywhere were seeking their fortunes; the Wars of Religion provided an opportunity for both captains of troops and great nobles to find their share in the luxuriant growth of royal finances.

The first appropriations of royal revenues

War came in March 1562 when some followers of François de Guise attacked a group of Huguenots worshiping in the little town of Vassy in Champagne. The Protestants, more or less united under the prince of Condé (Bourbon), quickly seized power in a dozen important cities in the north and center. They also made themselves the masters of some provinces in the south and west (Dauphiné, eastern Languedoc, and parts of Poitou, Guyenne, and Provence) where they were a large percentage of the population. After a few viciously fought but inconclusive battles around Rouen and Paris, François de Guise was assassinated; since Condé had been captured in battle two months previously the way was now open for Catherine to negotiate a peace, known as the "Pacification of Amboise," in March 1563.

Wherever Huguenots were numerous enough, they either set up bands

---

verified by the fiscal courts, explaining that because of the "malice du temps & troubles," such payments were necessary.

7. This famous cynical remark also is attributed during the Renaissance to Louis XI. See Dallington, *View of Fraunce*, p. Q2; Scipion de Gramont, *Le denier royal* (Paris, 1620), p. 201; Albèri, *Relazioni*, ser. 1, 4 : 196.

of militia to defend themselves or entered into pacts with local nobles who could provide some fighting men.[8] Thus the Huguenots of Auvergne hired the baron Des Adrets, a famous and brutal military leader, who was in fact colonel of the royal Languedoc *légion*.[9] Wherever they could, Huguenots seized monasteries and their lands, and used the revenues to pay their soldiers. Bands of soldiers seemed to spring up out of the ground, proclaiming themselves for hire. Even regular troops of the king, when they were not paid promptly enough, threatened to go over to the rebels.[10] Poor seigneurs, especially in the south and west of France, often extended their protection to Huguenots for pay, without entertaining any personal inclination toward Calvinism whatsoever.

One immediate fiscal advantage for the Huguenots was that where they were in control the region stopped paying the clerical tithe; indeed, there is evidence some of them had stopped such payments in 1561.[11] The Catholic clergy noted with apprehension that resistance to tithes was spreading into non-Huguenot lands. The church was still vulnerable as a result of the widespread attacks made during the Estates-General of 1560–61; these attacks had questioned not only the use of church wealth but the very legal and theological basis for the tithes.[12] The government of Charles IX did try to force the disaffected areas to resume paying the tithes after the Pacification of Amboise—with what success, we do not know.[13]

When the fighting began, the group under attack was forced to seize whatever fiscal resources it could. When an army of the opposing faith was deployed in the vicinity of a walled town, that town naturally used

8. H. G. Koenigsberger, "The Organization of Revolutionary Parties in France and the Netherlands during the Sixteenth Century," *Journal of Modern History* 27, no. 4 (1955) : 337–38. We know of one such agreement even before the outbreak of war: see Joseph Leclerc, *Toleration and the Reformation*, 2 : 67.

9. André Imberdis, *Histoire des guerres religieuses en Auvergne pendant les XVIe et XVIIe siècles*, pp. 66–67.

10. See the letters-patent of Blois, Feb. 1563.

11. Thompson, *Wars of Religion*, p. 118.

12. The era brought forth several tracts defending tithes; see François Grimaudet, *Paraphrase du droict des dixmes ecclésiastiques & inféodées . . .*, and René Benoist, *Traicté des dismes . . .* (Paris, 1564), which contains a refutation of the Huguenot argument that good Christians have no need to pay tithes to bad priests.

13. The fact that the same order is repeated in the pacification called the "Peace of Monsieur" suggests the problem had continued. See Isambert, 14 : 281.

the local revenues to buy immunity or to maintain defenses, without worrying too much about the legal implications of such an act. This was true of Catholic as well as of Protestant towns. These levies were usually made by assessing the rich burghers (*les plus aisés*) in a town roughly according to their wealth and then repaying them by assigning the local sales taxes and octrois to them. In Huguenot cities the Calvinists expropriated all of the church's wealth they could turn into cash; in Catholic towns the church authorities volunteered their wealth to local captains for the extirpation of local heretics.[14]

In the later years of Francis I, and increasingly during the reign of Henry II, the fiscal bureaucracy had been organized into well-structured, highly professional *bureaux des finances*, each généralité having one (see appendix B). Though the officials of the bureaux were dependent on the crown for permission to collect their salaries, they were actually paid out of locally raised funds. Most of the fiscal officials, of course, became involved willy-nilly in the political and religious struggles that entangled their own districts. It became quite hard for them to do other than obey the grandee or municipal council in control of their généralité or town.

The royal government did what it could to protect its revenues by warning governors and local magistrates not to collect taxes on their own authority; the crown affirmed that it would not be bound by debts incurred by towns or généralités in Protestant hands.[15] On this last point the crown had to reverse itself only a few months later. The debts contracted by Lyons while the city was under Protestant control, for example, were repaid with royal permission.[16]

At this stage, local seizure of royal revenues was an entirely empirical reaction; there was no open "fiscal disaffection" in the sense that people were ready to resist the king's power to tax. But even in these early days there were signs that some Frenchmen were getting ready to claim the

14. For Languedoc, see Dom Cl. Devic and Dom J. Vaissete, *Histoire générale de Languedoc*, 11 : 443, and 12: cols. 731–33; for Bourges in Berry, see the Vicomte de Brimont, *Le XVIe siècle et les Guerres de la Réforme à Berry*, 1 : 374.

15. The government issued several edicts on this point in the 1560s: see the royal decl. of Plessis-les-Tours, Nov. 29, 1565, in Isambert, 14 : 183, and the great edict of Moulins, Feb. 1566, art. 23, in ibid., p. 195; one edict was issued even before the fighting began, the famous "edict of January," the first toleration edict (1562), in ibid., p. 127.

16. Doucet, *Lyon*, pp. 63–68.

right to use local revenues under certain conditions. At an assembly in Nîmes (1562), the Huguenots of Languedoc declared that in addition to appropriating church wealth they had the right during emergencies to "borrow" funds from regular royal revenues; they promised they would account to the king for the way they spent these funds. In 1563 the burghers of Toulouse and other Catholic towns in the Midi swore to defend their faith by raising soldiers and imposing taxes on themselves. Similar declarations were made by the provincial Estates of Dauphiné and by the nobles of Guyenne in 1565.[17] These actions foreshadowed the more extensive tax power seized by Protestant assemblies and by towns of the Catholic League during the 1570s and 1580s. For the first time since 1484, at the time of the Estates-General of Tours, many Frenchmen seemed ready to challenge the sovereign power of the French crown in one of its key attributes—the power to tax.

The edict of Amboise, March 1563

The most dangerous expropriations of royal revenues in the first War of Religion were those carried out by Condé, "prince of the blood royal," and military leader of the Huguenots. During 1562–63 the Huguenots had been in control of large segments of the west as well as the south of France; in the north and center, Huguenots also ruled in Bourges, Orléans, Rouen, and many other important cities. However, unlike in the south and west, the best they could manage was to garrison the towns and control them by force, regardless of the religious convictions of the majority of the townsmen. In Huguenot areas Condé had been supported by grants from Huguenot town magistrates who diverted parts of the royal revenue system they controlled toward the Huguenot armies. Where the fortunes of war placed predominantly Catholic districts in Huguenot hands, Condé and other commanders seized royal cash boxes. He also assessed the Catholic burghers whenever he needed emergency funds, and in a few cases, he even authorized the striking of coins in royal mints under his control.

A legal problem of the utmost importance, therefore, remained to be resolved during the peace negotiations in 1563. The Huguenot leaders, and especially the prince of Condé, stood open to accusations of lese

17. Thompson, Wars of Religion, p. 215.

majesty by officials and private subjects of the king for seizure of these royal revenues. Therefore Condé tried to obtain blanket dispensation for his actions. Since Catherine de Medici was anxious for peace, and since she had plans to use the Bourbon-Condé and Châtillon families as counterweights to the Guises, she agreed.

The Pacification of Amboise granted Huguenot nobles the right to worship according to the new faith on their own manors; but lower-class Huguenots were given the right to worship in public in only one town in each bailiwick—except around Paris, which was to remain exclusively reserved for the Catholic faith. In return the Huguenots had to give back to the crown the towns they had garrisoned.

The edict of Amboise has been studied from many angles, especially for the question of why Condé, in effect, signed away the freedom to worship of so many of his lower-class coreligionists—those unlucky enough to live outside the one town per bailiwick where religious toleration was to be established.[18] The provisions concerning appropriated royal revenues, however, have not received much attention.[19] And yet these financial considerations are extremely significant since they pointed the way toward easy financing of future rebellions.

The edict of Amboise, in fact, proclaimed Condé "absolved for all the moneys which, by him and on his commandment and ordinance, have been seized and levied from our treasuries and revenues, for whatever sums to which these may amount." It spelled out carefully that where such funds had been appropriated, in "monasteries, towns, goldsmith shops, [or] churches," no charges could be brought against Condé in royal courts of law by royal officials or private citizens. Townsmen who had gone along with Condé's tax levies were to be forgiven their complicity. They were even forgiven for striking coins on their own authority. It was clear, furthermore, that other Huguenot leaders involved in the war, including the great admiral Coligny, were to be covered by the provision that any levies of funds made by them, presumably on order of Condé, were also to be excused. Their debts were not to be paid by them but by

18. The edict of Amboise, in Isambert, 14 : 135–40.
19. In the classic work by Mariéjol on the era, in Lavisse 6¹ : 74, this factor is not mentioned; nor does it appear in Thompson, *Wars of Religion*, p. 191; nor in two excellent recent handbooks: Georges Livet, *Les Guerres de Religion* (Paris, 1966); and Henri Lapeyre, *Les monarchies européennes du XVIe siècle* (Paris, 1967).

the royal tax system.[20] This pattern was repeated after subsequent "pacifications" during the Wars of Religion,[21] and particularly in the final settlement known as the Edict of Nantes (1598). The royal fiscal system, therefore, served the rebels by financing the war for them with few if any penalties.

From the edict of Amboise to St. Bartholomew's Eve

After 1563 the country enjoyed a few years of rather precarious peace, and the fiscal machine went back to work for the royal treasury—neither immediately nor everywhere, however. In many districts the Huguenots continued to raise taxes only for their own purposes. Writing in 1572, but referring to the period before the massacres of that year, the Venetian ambassador reported that the Huguenots could easily raise 800,000 livres a year, and two or three times that much given a major crisis; "everyone was taxed, even the lower classes, tradesmen, workers, and servants; everyone was rated voluntarily according to his conscience as to whether he could support more or less; and they pay with such promptness that it is a wonder to behold." [22]

Another grave problem was that a considerable number of empty fiscal posts had to be filled. Many collectors and other officials had deserted, some because they were known Huguenots, some because they feared (the edict of Amboise notwithstanding) that the way they had handled tax funds during the recent war could not be forgiven by the king.[23]

Catherine de Medici managed her famous "seesaw policy" rather well these years, swinging from the Guises to the Bourbons and back again.

20. It was partly to pay such debts, and partly to pay royalist troops, that, as we saw in chapter 4, the government forced through the first alienation of church temporel.

21. In fact we know the rebels asked for it. See the demands raised by the Huguenot assembly of Montauban, Aug. 1573, in Devic and Vaissete, *Languedoc*, 12: cols. 1054–55.

22. Albèri, *Relazioni*, ser. 1, 4 : 300. See also the letters-patent of Paris, Oct. 22, 1563.

23. B.N. Nouv. acq. fr. 2374, fol. 61, dated June 19, 1562, shows that a few months after fighting began the government forced the members of the Cour des aides to "faire profession de leur foy." See also the royal decl. of Paris, Oct. 22, 1563, in Fontanon, 2 : 657–58.

Meanwhile she tried to build up loyalty to her son Charles IX. In January and February of 1566 an important Assembly of Notables was held at Moulins, and fiscal problems were thoroughly aired. Some of the economy-minded policies of the Guises in 1559–60 were reimposed. A large number of alternatif tax officials were dismissed. The number of généralités was cut from seventeen to seven in an effort to reduce the number of tax officials attached to the provincial bureaux des finances. A strong effort was made to build up the value of the royal domaines revenues, chiefly by checking over and canceling as many of the recent alienations of royal lands and revenues as possible. The two edicts of Moulins that came out of this reform effort (both February 1566) stand with the two great ordinances of Orléans and Blois (1561 and 1579) as the main attempts to reform the French fiscal system in the era between Francis I and Sully.[24]

Renewed fighting (1567–70), interrupted only by a six months' truce, meant that the crown had to toss aside the praiseworthy fiscal reforms signalized by the Moulins edicts of 1566. In 1567 the fiscal posts in the office of the Parties casuelles that had been canceled, as well as those of the royal household, were all reinstated; in addition, the alternatif army paymasters who had been eliminated were returned to their posts, as were many others. The number of généralités was raised again from seven to seventeen, and all the dismissed bureaux des finances officials were allowed to take up their posts again. Worst of all, the crown returned to the practice of issuing new alternatif fiscal posts.[25]

SOUTH AND WEST FRANCE DISCARD ROYAL TAX POWER

The Huguenot-Politique alliance

The grim events we call the "St. Bartholomew's Eve massacre" (1572) completely changed the political situation in France. The Huguenots were jolted into realizing they had no real hope of forcing the whole country to become Calvinist; for one thing, so many Huguenot noble-

24. Edict of Moulins, Feb. 1566, in Isambert, 14 : 185–89 (on domaines); and see Fontanon, 2 : 666–69 (on généralités).
25. Edicts of Paris, Oct. and Nov. 1567, and Nov. 1570; edict of Blois, Oct. 1571. By 1579 the number of bureaux des finances was back to nineteen; see the "ord. of Blois" (actually, Paris), May 1579, in Isambert, 14 : 242.

men were killed in the massacres that the Huguenot cavalry was now dangerously weak. Estimates are that in the few days after August 24, 1572, perhaps 3,000 Huguenots were slaughtered in Paris and 8,000 elsewhere. The Huguenot cause now had to go on the defensive. La Rochelle itself came within an ace of being taken in a long and hard-fought siege. (This counts as the fourth War of Religion.)

The shock and horror of these massacres, however, forced the Huguenots to go into more open rebellion against the crown. As it turned out, the religious organizations of Calvinism—congregations, consistories, synods—proved themselves a good framework for obtaining a consensus and supporting administrative cadres; the tough and fervent Huguenot pastors made capable local bosses. Virtually the whole apparatus of the royal tax machine in Languedoc and other provinces of the south and west was in the hands of this "state within a state."

At a meeting in December the Huguenot assembly drew up a regular body of government rules, in effect a constitution for its territory. The fiercely independent Rochellais now came into the association, after a considerable amount of soul-searching, extending this strange new government farther into the west of France. The local (diocesan) and provincial assemblies still protested their basic loyalty to the French crown and claimed they were being forced into defying royal authority by threats to their own safety and by the need to purge the royal government of the evil influences surrounding it.

This essentialy Huguenot confederation was joined, before long, by the southern *Politiques*. The latter were an extremely mixed group, united only by their moderate position on the religious issue. This position was exemplified, in the eyes of their contemporaries, by the dangerous notion that the well-being of the country was more important than extirpating a heresy. Moderate Catholic Politiques increased in number and influence during the revulsion to the St. Bartholomew's Eve massacres.[26] Politiques were more numerous in the south and west, where there was a significant Protestant population; but as a faction they counted adherents all over the country, including the royal court itself. In fact, wherever opposition to "foreigners" (Italians and Guisards) was popular so were the Politiques. Their power in Languedoc was

26. Forerunners of Politique outlooks, however, can be found as far back as the 1540s. Leclerc, *Toleration and the Reformation* 2 : 38.

demonstrated by the fact that the royal governor of that province, Montmorency-Damville, came over to the alliance in 1574. The south and west of France, these years, were hardly as united behind the rebellion as, for example, the southern states during the American Civil War. There were many Catholic enclaves, such as Toulouse and its surrounding area, that supported the crown, and there were other Catholic towns that set themselves up as virtually independent city-states. At times the king proclaimed special fiscal favors "for the duration" for these Catholic enclaves; Henry III granted the garrison at Arles the right to levy a 2 percent octroi on all goods passing near the city.[27] Some seigneurial domains were ruled by war lords, including some bandits quite indifferent to religious or political issues.[28] It is also true that Huguenot-Politique control was relatively weak in the countryside as compared to the cities. But the framework was there for an effective and independent government for the southern portion of France.

Tax power in the Huguenot-Politique areas

For almost four years, from early 1573 to the end of 1576, the taxes of the west and the Midi were collected in the name of the Huguenot cause and its allies in rebellion. This was the part of France, of course, where local government traditionally was strong. As for tax administration, this area had few élus and no élections, and provincial Estates had considerable tax power: gabelles were relatively light, tailles were levied only after consultation with local Estates and by provincial tax officials, the équivalent was paid rather than aides, and the only important group of taxes corresponding to those of the rest of the kingdom was the traites. Portions of this territory continued to escape royal taxation even after the breakdown of the Huguenot-Politique alliance in 1577.

By the time of the Huguenot assemblies held at Millau in 1573–74, the main outlines of Huguenot taxing were established. The whole area was carved up for purposes of administration into "dioceses"—essentially towns and their neighboring countryside. Positions in all government bureaus were to be open to members of both faiths. A representative body for Protestants and Catholics in the whole rebellious territory was

27. Letters-patent of Paris, March 29, 1577.
28. See Pierre de l'Estoile, *Registre-Journal*, vol. 1, part 1, p. 62.

organized, grandiloquently entitled an "Estates-General." It was composed of three estates; but these estates, of course, could not include a
clerical First Estate. The nobles, therefore, counted as the First Estate,
magistrates as the Second, and commoners as the Third. These Estates-
General were to meet regularly, preferably every few months.

The royal system of recettes générales was retained. There were to be
eleven of these, each under the authority of a général. Diocesan collectors had the duty of transporting the restes to receveurs généraux.[29] The
bureaux des finances were to continue in operation with few changes,
but under the supreme authority of the assemblies. In this system there
was no sign of a central treasury corresponding to the Epargne of the
king. The Huguenot-Politique tax system was a federative rather than a
centralized one. Towns had much more fiscal independence than previously. The chief town magistrates were completely in charge of municipal finances. In theory, the central council guiding Huguenot affairs
between assemblies was supposed to act as the central executive of
financial affairs. In practice, towns took care of their own taxes except
when they were under the thumb of a grandee or a war lord.

The basic structure of taxes in the rebellious areas remained un-
changed; tailles, équivalents, and gabelles were collected as before.[30]
Décimes were still exacted from Catholic churchmen. Even the traites
were collected on the borders of this "state within a state." The royal
domaines lands, now in the control of the Huguenot and Politique généraux, were operated for the benefit of rebel treasuries. There is only one
departure visible in the Huguenot-Politique tax structure—according to
the declaration adopted at the assembly of Nîmes in 1575, one-fifth of
all booty and one-fifth of the payments from "ransomed" cities had to
be paid over to the receveurs généraux.[31]

Because of the emergency atmosphere in the south and west, taxation
took on a distinctly ad hoc character. Many of the towns and chieftains
relied on the mints they controlled to fill the revenues gap. They had no
regular system for borrowing, apart from forced loans—nothing like the

29. Léonce Anquez, Histoire des assemblées politiques des Réformés de France
(1573–1622), pp. 17–21. See also, for the declaration of the assembly of Nîmes,
Jan. 1575, Devic and Vaissete, Languedoc, 11 : 603, and 12: cols. 1112–38, esp.
col. 1116.
30. Devic and Vaissete, Languedoc, 12: col. 1123–24.
31. Anquez, Assemblées politiques, p. 19.

royal rentes. When forced loans were exacted, they fell most heavily on those whose enthusiasm for the new faith was questioned. When enemy territories were captured, the polite fiction of forced loans was dropped. Thus in 1575, after a Captain Merle retook the town of Issoire (Auvergne) for the Huguenots, he tried to force the burghers to disgorge 40,000 livres; they refused, and Captain Merle burned three of them at the stake "to encourage the others," who thereupon settled for a payment of 22,000 livres.[32]

In spite of this rather loose tax system and its different character from one district to another, there seems to be no question that essentially all of the royal tax structure was in rebel hands. Perhaps this explains part of the memorable and stubborn resistance of the Huguenots and their allies after 1572, in the face of such discouraging odds. The older accounts of the Wars of Religion hardly mention this factor; they prefer to emphasize that Huguenots, unlike royalists, served without pay and fought with fanatical courage. According to Sir Charles Oman, this devotion to the cause—plus the "extraordinary incapacity" of their adversaries—explains why Huguenots were able to give such a good account of themselves.[33] But all that we know about the financial aspect of military operations in the later Renaissance contradicts this view. At least part of the Huguenot-Politique forces had to be paid. Some of them were mercenaries of the lowest type. And even those Huguenots truly ready to fight and die for their faith had to be fed and equipped. It does not detract at all from the faith and heroism of these men to state that without their control over royal revenues their cause might very well have been lost.

Huguenot chiefs had a great interest—a material but not necessarily a selfish one—in keeping royal authority weak by throwing themselves into the quarrels between the factions. Huguenots justified their seizure of royal taxes by proclaiming themselves the nation's protector against the Guises. This being the case, the Venetian ambassador asked, in 1575:

How can there ever be peace in the realm, since it is the plain truth that for its own gain [each faction] stands ready to foment war? . . . Thus where the king spends thousands in the fighting, they spend

32. Imberdis, *Auvergne*, pp. 139–43.
33. *A History of the Art of War in the Sixteenth Century*, pp. 403, 407–08, 432.

nothing—at least nothing of their own, but rather of others and of the king. And while the king destroys himself, they, on the contrary, pile up their holdings, holdings they would lose if peace were to come, as they would lose their power and following, with the danger that these might never return again.[34]

Huguenots and Politiques denied that their assumption of tax power was a permanent arrangement. They proclaimed their loyalty to the crown, and insisted that they were levying taxes only by necessity.[35] Even La Rochelle, the Huguenot stronghold, resumed payment of royal taxes to the Epargne in 1573—until fighting began again.[36] The Millau assembly of July 1574 proclaimed the younger Condé "governor and protector in the name of, and under the authority of, the king. . . ." [37] As soon as more stable government returned, they said, they would recommence turning over taxes to royal fiscal agents. The king, to save his face, at times granted "permission" to hold these assemblies, which were clearly acts of lese majesty.[38]

Whatever king or rebels said, the operation of the tax system in most regions of the south and west constituted a significant denial of the king's right to tax his subjects. By their actions, Huguenot and allied rebels showed that they were not only preventing royal taxes from reaching the Epargne but also that they were appealing to a different ultimate authority—the people. The radical, medieval notion that taxation should be levied with the consent of the taxpayers was not only an interesting theory these years, it came closer to reality than at any other time in France since the 1420s.

The most intriguing aspect of "taxation by consent" in the west and the Midi was not the local self-taxing by municipalities nor the exercise

---

34. Albèri, *Relazioni*, ser. 1, 4 : 358–59.

35. Koenigsberger, "The Organization of Revolutionary Parties," p. 350, suggests that in general both Huguenot and Catholic party chiefs were not revolutionaries but rebels; they wanted "to capture the existing machinery of state without subverting the social order or radically changing the political or even the religious structure of the country."

36. James W. Thompson, ed., *The Letters and Documents of Armand de Gontaut, Baron de Biron, Marshal of France* (1524–1592), 1 : xxii.

37. Anquez, *Assemblées politiques*, p. 13.

38. Edward Armstrong, *The French Wars of Religion: Their Political Aspects*, pp. 37–38.

of some tax powers by provincial Estates. Both these developments had been visible many times in the past, and were to mark the rebellion of north and central France against Henry III and Henry IV after 1588. Self-taxing by a beleaguered territory is, after all, an almost automatic reaction to severe danger. The difference now was that consent to taxation was supposed to cover the entire rebel territory in a federative compact. By the terms of the 1574 agreement at Millau, every tax, every surtax, and even every important loan had to be authorized by the Estates-General of the Huguenot-Politique area.[39] All the important comptables, furthermore, were responsible to the representatives of the people in the assemblies and not to a prince or any other executive body. Even the *commissaires* who farmed out indirect taxes had to answer to the assemblies rather than to the fiscal généraux of the various tax districts, as was the case in the royalist lands. And the assemblies proclaimed at least lip service to the concept of popular consent for each tax levy—not only the first, but for each year and for all changes in the structure of taxes. The tax powers of the Huguenot-Politique representatives, at least in theory, was quite comparable to that of the English Parliament under Queen Elizabeth.

Inevitably, this interesting trend toward popular control over taxes was stopped. There simply was too tight a connection between the ability to lead armies and the ability to command taxes by fiat. When the Huguenot-Politique alliance was first formed, Montmorency-Damville was paid by the assemblies as their chief captain, and he was supposed to accept the guidance of a council chosen by the assemblies.[40] Before long, however, Montmorency-Damville had to order taxes levied on his own authority or see his armies crumble. Similarly, when Henry of Navarre first became the recognized leader of the Huguenots (1576) he was granted imposts by regular votes of the representatives. By the 1580s, however, Navarre assumed the power to impose taxes himself. By the time Navarre became king of France (1589), therefore, the transition to collecting royal taxes in the south and west was easy, since he had been collecting such taxes for years in a thoroughly royal manner.

39. Ibid., p. 34.
40. Devic and Vaissete, *Languedoc*, 11 : 602–04; Anquez, *Assemblées politiques*, Introduction.

The "Peace of Monsieur"

When Henry III first came to the throne in 1574 his position among
the various French factions was not at all clear. For a while there was
some hope he would support the Politiques; and he did, in fact, begin
negotiations with some Politique leaders. They, of course, were more
than suspicious of this man whose hands were badly stained with the
blood of the St. Bartholomew's Eve massacres. Within a few months
Henry was beginning preparations to wipe out the Protestant strongholds in the Midi; soon the fifth War of Religion had begun. Scenting
advantage to himself, Henry's younger brother, the duke of Alençon
(who would have inherited the crown if Henry, elected king of Poland
in 1572, had only stayed there after the death of Charles IX), formed
a powerful new faction to trouble the political scene, the "Malcontents."

From the beginning of the fighting Henry III was plagued by the most
disheartening financial problems. Most of the districts in Huguenot-
Politique areas were not paying him taxes; the cost of fighting was rising,
partly because of the many fronts and partly because of the extensive use
of German and Swiss mercenaries; loyal towns and provinces either
could not or would not respond to the crisis by making additional
financial sacrifices; and even the burghers of Paris, perhaps the most
fervent anti-Huguenots in the kingdom, had to be cajoled into lending
money. Royal bonds on the Hôtel de Ville, which had averaged about
2.6 million livres a year under Charles IX, fell to an average of about
220,000 livres per year between 1575 and 1584.[41] The provincial Estates
of Burgundy did vote the king additional subsidies, but the province had
been so weakened by German mercenaries in the pay of the rebels that
they could help very little. On the other hand, a meeting of representatives of twenty-six "good towns" in Paris in the summer of 1575 refused
to do more than listen to pleas by the king in person that his "grandes et
excessives dépenses" were ruining him; the deputies even refused to advise the king on possible solutions to the problem, arguing that they did
not want their decisions to bind towns not represented at the meeting.[42]

41. Schnapper, *Rentes au XVIe siècle*, pp. 172–73.
42. Augustin Thierry, ed., *Recueil des monuments inédits de l'histoire du tiers
état* (Paris, 1853), pp. 830–34.

In the few sections of Languedoc he controlled, the king kept royalist provincial Estates functioning as counterweights to the Huguenot-Politique assemblies. These Estates did grant him a few grudging additional taxes; but of course here the situation potentially was so explosive that the king dared not push his tax power too far.[43] Some Catholic cities precariously situated near the Huguenots actually proclaimed their neutrality and tried (though in vain) to avoid paying taxes to either side.[44]

The only way the government could keep its affairs moving, therefore, was to beg, to borrow, and to employ expedients. The king pawned some of his jewels, borrowed from his courtiers, and sold off the few domaines revenues still belonging to the crown; he also created and sold many new fiscal offices. When things looked black, the papacy made him a gift of 300,000 écus; and the city of Venice, in a noble gesture, canceled his debts to them and returned his pawned jewels.[45]

Henry III, like Charles IX, kept trying to frighten the men who were misusing his revenues by publishing edicts against lese majesty.[46] But such feeble efforts did nothing to close the gap between his income and his expenditures. It soon became apparent that the tax situation was hopeless and that the king would have to depend on borrowing. Without the support he obtained from the great Italian bankers in France (Adjacet, Gondi, Sardini, and Zametti) the government might have collapsed. Of course these bankers demanded control over the most sure and most lucrative revenues in return for their loans; and once this vicious circle became apparent to everybody it was obvious the king would have to cut his military expenses. He now determined to go to the peace table with terms his adversaries would accept.

The peace treaty that resulted from these negotiations is known as the "Peace of Monsieur," because to contemporaries it appeared to have been forced on the king by Alençon. Certainly it was generous to the Malcontents and their Huguenot and Politiques allies—generous enough to make the Catholic *zélés* ("zealots") furious when the terms became known. Alençon was given a large appanage for his own, covering most

43. Devic and Vaissete, *Languedoc*, 11 : 599–602.
44. Thompson, *Wars of Religion*, p. 492; Mariéjol, in Lavisse 6¹ : 166.
45. Thompson, *Wars of Religion*, p. 509.
46. Edict of Paris, Sept. 1575; royal decl. of Blois, March 30, 1577.

of Anjou, the Touraine, and Berry;[47] the Huguenot and Politique leaders were given governorships, cash payments, and fortified towns for strongholds, in addition to a total amnesty. The fiscal clauses in this 1576 settlement repeat all of the arrangements of Amboise in 1563. Condé, Navarre, Montmorency-Damville, and Alençon, together with all other rebel magnates and the agents who served them, were granted pardon for the taxes raised illegally since the St. Bartholomew's Eve massacres. They were also excused for having seized and sold clerical wealth, for holding towns for ransom, and for cutting down and selling the crown's tall timber forests.[48] They were not to be prosecuted in the royal courts for forcing fiscal collectors to honor their own warrants and décharges; and men who had obeyed them and paid them taxes were likewise to be pardoned. Agents and tax farmers who had worked for them were excused both for having leased out tax farms and for having kept the funds for themselves. La Rochelle was pardoned for striking coins on her own authority—a pardon that was extended all the way back to the years just before the Wars of Religion began. In Catholic districts, the magistrates and tax officials were warned not to discriminate against Huguenot minorities by taxing them in a punitive way. And as part of the gesture to rehabilitate the victims of the massacres that had touched off this war, the king extended a fiscal favor to their widows and orphans; these widows and orphans, if they were nobles, were excused from paying the *ban et arrière-ban*; if commoners, they did not have to pay "toutes tailles et impositions." In both cases the exemptions were to run for six years. Finally, and rather lamely, the edict of pacification announced that all these valuable fiscal concessions would operate only if there were no further depredations against the royal fiscal system. The king, without much apparent conviction, ordered all his subjects to resume paying the clerical tithes and announced that severe punishment would be meted out to anyone daring to raise taxes without royal authority.

One point not resolved by the Peace of Monsieur was the salt scarcity

---

47. From this time, the heir apparent is the duke of Anjou; but to avoid confusion I shall continue referring to the new duke of Anjou by his old title of Alençon.

48. On the merciless way forests were exploited during the wars, see Devèze, *Forêt française*, 2 : 227–45.

caused by Protestant seizures of certain of the better salt-producing districts. This gave the Protestants a means of profitably harassing the king. They worked together, at times, to prevent western salt from going into the northern and central provinces. Each time fighting flared up, the king found it difficult to supply north and central France with enough salt, and in consequence he was sometimes forced to rely on the less satisfactory Norman and Breton salt. This not only resulted in lower revenues for him, but also created hardships for consumers of salt. In 1577 the situation looked brighter when the duke of Mayenne, one of the Guises, stormed the great salt port of Brouage and captured it from the Protestants in La Rochelle. But control over most of western salt production remained in the hands of Protestants. In 1577–78 there was a bad salt famine in the royalist regions; to the disruption of the civil wars was added the misery of exceptionally wet weather, which meant that much of the Breton and Norman salt could not dry properly.

A group of courtiers, officials, and Italian financiers smelled the possibilities of large profits in the situation. In 1578 they formed a consortium known as the *grand parti du sel* and obtained a monopoly, a true *ferme générale*, to supply salt to all the *greniers* system lands—that is, to ten généralités of north and central France. The *grand parti* negotiated for supplies with Spanish producers and even attempted to make a deal with the Huguenot producers in the Saintonge district. The dearth of salt in the country (and famine-high prices) continued for another two years.[49]

---

49. Lapeyre, *Ruiz*, pp. 550–55; John U. Nef, *Industry and Government in France and England, 1540–1640*, pp. 103–04; Henri Hauser, *Les origines histor iques des problèmes économiques actuels* (Paris, 1930), pp. 53–69.

6

Efforts to Halt the
Disintegration of Royal Taxing

Henry III has been condemned as one of the worst kings ever to sit on a throne, both because of his repulsive personal characteristics and because of the costly mistakes he made. He was a clever and cultured person, however, and he certainly wanted to succeed in the business of kingship, which fascinated him. When the military campaigns of 1574–75 did not bring the success he craved, he quickly turned to conciliation. His new policy was to weaken his enemies by encouraging some of the troublemakers to pursue their ambitions outside France and by sponsoring reforms at home. These efforts were at least partly sincere. An Estates-General to hear the grievances of all sections and parties had been one of the terms insisted on by the Politiques and Malcontents during the settlement of 1576. But it was the king and his faction who worked most diligently to use this assembly for peace.

Unfortunately for compromise and conciliation, there now was a new factor on the political scene—an association of zealots known as the Catholic League. The Catholic League was formed in an attempt to prevent the king from carrying out the generous provisions of the Peace of Monsieur in favor of the Protestants. Burghers and nobles in scores of towns and provinces pledged troops and money for a new effort to crush Protestantism. The League could count on grandees, magistrates, and military captains controlling five provinces and an additional fifteen cathedral towns. Naturally the king followed this development with the greatest anxiety and tried to turn it into something beneficial for him. To remove some of the wind from the zealots' sails, he declared his sympathy with the aims of the League and proclaimed himself its patron and head.

As far as the Huguenots were concerned, the elections to the Estates-

General during 1576 were being rigged in ways that made it impossible for the Protestant faction to elect its fair share of delegates. This angered them so much that they made the mistake of not pushing their candidates or even cooperating in the elections with the Politiques. The moderate Politiques among the delegates, therefore, were at first definitely in the minority. The zealots seemed more than strong enough to carry a vote for another all-out war against the Huguenots. But as soon as the Third Estate began to debate issues other than religion it became apparent that the delegates were somewhat less than unanimous about many fundamental questions. They had much to worry about—the rampant corruption of royal officials, the deeply resented role of Catherine de Medici in government, and above all the incessant wars and the plague of soldier bands. The clerics appealed to the king to halt the ruinous series of debilitating little wars; the nobles, perhaps dreaming of a return to feudal self-rule, seemed ready to push through changes aimed at weakening central administration and royal justice in general.

The revenues issue at Blois

The position of the king soon became clear. He was willing to listen to grievances and to consider authorizing reforms, perhaps even important reforms. He also was willing, at least in the early weeks of the assembly, to go along with a resolution to finally crush heresy by force, although he insisted that enough funds be voted to carry the increased burden of such an effort. But first the deputies would have to advise him on how to cope with his *plus urgentes affaires*—his immediate need for cash. Henry III wanted higher revenues, plus an emergency grant of 8 or 9 million livres to deal with the more immediate claims on the treasury. The crown was in debt for the staggering sum of 100 million livres. Furthermore, the main revenues had been alienated for years to come.[1] In addition to helping the king raise money for a great crusade against Protestantism, the Estates-General were expected to deal with the existing debts. Part of the debt was a heritage from previous reigns, although a greater portion was accrued from the costly campaigns of 1574–75, as well as from the liberal grants that were part of the Peace of Monsieur.

1. Clamageran, *L'impôt*, 2 : 202; Picot, *Etats Généraux*, 3 : 32–33, 282, 299.

Chancellor Birague, in his presentation of the needs of the crown to the deputies, was less explicit about how funds might be raised than about how desperately these funds were needed. He and other members of the royal council suggested to the assembly, not very enthusiastically, that perhaps a high tariff on cloth exports could be instituted or the rate of the tax on spice imports could be increased. Neither of these devices was adopted; neither of them could have gone very far, in any case, toward satisfying the king's need for higher revenues.

Perhaps the king really hoped that some initiative would come from the Estates-General themselves, as it had in 1561, when the second and third orders had forced the clergy into regular and much higher annual payments.[2] This time, however, the deputies were in a much less cooperative mood. Their attitude was revealed in their reaction to the facts presented by Nicolay, président of the Chambre des comptes. Apparently they accepted the king's account of past expenses. But they refused to believe the figures pertaining to current expenses; and they denied that the royal revenues were as small as the crown claimed. Some of them grumbled that with proper management the French taxes, as they were then constituted, could easily bring in at least 20 million livres. The deputies showed they believed the widespread rumors that enormous pensions were being bestowed on unworthy court favorites, an unjustifiable expenditure, since so many of the recipients were Italians!

Toward the end of December, after weeks of fruitless quibbling over the true measure and condition of royal finances, the chancellor invited each estate to elect twelve delegates to confer with the président of the Chambre des comptes and to inspect the secret fiscal accounts so as to satisfy themselves. But when these thirty-six delegates reported back to their respective orders the assembly was more than ever convinced that the government had been lying. For, as Jean Bodin (a deputy at Blois) states, these men had been shown nothing but brief abstracts of the general budget, which told them little about precisely where all the French revenues were coming from and going to. More than ever, the deputies suspected the king had much to hide.[3]

2. Archbishop Pierre d'Epinac of Lyons shows he was apprehensive on this score in his *Harangue*, pp. 101–07.

3. Jean Bodin, *Relation iournalière de tout ce qui s'est negotié en l'assemblée générale des Estats.* . . . See also Picot, *Etats Généraux*, 3 : 33–34, 284–85.

The "taille égalée"

In January the king was forced to take the initiative and to propose to the Estates-General specific means for obtaining more funds. The chancellor brought forward a potentially important proposal for a graduated (*égalé*) tax on all commoners, with no exemptions, not even for the upper echelons of the fiscal and judicial bureaucracy. This taille égalée would range from one sou for the poorest peasant households up to as much as 50 livres for the richest merchants. A great attraction of this proposed tax was that it was to be, in modern terms, an *impôt de quotité* rather than an *impôt de répartition*, since its total yield was to be the sum of each rate (*quotité*) on every household or *feu*; it was not determined in advance and then apportioned out among the households as were the impôts de répartition like the regular taille and the *taillon*. It is most interesting that this early in tax history, even before the Old Régime, the technical evils of impôts de répartition were recognized. But the taille, of course, continued to be "repartitioned" right up until 1789.

The biggest inducement to accept the taille égalée was that it was supposed to replace all other main taxes, specifically the tailles, aides, gabelles, and traites. Thus it was an early version of a "single tax project," though in this case classes other than the commoners would continue to pay some direct taxes: the clergy would continue to pay the décime, and nobles would continue to bear the ban et arrière-ban and other feudal dues. The government estimated that the taille égalée would bring in an enormous revenue—between fifteen and eighteen million livres, enough to dispense with the other levies. Another inducement given was that such a tax would end the very large sums of money paid out to tax farmers.

The taille égalée, finally, would be infinitely more fair than the current tailles. Everybody knew that the main weight of the tailles fell on the poorest peasants. There would be no exemptions to the new direct tax— no "free cities," no wealthy burghers cowing or bribing local élus to give them a light tax. There would be only a regular rate payable by all, or rather, by every commoner, a rate depending on his wealth. The new tax would put the greater burden where it belonged, on the rich merchants, well-to-do artisans, professional groups, successful landlords, and officials. Probably this last feature was more attractive to the clergy and nobles at Blois than to the Third Estate deputies, who were made up of just those groups of wealthier bourgeois who now would be expected to pay a higher tax.

We do not know for certain what Bodin's attitude was toward the taille égalée while it was being debated. We should expect him to have supported it, since it fitted so well into his own ideas on fiscal justice.[4] But Bodin's later remarks on this proposed tax suggest he probably opposed it. In the third edition of his *République* (earlier editions were finished before the Blois assembly) Bodin attacked this proposal head on: he condemned it as hastily and poorly contrived; he ridiculed the inflated estimate of parishes to which the tax would apply. Even if the graduated tax could be forced on rich commoners, which he doubted, the taille égalée would bring in only a few million livres rather than the 15 millions or more estimated by the government. But the most telling argument Bodin used was that the king could not be trusted when he said this tax would be a substitute for the tailles, aides, and gabelles. Rather, it was much more likely that the king was plotting to make it an additional tax.[5]

Many other deputies must have suspected that while the king was talking about better taxes, he was really scheming for more taxes. At the end of January the Third Estate rejected the whole proposal. The lame excuse was that the deputies had had no mandate from their electorate allowing them to approve such a drastic change in the tax structure. The real reason was that by this time the moderates in the Third Estate were becoming stronger, and they were determined, reforms or no reforms, not to give the king large new grants of funds for fear he might use them to start another war.

Bodin at Blois

As the initiative in the Third Estate slipped from the hands of the zealots into those of the moderates, Bodin became more and more influential in the various debates and maneuvers. At one time he actually presided over sessions of the Third Estate.[6] Bodin's main purpose was

4. See Wolfe, "Jean Bodin on Taxes: The Sovereignty-Taxes Paradox," *Political Science Quarterly* 83, no. 2 (1968).

5. Jean Bodin, *Les six livres de la République*, pp. 890–91.

6. Bodin, *Relation iournalière*, p. 20^r.

to prevent a declaration of all-out war against the Huguenots. He threw his weight behind missions sent by the Estates-General to Navarre and to Montmorency-Damville, attempting to sound them out on a general settlement; at the same time he schemed to line up support against the zealots. He seems to have been aided by deputies from Brittany and, especially, from Burgundy, in addition to those from the Politiques in the south and west and from his own Ile de France. He cleverly isolated the zealot deputies of Paris by hammering home the idea that they had a selfish motive in supporting the royal demands for more taxes.[7] Everybody knew that the Parisians had not been paid any interest on their rentes on the Hôtel de Ville for a long time, and that they hoped higher national taxes would allow the king to resume these payments; this Bodin interpreted as an attempt to transfer money from the purses of provincials into those of the Parisians.

Bodin's method, in other words, was to demonstrate to the deputies the close connection between a war policy and a heavier tax burden. He led them in rejecting a royal request for an emergency grant of 2 million écus, claiming such temporary grants had a way of becoming permanent.[8] The king, who was drifting away from the Leaguers at this point, may secretly have been glad that no vote for war was forthcoming;[9] but he certainly was upset when he saw no financial aid whatsoever being granted him by the Third Estate.

It was apparent the Estates-General were not going to become an instrument for a holy war. Many of the more fiery zealots went home in disgust, without even obtaining their congé from the king. Several of the Paris delegates left abruptly when they were voted down on the proposal to grant the king an emergency levy of 2 million écus. This had the effect of leaving the moderates in the Third Estate at Blois even more firmly in command.

Proclaiming his desperation, the king asked for approval of a plan for a large-scale alienation of royal domaines, enough to bring in 300,000 livres a year.[10] However, by this time Bodin and his supporters were well in control of the Third Estate; and for them alienation of domaines

---

7. Bodin was a deputy from the Vermandois. Paris had its own deputies, and did not count as part of the Ile de France in elections for the Estates-General.
8. Picot, *Etats Généraux*, 3 : 58.
9. Roger Chauviré, *Jean Bodin, auteur de la "République"* (Paris, 1914), pp. 62–63.
10. Clamageran, *L'impôt*, 2 : 221.

was a most grievous evil.[11] Bodin insisted that domain lands, in particular, were not for sale; the king was only the *simple usager* of such property, which had to be kept inviolate as the main guarantee that the tax burden would one day be reduced to bearable proportions.[12] The Third Estate supported Bodin, and it was a stinging defeat for the king.[13]

According to Bodin's own account of these proceedings, the king was "strong dismayed" by this stand on alienation of the domaines. Previously he had openly supported Bodin against detractors, saying that although he regretted how things were going in the Estates-General, the great philosopher was obviously an *homme de bien*.[14] It is possible that the adamant stand Bodin took against the king was a factor in his inability to advance his career in the royal bureaucracy in later years.[15]

Bodin is honored as a great Renaissance intellectual, one of the founders of political science with his masterwork, *Six Books on the Republic*, as well as a founder of political economy with his *Reply of Master Jean Bodin . . . to the Paradox of Monsieur Malestroict*. It is fascinating to see him also as one of the chief participants in the drama of the Estates-General of Blois. Bodin was more than a detached philosopher; in 1571 he took a post as privy councilor to Alençon, and he played a part in several missions for the duke. What did Bodin hope to accomplish at Blois, apart from supporting the Politique position that national security and internal order were more important than crushing the Huguenots? Since he left no statement on this matter, we can only guess; but some of his arguments in the *République*, published the very year the Estates-General were convened, and his *Relation iournalière* (diary) of the assembly, published after his death, do seem to suggest what he had in mind concerning royal tax policy.

Certainly Bodin was not an advocate of limited monarchy. The whole atmosphere of the *République*, especially those passages where he works out his famous definition of sovereignty, rejects such an idea. "When edicts are ratified by Estates or parliaments," says Bodin, "it is for the purpose of obtaining obedience to them and not because otherwise a sovereign prince could not validly make law." It is true that Bodin

11. Bodin, *Relation iournalière*, pp. 38ʳ–39ʳ.
12. Henri Baudrillart, *J. Bodin et son temps* (Paris, 1853), pp. 124–26.
13. Mariéjol, in Lavisse 6¹ : 186.
14. Bodin, *Relation iournalière*, pp. 24ᵛ–25ʳ, 40ʳ.
15. Chauviré, *Jean Bodin*, p. 66.

definitely places the taxing process within the power of the sovereign "to impose laws generally on all subjects regardless of their consent," whereas elsewhere in this treatise, he makes it clear that he believes laws passed for the purpose of increasing the burden of taxes, or even for continuing previous taxes, must be subject to the consent of the Estates-General and of other representative bodies.[16] Bodin's ideal state, we would say, cannot have both a monarch as sovereign as Bodin believes he must be and a parliament participating in the levying of taxes.[17] But especially in his passages on taxation, Bodin indicates that he had other purposes than a search for consistent and universal political principles. His problem was not how to improve his countrymen's understanding of the taxing process but how to persuade them to do all they could to stop the wars.

If the records of the past teach us anything, according to Bodin, it is that "one cannot find more frequent upsets, seditions, and ruins of commonwealths than because of excessive tax burdens and imposts." [18] Similar observations are scattered throughout the *République*; they are especially numerous and quite pointed in the first three chapters of Book VI. Perhaps Bodin intended to demonstrate to the king that not only were the French dangerously antagonistic, but so far as tax grievances were concerned they had every right to feel that way.

Bodin seems to be saying that a successful king has to be a strong king. He implies that the government, particularly in 1576, should embark on a program of tax reform, not only because it would be proper "constitutionally" but also because it would be wise politically. The existence of the monarchy depends on the king's ability to gain the support of his subjects no matter what their religious beliefs or local loyalties.

A "constitutional tragedy"?

Looking at the whole span of French constitutional history in early modern times, it seems that the Estates-General of Blois in 1576–77 may have been the last real chance for the nation to turn down a road other than the one leading to absolute divine-right monarchy. Many factions

16. Bodin, *République*, pp. 40, 140, 223, 244–45.
17. See Wolfe, "Jean Bodin on Taxes," p. 275.
18. Bodin, *République*, pp. 881–83.

had deep grievances; talk of basic political reform was in the air. At times the king even seems to have invited discussion of constitutional reform as a part of a deal for more revenues. The political alignments and interests were fluid enough so that the Estates-General might have emerged with concessions which in time would have helped that institution develop into a regularly convened national advisory body, perhaps with even some of the "power of the purse strings" so important to the Parliament of England. The Estates-General of Blois, therefore, was one of those potential turning points in history at which France failed to make a turn.

There is no doubt that at Blois the government was extremely anxious to convince the delegates of its poverty.[19] In the first weeks of the assembly, at least, the king was willing to entertain a vote for a crusade against the Huguenots, provided that the deputies voted him higher taxes. When this did not seem to be forthcoming, the king begged, threatened, and reasoned with the Estates as groups, and he brought immense pressure to bear on influential delegates in his attempts to get more money. At one time he even sent his brother Alençon (whom he detested but who had some standing with the moderates) to ask the deputies to give up their opposition to the emergency grant of 2 million écus.[20]

Perhaps the greatest error, from the long-range "constitutional" point of view, came in January when the deputies rejected the king's offer to allow a second committee of twelve from each order to be appointed; this committee was supposed to confer with high crown officials and councilors on the fiscal crisis. In the world of "might-have-beens," this committee might have developed into an important popular check on royal tax power. But as it happened Bodin took the position that this proposal was simply a maneuver on the king's part to bend this smaller group to his will, since he had failed to convince the whole assembly of some 400 delegates.[21]

In spite of all his protestations of poverty, Henry III was not entirely

---

19. At least some of the more critical delegates were convinced. See Archbishop d'Epinac's remark to the king admitting that one reason revenues are so unsatisfactory is that "the greater part of finances and receipt centers are in the hands of the opposing party." *Harangue*, p. 91.

20. Bodin, *Relation iournalière*, p. 23^r.

21. Ibid., pp. 29^r–30^v.

without resources at this time. During the following Estates-General of Blois (1588), the king's position was truly desperate; all he really could depend on at that time were the daggers of his assassins. But in 1576 the king was still fairly well in control of most of north and central France, since the Catholic League had not yet joined the rebellion. If a crusade were to be unleashed against the Huguenots, the king would have to lead it; if basic "constitutional" reforms or an improvement of the administration were to be instituted, the king would have to grant them; if some fiscal concessions were to be forthcoming, the king would have to bestow them. In order to obtain concessions, therefore, the Estates-General would have had to give the king some highly important benefits in return. The form in which the king expected these benefits was quite clear. At the beginning of the assembly, some delegates tried to avoid the necessity of such an exchange; they attempted to push through a resolution to the effect that whatever measures the three Estates approved unanimously, the king would have to implement as the law of the land. The king rebuffed this maneuver firmly and it failed.[22]

The Third Estate rejected no less than nine proposals by the king or his supporters for higher revenues.[23] Wrangling over how to raise enough money to wipe out heresy turned into wrangling over whether, in view of the exhaustion of the country, the king should be awarded any money. Some of the nobles promised to serve in the army for a limited time without pay, and the clergy voted a subsidy of 450,000 livres. Such offers were better than nothing. The deputies of the Third Estate, on the other hand, demanded tax relief. They asked for an outright cancellation of all the gabelles, they demanded that the amounts taken as profits by tax farmers be reduced, and they also asked that no tax farms whatsoever be awarded to "foreigners" (*read* "Italians"). They requested a large number of specific reforms in tax administration, some of which were actually granted, three years later, in the great reform decree known as the Ordinance of Blois. They deplored the "unreasonable contracts" the king was allowing the financiers, which involved such huge charges that interest was eating up revenues. Instead they thought that the king should calculate the excessive interest he had been forced to pay in the past and fine the guilty financiers. They suggested that if the king needed

22. Mariéjol, in Lavisse 6¹ : 182–83.
23. Picot, *Etats Généraux*, 3 : 281 and passim.

money in a hurry he could get it in the form of forced interest-free loans from his overly rich tax officials. They wanted the inflated number of royal officials to be pared down and all recently granted royal pensions to be revoked. And they advocated the institution of a *chambre de justice*, a board of investigating judges who would inquire into the sources of tax officials' personal wealth and, where appropriate, force them to return it.[24] In the final days of the assembly, the rump of the Third Estate agreed to vote for the reestablishment of a unified faith for all Frenchmen, but only "sans guerre." The Parisians still present were defeated in their attempt to strike out this clause.[25]

Did the deputies at the Estates-General of Blois realize they were in a position to force important constitutional concessions from the king? Only speculations are possible on this score; but it seems unrealistic to expect that men in 1576 would have known, as we know today, that the parliaments which were to survive this era were those that gave their princes money, not those that withheld it. We must recognize, also, that even the Leaguer deputies were terribly suspicious of promises that might be wrung from this rather complex young prince; they suspected that he might take money voted for a holy war and dissipate it in gifts to his cronies. Finally, we must agree that the economic-fiscal situation in 1576 was against any bold new fiscal departure comparable to that of 1560–61. During the Estates-General of Orléans the large and relatively untapped wealth of the church had been on everybody's mind. But in 1576 all the French were crying poverty, and with good reason.

The deputies of 1576 wanted to strengthen the Estates-General as an institution; this we do know. In its final *cahier* the Third Estate asked that the people should have the right to regular convocations of an Estates-General and also that such Estates-General should have the right to consent to taxes—presumably to new or higher taxes.

In summary, we have to say that while the delegates to the 1576 Estates-General might have exacted concessions from the king, they were more interested in denying the king what he wanted than in obtaining such concessions. By refusing to share fiscal responsibility with the king, they were, in effect, voting for the fiscal system to continue fueling the civil wars.

24. D'Epinac, *Harangue*, pp. 98–100; Clamageran, *L'impôt*, 2 : 213–14.
25. Baudrillart, *Jean Bodin*, p. 121.

POLITICAL PROBLEMS AND ECONOMIC REFORMS

The monetary reform of 1577

The king and his brother, who had just finished fighting in 1575–76, soon were planning a joint campaign against Henry of Navarre. They even managed to bribe Montmorency-Damville away from his alliance with the southern Huguenots. This "diplomatic revolution" paved the way for the sixth War of Religion (1577). Just when it appeared that the divided, quarrelsome, and badly mauled forces of Navarre in the west were on the brink of final defeat, King Henry III intervened and granted Navarre rather generous peace terms.

Henry III liked to call the 1577 pacification the "King's Peace"— in contrast with the Peace of Monsieur of 1576. Whatever it is called, the period after 1577 forms a complex but exceptionally interesting era in fiscal history. This period is often called a "peace of exhaustion"; but France was so far from exhaustion that the government was able to support the enormously costly campaigns waged by Alençon to make himself master of the Spanish Netherlands (1579–83). The king still managed to obtain large revenues and to improve the fiscal system while holding down the rising price spiral. Henry III must be given credit for trying to effect several significant fiscal reforms.

The more financially perceptive among the French had realized for years that the paradox of two moneys—real coins and money of account—was itself a factor in the falling value of money. (For an explanation of money of account and its relation to *billonage*, see appendix F.) It was known that as freshly minted coins appeared they could be worth considerably more for their gold or silver content than in terms of money of account, since even the thinnest, most worn teston, for example, in 1575 was officially 14 sous 6 deniers. It also was known that the existence of "imaginary money" made it easier for the government to "cry down" (*décrier*) the livre, that is, to decree that in the future the same coin, say the teston, was to be worth not twelve sous as in the past but thirteen.[26] This was inflationary in its effects, just as was calling back circulating coins and reissuing them lighter or with a higher

26. See, e.g., the edict of Paris, June 9, 1573.

percentage of base alloy. Since debts and taxes legally had to be carried in money of account, they now could be paid off either in coins worth more in money of account or in "cheaper" coins. Both these types of payments greatly disturbed debtor-creditor relations.

These developments, as well as the inpouring of Spanish treasure, caused an upward pressure on prices, which tended to weaken the purchasing power of the money received by the king in revenues. When the government decided to eliminate money of account, therefore, it hoped that the reform would work to its advantage, as well as to that of the business community. The seigneur de Malestroict, who wrote a famous brochure in 1566 on the causes of what we now call the "price revolution," argued that "imaginary money" was one of the main reasons for the country's price problems. Jean Bodin, who answered this brochure with an even more famous one of his own in 1568, argued that price fluctuations came primarily from foreign treasure. But Bodin, too, was in favor of the 1577 monetary reform. It was also supported by many of the foreign bankers in Lyons, the group most knowledgeable in the ways of the money market—though the French in Lyons were not so optimistic concerning its effects.[27]

We call the monetary reform the *compte par écus*, since the government ordered that all accounts be kept in real coins—écus and their fractions—rather than livres, sous, and deniers. The écu was to act as the basic monetary unit; it was given a fixed and convenient exchange rate for large and small silver coins. Thus it was exchangeable for 60 douzains. The teston, which at 14.5 sous did not fit neatly into the new system, was abandoned; a large and handsome new portrait coin, France's first silver franc, was issued at three to an écu—exactly the old value of the "imaginary" livre, that is, 20 sous. Another new coin—and a significant departure in French monetary history—was the all-copper denier.[28]

This ambitious and well-intentioned reform had some limited success. Bookkeepers, of course, resisted the innovation because of the bother of learning a new system. But the government persisted; and for almost

27. Lapeyre, *Ruiz*, pp. 450–51; Doucet, *Lyon*, pp. 88–89.
28. Jean Lafaurie and Pierre Prieur, *Les monnaies des rois de France: François Ier à Henri IV*, pp. 97–98 and passim; and see the edict of Poitiers, Sept. 1577, in Isambert, 14 : 327–30.

twenty-five years most official accounts, if not merchants' accounts, were drawn up in conformity to the new order. The saving in the labor of reckoning and effecting transactions must have been considerable. More important, the compte par écus reform dampened speculation by bankers and merchants for profits gained in trading foreign coins for French, or gold coins for silver.[29] Unfortunately, after only a few years the upward drift of prices resumed; and the large silver franc had to be withdrawn in 1586, since it had become the object of enthusiastic attention by "clippers," persons adept in snipping off a bit of the edge of coins. The government soon was obliged to alter the weight of silver in some of the smaller coins. Gradually, merchants, followed by official comptables, fell back to reckoning in livres, sous, and deniers. The compte par écus finally was abandoned in 1602.[30]

The ordinance of Blois, 1579

Another exceedingly ambitious reform attempt in the period of the "King's Peace" was the ordinance of Blois of May 1579. It actually was issued at Paris; but it is called the ordinance of Blois because it was supposed to be a response to the complaints and suggestions of the Estates-General of Blois in 1576. The enemies of the king had accused him of stalling the reforms he had promised in 1576. The king excused the delay (in the preamble of the ordinance) by claiming that previously the country was so upset by civil strife there would have been no chance for enforcement. The fact that almost three turbulent years had elapsed between the opening of the Blois meetings and the issuing of this ordinance suggests that the king had reasons for postponing the reforms, which were more important than satisfying the demands of the delegates.

One reason for the great reform was the dangerous signs of resistance to royal taxes in regions other than the south and the west of France. There seem to have been dozens of violent outbreaks against the fiscal system in this period, though we know very little about most of them.

29. Henri Sée, *Histoire économique de la France*, 1 : 94–95.
30. The complex economic, monetary, and government policy background of this reform is studied in Frank C. Spooner, *L'économie mondiale et les frappes monétaires en France 1493–1680*, pp. 90–92 and passim.

In Burgundy, for example, the provincial Estates defied the king's order levying new subsidies; they threatened to pay nothing until the king complied with a long list of demands.[31] There were parallel outbursts in Normandy, Brittany, and Auvergne. Pierre de l'Estoile suggests that in addition to their uneasiness over higher taxes, the burghers in several of the chief cities were disturbed by the fact that the king had not made any efforts to pay off his debts, most of which were held by merchants and officials in these cities.[32] The great reforms of the ordinance of Blois were in part a reaction to these demonstrations, as well as to the demands of the Estates-General.

The ordinance is a long list of 363 articles, touching on almost all aspects of French government, military matters, and religious affairs.[33] It deals with the reform of judicial procedure, public services such as hospitals, and even municipal obligations in maintaining roads. The main articles dealing with taxes are those from 242 through 250 and from 329 through 355, although there are many others applying to finances scattered elsewhere in the ordinance. Both the length and the many subjects covered in this ordinance have led some authorities to see it as a sort of general law code, or at least a first approximation for codifying French law, a project in which Henry III was keenly interested.[34]

One of the chief features of the ordinance of Blois is that it shows the king realized that because of the wars many aspects of his power were slipping into the hands of his provincial governors. The governors were reduced in number and ordered not to appropriate royal prerogatives—specifically, granting pardons, borrowing money, authorizing markets and fairs, and especially levying taxes. The reference to the fiscal powers exercised by Montmorency-Damville and the Guises was obvious.

Other fiscal provisions of the ordinance simply repeated the work of previous tax reforms, and especially those of the two important ordinances of Moulins in 1566. Thus there was an attempt in the

---

31. Henri Drouot, *Notes sur la Bourgogne et son esprit public au début du règne de Henri III, 1574–1579*, pp. 139–44.
32. Pierre de l'Estoile, *Registre-Journal*, vol. 1, part 1, pp. 105–06, 116–17.
33. Isambert, 14 : 380–463.
34. Henri Hauser, *La prépondérance espagnole, 1559–1660*, 3d ed. (Paris, 1948), pp. 127–28; Maurice Wilkinson, *A History of the League or Sainte Union, 1576–1595*, p. 9.

ordinance of Blois to improve collections of domaines revenues, to eliminate fraud in granting tax farms, and to reduce the vast number of exemptions to tailles and other imposts (articles 323 and 336). In addition, all royal gifts made in the form of forest lands were canceled, and a large number of redundant fiscal offices were cut out. The important posts of trésoriers généraux and receveurs généraux were to be reduced from five to one for each généralité—not immediately but *vacation avenant*; that is, the king simply promised he would not fill a post scheduled for elimination after each officeholder left or died (articles 242–45). Otherwise, of course, the king would have had to buy back the office. There were similar provisions to reduce the recently inflated number of élus, grenier officials, and collectors of the taillon.

Some fiscal aspects of the ordinance of Blois amounted to nothing more than attempts to create good will by promising reforms that the king must have suspected had little chance of becoming a reality. Thus Henry announced a reduction in the tailles and other taxes; he ordered a severe limitation of, and accounting for, all royal gifts to favorites amounting to more than 1,000 écus; and he declared that there would be an end to the brutality of the constables enforcing tax collections (articles 341–51). Some of the articles, however, seemed to be more practical, pointing toward worthwhile reforms. This category included the order that all pensions would be assigned at the central Epargne rather than at the généralité treasuries; this had been a source of grave abuse since the days of Henry II (article 335). The clergy, also, were compensated by the king for the recently repeated forced alienations of temporal wealth by an order enforcing their rights to collect tithes everywhere (article 49). And a chambre de justice was set up to investigate improper activities by tax officials—which, as everyone knew, really was an order to extort a grant to the treasury from these very rich men (article 353).

Contrary to the belief of some historians, the ordinance of Blois was something more than a hypocritical attempt at appeasing the would-be-reformers.[35] Probably it erred in promising too much.[36] But

35. Picot, *Etats Généraux*, 3 : 91; Mariéjol, in Lavisse 6[1] : 223; Clamageran, *L'impôt*, 2 : 252.
36. See Pierre de l'Estoile's mocking comment, "It is to be feared that one can say of this edict, as of . . . so many other fair ordinances made in France, 'Not valid after three days.'" *Registre-Journal*, vol. 1, part 1, p. 119.

the king was at least partly sincere in his desire to work some improvements in fiscal affairs and in other matters of government. It would have required a stronger leader than Henry III, however, and more propitious times than the early 1580s, for the ordinance of Blois to have become a success.

Other fiscal reforms after the "King's Peace"

In addition to heavier old taxes, Henry III called up a number of new taxes and other new fiscal devices. Several taxes seem to be more bother than they were worth, such as the tax on "gifts" paid by litigants to judges (the *parisis des épices*) and the tax on playing cards and dice (1583). Some devices probably brought important amounts to the treasury, however, such as the sale of exemptions to tailles for one person in each parish.[37] Others probably were useless either as reforms or as revenue measures; one example is the decree promising that any person revealing graft at any level of fiscal administration would receive one-eighth of the fines recovered from guilty officials.[38]

Some fiscal measures were announced as improvements but were all too transparently aimed at higher revenues. One example is an act creating a new bureau with no other duties than the payment of interest charges on the Hôtel de Ville rentes. A huge number of new and redundant fiscal offices were decreed, notwithstanding the promises made in the ordinance of Blois.

But other measures were aimed at useful improvements in fiscal administration. In 1581, at a time when the rates of the traites were being increased, the export tariff bureaus were all moved to the frontiers of the entire area where the aides were collected, a great improvement over the older system of check points and collection stations for exports en route inside France. When the king could (as in 1579–80 and 1583–84), he canceled at least some of the redundant offices he had created during the worst emergencies. In 1585, however, the loss of so much

37. Clamageran, *L'impôt*, 2 : 243. The payment for this privilege was 150 livres per person. Since the edict announced that payments were to be made "au pied de denier 15," it follows that 150 livres must have been considered purchase of exemption from a taille of some 10 livres or more annually. This suggests that 10 livres was considered a taille for a fairly wealthy person.

38. Royal decl. of Paris, April 25, 1587.

French territory to the League meant that these offices had to be restored.[39] The levy of *sel par impôt* was limited in December 1584 by prescribing the exact amount each person had to buy and by clearly drawing the boundaries of areas subject to it.[40] Also in 1584 a large number of indirect taxes in central France were gathered together and farmed out to a single syndicate. This was the origin of the famous *cinq grosses fermes* that figured so importantly in the reforming attempts of Sully and Colbert in the seventeenth century.

Other evidence of the king's use of reforms as a regular policy can be found in measures partly outside the area of taxation proper. In 1577 and 1581, for example, Henry III increased the powers of town magistrates to set prices of foods and other necessities by decree; clearly this was another attempt, though a feeble one, to offset the bad effects of the "price revolution." In December 1581 the king strengthened the corporate structure of French artisan manufacturing by decreeing the admission of guilds (*métiers jurées*) to towns that had not possessed them previously and by increasing the number of master craftsmen in each guild. Whether this was intended to gratify the treasury or to strengthen French manufacturing is hard to say, since each new master craftsman had to pay a fee into the fisc (amounts differed depending on the location and craft), in some cases amounting to as much as thirty écus.[41] There is also some doubt concerning the purpose of the *droit de marque* reform in 1582, obliging all manufacturers of woolen cloth to submit to an inspection of their products, which then were marked with a lead seal attesting to their quality—for which, of course, the manufacturer had to pay a fee. Whether this reform was primarily "bursal" or not, it is significant as the first national tax on manufacturing as such in French tax history.[42]

Another interesting semifiscal reform was an elaborate and seemingly effective system for registering private contracts, a measure which

39. Examples of orders restoring suppressed offices are the edicts of Paris of April and May 1585. And see Pierre de l'Estoile, *Registre-Journal*, vol. 1, part 1, p. 169.

40. Clamageran, *L'impôt*, 2 : 261.

41. Emile Levasseur, *Histoire des classes ouvrières et de l'industrie en France avant 1789*, 2d ed., 2 vols. (Paris, 1900–01), 2 : 138–43.

42. Rolland du Plessis, *Remonstrances*, p. 81, complained that since poor people wore this cloth the tax innovation came out of the poor people's blood.

replaced the *insinuation* of 1539.[43] The edict establishing the reform explains that legal instruments involving property transfers were in such confusion that the courts were clogged with disputes and the king and other landlords could not collect the revenues due them. Therefore the king ruled that in order to have all such records "in one sole spot and locality," a new comptroller of such papers would set up for business in every town with a royal judge. All gifts, inheritances, leases, and sales of property over a certain value now had to be registered and copied by this comptroller; and for this service the government exacted a fee of 10 sous. This *droit de contrôle* was a sensible reform which apparently worked satisfactorily, and it survived to the end of the Old Régime. It did bring a small amount of additional revenue to the crown.

Perhaps the most bizarre and transparent attempt to call attention to the king's good intentions was the reform ordinance of Paris, April 26, 1582.[44] This proclaimed the king's irritation over the fact that so many persons were annoying him with *requestres & placets*. Therefore the king forbade his subjects to put forward any plans for additional venal offices (a reference to the operations of the *traitants*) "and other devices and inventions for making money, which go to the downtreading of his people" on pain of suffering disgrace (a reference to the insistent pleas of the courtiers). Chancery officials were commanded not to provide the proper forms for such requests to persons wanting to make them. The king announced that no more gifts or favors of this sort would be granted unless they could be accommodated on Saturdays only, after dinner, and while the king was still seated at his table.

THE ASSEMBLY OF NOTABLES OF ST. GERMAIN-EN-LAYE, 1583–84

Henry III continued his interest in fiscal reforms during the remainder of his reign.[45] But his efforts during 1583–84 are especially interesting.

43. Edict of Blois, June 1581, in Isambert, 14 : 493–99.
44. B.N. F23610(436).
45. The great *Code du roy Henry III, roy de France et de Pologne*, ed. Barnabé Brisson, is the best example of the king's interest in law codification. On the king's genuine interest in tax reform these years, see Aline Karcher, "L'Assemblée des Notables de Sainte-Germain-en-Laye, 1583," *Bibliothèque de l'Ecole des Chartes* 114 (1956) : 115–18.

In 1583 the financial situation was critical but not yet hopeless. The tax system was terribly strained by the costs of past religious wars and by the enormous subsidies required for the Netherlands campaigns. Meanwhile the French were showing signs of increasing irritation with their tax burden. Therefore the king determined to sponsor a full-dress and well-publicized investigation of the total royal financial picture.

This investigation was put in the hands of an Assembly of Notables, brought together at St. Germain-en-Laye in November 1583 to deal with the fiscal crisis and to advise the king on other matters. Like other such assemblies, it was not composed of representatives of the French Estates but rather of high officials, great nobles and clerics, and valued advisors chosen by the king. In this case, the assembly also included a large number of fiscal experts. To help the notables in their work the government, in the preceding months, had made a strong effort to survey the fiscal situation in the provinces. Reports were written concerning the fiscal situation in general and the central Epargne in particular; and one report dealt with the king's indebtedness. The government asked the notables to give their advice in the form of answers to a long set of questions; the questions were, in effect, a blueprint of suggested reforms of the tax system.[46] The questions themselves demonstrate a quite sophisticated appreciation of the fiscal problem, together with an apparent concern not only for improving revenues but also for making the tax burden more equitable and more bearable. Is it possible to make the aides more valuable through better administration (*bon ménage*)? What can we do to increase the value of tax farms without authorizing higher rates? What must we do to improve the general quality of lower-echelon fiscal administrators? Some of the queries suggest the king was willing to lighten the tax burden on poor peasants and increase it on nobles (by raising the value of the ban et arrière-ban) and on the clergy (by forcing the church to redeem the rentes which had been issued on the security of the décimes).

Most of the advice given by the notables was neither imaginative nor new. Often it consisted of pointing out that the situation was covered under the great reform edict of Blois of 1579 and merely required that the pertinent clauses of this edict be enforced. Rather than recommending basic functional changes, the notables seemed to

46. A summary of the questions appears in Clamageran, *L'impôt*, 2 : 253–60.

feel that the system was adequate and mainly required removal of obvious abuses. For example, they did not call for any changes in the nature of the tax bureaucracy, but only for a reduction in its size.[47] In only one area affecting taxes did they make what could be considered a striking departure. They suggested that revenues could be improved and artisans and merchants helped, if a set of import tariffs were imposed at the frontiers so as to hamper foreign competition. This counts as perhaps the first clear evidence of mercantilist thinking in Renaissance France.[48]

The notables demanded that all important royal gifts of lands or revenues be canceled by the state without compensation, that alienated domaines which were worth more than the *denier douze* (8⅓ percent) of their sale price be repurchased, that the government call in its leases of tax farms and renegotiate them at higher prices, and that the salt tax burden be increased in some of the unfairly favored provinces. They also demanded another chambre de justice to investigate complaints against tax officials and, of course, to squeeze a *composition* out of them. Royal commissaires, sent out on this mission, worked through much of 1584 and into 1585, managing to force the very respectable sum of 240,000 écus from their victims.[49]

Were all the king's reforms these years, plus the work of the Assembly of Notables, adequate to the task of pulling France out of its fiscal crisis?[50] Obviously not; the situation called for more drastic changes, especially for a long period of peace. But France was to enjoy neither peace nor the precarious and interrupted type of truce that marked the

47. In fact a large number of offices were ordered suppressed in 1584; but the deepening crisis of the following year made it necessary for the government to reconstitute them.

48. On dating the appearance of mercantilist thought, see Wolfe, "French Views on Wealth and Taxes from the Middle Ages to the Old Régime," *Journal of Economic History* 26, no. 4 (1966). See also Karcher, "L'Assemblée," pp. 150–51.

49. Letters-patent of St. Maur-des-Fossées, May 29, 1584, and of Fontainebleau, July 1584; see also the letters-patent of Paris, July 11, 1586, enjoining the Chambre des comptes to stop prosecuting financial officials for crimes for which they had paid as a result of this chambre de justice. See also Clamageran, *L'impôt*, 2 : 261.

50. Karcher, "L'Assemblée," p. 161, believes that budget figures presented to this assembly show that with the reforms undertaken the budget was close to being balanced, and that if peace had lasted the fiscal crisis would have been resolved.

years 1577–84. In June 1584 Alençon died, precipitating France toward her most dangerous trial during the Wars of Religion.

THE SECOND ESTATES-GENERAL OF BLOIS, 1588–89

With Alençon dead, it was obvious that the Valois line was near extinction since Henry III was incapable of having children. This made the Huguenot Henry of Navarre, the king's nearest male relative, heir to the throne by a well-established tradition, which, however, dated from the days when Calvinism was not a problem. Rejecting the king's pleas for calm, revolutionary councils sprang up in Paris and many other large towns.[51] The Catholic League was revived, this time in an exceedingly menacing form. The Guise family and its supporters easily made themselves the chiefs of the League and at the same time masters of Champagne, Brittany, and much of Burgundy and Normandy. Yielding to Catholic pressure, the king proclaimed the highly unrealistic edict of Nemours (July 1585), which gave the Huguenots six months to return to the Catholic church or leave the country. This surrender caused the Guises and the rebellious Catholic town councils to recognize, somewhat apprehensively, the suzerainty of Henry III. For the last time before he died, Henry III was able once again to control at least most of the tax system of the north and central provinces; that is, all territories not in the hands of Huguenots or Politiques.[52]

In 1584 and 1586 the king was able to force his burghers to accept almost 7 million livres in additional rentes, to be supported by yet another alienation of church temporel. But of course in these frantic times funds were almost impossible to raise. The government tried all the worst expedients: imposing new excises, raising salt taxes, creating additional alternatif officials, and flooding the provinces and Paris with other new officials.[53] Blustering, useless edicts were issued ordering con-

51. See the remarkable and eloquent *Déclaration de la volonté du roy sur les nouveaux troubles de ce royaume* (Paris, 1585).

52. As part of the price for this return to obedience he had to agree to pay the troops Guise had raised. Guise reminded Catherine de Medici of this promise in a quite insolent letter: see Georges Hérelle, *La Réforme et la Ligue en Champagne*, 2 : 143–45.

53. Edicts of Paris, Feb. 25, Sept., and Dec. 1587. For an amusing account of how the king announced a new forced loan to the burghers of Paris, see the *Registre-Journal* of Pierre de l'Estoile, vol. 1, part 1, pp. 213–14.

fiscation of lands and goods of Huguenots and of others who took up arms against the king.[54]

Perhaps because the Guises could not conceive of the possibility of France's ever accepting a heretic king, they bided their time, accepting promises from Catherine de Medici and secret financial support from the pope and from the king of Spain. A stalemate developed, signalized by the complex series of campaigns in 1587 called "The War of the Three Henries" (Navarre, Guise, and Henry III). In the summer of 1588 Guise was able to take over Paris; he forced the king to name the old Cardinal de Bourbon as royal heir and to bow to other humiliating conditions.

One of these conditions was that another Estates-General be convoked. The complete disaffection of so many areas made the Guisards hope that an Estates-General would force Henry III to name Guise heir to the throne after the Cardinal de Bourbon. Some zealots came to this meeting at Blois (September 1588) hoping to find support for an all-out war against the Huguenots; some nobles came because they thought they saw a chance to make fundamental changes in French government in the direction of feudal independence; some burghers and officials wanted more self-rule for municipalities and provinces. Given the hysterical state of public opinion, it was easy to rig the elections so that almost no Politiques, let alone Huguenots, were chosen as deputies.

The fiscal business taken up by this Estates-General is more interesting for what it reveals about French opinions on taxes than for any direct effects on French tax history.[55] The delegates were adamant in their insistence that no new levies could be raised; they pointed out that Henry III had promised France a cut in taxes in the ordinance of Blois (1579) but that since 1579 the nominal rate of the taille had doubled. They demanded, as in 1576–77, that the practice of *sel par impôt* gabelles be abolished completely and that no man be required to buy more salt than he really needed. They insisted that all taxes be lowered at least to the level of 1576.

Some of the most moving discourses on popular misery in the six-

54. Edicts of Paris, Nov. 11, 20, and 26, Dec. 23, 1585; Apr. 26, 1586; and March 12, 1587.
55. Picot, *Etats Généraux*, 4 : 44–53.

teenth century are to be found in the complaints of this Estates-General on taxation.[56] Several of the delegates published their harangues, which show that they felt that continued internal war and excessive taxation were feeding on each other. Renaud de Beaune, the archbishop of Bourges, told the king that France was "a sick body which has been too much bled"; to his poor subjects "there remains naught but the tongue for crying out to God and the eyes for weeping [since there are] no ways or means of extracting money not already thought upon and invented, even from things most basic for human needs. . . ." With people fleeing their homes for fear of tax collectors, soon the king would be nothing but "king of a large and broad land of empty spaces." [57]

But the king persisted in begging the delegates for money. In his principal address he asked how a "dignified" war on heretics could be waged without funds. He humbly admitted that fiscal administration in the past had been inefficient and promised to do better in the future.[58] He even volunteered to cut household expenses to a *petit pied*, if the delegates would only vote him an emergency grant to tide him over for a few months.[59] The delegates, however, were bound by the rather contradictory League propaganda that heretics should be exterminated and taxes lowered at the same time. They were infuriated by the revelation that even while they had engaged in dickering with the king on lowering taxes, royal commissioners had been out scouring the provinces trying to raise more money for the crown by loans and forced loans.[60] In the end they restricted themselves mainly to giving advice. They told the king to use misconduct fines or other *casuelles* to buy back the royal domaines, which they felt would provide more than enough revenue for any legitimate royal needs. Again, as in 1577, they advised the king to squeeze "the overly swollen sponge" of financiers and tax officials through a chambre de justice.[61] However, the delegates agreed that if the king would enforce the tax concessions and fiscal reforms he had promised them, they would undertake (in very vague

56. E.g., the *Remonstrances* of Rolland du Plessis, pp. 38–39.
57. Renaud de Beaune, *Première remonstrance faicte au roy . . . de ce qui est accreu des tailles & impositions . . .* , pp. 7, 12–13.
58. Picot, *Etats Généraux*, 3 : 383–84.
59. Clamageran, *L'impôt*, 2 : 270–71.
60. Beaune, *Première remonstrance*, pp. 11–12; Clamageran, *L'impôt*, 2 : 270.
61. Clamageran, *L'impôt*, 2 : 280–81.

terms) to raise enough additional funds for subsidizing a new religious crusade and to begin, at least, to pay off the king's debts. But they adamantly refused to translate this vague concession into an immediate grant of new taxes.

At one point, toward the end of these long and confused negotiations and maneuvers, the king suddenly announced he had determined to give in to all the demands for fiscal reform raised by the delegates. The spokesman for the Third Estate, Etienne Bernard (who wrote a *Journal* of this assembly), tells how the delegates were stupified at the far-reaching implications of this apparent surrender. The king explained, in a most revealing statement, that while his council had warned him such a step would be *demi-démocratique* he had still resolved to go ahead: "For I have known that the queen of England, however wicked she may be, supports herself by such means only, and this her subjects, in case of necessity, grant her more willingly than that they would, being tallaged. . . ." [62] Even more specifically than in 1576–77, the king insisted the Estates-General would indeed be invited to share in some of his taxing powers in return for support in raising emergency levies.[63] The delegates, understandably suspicious, pressed the king to make additional promises of reforms; but they still would not satisfy his request for quick cash relief. This chance for the Estates-General to gain some tax power, never very promising in view of the unhappy relations between the crown and the delegates, was snuffed out by the assassination of the duke of Guise.

One of the memorable ironies of fiscal history in this era is the role of the doomed Henry of Guise in these bickerings. At first Guise was delighted to see the king so frustrated and humiliated in his negotiations with the delegates over funds. Then, when it became apparent the king would not get a sou, Guise became alarmed; after all, money now paid to the crown would go to support an anti-Huguenot army, which he, undoubtedly, would lead. Therefore Guise switched attitudes abruptly, and began to use his influence to get some extraordinary funds voted to the king.[64]

While Guise was far from clear as to how he should deal with the

62. Picot, *Etats Généraux*, 3 : 413.
63. Dur, "Constitutional Rights," pp. 87–88.
64. Picot, *Etats Généraux*, 3 : 406–07.

king, Henry III was burning with resentment and hopes for revenge against the man he blamed for all his troubles. The month following the execution of Mary Stuart, niece of the Guises, Henry ordered her dowry rights and properties in Champagne and Poitou to be confiscated and sold at auction.[65] In the summer before the convocation of the Estates-General, the position of the Guises had been weakened when their chief ally, the king of Spain, suffered the defeat of the Spanish Armada. This encouraged Henry III to scheme to assert himself. On December 23, 1588, when Guise was on his way to a council meeting ostensibly called to discuss concessions to be made to the Estates-General regarding the salt taxes and other fiscal burdens, he was cornered by the king's assassins.[66] Henry III showed he was still king by butchering both the duke and his brother the Cardinal de Guise, and by intimidating the deputies to the Estates-General with his soldiers.

This gruesome deed threw Paris and other League centers into a frenzy. Mobs yelled for the king's blood. The Sorbonne faculty solemnly declared all men relieved of their oaths of loyalty and of all duties to the king, including their obligations to pay royal taxes. But so long as the Guise faction remained confused by the loss of their leader and the king remained in control of a small part of central France, there was nobody to call Henry III to account for this crime except, seven months later, another assassin.

The king was now almost completely without funds or support. He was also without his mother's very important help: Catherine de Medici died only a few days after Guise had been struck down (January 13, 1589). Money trickled in from some towns of the Loire valley and a few others in the heart of France. At the news of the assassination, most of north France, from Brittany to Picardy, went into open revolt. Some towns remained loyal, so that the king could transfer his Chambre des comptes, Cour des aides, and parlement from Paris to Tours—or rather, transfer those officials who chose to obey his commands. Boulogne, Châlons, Calais, Compiègne, and one or two other northern towns also remained royalist. One of the more macabre bits of fiscal history in

---

65. Edict of Paris, March 1587.

66. Estienne Pasquier, *Lettres historiques pour les années 1556–1594,* ed. D. Thickett, pp. 352–53, believes that the king had sent word to Guise that he was wanted at a meeting of the Conseil des finances.

this period was Henry III's letter to the magistrates of Châlons, ordering them to raise 12,000 écus for his Swiss mercenaries; he authorized them—if the money could not be obtained from other sources—to melt down into ingots the "buffet d'or" which had belonged to "ledict feu duc de Guyse." [67]

The king had to accept an alliance with Navarre, on Navarre's terms. He was forced to name Henry of Navarre as the recognized heir to the throne in spite of his religion. Henry III and Henry of Navarre managed to raise a large army between them, and they marched on defiant Paris. Not long after the siege was established, an assassin managed to reach the king (August 2, 1589). Henry IV was now king of France as well as of Navarre, but only in the eyes of his own supporters.

67. Hérelle, *Champagne*, 1 : 190–91, 197.

7

The Fiscal System in
the Grip of the War Lords

THE COLLAPSE OF CENTRALIZED TAXING

Tax power in the Guise-League areas

The worst of the fiscal crisis came before the death of Henry III. It was the assassination of Guise, not the accession of Henry IV, that brought the royal tax system of France to its lowest point since the era of Joan of Arc. Writing to Marshal Biron to get his support, only one month after Guise's death, Henry III revealed: "Champagne, Picardy, Burgundy, Dauphiné, Provence, Languedoc, Poitou, Paris and its district, all give no help at all, and there remain only the little lands in the heart of France who can give some, and that will be only feeble support." [1]

This geographic picture of fiscal disobedience, of course, changed radically when Henry of Navarre became king. Huguenot and Politique town councils and assemblies, which had supported Henry before he was king, continued to make their net revenues available to him. The fiscal apparatus of most of Guyenne, Poitou, and parts of Languedoc, Provence, and Dauphiné, therefore, could be counted as royalist. Those towns in central France that had remained loyal to Henry III after the murder of Guise also rallied to the Huguenot king. Henry IV established Tours as his administrative center, while he worked, fought, and schemed to take Paris.

The provinces north of a line from Nantes and east along the Loire down to Lyons remained almost solidly in the control of the Guises, however. In addition, a host of districts and cities south of this line were either pledged to the League or controlled by war lords also fighting against Henry IV. Most of these areas recognized Cardinal de

1. Thompson, *Biron*, 2 : 457–63. See also the armistice declaration of April 1589 (with Navarre), in Isambert, 14 : 645–50.

Bourbon as "Charles X"; but this prelate, a prisoner of Henry IV, died in 1590. The larger rebel areas had complex, highly integrated fiscal institutions available to their rulers; and in the bureaux des finances, especially, they had agencies trained to keep the provincial and local fiscal machines going with a minimum of attention from the ruler. The importance of the bureaux des finances was underlined in the winter of 1588–89. At that time Henry III, desperate to keep as large a territory loyal to him as possible, created rival bureaux wherever he could find a loyal town in the midst of a Leaguer district. In Auvergne, for example, a new bureau des finances was authorized in the royalist town of Clermont, in competition with the regular bureau in the Leaguer town of Riom.[2]

In rebellious Champagne, however, there were some royalist towns, for at least part of this period. Châlons, for example, at times paid revenues to Henry III and Henry IV. Even in Burgundy, some towns refused to contribute to the League's cause.[3] For the most part, however, tax power in the belligerent provinces can be characterized by stating that the grandee simply replaced the king. The chief difference in the fiscal situation was that now the revenues collected at Dijon, Troyes, Rouen, Rennes, and many other provincial tax centers were denied to the king. In addition to the bureaux des finances, the various branches of the Chambres des comptes and the Cours des aides continued to function, operating under the authority of the ruler in control of their territories.

Tax power in Guisard Brittany was particularly confused. The governor of Brittany after 1582 was the duke of Mercoeur, a cousin of the Guises. In 1588 he managed to make himself ruler of most of the province, though in Rennes, Brest, and St. Malo the town magistrates professed loyalty to the king while managing to increase their already large degree of municipal autonomy. There seems to be no doubt that while Mercoeur took all the money he could from Philip II and pretended to further Spanish pretensions to the French throne, what he really was working for was an independent principality for

2. Imberdis, *Auvergne*, pp. 581–88; see also the letters-patent of Tours, April 17, 1589.
3. Drouot, *Notes sur la Bourgogne*, p. 105; idem, *Mayenne et la Bourgogne, 1587–1596*, 2 : 37.

himself. But Brittany was badly hurt by internal struggles between religious and political factions. In many of the poor and less accessible areas minor nobles and war lords took over as effective rulers, setting up local systems of defense and keeping local revenues for themselves.[4]

Auvergne also counted as a League province, and its governor, Count Randan, was an ally of the Guises. Randan decided to revive the Estates of Lower Auvergne and directed this assembly to assist him in raising taxes. The Auvergne Estates seemed anxious to cooperate with their local ruler, especially since this new arrangement allowed them to cut the rates of the tailles. But in 1590 Randan was killed in battle, and several Auvergne cities declared for Henry IV. Auvergne broke up into a confused mass of quarreling districts and towns, wracked by desperate sieges and bitter skirmishes until 1594.[5]

One point that seems clear is that in contrast to the Huguenot-Politique areas when they had been in rebellion, the Guise-Leaguer lands produced no single overall coordinating authority. The south and west assemblies of the late 1570s had spoken for all the Huguenot-Politique territories; they had issued general as well as specific tax edicts and had even prepared rules and regulations for administrative procedure in tax matters. It is true, however, that the League had a general council, based in Paris, to which other towns and provinces sent delegates; this council named Mayenne, a younger brother of the murdered duke of Guise, lieutenant general of France. And in 1593 the League did manage to convoke an Estates-General for its territories.[6] But each of the League areas, large and small, had its own ruler who jealously monopolized its own revenues. Delegates to the Leaguer Estates of 1593 drafted despairing petitions to Mayenne for help in stopping Catholic war lords and governors from looting under the cover of taxing, "it being the case that Catholics are as badly treated as the enemy." [7] Even the Guises were too interested in turning the provinces they controlled into principalities to subordinate their affairs to nation-wide issues.

There was also a significant amount of tension between the Guises

4. Abbé H. Poisson, *Histoire de Bretagne*, pp. 226–27.
5. Imberdis, *Auvergne*, pp. 344–55.
6. Chaos in France, however, permitted only a relatively small number of delegates to get through. They accomplished little.
7. Arthur Desjardins, *Etats-Généraux, 1355–1614* (Paris, 1871), pp. 589–90.

and lesser Catholic nobles. The League municipalities, furthermore, rarely cooperated with each other or with the Guises. Many of the minor nobles were repelled by the tendency of Leaguer clerics and town magistrates to preach rather radical political doctrines, including that of "no taxation without consent." They tended, therefore, to deny their support to League towns and to retreat to their own castles or to attach themselves to the nearest war lord. The Catholic League was far from becoming "a state within a state." [8]

The most important of the Guise tax machines, and the one we know the most about, is the one under the control of the duke of Mayenne.[9] Mayenne ruled a vast principality based in Burgundy. It included most of Champagne and parts of Picardy and other provinces. When Henry of Guise had been alive, the two brothers had almost established themselves as the effective rulers of Champagne and Burgundy in their position as governors; they had built fortifications, garrisoned towns, commissioned the manufacture and purchase of cannon, and had even taken oaths of loyalty from their troops—all acts of lese majesty. Thus it was no great step for Mayenne to take over the remaining functions of rulership in 1588, including taxation.

Burgundy had traditions of autonomy; it had its own Estates and parlement. Taxation in Burgundy was carried on with at least the appearance of cooperation, if not consent, by representatives of the people. The county of Champagne, on the other hand, had been ruled directly by the crown since the thirteenth century. Here the levying of taxes by Mayenne was decidedly arbitrary. Immediately after Mayenne took over control in Champagne he ordered an investigation of the personnel of the bureau des finances at Troyes. All fiscal administrators suspected of Politique or royalist sympathies were discharged.[10] All the royal taxes raised in Champagne were continued, and, to the disappointment of the taxpayers, they were continued at the same rates as under the king. Ironically, several of the tax edicts imposing new levies in Champagne, which had been issued in the last months of Henry III's reign, were first put into operation by the bureau des finances at Troyes, acting now under the orders of Mayenne.

In Burgundy, as in Champagne, Mayenne had the same tax powers

8. Wilkinson, League, p. 3.
9. Drouot, Notes sur la Bourgogne, pp. 104–25; Mayenne, 2 : 104–05 and passim.
10. Hérelle, Champagne, 2 : 255–58.

as the king. And Mayenne raised forced loans on the wealthier burghers in his cities in a royal manner; here the Burgundian Estates were of great assistance, since they had the obligation of deciding what tax measures to employ in order to repay these loans.[11] At times he increased the rate of old taxes, especially those for the aides and the traites. He increased the export duties on wine, for example, thus putting an additional burden on one of Burgundy's chief sources of income.[12] He created and sold offices to the point where he had to have his own office for Parties casuelles, just as did the crown. He seized and operated domaines revenues for his own benefit, including those from the royal forests. He even had his mints coin money. Clerics in his territory paid him décimes,[13] and he prevailed on churchmen to alienate more of their temporel and to turn the proceeds over to him. Finally, he forced the Burgundian Estates to provide him with funds for the support of his own court and household—a sort of civil list, but labeled "gifts." He justified them, in a rather twisted way, as a substitution for the money he formerly had collected as governor.[14]

The fact that Mayenne took advantage of the whole panoply of royal taxation does not mean, of course, that his treasury was overflowing. Even before 1589 Burgundy and Champagne were on the invasion route for the German mercenaries called into France, and they seemed to delight in laying waste to east France. We know that, far from building up a personal fortune from his revenues, Mayenne was constantly harassed because of lack of cash. When he finally laid down his arms (1596) one of the conditions of his surrendering was that the crown take over his most pressing debts.

In spite of the poverty and exhaustion of Burgundy, Mayenne increased the tax burden there. Towns were forced to pile up a great burden of debt; they were allowed to float their own rentes, using as security the value of town tolls and other levies.[15] Often this increased

11. Drouot, *Mayenne*, 2 : 108.
12. Drouot, *Notes sur la Bourgogne*, p. 122 and nn.
13. This seems to have been against the wishes of the leaders of the League. See Clamageran, *L'impôt*, 2 : 303.
14. Drouot, *Mayenne*, 2 : 105–07. In Vienne, too, Saint-Sorlin, the Guise captain struggling with the Huguenots and Politiques for control of Dauphiné, raised all the royal taxes. Pierre Cavard, *La Réforme et les Guerres de Religion à Vienne*, p. 345.
15. Drouot, *Mayenne*, 2 : 111–12.

expense was for the purpose of provisioning and quartering mercenaries or other foreign troops. The Burgundian Estates claimed, in 1591, that they were paying higher taxes under Mayenne than they had paid to the late king. They even advanced figures to show that total annual revenues from their province had risen from 152,000 écus during the period 1575–77 to almost a million écus in 1590.[16]

One of the Guises' problems was that they did not have full access to powerful syndicates of Italian financiers. The clouded future of royal power in France, in addition to the collapse of centralized taxing, made these bankers hesitant to turn over their resources. Of course, subventions from the king of Spain found their way into Guise treasuries; but these were never enough. Philip II is often characterized as being catastrophically shortsighted in the niggardly way he doled out money to his French allies. When the body of Henry of Guise was searched after his assassination, it was reported that an unfinished letter was found asking the king of Spain for more cash. But Philip had not really trusted the Guises to further Spanish plans for France; and in any case, especially after the defeat of the Armada, Spain had her own financial problems.

Feudal lords and communes

An even more dramatic aspect of the collapse of centralized taxing is the manner in which fiscal matters were handled outside of the grandees' territories. Here it is much more difficult to make useful generalizations. Some cities, such as Paris, Marseilles, St. Malo, and Lyons, were at times virtually self-governing communes. There were also Leaguer enclaves inside predominantly royalist provinces controlled by war lords where regular taxing almost disappeared; and there were two or three small fiefs whose feudal lords assumed tax powers similar to those of the Middle Ages. Some seigneurs began to levy an occasional seigneurial taille, a right denied them since 1439, when the crown established its power over the royal taille.[17] Modern historians, looking

16. Ibid., 2 : 104–06. But an increase of this order during the later Wars of Religion hardly seems possible.

17. Doucet, *Institutions*, 2 : 576 n. 1. Several royal edicts in 1565 and 1566 complain of this and warn seigneurs against levying tailles on anyone but their serfs. See also the great ord. of Blois in May 1579, art. 280, in Isambert, 14 : 443.

at all of France in this era and seeing nothing but fiscal chaos, interpret this development as a reversal toward feudal government, a sort of "féodalité financière." But this concept really does not apply to the large portions of France that were under the control of a great lord. In most of the kingdom, for at least the greater part of the crisis years 1584–98, monarchical institutions were maintained vertically, though of course they were broken up horizontally among many possessors.

In only one of the great fiefs did the lord take advantage of the crisis to resume medieval tax powers, namely the county (later duchy) of Nevers. The lords of Nevers had enjoyed a large degree of autonomy in the fifteenth century, including the right to assemble their provincial Estates to aid in the levy of local taxes. Nevers's self-rule was chipped away in the late fifteenth and early sixteenth century by the usual infiltration of royal officials; and control over its Estates passed to the king, who allowed this representative institution to wither away. But Nevers, during the Wars of Religion, was fortunate in its new duke, Louis Gonzaga (who married the heiress to the fief), a capable, ambitious, and rich Italian noble who soon put the Valois kings in his debt by lending them large sums from his own wealth and supporting their requests for loans from Italian bankers. Nevers was also fortunate in having as chief administrator Guy Coquille, an extraordinarily competent legist and a stalwart proponent of provincial patriotism.[18] Until the very end of the sixteenth century, when Henry IV was firmly on the throne, the rulers of Nevers were able to control all the instruments of government in their province, including the entire tax structure and all its revenues. They had their own bureau des finances, Chambre des comptes, and even an administration of their *eaux et forêts*. An Estates of Nevers reappeared, responsible only to the duke; the Estates gave him important assistance in levying, apportioning, and collecting taxes. The duke wielded his power not as governor in the name of the king, and certainly not as an agent for a city or an administrator for the League (or any other party). He ruled as the feudal lord of his land—though it is true he enjoyed additional powers that came from the large number of royal officials who were now under his control.

There were also one or two other small fiefs in which the local tax structure was controlled once again by a feudal lord: the vicomté of

18. Despois, *Nivernais*, pp. 282–86; Church, *Constitutional Thought*, chapter 5.

Turenne is the best example. Other small fiefs on the southern and eastern borders of the country (e.g. the duchy of Bar and the county of Comminges) had retained their feudal autonomy from before the Renaissance. But "féodalité financière" in the later Wars of Religion was an exception, not a rule.

Much more significant were the instances of self-government and self-taxing in the cities of France. We have seen that the growth of royal power in the late Middle Ages turned municipal governments into subordinate agencies of the crown. But when in 1588 rebels threw off royal authority they found it convenient to appropriate the royal taxes and the royal fiscal machines in their area. Often this was unavoidable: towns had to act on their own initiative in financing their defenses, rebuilding or improving their town walls, arming their citizens, and hiring soldiers from outside. They had to guarantee and pay interest on their municipal debts—held, of course, by their own richer burghers, who had no wish to see their towns declare bankruptcy. In the Leaguer towns, some of the higher royal courts and tax bureaus tended to be lukewarm toward the rebellion. In Paris such men were jailed and replaced by enthusiastic Leaguers; but elsewhere town councils simply bypassed uncooperative fiscal bureaucrats and raised revenues on their own authority and with their own men.

Zealous Leaguers developed some new fiscal devices. They employed clerics to make door-to-door canvasses of all residents for contributions. Property belonging to Huguenots and suspected Politiques, which until 1585 had been protected by the crown, finally was seized and sold. In Paris the richer burghers who were known royalists were tossed into the Bastille and forced to pay ransom. In Lyons the consulat drew up its own budgets, increased the rates of its taxes when it had to, and even devised new taxes.[19] But the tax burden remained heavy on the faithful, too, which was the source of severe unrest especially among the poor artisans and peasants who found it difficult to understand why they were still called on to pay taxes.[20]

Municipal self-taxing was found outside of League areas, too. As early as the summer of 1587 the town magistrates of Bordeaux were

19. Doucet, Lyon, pp. 112–17.
20. Drouot, Mayenne, 1 : 125–27; Wilkinson, League, p. 25; Armstrong, Wars of Religion, p. 80.

appropriating and spending royal revenues for municipal purposes, pushing aside the royal tax collecting officials.[21] The Huguenot burghers of La Rochelle, though they adhered to the Huguenot-royalist alliance of 1588, continued to manage their own fiscal affairs and to spend local revenues on local needs. The royalist city of Compiègne, sandwiched between Leaguer districts, was forced to run its own fiscal machine; it had been provided with a bureau des finances and a mint by Henry III in the spring of 1589, as a sort of fiscal counterweight to rebellious Paris. Compiègne taxed not only the burghers of the city but also the peasants in surrounding villages. It provided for its own administration and defense, and it paid the troops of Charles de Humières, a captain operating out of Compiègne. During the crisis, Compiègne managed to increase the level of its revenues by relatively enormous amounts.[22]

The last category in this survey of fiscal decentralization comprises lands that the fortunes of war placed in the hands of petty war lords, who might or might not be entitled to call themselves governors. Some of them were important captains who asked only support for their troops from the districts in their control. This was the case with Villars-Brancas, who in the winter of 1591 withstood a siege of Rouen by Henry IV and Biron; for a while he was the effective ruler of eastern Normandy. Similarly, Lesdiguières, in his capacity as head of the Huguenot forces in Dauphiné, at times commanded that revenues be raised for him by provincial and municipal authorities. The duke of Aumale, who was governor of Amiens, used the town's finances to support his rule over Picardy and to facilitate the entry of Spanish troops from the Netherlands into northern France. On the other hand, the duke of Nemours, Henry of Savoy, obtained control over Lyons and its district in 1593 and ruled "as king rather than as governor"; his aim seems to have been either to annex as much of the Midi as possible to the duchy of Savoy or to carve his own principality out of these troubled lands.

The eccentric and fiercely ambitious duke of Savoy himself, Carlo Emmanuele I (who for a time after 1589 hoped the French Catholics would offer him the throne), ruled parts of Provence. He was formally recognized as the count of Provence by an Estates of the Catholic

21. Edict of Paris, July 11, 1587, in Fontanon, 2 : 683.
22. Baron de Bonnault d'Houët, *Compiègne pendant les Guerres de Religion et la Ligue*, pp. 76–77, 97, 218–19.

elements of that region (Aix, 1591). Some of the Provençal towns raised funds for Carlo Emmanuele's troops operating in the Midi. But the Provence city he wanted most, Marseilles, kept out of his grasp by playing Savoyards off against Spaniards while remaining, in effect, a self-governing commune.

These great and petty lords and communes, in addition to the great principalities, continued to levy their own revenues for years after Henry IV became king and even after he embraced Catholicism. This was especially the case in Provence, Brittany, and parts of Languedoc and Normandy. In Languedoc the hodge-podge of competing authorities milked the countryside so dry that toward the end of the war, some of the antagonists signed agreements with their enemies not to collect back taxes on territories recently captured—so as to avoid killing the geese laying golden eggs. In Normandy, La Barre recalled, between the king and the Leaguers on the one hand and the "Capitanneaux" and "tyranneaux" on the other some fifteen or sixteen surtaxes were levied on peasants in 1596 and 1597. The townsmen were taxed to raise a fortification; then they were taxed again to tear it down.

> Then after all their evildoing and destruction, in order to save themselves from harm [these petty captains and tyrants] struck a bargain by which the king took them under his protection, [and] acknowledged that all had been done in his service. You casuists judge by what sort of advice.[23]

One interesting trend in both these smaller areas and in the Guise-Leaguer provinces is that here we find a definite attempt to base taxing on popular consent. In general, after Henry of Navarre became the heir to the throne, League territories embraced radical political philosophies, while Huguenots, who had preached limited monarchy before 1584, now became thoroughly "absolutist" and even came close to the theory of divine right monarchy. This reversal in the arguments of publicists and magistrates was paralleled by actual fiscal institutions and procedures. In a half-dozen provinces between the Leaguer north and the Huguenot-Politique Midi, there was a fascinating revival of provincial and local Estates where none had operated since the fifteenth century—in Auvergne, Berry, the Limousin, Périgueux, and one or two smaller *pays*.

23. La Barre, *Formulaire*, p. 357.

All of them, in the few years they operated, participated in the taxing process, as did the even more important provincial Estates of the Nivernais. In the Huguenot lands, on the other hand, at least outside their pays d'états, while representative assemblies continued to operate, they had little to do with taxation. Henry IV saw to it that they restricted themselves to authorizing expenses for religious purposes only, that is, for their pastors and church organizations. In the south and west, outside of Leaguer districts, taxes were raised in the name of the king of France, not of the peoples' representatives. Ironically, then, while in most of the Leaguer districts the towns and Estates were experiencing their first real popular control over taxation since the beginning of the Renaissance, the Huguenot lands were now being taxed and administered more and more as they had been before the fiscal crisis.[24]

War lords and governors

At this point it is important to consider another factor in this already complex picture—the role of soldiers in the fiscal crisis. No military leader was foolish enough to believe that there was sufficient money in the treasury of his employer to pay the wages of both his men and himself when his troops were called up for service. The war chests of Francis I were now only an admired feature of a more affluent past. Captains of troops, both mercenary and regular, understood quite well that the machinery of the revenue system, aided by the mechanism for raising emergency loans from towns, would provide the bulk of their pay. When they had to, or when the temptation was strong, troops sold their services to another faction or supplemented their pay with plunder. But what they were promised, and what they usually sought, was pay out of funds raised by regular tax officials.[25]

The famous Renaissance aphorism, "no money, no Swiss," really meant, therefore, "no revenue-raising authority, no money, no Swiss."

24. Clamageran, *L'impôt*, 2 : 301.
25. A. Boulay de la Meurthe, "Histoire des Guerres de Religion à Loches et en Touraine," *Bulletin et Mémoires de la Société Archéologique de Touraine* 45 (1896) : 458, publishes a letter from Henry III to the trésoriers at Tours, reporting rumors of a plot to turn over the great fortress of Loches to the Leaguers; the king ordered the trésoriers to advance the Loches soldiers 200 écus toward their back pay "afin de ne laisser occasion à iceulx soldatz d'estre praticquez."

So long as the revenue-raising authority in France was firmly centralized in the hands of the king, the paid troops in the country, by and large, were the king's men. Beginning in the earlier Wars of Religion, however, German, English, and Spanish rulers, in addition to leaders of factions inside the country, paid for invasions of France by foreign mercenaries. And now that the Wars of Religion were splitting up the tax system among great nobles, faction leaders, and confederations, another Renaissance expression "money is the sinews of war," began to take on a new and sinister meaning. So long as the factions and the war lords retained their grip on pieces of the royal revenue system, they could raise more troops to fight another day. The fighting could not be pushed toward any lasting conclusion while so many war lords and grandees could depend on seizure of revenues to support their constant search for power and glory. The French revenue system, once a prime agency of centralized power and internal stability, was now an apparently inexhaustible sower of dragon's teeth.

For the minor war lords, the line between taxing and plundering was very thin. Some captains controlling important roads periodically waylaid merchants, appropriated their goods, and held the merchants for ransom; others preferred to sell safe conducts to them. These military leaders did not care if a town or village they had recently captured had already paid taxes to their enemies; the new masters forced the inhabitants to pay the same taxes again.[26]

Often when troops turned to plunder, it was not entirely their fault. Time after time, a campaign beginning with troops in fairly good order would end with the same men, or what was left of them, turning into a horde of armed bandits, devouring everything in their path. At the start of a campaign, after a period of peace, the revenue system would be functioning well enough for the employer of troops to advance at least a "down payment" for his soldiers. For a while, order was maintained; the troops were moved along main roads, and they bivouacked at safe distances from vulnerable towns. But provisions and supply lines were rarely adequate, and money to buy food and other necessities from civilians soon ran out. Then the troops were on their own and life became very hard for towns and villages in their line of march. Thus Bodin asks, in his *République*:

26. Wilkinson, *League*, pp. 24–29.

Who is a greater enemy to a man of peace than the violent soldier, to a worthy peasant than the bloody warrior, to a philosopher than the captain, to the wise than the fools? What the fighting man most enjoys is to devastate the countryside, rob peasants, burn villages, besiege, storm and sack cities, massacre good and evil alike, young and old of whatever sex or age, rape women, drench himself in blood of those murdered, defile sacred things, raze churches, blaspheme the name of God, and tread underfoot all rights human and divine. Such are the fruits of war, pleasing and agreeable to men of war, abominations to men of good will, and detestable to God." [27]

Today, as during the Renaissance, the impulse to loot is close to the surface among soldiers in enemy territory. Even the self-righteous Sully tells us, rather shamefacedly, that during the abortive attack by Royalist and Huguenot forces on Paris in 1589 the troops at one point fell to plundering the suburbs, and as his share Sully got two or three thousand écus.[28] But this gives only an incomplete picture. Soliders preferred to be paid and to pay for what they took. When a Leaguer general, Carcès, wrote the parlement at Aix for money for his troops, he pointed out that the soldiers had to be maintained somehow, and that, unlike some captains, "I never have fattened myself at the expense of the countryside." [29] Of course, soldiers did sometimes pillage for no other reasons than greed and brutality. It was more likely, however, for Renaissance soldiers to turn to pillage because they were furious at not having been paid for long periods, or because they were truly close to starving, so that plundering was at least partly for self-preservation.[30]

Johann Casimir, son of the elector of the Palatinate, the famous "Protestant condottiere," once made it clear that his troops were forced to turn to plunder as a last resort. He had brought them into France during the campaign of 1575 to serve under Condé and Alençon; and their pay (as well as their back pay) had been guaranteed by Henry III

27. Bodin, *République*, p. 755.
28. Sully, *Mémoires des sages et royales oeconomies d'estat* . . . , 1 : 74.
29. Wilkinson, *League*, p. 12.
30. On the attitudes of the age toward looting and booty, see Fritz Redlich, "De Praeda Militari," *Vierteljahrschrift für Sozial-und-Wirtschaftsgeschichte* 39 (1956).

as a condition of the "Peace of Monsieur." But then the king claimed that the money could not be found; and the surintendant des finances, Pomponne de Bellièvre, sent to negotiate with Casimir, could not persuade him to leave France without his due. Casimir's mercenaries settled themselves down in scores of French villages, appropriating what they wanted and behaving abominably. They gradually worked their way back through eastern France, leaving devastation behind them. When it became apparent that Pomponne de Bellièvre was not going to be able to persuade the king to disgorge the promised money, Casimir seized him and carried him back to Germany as a hostage.[31]

Johann Casimir and all other military commanders, when they could, used methods of raising funds from lands they dominated that were quite like the "extraordinary" tax measures of the crown. They exacted forced loans from towns and surtaxes on tailles from peasants. If town magistrates resisted, as they often did, they were forced to draw up a list of the wealthiest burghers, and the war lord simply set an arbitrary amount for each of them.[32] If the town's defenses were strong, of course, it could refuse and take its chances. Toward the end of 1574, German reîtres brought into the country by Henry of Guise settled down around Châlons, in Guise's own county of Champagne, and demanded a "loan" of 2,000 écus—which they claimed would be repaid promptly by the crown. But the magistrates insisted that before they would pay any money the mercenaries would have to be camped at least eight leagues away from the town walls. When the soldiers, instead, moved menacingly closer, the burghers shut their gates and armed their citizens.[33] One suspects, however, that the soldiers usually got their way. The Catholic town of St. Antoine in Dauphiné, for example, suffered periodic visits, sometimes several a month, from the nearby garrisons of Huguenot mercenary troops, who never left before they had forced one or two hundred écus out of the town consuls or the richer inhabitants.[34] Even the gendarmerie, the core of royal regular troops, sometimes raised taxes on their own authority. In a bitter remonstrance to the crown late in 1575, just before the first Estates-

31. Mariéjol, in Lavisse 6[1] : 171–72; Sutherland, Secretaries, p. 195.
32. Thompson, Biron, 1 : 159–60, 296.
33. Hérelle, Champagne, 2 : 82–83.
34. Dom H. Dijon, Le bourg et l'abbaye de Saint-Antoine pendant les Guerres de Religion et de la Ligue, pp. 161–66.

General of Blois, the Parisians complained that royal troops, in addition to rape and pillage, "deliver themselves over to such great license as to raise tailles in several provinces of this kingdom without your permission." [35]

When they could, towns tried to get the soldiers to accept settlement in installments. However, if a truce intervened, the towns would attempt to obtain cancellation of their "debts," at least those to enemy mercenaries, in the truce terms.[36] A menaced town might try to bribe a captain with a secret gift that would not have to be shared with his troops. Thus in 1586 Marshal Biron boasted that his son, camped around the town of Montmorillon (near Poitiers), had been offered a bribe of 600 écus and had refused.[37]

Of course for inhabitants of the *plat pays*—the villages and small towns with no walls to protect them—resistance to demands for money was out of the question. They had no alternative but to pay or flee when the "tax collectors" of armies in the vicinity descended on them. The open country was horribly vulnerable to the slow tide of desperate soldiery, and it hardly mattered whether the district being stripped happened to be in sympathy with the political or religious opinions of the leaders for whom the captains were supposed to be fighting. The crown issued several warnings to its governors and captains that animals and farm tools of the peasants could not be seized for nonpayment of tax levies; but such decrees could have meant little to hungry troops.[38] Particularly in Dauphiné or Brittany, troops would fasten on to a district of relatively isolated villages and settle down to living on what they could gouge out of the peasants. As late as 1596 there was still a great deal of ugly work to be done by Henry IV in prying these bands loose from the villages they dominated.[39]

In theory, if not in fact, the fiscal powers of a war lord depended in part on whether he was able to obtain as a base of operations a town or province he could rule as the rightfully appointed governor. In the latter stages of the Wars of Religion governorships were given out more

35. Mariéjol, in Lavisse 6[1] : 226.
36. Wilkinson, *League*, p. 41.
37. Thompson, *Biron*, 2 : 449.
38. Royal decl. of Blois, Oct. 8, 1571; and of Paris, March 16, 1595, in Isambert, 14 : 238–40, and 15 : 98–101.
39. Albert Chamberland, *Un plan de restauration financière en 1596*, pp. 14–16.

and more freely—and not only to grandees like the Montmorencies and
the Guises. In the Middle Ages and early Renaissance, governorships
had gone mainly to important nobles who undertook the defense and
military organization of key frontier provinces. Minor nobles who were
successful war lords often were given districts to govern, to repay them
for their services or to consolidate their loyalty. By a complicated process that remains poorly understood, in the later Renaissance *gouverneurs* began to be "governors" in the modern sense of the word—that
is, high dignitaries responsible for administrative, judicial, and economic
affairs in their *gouvernements*, as well as for soldiers and fortifications.
What is even more significant, the number of such posts and the
area they controlled increased; by 1560 all of France was covered by
gouvernements.[40] Early in the reign of Charles IX governorships were
created over certain key towns in addition to provinces. Although the
frontiers of such governorships were constantly shifting and hard to
define, they were becoming significant entities in Renaissance France;
this is shown by the fact that for the Estates-General of 1561 (at
Pontoise) the delegates were grouped by gouvernements rather than by
bailiwicks and *sénéchausées*, as before. Governors were now potentially
viceroys in their provinces, their actual power depending on their
family resources, their standing with the king, and their personal ability
in focusing local loyalties on themselves.[41] Also, the more important
governorships were becoming hereditary, in fact if not in law. Apparently this development, so dangerous from the point of view of monarchical centralization, had been accelerated by Henry II as a means of
bestowing valuable and honorific positions on his favorites. Perhaps it
can be viewed as a sort of "feudal reaction" paradoxically abetted by
kings who temperamentally sided with their fellow aristocrats and
sympathized with their drive for wealth and power; or perhaps the
kings saw in governorships a way of appeasing the grandees and turning
their attention away from the rising tide of royal power.

After the death of Henry II a governorship became the most impor-

40. Gaston Zeller, "Gouverneurs de provinces au XVIe siècle," *Revue Historique* 185 (1939) : 225–56.

41. The delicacy of the king's relations to the governors is suggested by the
fact that the four chief secretaries of state were given the task of liaison between
governors and king. Sutherland, *Secretaries,* pp. 30–33.

tant single prize in the complicated game of dynastic and religious factionalism in France. The Montmorencies in Languedoc and the Guises in Burgundy built up their family power through their role as governors to a point where even if the king happened to be desperately opposed to them he dared not relieve them of their posts. Less noble families, following the lead of these grandees, begged and schemed for other governorships over towns or smaller provinces which might or might not have any connection with their family fiefs. Thus lords of Nevers managed to get themselves named governors of that province; but they also controlled several others in the name of the king. Henry III made his *mignons* presents of governorships in wholesale lots; thus d'Epernon was governor of Metz, Toul, Verdun, the Boulonnais, Aunis, Saintonge, Touraine, Anjou, Provence, and Normandy, as well as of his family fiefs (the Angoumois and Foix).

The rising power of governors, therefore (though it was a phenomenon to some extent prior to and independent of the Wars of Religion), accentuated the collapse of centralized tax collection in this era. We know that even before 1562 the crown found it necessary to warn governors to permit royal tax collectors to operate unhindered and to raise no taxes without royal authority. But as soon as the fighting broke out governors moved quickly to replace royal tax officials with their own men. In the larger districts, governors seized control of the bureaux des finances, established their own Chambres des comptes and Cours des aides, and negotiated with provincial Estates for higher tax rates and special *dons*.

A fascinating glimpse of the fiscal powers of a man who was both a war lord and (at times) a governor is found in the published correspondence of Armand de Gontaut, Marshal Biron.[42] Biron was a greedy and unscrupulous would-be princeling, and one of the most highly regarded captains of his day. After the Peace of Monsieur (1576) his principal mission was to contain Henry of Navarre in the southwest corner of France, which meant in effect keeping Navarre from taking over Guyenne. Biron, like many governors of the period, attempted to turn his base of operations (the district from Bordeaux to Agen) into

42. Biron played a part in a chilling "might-have-been"; at the siege of Epernay (July 1592), when he was riding almost shoulder to shoulder with Henry IV, Biron's head was blown off by a cannon ball.

his own province. When he was in complete control of this district he used the entire apparatus of the fiscal administration. For example, in Bordeaux and Agen he levied his own taxes; he decided whether his peasants could support a surtax on the tailles; he ordered merchants of Bordeaux and other towns to loan him funds; and he disposed of collected revenues as he saw fit, paying little attention to remonstrances that came to him from the king or the royal council.[43] On one occasion he even ordered a forced loan raised from foreign (Spanish and Portuguese) merchants in Bordeaux. Of course he claimed the authority over taxes and their "acceleration" had been given him by the king; but his correspondence shows that the king at times was furious at the way Biron used the royal tax system for his own purposes.

When he was not in control of a district, Biron had to supplement the meager amounts of money doled out to him by royal treasurers with what he could raise himself. His letters about money written under these circumstances are full of interest. They show it was Biron, and not the distant king, who was held accountable by his troops for their food and their wages. Time and again he complained of having to face the "crierie" of the Swiss and other mercenaries. His letters detail the indignities he had to suffer to prevent his troops from drifting away because they had not been paid.[44] When necessary, Biron ordered his clerks to present local towns with états listing demands for food, wine, hay, and cloth. He also forced towns in the vicinity of his troops to sell communal property (or to levy a town octroi) to meet his cash demands. Once he authorized the imposition of a taille on a town, claiming that the town had not paid tailles for the previous two years.[45] When he was hard pressed he traveled to financial centers (including Amsterdam) in order to arrange for loans with bankers. When everything else failed he even drew on his personal resources, pledging his own property, down to "my cup from which I drink." Even so, there were occasions when Biron had to disband his troops without paying them. This was a ticklish operation; when he managed it successfully— that is, without having his troops go on a rampage—he boasted of it.[46]

43. Thompson, *Biron*, 1 : 135–61; 2 : 420, 428.
44. Ibid., 1 : 267, 307; 2 : 483–91.
45. Ibid., 2 : 479–80.
46. Ibid., 1 : 205, 263, 273–76, 301, 336; 2 : 420–21.

As long as the revenue system continued to supply the means for keeping Biron in the saddle, he could hardly be expected to use his high position to work for peace. In 1591 Biron is supposed to have kept his son from ending a battle too victoriously, saying that it was not his intention to go back to planting cabbages on the family farms. For such men the periods between fighting were only breathing spaces, or rather periods in which the economy was allowed to function relatively unmolested while the revenue system filled up to the point where it could once again support cash advances from merchants and tax officials—in other words, until the fiscal sponge could be squeezed again.

Seizure of the mints

Symbolically, if not financially, the most important cases of appropriation of royal revenues came when towns, war lords, grandees, or Huguenot assemblies seized that precious attribute of sovereignty, the right to strike coins. Protestant strongholds had dared to coin money as early as 1563, especially when their towns had been under siege; for the most part, however, they continued to use royal portraits and legends. In the 1570s there were a half-dozen important mints and several minor ones striking coins under Huguenot authority and for the profit of Huguenot treasuries. Others coined money under the authority of Montmorency-Damville.[47] Some of these coins, especially the lower denominations, were seriously debased compared to royal coins and were therefore a source of considerable profit to the coining authorities.[48] When Henry of Navarre became Henry IV, of course, all the Protestant mints became royal mints.

Almost every city with a mint in the control of the League after 1588 continued to strike coins for the rebellious towns and grandees. These included some of the most important mints in the kingdom, such as Paris, Rouen, Lyons, Dijon, Troyes, Amiens, Bourges, Aix, and Toulouse. At Toulouse great masses of coins were struck, thereby providing an important source of revenue for League supporters in the

47. See the ord. of Paris, Nov. 15, 1585, ordering coinage in Montpellier to stop.
48. A. Blanchet and A. Dieudonné, *Manuel de numismatique française*, 2 : 171, 174.

Midi.[49] Perhaps nothing else demonstrates the breakdown of the central government as much as this rebel coinage. But from a symbolic point of view the rebels might have gone much further. When one looks at these coins, struck for so many towns, provinces, and factions—apparently engaged in wars of extermination against each other—one fact stands out: they still look like royal coins. There is only one noteworthy exception: besieged Orléans in 1562–63 struck a few écus and some testons with a portrait of Condé. All the other coins bear legends similar to those minted before 1562; the effigy of a king of France is still on the obverse; and (except for the more debased varieties) they circulated at well-established national rates. There seems to have been little demand to use the propaganda opportunity coinage presented in order to appeal to provincial or feudal loyalties. True separatist feeling in France, it seems, had not developed far enough to be reflected in its coinage.

However, no less than fourteen League towns struck coins to signalize their support for a rival king. These coins appeared with the legends and effigy of "Charles X," many of them even after this unfortunate figurehead died (May 1590).[50] The mint of Mercoeur in Brittany, in fact, struck "Charles X" coins until 1598.[51] Other Guise-League mints continued to use the bust and legend of the long-dead Henry III rather than recognizing the heretic Béarnais who now pretended to the title of Henry IV.

This confusing situation was further confounded by the establishment of additional mints in areas under dispute. When Mercoeur lost the Breton mint at Rennes, for example, he created another at Dinan. Henry IV struck "royalist" coins at St. Jean de Losne in Burgundy to compete with Dijon, at Compiègne and Melun in the Ile de France to compete with Paris, and at several other enclaves of his in Guise-League territories.[52] In 1594, after Henry's conversion and the surrender of Paris, a great number of rebel mints went over to the king. But it was not until 1598 that the coinage of France was once again controlled by a single authority.

49. J. Bailhache, "La monnaie de Toulouse pendant la Ligue, 1589–1596," *Revue Numismatique*, 4th ser. 35 (1932) : 199–230.
50. Lafaurie and Prieur, *Les monnaies*, 126–30.
51. Blanchet and Dieudonné, *Numismatique*, 2 : 138.
52. See the excellent map in Lafaurie and Prieur, *Les monnaies*, p. 123.

In spite of the turmoil of war, civil strife, and the terrible dislocation of the economy, the total volume of coinage continued at a high level after 1588; in the case of some mints it was even higher than 1578, the peak year for France as a whole. Paris, for example, struck 675,000 livres in coins in 1578, but turned out 1.2 millions in 1590 and about the same amount in 1591.[53] Meanwhile, many mints, some of which had not been in use before 1588, were busy striking coins for political and military purposes, rather than for the needs of the business community. An increased flow of debased coins entered on the scene (speeding up the operation of "Gresham's Law"), making it difficult for merchants to find adequate supplies of large silver and gold coins to pay their debts. This in turn made it necessary for mints everywhere to turn out larger amounts of small coins, which aggravated the vicious circle of debasement. Thus in 1590, when Lyons found its silver vanishing, driven out by the heavily debased *gros de nesle* struck in Le Puy and Trévoux, the consulat of the city decided that since their merchants had to use such coins anyway the profit of striking them might as well go to the Lyons mint.[54]

WHAT WERE THE CROWN'S TOTAL REVENUES DURING THE LATER WARS?

The fiscal records of France for most of the Renaissance, sketchy and imprecise though they may be, at least indicate the magnitude and the trend of royal revenues. But what of the era when centralized taxation was collapsing? Of what use is the concept "total crown revenues" these hectic years when France was so divided? Modern treatments of this subject are perplexing. On the one hand, we are told that revenues soared from about 14 or 15 million livres in 1575 to 30 millions in 1581, and that they remained at this high level in the 1580s and 1590s; on the other hand, we read of one province after another cutting itself away from the royal tax structure. In spite of this anomaly, general histories continue to state that the king's revenues doubled.[55]

53. Spooner, *L'économie mondiale*, esp. pp. 393–94.
54. Doucet, *Lyon*, pp. 122–23.
55. Fernand Braudel, *La Méditerranée et le monde méditerranéen à l'époque de Philippe II*, rev. ed. (Paris, 1966), for example, contains a chart (p. 31) showing that the "budget" of France virtually doubled during the reign of Henry III, both in livres tournois and in the gold value of these revenues.

As in so many aspects of Renaissance tax history, the picture of the volume of royal revenues during the years 1574–98 depends on the work of J.-J. Clamageran written one hundred years ago. Clamageran found that the range of royal revenues was from 10 to 13 million livres in the 1560s and early 1570s; they then rose to 14.3 million livres in 1575, and to 15 or 16 millions in 1576.[56] While he has no summary figure for any single year from 1577 to 1587, Clamageran gives a good deal of information on individual tax rates and partial revenues over this period. He believes there was "an almost unprecedented upward march" in revenues and that the level for 1588 (about 28 millions) was reached around 1580 and maintained from 1580 to 1588.[57] He shows, for example, that direct taxes (tailles, taillon, and the "subventions" on walled towns) more than doubled—from some 8 million livres in 1576 to about 18 millions in 1588.[58]

The concept "total crown revenues" seems even more deceptive for the years 1589–94—that is, until Paris was won by Henry IV—since obviously so much of the country was paying the new king nothing. Clamageran reports that Henry IV reduced the burden of the tailles and other direct taxes from a level of about 17.5 millions to about 11.8 millions in 1593, with comparable reductions for aides and gabelles,

56. Clamageran, *L'impôt*, 2 : 197–98. For 1567, the état au vrai studied by Roger Doucet indicates that there were 10.2 million livres in "normal" receipts, that is, not including loans and windfalls. The "estat abrégé" for 1574, transcribed by Dur, "Constitutional Rights," pp. 217 ff.—which from its careful detail appears to be an état au vrai—shows a global total of 11.1 million livres.

57. The total for 1588 given by Clamageran, *L'impôt*, 2 : 244, as 27.9 million francs is really three times the given figure of 9.3 million écus: see the états for 1588 transcribed in Dur, "Constitutional Rights," appendix 6, esp. p. 305. Rolland du Plessis, in his 1588 *Remonstrances*, p. 43, accepts the figure of 10.5 million écus, or 31.5 million livres. Both Pierre de l'Estoile, *Registre-Journal*, vol. 1, part 1, p. 205, and Scipion de Gramont, *Le denier royal*, pp. 269–77, accept 30 million livres as the level of revenues under Henry III after 1580. Clamageran, *L'impôt*, 2 : 227, also suggests that the level of 30 millions was maintained for the years 1594–98. However, see Dur, "Constitutional Rights," p. 261, where an obviously retrospective budget gives total receipts for "around 1580" as 14.5 million livres. And see the provisional budget in B.N. Fonds fr. 6413, fols. 116–22, dated Dec. 10, 1584, at St. Germain-en-Laye; the total of revenues is 3.9 million écus, or only 11.6 million livres. This budget does not seem to have been studied by Clamageran or others.

58. For direct taxes, see Clamageran, *L'impôt*, 2 : 198, 230. Clamageran shows that excises and salt taxes almost tripled over the same period.

suggesting total revenues of about 22 millions for that year.[59] But everything we know about the desperate state of Henry's IV's affairs makes
it difficult to accept the notion that he was able to control such a huge
amount of cash at that time.[60]

The estimates of Clamageran for the reign of Henry III and the early
years of Henry IV are based on his use of a large number of documents
giving summary as well as detailed and partial accounts of royal
finances.[61] Perhaps his use of these documents explains why, in the past
one hundred years, his estimates have been questioned only in minor
details.[62] But when one looks at the documents themselves it becomes
obvious that the figures they afford may in some instances be more
misleading than enlightening. In the first place, most of these documents were drawn up, not in the years to which they apply, but sometimes many years later.[63] In other words, they are retrospective documents, not records generated by the normal workings of the fiscal
machine. They owed their existence to a special purpose—often the

59. Clamageran, *L'impôt*, 2 : 284–85.
60. Forbonnais, *Recherches et considérations*, 1 : 28–29, also accepts revenues
for 1596 as about 23 million livres. But see the "Abrégé de la Valleur des finances," B.N. Fonds fr. 6413, fols. 158–62, which compares income and expense
for 1588 with those for 1593 (fols. 158[r], 159[r]–162[v]) and gives a total of 3.4 million écus, or 10.3 million livres, for 1593 (fol. 161[r]).
61. See Clamageran, *L'impôt*, notes for vol. 2, book 2, chaps. 2–5, esp. p. 189
n. 1.
62. Clamageran's estimates are enshrined in J. H. Mariéjol's classic volumes
on this era in the Lavisse series, and reenshrined recently in two excellent and
widely used manuals: Lapeyre, *Les monarchies européennes*, p. 307, and Livet,
Les Guerres de Religion, p. 81. Clamageran's summary figures, while suspect as
to specific values for each year, are still the best we have for indications of long
range trend. The following total "normal" revenues (in millions of livres)—
without "outside" loans and some of the fiscal expedients—are taken, unless
otherwise indicated, from *L'impôt*, 1 : xxiv.

1453	2.5	1546	9.0 [a]	1588	27.9 [d]
1482	4.5	1547–49	13.6 [b]	1596	28.0 [e]
1523	5.6	1576	15.0 [c]	1607	27.7

[a] *L'impôt*, 2 : 130–31. [b] Average for these years. [c] *L'impôt*, 2 : 197–98. [d] *L'impôt*, 2 : 244; but see 1 : xxiv,
where the figure given is 22.0. [e] *L'impôt*, 2 : 285.

63. In a few cases this is obvious; thus B.N. Fonds fr. 6413, fols. 158[r]–162[v] is
entitled "1588. Abrégé de la Valleur des finances dont le feu Roy faisoit estat en
Lannée 1588 . . ."; but at the end of the document the date 1593 appears.

need of Henry IV to know (while he was struggling to establish himself) what had been the legal burden of taxes in the past, so as to discover what he could impose. Henry IV also needed to know where imposts had been levied but not collected during the previous régime, since the amounts past due constituted debts to the new king.[64] Until 1594 Chambre des comptes records were not available to the new king. Some documents appear to have been drawn up by members of the Conseil des finances to justify themselves against Sully; others were drawn up apparently on Sully's orders.[65] This, of course, does not mean that these materials necessarily are unreliable; there is a chance they might all accurately duplicate or abstract the original états. But until this is proven, they cannot have the same authority as, for example, the documents for the clearly authentic budgets of 1523 and 1567 studied by Roger Doucet. One of the reasons some of them were preserved, in fact, is that they were in the private papers of some royal advisor and so escaped the disastrous Chambre des comptes fire of 1737.

There are other problems involving these documents. Some of them, especially those of the late 1580s and early 1590s, are only summaries and do not show both income and expenses; therefore it is difficult to know whether the totals given are gross or net.[66] At times it is difficult to ascertain whether listed figures are meant to be livres tournois or écus.[67] Some of the accounts purporting to be *états des finances* are so brief that important categories of revenues seem to have been forgotten, if not deliberately omitted.

64. See, e.g., B.N. Fonds fr. 15893, fols. 345ʳ–350ᵛ, a letter from Bellièvre to Henry IV in 1595 on unpaid clerical imposts for the years 1586, 1587, and 1588.

65. Some of these papers, collected by Bellièvre, seem to be in his own hand, e.g., B.N. Fonds fr. 15893, fol. 393ᵛ. Bellièvre was chancellor, 1599–1605, and would have had charge of such papers. After 1596, Sully ordered extracts made from Chambre des comptes records in order to check on some trésoriers whom he (often unfairly) accused of corruption. See his *Oeconomies*, 1 : 224, 228–30, and 290–94; see also David Buisseret, *Sully and the Growth of Centralized Government in France, 1598–1610*, pp. 43–44, 63–64.

66. The highly interesting document, B.N. Fonds fr. 6413, fols. 112–13, for example, dated St. Germain-en-Laye, Dec. 10, 1584 (one of the several in this group signed by the king and Brûlart), and entitled "Abrégé des Recept et despence à faire durant lannée prochaine 1585 suyvant lestat qui en a estre faict et resolu par le Roy," has, in spite of its title, only one summary figure for income; the état is, rather, an estimate of anticipated expenses.

67. "Ecus" usually appears as a small *w* with a line across the top, confusingly like a scribbled *lt*, since the bar for the *t* goes across the *l*. Forbonnais, who gives

But the most baffling problem is that for the most part these documents gloss over the chief reality of the Wars of Religion: they list,
as usual, revenues from each and every généralité, as though none of
the provinces were in rebellion. A scholar would be able to search
through a dozen of these accounts and find little evidence of what
are known to be the political-fiscal realities.[68] All of the provinces
appear in the documents as usual, with figures for income from the
main categories of taxes, including the domaines, estimates for special
levies and clerical imposts, together with the expenses and deductions
imputed to each district.

Modern scholars, of course, want to know what funds were actually
available to the king, rather than those officially available. It would be
out of the question, however, to attempt estimating a more realistic
figure by simply eliminating returns for an entire province in a year
when the province was known to be in rebellion. In the first place,
fiscal years and the duration of rebellions hardly coincided. In the
second place, certain towns and districts, even in provinces in revolt,
continued to be controlled by royalists and thus paid taxes to the king's
agents. Even in the Huguenot-Politique "state within a state," some
towns, or entire districts for some years, paid taxes to the crown. La
Rochelle, for example, paid the king some taxes in 1573; that is, until
fighting broke out again in 1574.[69] As late as 1583 in Brittany, and
possibly even to 1585 in Burgundy, these provinces were making partial
payments to the crown.[70]

The king enjoyed fairly good control over most of the country by

---

the summary for the budget of 1581 (*Recherches et considérations*, 1 : 15) as
11.5 million livres, was mistaken; the figure is for écus (actually, the corrected
figure is 10.5 million écus). See Albert Chamberland, "Les recettes de l'Epargne
en 1581 et une erreur de Forbonnais," *Revue Henri IV* 3, no. 1 (1909): 102–07.

68. An exception is the account for 1588, B.N. Fonds fr. 6413, fol. 156ʳ, probably done (or copied) in 1593; after listing all the free and clear revenues, it
stipulates that "from this one must deduct the nonpayments [*nonvalleurs*] for the
occupied lands and for the impoverishment of the people."

69. Thompson, *Biron*, 1 : xxii.

70. Zeller, *Institutions*, p. 63; Drouot, *Mayenne*, 2 : 39–45. However, B.N.
Fonds fr. 6413, fol. 105, dated St. Germain-en-Laye, Dec. 10, 1584—which is
an "Estat des deniers que le Roy veult estre Recuz par le Trésorier de lordinaire
de la Guerre en chacune des Receptes . . . ," signed personally by the king and
by his secretary Brûlart—does not list the bureaux dominated by the Guises, that
is, Amiens, Soissons, Châlons, Nantes, and Dijon; Lyons and Riom are not
mentioned either.

1597; thus it is easier to believe evidence concerning that year (and subsequent years) which suggests very high total crown revenues. At this
time, Sully and the former high advisors were jostling each other for
precedence; one way of asserting their superiority was to project schemes
for setting the treasury on its feet. Pierre Forget de Fresne, a secretary
of state and one of the most knowledgeable of Sully's rivals, advanced
a plan for financial reform.[71] To this plan was appended a survey of
the kingdom's revenues. The survey estimates that about 7.8 million
écus, or 23.4 million livres, were available from all established forms
of taxation, and a surtax of 2.5 million écus could be supported,
amounting to revenues of some 10.3 million écus or 31 million livres—
which he expected to result in a very large deficit. And there is other
evidence suggesting that national revenues of the king were near 30
millions by 1597.[72] While some doubts remain concerning details of
the royal budgets after peace was achieved, it is fairly certain that
revenues were reduced by substantial amounts between 1598 and 1604,
and that they rose again during the years 1605–10—but probably not
beyond the heights of 1596–97.[73]

Given the erosion of centralized taxing during the later 1570s and
1580s, it is difficult to see how the king could have brought about
any increases in his tax revenues. But there are signs that apparently
well-informed contemporaries of the king indeed believed this was
happening.[74] The writings of the period contain many bitter comments
on the more lurid examples of Henry III's spendthrift ways, such as
his gift of 1.2 million écus to one of his favorites when this man performed the service of marrying the queen's sister.[75] Where did the

71. This plan is reprinted in Chamberland, Restauration financière. Devèze,
Forêt française, 2 : 217–18, accepts Forget de Fresne's estimates for forest revenues.

72. Chamberland, "Le budget de 1597, exposé du projet de l'Assemblée de
Rouen," Revue Henri IV, 2d ed., 1 (1912).

73. Buisseret, Sully, chapter 4. See esp. Buisseret's remarks concerning double
counting in these budgets.

74. Dur, "Constitutional Rights," pp. 318–22, transcribes B.N. Fonds fr.
6413, fols. 71–72, which purports to give all the revenue increases from 1576
to 1581. This document's complaining tone and other features suggest it is the
work of an outsider. See also Chamberland, Recherches critiques sur les réformes
financières en Champagne à l'époque de Henri IV et de Sully, pp. 8–9.

75. Pierre de l'Estoile, Registre-Journal, vol. 1, part 1, p. 137. This was in
Sept. 1581. In the even more critical year of 1586, Henry authorized his agents

money come from? A partial explanation for the paradox of collapsing taxation and unprecedented largesse, of course, is that Henry III borrowed from everybody possible, foreigners as well as his own subjects.[76] Catherine de Medici was still able to raise some loans in Italy, though at increasingly onerous rates; [77] and of course the king did exploit the usual expedients in order to fill the gap. In addition, the larger cities staggered under an increasing burden of forced loans. In the published edicts of the year 1581 alone there are no less than thirteen edicts creating special offices for the entire realm, in addition to innumerable special purpose offices for particular areas. The budget for 1581, if we can believe it, shows that the government expected to realize the huge sum of 3.5 million écus from the sale of venal offices, or about one-third the entire income for the year.[78] Other bitterly resented expedients included forcing additional masterships on the guilds, pressuring some cities to turn local revenues over to the crown, and creating dozens of new tolls and octrois. Even the fees and perquisites (*épices*) of judges were taxed, as were dowries, lawsuits, dice, playing cards, and much more.[79] In his harangue before the Estates-General in 1588, Rolland du Plessis stormed at the king for stooping so low as to place tribute on "infant baptisms and marriages, and even on those who empty their bladders in the streets and throw their wastes out of their houses; [and] on usurers, pimps, whores, brothels, and tolerated Jews; and for the pinnacle of such action, we even have [taxes] on [sacred] relics and sepulchres." [80]

We are left with many interesting questions. Did the level of total crown revenues actually double from 1576 to 1581, or are the accounts which seem to show this merely spurious figures produced much

to spend 100,000 écus on rare lap dogs and other little dogs, an intermittent passion of his.

76. Alfred Joubert, *La rente et l'impôt. Leur origine—leur histoire*, 2d ed. (Paris, 1893), pp. 139–40.

77. Eletta Palandri, *Les négotiations politiques et religieuses entre la Toscane et la France* . . . (Brussels, 1908), pp. 107–09, 223. Catherine stalled shamelessly on repaying these loans, hoping her creditors would write them off as a subsidy in the common cause against heresy.

78. That is, one-third the corrected figure of 10.5 million écus.

79. These seem petty; but the tax farm on playing and tarot cards went for better than 50,000 livres annually. Doucet, *Lyon*, pp. 107–08.

80. Rolland du Plessis, *Remonstrances*, pp. 93–96.

later by Henry IV's government in order to justify its own tax rates? Is it possible that in some years, such as 1581 and 1588, the budget actually was set at around 30 million livres, but that in other years (for which we have no figures) the budget was dramatically lower, so that the concept of a "level of revenues" is itself misleading? Did Henry III double the burden on loyal provinces in order to make up for losses from the break-away provinces? Was the purported increase in revenues from 1576 to 1581 the result of the need to raise huge funds for Alençon's Netherlands campaigns? Or was the government goaded into raising its revenues because of the "price revolution"—that is, because of the decline in the purchasing power of its revenues? Did the deputies at the 1588 Estates-General accept the figure of 30 millions because this is what the records revealed or because they wanted to exaggerate the country's need for tax relief? Did the disaffected provinces take advantage of the announced higher rates of specific royal taxes to increase their own collections, so that the country as a whole did pay the huge amounts reported in these documents? We cannot say. La Barre, writing in 1622 but referring to the 1590s, says, "Even as more revenues were being raised, the king had less of them." [81] In the present state of our knowledge, this sentence may sum up the situation as well as anyone can.

While the problem of the true level and trend of royal revenues during these years is awesome in its complexity, it is worthy of attention. "Total crown revenues," if we but knew them, would illuminate more than fiscal history. The existing accounts of the era show a country where the nobility were being driven to sell their ancestral lands, where the bourgeoisie were being ruined by depredations against commerce and industry, and where the peasantry looked like troops of starved scarecrows. How could such a land double its revenues for the king— in addition to paying illegal and unreported revenues to war lords? Should we not, therefore, abandon the concept that revenues doubled between 1576 and 1581 and remained at this very high level thereafter? On the other hand, if the country truly was able to support such a huge fiscal burden, have we exaggerated the seriousness of the economic setback caused by the wars?

81. Formulaire, p. 358.

There is one point on which we can all agree. From 1588 to 1594 the fiscal system lay smashed in pieces, some large, some tiny; some still generated large revenues, others were almost valueless. But, once certain conditions were met, the nature of these shards was such that they could be put together easily. And, once together, they could provide the basis for reconstructing a powerful monarchy.

8

The Restoration
of Royal Taxing

The revenues still not recovered

So long as the revenues of France remained available to feudal lords, town councils, and war lords, the proper question to ask, it seems, is not why the Wars of Religion went on as long as they did, but rather how they ever could have ended. France was caught in a deadly equilibrium of fighting and revenues. No matter how desperate the financial plight of any grandee or faction, no matter how many battles lost or armies dispersed, it was still too simple to raise more troops (from inside or outside the country) with a promise of pay or a license to loot. The situation could not be resolved by battle, but only by a changed relationship between the king and chief nobles opposing him, a relationship that would again centralize control over the French revenue system.

Henry of Navarre showed that he could win battles; but by 1593 he was no closer to crushing his enemies than in 1588, when Henry III first openly accepted him as successor to the throne. Hauser says that at first Henry IV was "only king of his armies." [1] In reality, however, these armies had a disconcerting tendency to drift away when most needed. The fundament of Henry IV's power, aside from his "Salic Law" claims, was his right to obtain cash from the royal revenues.

The fighting and the disaffection, the crumbling of central authority, the maneuvers of local and general Estates—none of these changed the fact that the only authority in France with a valid claim over the national revenues was the duly annointed king. Once the crown was firmly on Henry's head—that is, once the main religious objection to

1. Henri Hauser, *La prépondérance espagnole*, 1559–1660, 3d ed. (Paris, 1948), p. 151.

his rule had been removed—the fiscal potential for maintaining that crown was assured. It is significant that even the most radical pamphleteers never claimed that the revenue system of France should be broken up; they only asked that the system be reformed by lightening the burden of the taxes, giving provincial and general Estates some authority in fiscal matters, and freeing the country from foreign bloodsuckers.

As late as 1596, perhaps one-fifth of French tax revenues were still being diverted into purses other than the king's.[2] It was not only the die-hards among the Leaguer towns and Guise supporters that gave the king trouble on this score. There is a curious episode in 1595, at the time of the siege of La Fère by Henry IV's armies, that shows some revenues still being appropriated by Protestants. At this time the Huguenots among Henry's captains were urging him to make a public pronouncement that all offices in France would be open to Protestants as well as Catholics; when they did not get a satisfactory answer, they abandoned the siege, retreated to Huguenot strongholds, and seized the royal treasuries there to pay their troops.[3]

Between 1589 and 1594, while Henry IV still believed that without deserting Calvinism he could take Paris and reduce all the rest of France by force, royal finances were in a desperate situation. The king was forced to use expedients that made those of Henry II and Henry III appear mild in comparison. These devices were authorized by edicts that still convey their emergency atmosphere to us, since they were proclaimed from military headquarters during various campaigns rather than from cities or from royal chateaux: "au camp du Provins," "au camp devant Rouen," and so on. The king issued the sternest warnings to rebels not to misappropriate royal revenues; but few, it seems, took these threats seriously. Offices were created and sold by the hundreds, some for posts in rebel lands. Domaines revenues and lands were sold at ridiculously low prices, including those over which the crown had little or no control. In royalist towns the king begged money from everyone; at the same time he raised the rates of tailles and gabelles (the easiest taxes to collect) to new heights. He also created two additional masterships for all incorporated guilds (*maîtrises jurées*) in

2. Clamageran, *L'impôt*, 2 : 284.
3. Mariéjol, in Lavisse 6[1] : 416–17.

every town.[4] To calm his new creditors, the king assured the crown's old creditors that he would pay off the debts of Henry III—that is, those held in towns that came over to his side.[5]

When the king's captains took over a rebel district they taxed it unmercifully. His agents furnished the royalist troops with lists of which taxes were due and past due in all areas, with no regard for questions of whether such districts had been paying taxes to other authorities. But even in Henry IV's own lands of west France, taxes were raised so cruelly that in 1593 there was a rash of peasant uprisings against them. The main vehicle for increasing tax revenues in central France seems to have been the gabelles; the salt taxes in the *grandes gabelles* lands, which had been raised to 150 livres per *muid* by Henry III, were more than doubled by Henry IV.[6]

For some months, the new king was able to obtain the services of Swiss troops without pay. Some timely emergency funds were sent to him by Elizabeth I of England and by the city of Venice. But soon the good will of his foreign allies and his mercenary captains ran out; as a result the king could not keep his forces together. Henry tried to maintain his armies by sending fiscal officials to expedite raising funds from the lands they occupied; but these commissaires seemed to have accomplished little. Biron had to threaten the king with the prospect of all his mercenaries going over to the other side, especially now that the enemy was holding out "a bridge of gold." [7]

"Dîtes plutôt vendu"

It was a great relief for Catholics in many parts of France when Paris surrendered rather easily to the king (March 1594) after his conversion. Henry IV displayed his now famous magnanimity to the city that had rejected him for so long. The burghers of Paris were granted a sweeping pardon for "seizures of funds from the receptes générales, décimes, gabelles, and sales of salt, taxes placed upon the same, and all other taxes and levies of funds, as much in the said city as in the environs,

4. Edict "Au camp d'Alençon," Dec. 1589.
5. Royal decl. "Au camp de Rouen," Dec. 12, 1591, in Isambert, 15 : 34–36. This had to be pushed through the Chambre des comptes with *lettres de jussion*.
6. Clamageran, *L'impôt*, 2 : 284–85.
7. Thompson, *Biron*, 2 : 479–92.

[plus] traites and *impositions foraines* placed on commodities and merchandise. . . ." [8] Frenchmen of all faiths and politics already had developed an admiration for Henry's dashing military leadership and his chivalrous treatment of defeated enemies. In Burgundy, Champagne, and Picardy (areas until now solidly in rebellion), several cities threw open their gates to royal captains; some even overthrew the local Guisard garrison in order to be able to declare for the king. Thus the burghers of Troyes forced out the prince of Joinville, a member of the Guise family and governor of that city. The grudging acceptance by Pope Clement VII (September 1594) of the validity of Henry's conversion seemed to settle the matter, so far as the great mass of Frenchmen were concerned.

Henry IV wisely decided not to use his improving position to attack the Guisard chiefs still in rebellion. The Guises and their followers had never been able to turn up an effective national leader. Henry IV was quick to let them know that it would be much more profitable to make a deal with the king than to maintain resistance in the name of a fading cause. They were now ready to consider terms. In 1596, the king stated that God had given the royalists military victories; but He also had given them "the wherewithal to conquer through peaceful means [i.e. money] those who render themselves worthy of this." [9]

The nature of these settlements is interesting. One after another, rebelling chiefs allowed themselves to be bought out with gifts, pensions, transfers of their debts to the crown, and promises of lucrative offices. In return, the grandees and war lords allowed their territories to come back under royal authority, which meant, of course, that their local revenues once again became part of the royal revenue system—even though, for a few years at least, their main function was to pay off the king's obligations to their recent masters.

A famous bon mot of Henry IV highlights the mechanism by which the worst crisis in the Wars of Religion was liquidated. After one of the last important die-hards accepted surrender terms, the king was complimented in a speech in which he was told his subjects had finally "rendered (*rendu*) unto Caesar the things which are Caesar's." Henry IV, the best phrase-monger ever to sit on the French throne, was equal

8. Edict on the subjugation of Paris, March 1594, in Isambert, 15 : 76–85.
9. Preamble to the edict of Folembray, Jan. 1596.

to the occasion. "Don't say they have rendered [*rendu*] it to me!" he exclaimed. "Say rather that they have sold [*vendu*] it!" [10]

A few important Catholic nobles had rallied to Henry IV even before his conversion. Of course, it was more than money alone that brought the new king this following. Henry's tremendous appeal as a brave and eloquent leader certainly had much to do with his success. When Henry IV wrote to Marshal Biron in 1589 to solicit his support, he stated that he was "a king without a kingdom, a husband without a wife, a warrior without money." [11] But it is unlikely that a tough and selfish old soldier such as Biron would have been moved by such eloquence alone. Certainly Biron was more convinced by the pledge of a desirable governorship and a substantial pension—and by the conviction that the king had the authority and the means to make that pledge good in the near future, if not immediately.

Another factor that caused some Guisard chiefs to surrender, especially after Henry's conversion, was simple patriotism; they feared that Philip II's motive in supporting the Catholic League with Spanish troops was to capture the French throne for his own family. But whatever the motives, a substantial financial settlement accompanied the rebel chiefs' surrender to the king. The size of the payments and pledges of pensions involved seems to have been determined by the importance of the territory to be surrendered and the magnitude of the debts incurred by these chiefs during the wars. The governor of Orléans received 250,000 écus for opening the gates of his city. Villars-Brancas, the Guise chief who delivered Rouen and several other northern towns, is supposed to have received 715,000 écus and the office of admiral of France.[12] Even more princely settlements were bestowed on the duke of Aumale, in Picardy; the duke of Epernon, for parts of Provence and other districts; and the young duke of Guise, son of the murdered Henry of Guise, who relinquished control of Rheims.

The most significant settlement with a rebel leader was that made in November 1595 with the duke of Mayenne. Mayenne had controlled

10. There are various versions of this witticism. See Oman, *History of the Art of War*, p. 532; Wilkinson, *League*, p. 149; Pierre de l'Estoile, *Registre-Journal*, vol. 1, part 2, p. 218.

11. Thompson, *Biron*, 2 : xxxix.

12. Mariéjol, in Lavisse 6^1 : 391–92. This amounts to about 2,145,000 livres; but Clamageran, *L'impôt*, 2 : 353, gives the sum as 3.5 millions.

Burgundy and much of Champagne and Picardy; in addition, until 1594 Mayenne was acknowledged by the Parisians as their military chief. He was the most important of the remaining Guises. There were times, before Henry IV's conversion and acceptance by the pope, when it appeared that Mayenne might have been gearing up his courage to demand the throne for himself.

We know the terms of Mayenne's settlement with Henry IV, since it was issued as a "general edict of amnesty" at Folembray in January 1596.[13] Few documents of the era reveal in such detail the special role taxation had played in the Wars of Religion. In fact, a large portion of this decree involves tax affairs—that is, pardoning Mayenne for his past deeds of fiscal disobedience. The articles in the Folembray edict parallel in a fascinating manner similar concessions that had been extended to Huguenot leaders, and especally to Condé, in the edict of pacification of Amboise in 1563, at the end of the first of the Wars of Religion. But the 1596 edict is even more revealing; Mayenne, after all, had been exploiting a large portion of the royal fiscal apparatus for about ten years.

Perhaps the most important fiscal clause in the amnesty of Folembray is article 9, which acknowledges Mayenne and all who had followed him to be "quit and discharged from all prosecution for public or private funds which have been levied by them. . . ." This pardon was to include seizures of money chests at receptes généraux, local receptes, and greniers; also pardoned were appropriations and sale of jewels, furnishings, plate, salt, and tall timber belonging to the king, clerics, nobles, or any individuals; any "traictes et impositions" laid on wine, meat, and other foods also were to be forgiven, as were any levies on the rich ("cottes sur les particuliers"); in general Mayenne and his followers were "quit and discharged for [levying] any funds, imposts, and anything else whatsoever, even actions not more particularly listed here. . . ."

No less than thirteen articles in the amnesty of Folembray (out of thirty-two) were taken up in whole or in part with fiscal and financial affairs. These articles provide a precious insight into the manner in which portions of the royal fiscal system had been used by the grandees. Article 22, for example, provides pardon for clergy who had turned

13. In Isambert, 15 : 104–16.

over clerical tenths to Mayenne and who had paid him money from alienation of church temporel. Articles 17, 18, and 20 discuss the problems arising from Mayenne's own "recepte des parties casuelles"; officials he had appointed were to be maintained in their positions, and those who had paid Mayenne for such offices were enjoined from taking him to court for any matters arising out of these payments. Article 10 forgave Mayenne and his followers for many "actes d'hostilité," including coining their own money.[14] Article 30 is an agreement to take over 350,000 écus of Mayenne's debts, on the excuse that this money had been spent "in war and for other affairs concerning his faction, and none of it has been employed for his own individual profit. . . ." This was to be considered a royal debt, and provisions for paying it were made by assigning it to one of the royal receptes générales. In addition, the king promised to pay all the money owed to mercenaries Mayenne had employed, "and to place these [sums] among the other debts of the crown . . ." (article 31). Article 23 of the Folembray amnesty provides for the complete absorption by the crown of financial accounts kept by Mayenne's comptables. All such fiscal records were to be turned over to the nearest royal Chambre des comptes, and they were to be accepted as valid even though they might not be in the proper form and style.[15] As for the comptes still in the process of being completed, they were to be submitted to a branch of the Chambre des comptes within a year from the issuing of the edict. Articles 26 through 29 invited all the remaining Guisard chiefs who had not yet made their peace with the king to do so within six months. If they complied they were to be granted all the pardons specified for Mayenne.[16]

Only a few territories returning to the king's obedience after 1593 did not cost Henry IV substantial money payments. Duke Carlo Emanuele of Savoy, it is true, was pushed out of his part of Provence by an invasion of Savoy itself (led by Lesdiguières, the Huguenot hero of

14. See also Bailhache, "La monnaie de Toulouse," p. 225.

15. B. Zeller, ed., *L'histoire de France racontée par les contemporains: Les Etats Généraux de 1593* (Paris, 1888), p. 176, claims that the king ordered that all the records of all financial agencies that had adhered to the League be burned.

16. Amnesty granted to Mercoeur (edict of Angers, March 1598), however, gave him concessions similar to those of Mayenne, even though the six months time limit was far exceeded. Fontanon, 4 : 834.

Dauphiné) in June 1597. Some towns held by the Catholic League surrendered to the king in return for religious and political guarantees rather than financial concessions; they sometimes obtained, for example, the right to exclude Protestant worship from their town or a promise from the king not to prosecute town councilors who had taken charge during the period of rebellion. Even so, Guisard chiefs in charge of armies operating out of such towns, as well as governors of the towns themselves, demanded and usually got some cash payment. However, some exceptions stand out. Sesseval, governor of Beauvais, immortalized himself by giving up his command without a bribe.[17] Du Bourg, in charge of the Bastille at the time Paris surrendered, "would accept no money for it," according to Pierre de l'Estoile, "showing his generosity and his worth." [18]

"Faire la France coûtait cher," said Jacques Bainville concerning the financial problems of Philip IV; and the same can be said of Henry IV. Sully, writing many years later, estimated that in 1596 about one-quarter of the crown's available revenues were expended to pay the Catholic grandees the necessary installments on the monetary concessions they had wrung from the king. He claimed that the king's commitments on this score amounted to a staggering 32 million livres.[19] Other evidence suggests that the Assembly of Notables in 1596 was told that the sum promised to "buy back" France was not 32 but 19.5 millions.[20] At that time, it is true, Mercoeur had not yet surrendered; he is reported to have received 4.3 millions.[21]

Let us accept, then, a total figure of approximately 24 million livres. The point to emphasize is that 24 millions—give or take a few millions—does not seem an impossibly heavy additional burden of debt for a fiscal system as large and powerful as that of France. It amounts to five-sixths of one year's income. Most of the payments were not given out in a lump sum but were simply carried on the books as an addition to the royal debt or as additional pensions. Estimating that maintaining this debt cost the crown, say, 10 percent of the principal sum annually, we arrive at an additional burden on the revenues of only 2.5

17. Mariéjol, in Lavisse 6¹ : 391.
18. Pierre de l'Estoile, *Registre-Journal*, vol. 1, part 2, p. 211.
19. *Oeconomies*, 2 : 29–30.
20. Mariéjol, in Lavisse 6¹ : 392 and n. 2.
21. Clamageran, *L'impôt*, 2 : 353.

million livres. In the end, of course, the crown got much the better of the bargain. It is true that for many years the rebel grandees and war lords continued to be served pieces of the revenues pie;[22] but such payments were simply amalgamated into the pensions to nobles that had been a feature of royal finances since the late middle ages. Meanwhile, the revenues pie was being cut again by only one knife instead of many. Before long, some of the former rebels fell out of favor; others died without proper heirs, and their pensions were canceled.

In provinces with Estates, the king was able to lay part of the burden of bribing the rebel chiefs on the shoulders of the "liberated" towns themselves; in 1598, for example, the king asked the Estates of Brittany to grant him 800,000 écus for his obligations to Mercoeur and for the costs of his military operations there.[23] Sometimes the king financed these expenses by placing new taxes on specific areas; these taxes were collected long after their purpose was fulfilled. Thus in 1595 Henry IV bought out the governor of Vienne by assigning him the proceeds of a new toll on the Rhône (the *droit de Vienne*) on all goods passing near that town. This tax lasted until 1789.[24]

THE ASSEMBLY OF NOTABLES OF ROUEN, 1596–97

In April 1596 the Spaniards surprised everybody by storming out of their Netherlands bases and capturing Calais. It was a discouraging setback for the king. Funds to organize yet another major campaign were simply not available. For the first time the king was forced to consider seriously making some important alterations in the structure of French taxes.

The reforms that were contemplated would have had to involve a heavier tax burden; it was advisable, therefore (considering the highly irritable state of mind of his subjects), for the king to produce at least the appearance of popular consent to these changes. To have called an Estates-General for this purpose, however, would have been out of the question. The country was too confused and agitated for

22. An "état de pensions" for 1605 shows a pension of 50,000 livres for Mayenne and the same for "Monsieur d'Elbeuf." B.N. Fonds fr. 11165, fol. 239.
23. Poisson, *Bretagne*, p. 227.
24. Mariéjol, in Lavisse 6[2] : 17.

the king to risk general elections. Henry IV decided to fall back on another device, an Assembly of Notables, traditionally a smaller convocation and one whose members were appointed by the king rather than elected. It consisted of about eighty princes, nobles, prelates, royal councilors, a large number of fiscal officials, and a highly selected group of town magistrates. It was to prove the nearest approach to a general representative assembly ever called by the first of the Bourbon kings.

There was little the Notables could do, however, to help the king. Even though the fiscal system was almost entirely put together again, it still was not functioning well. The economy, furthermore, had been bled white, and satisfactory finances had to wait for economic recovery that only peace could bring. But the king had to move immediately against the Spaniards in north France. The Notables, therefore, had no choice but to scrape the bottom of the barrel of expedients, the nature of which suggest the dimensions of the crisis. The Notables proposed that a full year's moratorium be declared on the payment of all judicial and fiscal officials' salaries—in other words, on virtually the whole bureaucratic apparatus. There was to be an additional sacrifice demanded of the fiscal officials. They were to be threatened with an investigating commission, a chambre de justice, to check on the sources of their wealth in recent years. This was, of course, only another cynical move for a *composition* from the tax officials; later, they duly bought their own way out of this investigation by turning over 3.6 million livres to the crown. The Notables suggested too that recently purchased offices had been sold so cheaply that salaries on all of them should be reduced considerably; the French officials also fended off this proposal with another collective payment of 3.6 million livres.[25] The Notables encouraged the king to raise 900,000 livres in forced loans from the rich burghers and officials in Paris alone.

Some tax reductions, too, were suggested by the Notables and accepted by the king in order to make it appear that while the burden was getting worse in some respects, it was improving in others. The crue on tailles for 1596, for example, was canceled, as was a special levy that the king had announced he would impose on the rich burghers of the chief towns. A few recently imposed river tolls were removed. And the king

25. Clamageran, *L'impôt*, 2 : 337–38; Mariéjol, in Lavisse 6¹ : 408.

agreed to forgive his subjects all the unpaid tailles, taillons, and gabelles that had fallen due in 1595. A general reform edict for the tailles
was issued, designed mainly to show that the government was determined to eliminate abuses that had become encrusted in the system
during the Wars of Religion.[26]

The most famous tax proposed by the Notables of Rouen—and
one which actually was implemented, at least for four or five years—was
the *pancarte*, an additional levy of 5 percent (one sou per livre) on
almost all important commodities in internal French trade, to be collected as the goods passed through town gates. There was such a large
amount of commodities involved that the tax officials resorted to printing placards, or *pancartes*, with lists of such goods, and posting them
at every town gate. This tax did not cause any lasting change in the
French tax structure, since it was suppressed by an edict given at Fontainebleau, November 1602.[27] But the pancarte, according to Sully,
was tied in to an attempt to change the whole basis of royal tax power
by denying the king the right to spend the proceeds of this tax as he
saw fit. The pancarte levy was to be administered by a commission
appointed by the Assembly of Notables (after 1597, by the chief "sovereign" courts, that is, Parlement, the Chambre des comptes, and the
Cour des aides), which would be given the right to control such revenues, applying them to certain types of expenditures—including wages
and pensions—and to the liquidation of a designated group of royal
debts. This committee was the much-discussed "Conseil de raison."
According to Sully, this would have limited royal control over expenditures to national defense, the royal household, and the royal court.[28]

It is now known that this Conseil de raison was at least partly a
figment of Sully's imagination. The story gained a certain amount
of stature because of a famous incident at the opening of the Assembly
of Notables (November 4, 1596).[29] At that time the king made a

26. Edict of Rouen, Jan. 1597, Archives Nationales AD[IX-471].

27. In Isambert, 15 : 131, 276–77.

28. *Oeconomies*, 1 : 237. It is possible that this scheme was supported by Forget
de Fresne. See Chamberland, *Un plan de restauration financière*, pp. 17–18.

29. Another reason for its acceptance was that Forbonnais repeats the story.
Recherches et considérations, 1 : 24–25. It is accepted by Picot (*Etats Généraux*,
4 : 118–21), by Clamageran (*L'impôt*, 2 : 341–42), and by Nef (*Industry and
Government*, pp. 124–25). But see Albert Chamberland, "La légende du Conseil
de raison," *Revue Henri IV*, 2d ed., 1 (1912) : 147–48; and Doucet, *Institutions*,
1 : 151.

remarkable address, inviting those present to participate in the work of finishing the pacification of the country and the war against Spain. Henry IV admitted that basic reforms were needed, and offered to put himself in their hands as to the nature of these reforms, "to receive your advice, to believe it, to follow it—in brief to put myself in your hands as guardians." [30]

It has been well established that Henry IV made this offer tongue in cheek. Sully gives the impression that the king was at the point of rejecting the whole presumptuous proposal when he (Sully) pointed out to him that the Conseil de raison was a self-defeating arrangement. He predicted (correctly, according to him) that the Notables had vastly overrated the revenues of the pancarte; they expected it to produce 4 or 5 million livres, whereas Sully thought it would bring less than a million. (The November 1602 edict canceling the pancarte seems to show that it was valued by the crown at about 1.3 millions.) Sully presumed that when the Conseil de raison saw that the revenue it controlled was entirely inadequate for its tasks, it would throw in the sponge, dissolve itself, and so return to the crown control over all its revenues.[31]

But there is no evidence the Conseil de raison controlled the revenues coming from the pancarte; there is not even any firm evidence that such a council actually functioned. The Notables were designated by the king himself and entirely responsible to him; it is unlikely such a group would have demanded that the king divest himself of an important segment of his tax power. Besides, Henry IV was not the sort of king likely to implement such a request. Possibly the Conseil de raison was intended as a gesture, an affirmation by the king that pancarte revenues would be reserved for retiring royal debts and that a special commission (of the Conseil des finances?) would see to it.

THE EDICT OF NANTES AND THE END OF THE FISCAL CRISIS

By 1596 only a few important Guisard nobles and Leaguer towns remained in arms against the king. Dreary, exhausting fighting continued, however, against Spanish forces which had come into the coun-

---

30. Picot, *Etats Généraux*, 4 : 114–15; Doucet, *Institutions*, 1 : 333–34.
31. *Oeconomies*, 1 : 238–40, 245. Sully writes that the Notables wanted to divide the kingdom's revenues into "deux esgales portions."

try as allies of the Catholic League. The war had changed from a quarrel between the king and his zealot Catholic subjects to a quarrel between France and Spain. Both kings were near the end of their strength. But the Spaniards in the Netherlands somehow managed to mount some successful campaigns against nearby French cities. In 1596 they took Calais; in March 1597 they dealt the French another hard blow by seizing Amiens, on the invasion route into the heart of France.

Henri Hauser claims that Henry IV galloped off for the siege of Amiens "sans argent." [32] This obviously is an exaggeration, since returns from the pancarte and the expedients authorized by the Notables in 1596 must have begun to come in to the Epargne at this time. It was clear, however, that scraping together enough funds for yet another major campaign after Amiens would have been out of the question. When Amiens was retaken by the French after a hard six-month siege, Henry IV was more than ready to try to reach an effective peace with Spain. After some hard bargaining, the treaty was signed at Vervins, in May 1598. Ironically, as far as territorial disputes were concerned, this treaty brought France and Spain back to about the same situation as in 1559, when the treaty of Cateau-Cambrésis had been signed. The French civil-religious wars and their postlude, the war with Spain, were over.

The famous Edict of Nantes was the act by which, for the first time in Europe, an important country successfully authorized a certain measure of religious toleration for its subjects. It was promulgated on April 13, 1598, while the final details of the Treaty of Vervins were being worked out. This long and complex settlement accomplished much more than establishing rules and regulations for tolerating the Huguenots.[33] It was a general edict of pacification, the main object of which was not so much protecting the Huguenot faith as bringing back all of the French into obedience to the crown. Therefore the Edict of Nantes was, for the most part, a series of carefully spelled out concessions, mainly to Huguenots, regarding not only their religious rights, but also military rights (a large number of cities were to be held as security with Huguenot governors and garrisons), rights to hold royal

32. *La prépondérance espagnole,* p. 160.
33. In Isambert, 15 : 170–99.

offices and pensions on a basis of equality with Catholics, and special rights of Huguenots in judicial procedure. This part of the Edict of Nantes is well known. Not so well known is the fact that the edict also included important concessions to the Huguenots and their allies regarding tax affairs.

The Catholic grandees and Leaguer towns, as they surrendered one by one to the new ruler, had obtained, as part of their concessions, royal forgiveness for both the taxes they had levied and the royal revenues they had appropriated. But there had been no general settlement between the king and his Huguenot nobles and towns for their acts of fiscal disobedience. The tax decrees of the Huguenot assemblies in the south and west, assemblies which had been revived and active since 1585, were also open to interpretation as acts of lese majesty. Of course the Huguenots had for the most part been working for the cause of Henry of Navarre, now king; but after his conversion to Catholicism (1593) the Huguenots became aggrieved at what they regarded as the ungrateful lack of attention to their demands on the king, for whom they had sacrificed so much during the lean years. They were apprehensive, also, that if the king turned entirely away from them, they would be open to prosecution by vengeful Catholics for having levied taxes during the recent wars.

We have seen that the last Valois kings, in the various "pacifications" after 1563, had forgiven past acts of fiscal disobedience committed by those who had seized royal revenues. It now remained for the first Bourbon king to do the same. The clauses of the Edict of Nantes that deal with this problem (articles 75 through 87) are highly interesting and are a testimony to the significant role of taxes during the Wars of Religion. As an integral part of what is perhaps the most famous single document of early modern history, they deserve more attention from historians.[34]

The first of these fiscal articles in the Edict of Nantes (75–76) granted a sweeping pardon for those, both Protestant and Catholic, who had imposed taxes on Frenchmen under their control since the proclamation of the last pacification—that is, beginning with March

---

34. Perhaps this aspect of the Edict of Nantes has been disregarded because the classic account of the era by Mariéjol in the Lavisse series, vols. 6¹ and 6², does not mention it.

1585 and extending up to the time Henry became king, in August 1589. Those who had refused to collect and turn over to royal officials the duly authorized royal imposts were also pardoned.

We do not wish that those of the said [Protestant] religion and others who were of their faction, nor Catholics who taxed towns and other places held by them, be prosecuted for the [unpaid] tailles, aides, crues, octrois, taillons, utensils, . . . and other imposts and subsidies levied [*escheus*] and imposed [by the kings] during the troubles before and up to our advent to the crown. . . .[Article 75]

All chiefs, lords, nobles, gentlemen, officials, town councils, or those who aided and succored them, or their widows, heirs, and successors are to remain quit and discharged of all money levied and taken by them and according to their orders; this includes royal revenues, town and private funds, money, jewels, and buildings of clerics, tall timber from the [royal] land or elsewhere; plus booty, ransoms, or any sort of funds taken by them . . . and no inquest is to be made of these matters now or in the future. . . . [Article 76]

So far as the Huguenots were concerned, the most important fiscal clauses in the Edict of Nantes were those that protected them from prosecution for their fiscal actions during the reign of Henry IV after 1589. The chief article on this matter is number 77, which states:

The general and provincial assemblies of the said [Protestant] religion, since that of Mantes [October 1593 to January 1594] and down to the present day, plus the councils [executive committees] established by the assemblies, are to be discharged . . . for levying and seizing our revenues, either those in the hands of receveurs généraux or particuliers, parish collectors, or others, in whatever manner it was done; [and they are also pardoned] for stopping the delivery of [our] salt, continuing or decreeing new tariffs and tolls and bureaus to collect these at Royan and on the Charante, Garonne and Rhône and Dordogne rivers . . . and all incidents and excesses befallen in the levying of such tariffs, tolls, and other revenues . . . [and also] impositions of taxes and corvées, bureaus for collecting taxes, depredations against our collectors and tax farmers and other officials . . . and generally everything which was done, deliberated, written, and ordained by the said assemblies and councils. . . .

In addition to the members of Huguenot assemblies and executive committees themselves, officials who had operated under their authority were also to be forgiven for the sums they had paid out, up to the month when the Edict of Nantes was proclaimed. The governors, captains, town magistrates, and others who had obtained money from royal tax officials by forced loans were likewise "deschargez," provided the money had gone for the payment of troops in the towns garrisoned by the Huguenots (articles 80–81).

There were certain formalities, according to the edict, before all their tax depredations could be forgiven Huguenot officials. They would have to prove that the sums they had raised or appropriated had been authorized by the Huguenot assemblies or by one of the Protestant or Politique chiefs. The form of such proof was to be their own financial accounts. These accounts would be accepted as valid provided they were transported to the Parlement of Paris within three months (articles 76 and 78). Henry IV, like the founders of all royal dynasties, was anxious to expunge from the record evidences of past situations where his authority had been weak. It is well known that the king ordered that fiscal records of the Catholic League chiefs and towns be destroyed; but we should recognize that, effectively, the same fate befell Huguenot records once they were swallowed up in the secret archives of the royal "sovereign" courts.

There was one group of "fiscal criminals" that was not to be pardoned, however, either by individual settlements such as those made with Catholic grandees or by the general concessions to Huguenots. There remained those men who had carried out "levies and exactions of revenues . . . on their own authority," and not "according to the necessity, law, and order of war" (article 87). This passage is aimed at the minor war lords and bandits who had plagued France so cruelly during the last years of the wars. What had been done on a large scale by the faction chiefs was not to be forgiven these smaller fry. Some bandit gangs were still harassing the French even in 1598: there were several of them in Brittany, which did not surrender to the king until just before the promulgation of the Edict of Nantes. There were other such bandits in the mountains of the southeast, and in the more desolate areas of the west and the Massif Central; they still had to be pried loose—one by one and painfully—from the towns and villages they terrorized. Such men, the edict stipulated, would be brought to justice and tried for appropriating money, as well as for their other crimes. The line was drawn between what would be considered taxing and what stealing.

There are several interesting miscellaneous provisions in the Edict of Nantes affecting French finances. In addition to seizures of revenues, the Huguenots were to be forgiven their past appropriations of church lands, as well as their issuing of coins. The garrisons and governors in towns now turned over to the Huguenots as security were to be paid from the royal treasury.[35] And Huguenot pastors (like Catholic priests) were to be paid tithes and were to be exempt henceforth from paying tailles.

All in all, the Edict of Nantes does not seem a great fiscal innovation; many of these clauses remind us of the edict of Amboise of 1563 (examined in chapter 5), though perhaps in the later edict the rights and pardons are spelled out more carefully and in more detail. For that matter, some of the religious and political privileges granted in 1598 to the Huguenots also had been foreshadowed in several prior settlements. The Edict of Nantes by itself, therefore, did little to bring peace to long-suffering France. Rather, it cemented the peace that had come because of the general exhaustion of the factions in France, the acceptance of Henry IV's conversion to Catholicism, and the fact that the Huguenots now had a king they felt they could trust—though perhaps not too far. The basic political, economic, and military situation in the later 1590s was not very different from that of many periods in the previous three decades. The greatest change, of course, was that an ex-Huguenot now sat on the throne.

THE WORK OF SULLY

The Renaissance fiscal system did not end when the Wars of Religion were over. There are grounds for arguing that few important breaks with the Renaissance fiscal system appear until the second quarter of the seventeenth century. This is certainly the case for the period of fiscal history dominated by the admirable figure of Maximilian de Béthune, marquis of Rosny and (after 1606) duke of Sully. Sully had

35. This is in an edict appended to the great one, dated the end of April 1598.

been a member of Henry IV's inner circle of advisors and fighting companions since 1580. In 1598 he became the king's chief finance minister. His main drive in this postion was "a judicious return to the past." [36] Knowing the dark role played by the fiscal system during the later seventeenth century, it is tempting to speculate on the impact a man of Sully's drive and patriotism might have had if he had taken advantage of his powerful position to effect sweeping innovations in the workings of the fiscal system. But his work has to be judged against the background of the crippling effects of the last stages of the Wars of Religion and not on the basis of what an improved system might have accomplished in the seventeenth century. If Henry IV's throne was to be made secure (and with it, the religious settlement) the tremendous potential of the French fiscal system would have to be realized—and quickly.

When Sully entered "the dense forest of abuses . . . sword in hand," [37] therefore, his aim was not to carve out a new fiscal system. He had a good idea of what revenues were rightfully due the king— revenues that would flow automatically if only the tax system were set into motion again. Given the circumstances, Sully's success in reestablishing the tax system of the mid-sixteenth century should be seen as a true achievement and not as a missed opportunity.

Sully's fiscal accomplishments were abundant and impressive; they were carried out with a certain amount of dash that matched the rest of Henry IV's reign. Sully threw out many of the most corrupt officials and bullied the rest into keeping better records. He sought out tax farms that were being sold for ridiculously low leases and forced them up to more gratifying prices.[38] He built up the value of the royal domaines by seizing those that had been alienated illegally or sold at distress prices, and he found new buyers at higher rates. Whenever he could, he used budgetary surpluses to buy back alienated royal forest lands, tolls, crop lands, and other domaines, so that by the end of his régime this category of revenue actually was bringing in important

36. Clamageran, *L'impôt*, 2 : 393.
37. Jules Michelet, *Histoire de France*, new ed., 19 vols. (Paris, 1879), 13 : 109–10.
38. Forbonnais, *Recherches et considérations*, 1 : 63, reports that from "almost nothing" Sully increased income from aides and Parties casuelles by more than 3 million livres.

funds to the Epargne—for the first time in more than two generations.[39] He reasserted royal auditing and other forms of control over
town finances, often with the aim of preventing exploitation of lower-
class townsmen by the richer burghers. He worked hard to improve the
administration of the tailles, both in a technical sense and by cutting
down on unjustified exemptions (perhaps by as much as 40,000 persons)
which of course had the effect of lightening the burden on the other
(usually poor) taillables.[40] On the other hand, he demonstrated few
compunctions against imposing heavy surtaxes on tailles when he found
it necessary; and he increased the rates of the grandes gabelles no less
than four times, so that by 1602 they had risen from 305 to 400 livres
per muid.[41] A rather surprising aspect of this Huguenot's tax policy is
that he treated the church rather gently, collecting only the usual tenths
(about 1.3 million livres annually) plus some "free gifts."

The aspect of Sully's success as finance minister that has received
the greatest attention is that for most of his years as surintendant
des finances he managed to hold expenditures below income. The
writers of older accounts, sensitive to the appeal of budget-balancing
endeavors, have been lavish in their praise of Sully's ability not only to
meet all demands for payment but even to lay aside a bit of cash each
year after 1601. Given the heavy outlays required by the king for court
and favorites, the costs of the surrender of Leaguer chiefs, the later
obligations of the Edict of Nantes, and a minor but expensive war in
1600, these surpluses were indeed a tribute both to Sully and to the
great potential of the French tax machine, especially since the burden
of taxation rose only moderately these years.[42] In addition to national

39. If we can believe his memoirs, this "disengagement" of the domaines was
the aspect of Sully's financial stewardship that pleased him most; see *Oeconomies*,
1 : 294; see also A.N. AE II[769], Paris, Dec. 24, 1601, where he approves the repurchase of the alienated *géolles* (income from prisoners) by trésoriers généraux at
Limoges.

40. For good insights on this reform effort, see Bernard Barbiche, "Les commissaires deputés pour la 'régalement' des tailles en 1598–1599," *Bibliothèque de
l'Ecole des Chartes* 118 (1960) : 58–59. See also the edict of Paris, March 1600,
in Isambert, 15 : 226–45; and an earlier edict on exemptions in Jan. 1598, in
Fontanon, 2 : 876.

41. Sully appears to have favored gabelles as equitable taxes, that is, as taxes
the rich had to pay as well as the poor. See Clamageran, *L'impôt*, 2 : 369–71.

42. Buisseret, *Sully*, chap. 4; Albert Chamberland, "Le budget de l'Epargne en
1607," *Revue Henri IV* 2, no. 5 (1908) : 325.

expenses, the king managed to accord the Dutch a very high subsidy for their struggle for independence from Spain (about 2 million livres in some years), and Geneva also received a small but regular subsidy after 1603.[43] Sully was able to accumulate a remarkable war chest in the new Bastille treasure chamber of some 7 million livres by 1607; when Henry IV died, there still remained 5 millions in the Bastille and possibly as much as 10 millions in other reserves.[44]

Another famous accomplishment was the manner in which Sully reduced the crushing royal debt. This debt, which had been building up at a dismaying rate since the later years of Charles IX, may have reached as much as 297 million livres by 1600.[45] Much of the debt was in the form of rentes bearing about 8 percent interest or more. Sully acted most vigorously, not to say despotically, to squeeze whatever he could out of this massive obligation. He set up a royal commission to investigate the validity of all outstanding rentes, and rather ruthlessly canceled those without a clearly valid legal claim on the crown. Sully then negotiated, in a rather high-handed manner, with the owners of the remaining debt claims—including those lingering on from the Grand Parti of the 1550s (see chapter 4), and forced them to accept only a fraction of their outstanding claims. Still other debts, especially those owed to foreign bankers and governments, were wiped out by using the budgetary surpluses.[46] However, Sully did nothing to improve the basic system of royal borrowing; in effect he left French public finance dependent on continued surpluses of current revenues over expenditures, and therefore just as vulnerable to harm from future expensive emergencies as it had been in the days after the collapse of the Grand Parti.

43. Buisseret, *Sully*, pp. 82–84.

44. Louis Batiffol, "Le trésor de la Bastille," *Revue Henri IV* 3 (1909). La Barre, *Formulaire*, p. 412, refers to this war chest. See also Buisseret, *Sully*, p. 80.

45. This is the same figure given by Forbonnais, *Recherches et considérations*, 1 : 28, for the "Etat des dettes" of 1595, presumably that furnished to the Assembly of Notables. It includes alienated domaines and foreign debts. But see Mariéjol, in Lavisse 6² : 53, for a discussion of the probable exaggerations in this statement of debt.

46. In the Champagne and Rethel districts, for example, Sully cut the annual interest burden of rentes assigned there from 115,000 to 63,000 livres. Chamberland, *Recherches critiques*, p. 14. In another case Sully appears to have bullied the Swiss into taking less than was due them. Albert Chamberland, "La comptabilité imaginaire des deniers des coffres du roi et les dettes suisses," *Revue Henri IV* 2, no. 1 (1907–08).

Sully liked to give the impression that he was waging a single-handed fight for fiscal reform. In his memoirs he often attacked others in the royal council who had some responsibility for public finance. But Sully did receive valuable help from several of these men in his reform campaign; in fact, a considerable amount of good work in restoring French finances was done before he was admitted to the council. Accounts of his contemptuous treatment of his supposed rivals for royal favor, therefore, have to be treated with suspicion.[47]

There seems to be no doubt but that Sully cherished a real and lively hatred for *partisans*, tax farmers, and especially for middle-echelon officials in the provinces, "the greatest destroyers of the kingdom's revenues," against whom he directed a long campaign of vilification.[48] In his zeal to investigate these men Sully often overrode the Chambre des comptes and audited their records himself, correcting their expense items and inserting caustic observations on their records in his own hand. And he unleashed against such officials four chambres de justice, that is, full-scale (threatened) investigations of all their affairs, a maneuver which invariably resulted in *compositions* by which officials purchased cancellation of the threatened inquests (1597, 1601, 1604, and 1607).[49]

Since Sully could truly boast of so many outward and visible signs of success (i.e. his surpluses), it was easy to believe his repeated assertions of the great savings he effected in cracking down on graft and corruption. But now historians are not so sure. One of the most famous accounts of such achievements, his pressuring of fiscal officials during a personal inspection tour at the time of the Rouen Assembly of Notables, is suspect. In his *Oeconomies*, Sully describes how he confronted the guilty financiers on their home ground, cleverly uncovered

47. Chamberland believes Sully's famous letter from Henry IV, in *Oeconomies*, 1 : 206–08, echoing Sully's harsh judgments against the fiscal experts in the council, either is badly mistaken or a complete fabrication. "Le Conseil des finances en 1596 et 1597 et les *Economies royales*," *Revue Henri IV*, 2d ed., 1 (1912) : 24, 153–63, 284. We know Sully often wrote friendly and appreciative letters to the same men he attacked in his memoirs after retiring.

48. *Oeconomies*, 1 : 172–73, 250, 267, 305, 557–58; 2 : 96. See also Mariéjol, in Lavisse 6² : 62.

49. The success of the 1607 squeeze is praised in Jean de Beaufort, *Le trésor des trésors de France* . . . (n.p., 1615), and in Jean Bourgoin, *Le pressoir des esponges du roy*.

their secrets, and by an adroit combination of threats of trial and promises of immunity, managed to make them disgorge the huge sum of 500,000 écus—enough to fill seventy carts, with which he returned in triumph to Rouen. The truth may be that whatever sums Sully did collect (undoubtedly less than he claimed) came, for the most part, from normal funds quite legitimately in the hands of généralité officials—funds needed for provincial wages, expenses, interest on rentes, and other amounts assigned for local handling.[50] There is also evidence that Sully—covered by royal approval, since this was a time of terrible emergency—simply seized and carried off this cash.

There were other than purely fiscal reasons for Sully's animosity toward middle-echelon fiscal bureaucrats. Many of these officials, especially those in the outlying provinces, were a potential threat to the centralizing power of the crown. Cadres of provincial officials had been transformed during the Wars of Religion into agencies supporting breakaway governments of grandees, war lords, or Huguenot confederations. By 1598 hundreds of these officials had received their posts from other hands than those of the French monarch. As part of the general settlement, Henry IV had given them repeated guarantees of security of office.[51] But could such men be trusted to transfer their loyalties away from their patrons? Many Guisard and Huguenot chiefs were still on the scene in areas they formerly had ruled as princelings, though now some of them were royal governors. The fiscal wherewithal for financing future rebellions was all too obviously still in place.

Small wonder, then, that Sully was likely to fly into one of his famous rages at signs of obstruction in fiscal matters from provincial officials and magistrates of the larger towns. He saw such action as subversion of royal revenues; and he saw the officials responsible for it as a threat to the unity of France. Especially after 1602, when the budget was balanced, it seems likely that considerations of royal power and not higher revenues would have been uppermost in Sully's mind.

In the matter of overlapping political and financial worries, a special danger for Sully lay in districts where provincial fiscal courts and

50. Sully, *Oeconomies*, 1 : 229–31; cf. 2 : 101, where Sully claims not 500,000 but 600,000 écus, i.e. 1.8 million livres. Albert Chamberland, "La tournée de Sully et de Rybault dans les généralités en 1596," *Revue Henri IV* 3, nos. 3 and 4 (1909); and see Mariéjol, in Lavisse 6² : 49.

51. E.g., in the edict of Folembray, Jan. 1596; see items 17–20.

branches of parlement decided to support those who were resisting him. The courts of parlement, especially, were enjoying new prestige among those who were seeking ways of limiting royal power. Parlement and the fiscal courts made increasingly greater use of their right to hold up or even refuse the registration of royal ordinances.[52] They encouraged fiscal officials to refuse to release their records for scrutiny by Sully's personal agents, claiming these officials were responsible only to the Chambre des comptes in such matters.[53] They also protested strenuously against Sully's high-handed reduction of the volume of rentes and of royal interest rates. (Since officials were saddled with more royal bonds than other groups, their concern here is understandable on simple and apolitical grounds.) At times the courts thwarted the awarding of tax farms; this was done by having the Cour des aides condemn the leases as illegal and unworthy of registration. Time and again Sully had to crash through such resistance—which of course he blasted as obstructionism rather than accepting it as protection of due process and local rights—by imposing direct royal commands to comply with the king's will (*lettres de jussion* and even *lits de justice*).[54]

The most spectacular cases of Sully's concern with the politically dangerous atmosphere surrounding provincial fiscal courts and officials are found in the pays d'états; here, provincial Estates represented yet another corporate body that could thwart royal power. Sully's attitude toward provincial Estates was that they talked about traditional rights but acted to perpetuate the unfair situation in which the delegates themselves paid less than their share of the country's royal imposts. He asserted that in situations where fiscal administration was partly in the hands of the Estates, record keeping tended to be more confusing, expenses of tax collection higher, and instances of corrupt practices more numerous.

On the whole, Sully had his way against this combination of fiscal courts, fiscal administrators, and provincial Estates. For the most part his reforms were enforced no matter how strenuous the objections.

52. There is an amusing account of one such confrontation in Albert Chamberland, "Jean Chandon et le conflit entre la Cour des aides et le Conseil du roi (Mars 1597)," *Revue Henri IV* 2, no. 2 (1908).

53. Buisseret, *Sully*, chap. 5.

54. Thus in 1597 Sully forced the Rouen parlement to register a long-contested decree imposing the *sel par impôt* regime of central France on Normandy.

Significantly, the proportion of royal direct taxes paid by the pays d'états increased over those paid by the pays d'élections.[55]

Provincial Estates, of course, were found in those areas where royal power during the Wars of Religion had broken down most completely. Certainly this is one reason Sully was so antagonistic to them. He announced that in his opinion the government should abolish them everywhere and spread the system of élections and élus uniformly through France. Such a sweeping change would have been beyond the capacity—and perhaps beyond the wishes—of the French in the late Renaissance; but in parts of Guyenne, Sully did take advantage of weak Estates and a confusing legal situation to enlarge the scope of the élections system. In the généralité of Guyenne the two largest cities, Bordeaux and Périgueux (and their districts) already were pays d'élections; but to the south and east were eight small districts (the Agenais, Landes, Condomois, Armagnac, Rivière-Verdun, Comminges, Rouergue, and Quercy) which either were pays d'états or possessed towns with a considerable degree of fiscal autonomy. In 1603 the government decreed that these districts would have to accept the regime of royal élections. A long, highly interesting, and extremely bitter clash began, with agents of these districts working hard to convince, bribe, or otherwise influence members of the royal council to stand up to Sully on this issue.[56] But Sully was able to show that not only would royal power be advanced in troublesome areas but additional royal revenues would come from sales of the new posts of élus and other officials. The king persisted in supporting Sully; and in 1609 the new fiscal regime was extended to these parts of Guyenne.

The same mixture of political and fiscal motives can be seen in Sully's sponsorship of completely inheritable offices—the system known as the *droit annuel* or, more informally, the *paulette*, instituted in 1604 (see appendix F). Certainly Sully welcomed the additional revenues brought in by this annual tax; and he also approved the manner in which the new device cut through the quagmire of rights and regulations concerning the voluntary surrender and transfer of royal office. Pehaps more importantly—and this is a point that could be missed—the paul-

55. Buisseret, *Sully*, p. 76 and table 3.
56. J. Russell Major, "Henry IV and Guyenne: A Study Concerning Origins of Royal Absolutism," *French Historical Studies* 4, no. 4 (1966).

ette tended to consolidate loyalty to the crown. One could argue that the inheritable venal offices in France would weaken the king's power over the quality and reliability of his own administrators; since these offices were somewhat like private property, the king could no longer appoint new officials. The immediate political effect of the paulette, however, was to remove the influence of governors and magnates who had been building support by appointing officials (through favoritism or family power) in regions where they had a particular interest.

Sully's career as surintendant des finances gave that post strength and prestige. As a result, he helped make a powerful finance minister a permanent feature of French administrative life. From the time of Semblançay to 1564, French kings had refused to give responsibility for the conduct of public finance to any one member of the council (see appendix E). In 1564 the office of surintendant was established; but for another generation rulers still hesitated between a surintendant and collective responsibility in a more or less distinct Conseil des finances, either within or attached to the inner royal council.[57] At the end of Henry III's reign, one of his *mignons*, François d'O, was operating as surintendant. D'O declared for Henry IV in 1589 and was allowed to retain his office. But d'O died in 1594, and Henry IV once again relied on a Conseil des finances. Sully was taken into this group in 1596 and, according to his memoirs, immediately set out to demonstrate that, far from possessing the energy and leadership necessary to hammer the fiscal machine into shape, the royal fiscal council members were themselves involved in the miasma of graft and conspiracy that was making the tax system a disappointment to the treasury and an abomination to the people. When Sully succeeded in reserving for himself the chief direction of finances in 1598 or 1599, the Counseil des finances was retained, presumably to collaborate with him.[58] But Sully managed to push the council further and further into the background. He made the key decisions on his own or after consulting with the king or other very high members of the inner council; and he organized a

57. Paul Viollet, *Le roi et ses ministres pendant les trois derniers siècles de la monarchie* (Paris, 1912), p. 218.

58. Sully, *Oeconomies*, 1 : 310, 323. On the question of just when Sully became surintendant and whether or not this was a regular office, see David Buisseret and Bernard Barbiche, "Sully et la surintendance des finances," *Bibliothèque de l'Ecole des Chartes* 123 (1965) : 538–43.

top-level staff of financial technicians responsible only to him, with auditors to cope with records and with the Epargne, and with financial intendants to exercise authority over the provincial bureaux des finances.

Marie de Medici, regent after the assassination of Henry IV in 1610, obviously did not want an independent-minded finance minister like Sully. When it became painfully clear he would not do her bidding, she accepted his resignation (1611); and she returned to using a Conseil des finances. But even before she was forced out of the regency it became apparent that a Conseil des finances was no longer adequate. The government of France required a powerful and responsible person in charge of public finances; thus the office of surintendant was revived. Richelieu depended heavily on the finance superintendency, which he sometimes split between two or three men. It is true that the office of surintendant was canceled in 1661 (when Colbert brought about the disgrace of Fouquet and determined to call attention to the scope of the new broom he was ready to wield). But the office of *contrôleur général des finances*, which Colbert instituted, essentially brought a new name to the same function.

9

Conclusions and Conjectures

Tracing the changes in a complex set of institutions over a very long time span can be a frustrating business. But it has virtues. It enables one to see which traditional explanations of details hold up well when looking at the entire picture, and which require reinterpretation. It also helps one bring into focus developments overlooked by scholars who have concentrated on only one facet of the subject or on only one episode.

Much of the effort in this book has been devoted to these matters of reinterpretation (such as the level of revenues during the later Wars of Religion), as well as topics not previously studied (such as the role of certain features of the fiscal system in prolonging the Wars of Religion). There remains the problem of greater interest to students of the early modern era: the overall significance of French Renaissance fiscal history. One aspect of this problem was treated in chapter 1, where an attempt was made to demonstrate that the fiscal history of the Renaissance does indeed mark a break with that of the Middle Ages. Another aspect is the relations between fiscal and general history during the Renaissance era.

For all its faults, and for all the pain it brought the people of France, the Renaissance fiscal system was a success. It succeeded in that it proved equal to many of the tasks demanded by the monarchy, the aristocracy, and the upper middle class of the country. It provided the wherewithal to drive the English from the land at the end of the Hundred Years' War, and it strengthened the king's hand in dealing with magnates bent on promoting disruption. At the same time, it allowed the aristocracy as a group to escape most taxation. The system enabled the king to maintain a magnificent court and to add to France's glory by incursions into Italy, the Netherlands, and Germany—even if he failed to appropriate much foreign territory. It provided the money for defending France's frontiers when her enemies mounted an on-slaught, as well as for defending the church against a complete Hugue-not victory. It presented wealthy commoners with the chance to gain status, honors, salaries, and profits. And, perhaps most important of all, the Renaissance fiscal system allowed for a remarkably rapid recovery of royal power and national security after the terrible dislocations brought by the Wars of Religion.

The overriding success of the fiscal system does not mean that if it had not developed in the manner it actually did, or if it had not exhibited all the main features we see at a given point during the Renaissance, it would have been a failure. These "iffy" questions—the sort that profoundly disturb historians—must be faced squarely.

First we have to summarize the chief features of the Renaissance fiscal machine. It possessed a broadly based tax structure, capable of drawing revenues from many different forms of wealth and types of transactions. It was manned by an overabundant body of officials and entrepreneurs, who operated at every level of French society throughout the land. It provided no less than three sets of expedients for coping with emergency needs: "outside" loans from wealthy individuals and money markets, "inside" credit such as forced loans and the "fiscal sponge," and sales of venal offices. It was an "absolutist" system in the sense that policy matters were virtually monopolized by the king and the advisors he chose; representatives of the French participated to only a small extent in determining the structure, administration, and burden of French taxes. And, finally, the system brought the king a very large volume of revenues which increased irregularly in some periods, steadily in others; so that at the end of the Renaissance the king was collecting perhaps ten times as much money as at the begin-ning—a far greater rate of change than that of the declining value of the coinage.[1]

For the purposes of this analysis, we can combine these characteristics into three groups: the chief constitutional arrangements, principally the system's "absolutist" elements; the remarkable complexity of the

1. For the trend of revenues, see chap. 7, n. 62; for the trend in the bullion value of the coinage, see Lafaurie and Prieur, *Les monnaies*, 2 : vii–x; and for the general price trends, see Frédéric Mauro, *Le XVIe siècle européen: aspects écono-miques*, Nouvelle Clio, vol. 32 (Paris, 1966), pp. 209–34.

system; and its large and increasing revenues. This device allows us to distinguish between means and ends. In order to accomplish what the French felt they had to do, what was needed was not a particular combination of fiscal attitudes and institutions. What was required was money—great and increasing quantities of it—when and where the need arose. It is quite conceivable that the French government could have enjoyed about as much revenue as it actually did receive with a less "absolutist" system (and indeed with elements of popular consent to taxation somewhat like England's). We can imagine alternative arrangements entirely appropriate to sixteenth-century society which would have resulted in a much simpler tax machine (e.g., without redundant venal offices) that could have been equally productive insofar as the level of revenues is concerned.

It is clear that the king's commitment to obtaining what he regarded as an adequate level of revenues was rigid and uncompromising. But he was less committed to any particular mechanism of his tax machine. The many attempts by Francis I to improve his tax system and to build up war chests show how interested a king could be in different institutional arrangements—provided this did not result in his receiving less money than he meant to have.

After defeating the challenge to its tax power at the time of the Estates-General of Tours (1484), the monarchy enjoyed three-quarters of a century without a comparable crisis—that is, until the Estates-General of 1560–61. Of course the king could not be expected to see that, for the most part, the high level and continued rise of his revenues was a function of France's growth in population and the more or less steady development of her economy. Since both these developments came after the great reforms of Charles VII—reforms which resulted in strengthening France's tax structure and elaborating its already highly articulated fiscal administration (as well as implementing fiscal "absolutism")—the government was provided with an enormous tax machine just in time to take full advantage of these favorable socioeconomic trends. But we can well imagine that in the minds of the kings and their advisors, the real explanation for the success of the fiscal system during this long era was fiscal "absolutism."

While the monarchy began to prize its great tax powers ever more highly, pressures for some abridgment of these powers continued to increase. As we have seen (chapter 3) Francis I, at the pinnacle of his strength, never dared to assert fiscal "absolutism" de jure. Many options regarding the king's tax power still seemed open. During the 1540s, the government showed it was quite sensitive to the bitter criticism directed against its tax system.[2] Why then did the king refuse to relieve some of these pressures through a few concessions to the principle of popular consent? This could have been done easily by calling a national Estates-General every five years or so; and a similar result could have been achieved by reconstituting provincial Estates in the pays d'élections or by devising some other mechanism to push some fiscal responsibility into the hands of local notables, as in England.[3] But the reforms of Francis I drove the fiscal system in the direction of even greater centralization and even more responsiveness to direction from the royal council rather than toward local responsibility. Henry II showed he preferred a bizarre panoply of expedients (plus a huge increase in borrowing) to appealing to his subjects for a voluntary concession of more funds.

Can we take seriously Henry III's explicit avowal to the Estates-General of 1588 that in exchange for monetary concessions he stood ready to share tax power with the people's representatives? Probably not. It is not likely that this erratic and troubled man would have undertaken the task of implementing fundamental changes aimed at seriously weakening his own powers of command. For Henry III (and his mother), such a step would have been too dangerous a departure from a policy of nurturing fiscal "absolutism" that had been a feature of royal government for almost a century and a half. Furthermore, control over the nation's revenues remained the chief resource available to the government for coping with the desperate political, military, and religious problems of the day. All depended, then, on whether the antiroyalist factions were strong enough and united enough to push through a significant abridgment of fiscal "absolutism." But because

2. This sensitivity is one reason for the concessions made by the government after suppressing the tax revolt of 1548; see also the preamble to the edict of Fontainebleau, June 17, 1540; edict of Châtelleraut, June 1, 1541; the royal decl. of St. Germain-en-Laye, May 17, 1543; and the edict of St. Germain-en-Laye, March 1, 1546, in Isambert, 12 : 902–06.

3. Kenneth Pickthorn, *Early Tudor Government*, 2 vols. (Cambridge, 1934), 1 : 61–62, 71.

of the religious struggles, and because of Catherine's adroit political manipulations, the factions had to accept a stalemate that left fiscal "absolutism" about where it had been before the wars. The vociferous and repeated demands for popular consent these years seem more a reflection of generalized discontents than a sign the country was determined to bring about specific and basic fiscal changes.

In the end, a decision regarding the relationships among "absolutism," the high level of royal revenues, and the characteristics of fiscal administration in Renaissance France must be made on the basis of one's own philosophy of history. Marcel Marion, our greatest authority on Old Régime taxation, says, "Nothing reflects more faithfully [a nation's] class relations, politics, economics, and even its moral outlook, than the manner in which revenues are imposed, collected, and spent. . . ." [4] But this comment apparently "reflects" a rather naïve determinism. We have seen that in many instances it is not at all clear whether changes in the fiscal system arose out of fundamental social, political, or economic features of French society. All-out venality, for example, if it "reflects" anything, seems to come chiefly from the government's ability to improvise in the face of the unprecedented costs of the wars against the Hapsburgs. Once it was on the scene, of course, all-out venality became a fixed feature of government and an important element in the upward drive of the bourgeoisie. Therefore, in this case, France had to adjust herself, and painfully, to a change in the fiscal system, not the other way around.

Did the chief features of the Renaissance fiscal system arise out of "structural" aspects of French society, that is from basic and lasting matters such as class relations or economic institutions? Or were they rather shaped by "mere events" and the personal decisions of France's political leaders? One of the arguments that might be used to support a determinist position can be labeled the "French Peru" approach: characteristics of the fiscal system "reflected" the rapidly growing wealth that came with economic expansion at this time, wealth the head of the state was bound to exploit as vigorously as he could. [5] The weak-

4. Marcel Marion, *Histoire financière de la France depuis 1715*, 6 vols. (Paris, 1914–31), 1 : v.
5. E.g., Doucet, *Lyon*, pp. 124–25.

ness of this concept, of course, is that it must apply equally to England, or for that matter to Holland; but in these countries the relationship between the fiscal system and the government turned out to be significantly different from that of France.

An important adjunct of the "French Peru" argument is the perennial favorite among economic explantions, the "price revolution" of the sixteenth century. In chapter 4 we saw that the greater reliance on loans during the reign of Henry II probably was related to the erosion of the king's tax income, an erosion caused in part by the price revolution. The upshot of this crisis, however, was that the king abandoned the new loan mechanisms and returned to "inside" credit and to the "fiscal sponge"—devices that had been favored by Francis I. The factor that allowed the king to dispense with the services of the great international merchant-bankers was his "absolute" power over the imposts and over the fiscal bureaucracy. In this case, therefore, the political or "constitutional" aspects of the fiscal system proved strong enough to prevent an economic development, the price revolution, from effecting basic changes in the fiscal system.

Another "structural" explanation is the relevant aspects of that venerable explanation of preindustrial socioeconomic development, "the rise of the bourgeoisie." From this point of view, the king's abuse of his "absolute"powers in order to create venal offices appears as a result of his decision to make political allies of the middle classes.[6] The bourgeoisie was allowed to take over many of the functions of royal administration partly because of the king's need to combat the centrifugal forces of the higher aristocracy, partly because it had to be from the wealthy that the king drew the loans he needed.

Obviously, without large numbers of ambitious and wealthy men, venal offices would never have grown to the proportions we see by the later sixteenth century. But this is hardly a sufficient explanation for venality, let alone for other main features of Renaissance fiscal institutions. It does not explain why the king chose to tap the wealth of the bourgeoisie by allowing them to take over portions of the tax machine,

6. Barrington Moore, *Social Origins of Dictatorship and Democracy: Lord and Peasant in the Making of the Modern World* (Boston, 1967), p. 58; Joel Hurstfield, "Social Structure, Office Holding and Politics, Chiefly in Western Europe," in *The New Cambridge Modern History*, vol. 3 (Cambridge, 1968), pp. 139–43.

rather than by inducing them to grant subsidies through representatives in the Estates-General. Neither does it show why the French ruler found it necessary to rely so heavily and so often on such an unpopular expedient as venal offices.

In the sixteenth century the kings of France did not, to put it mildly, seem to be courting the bourgeoisie deliberately with a view toward making them allies, either financial or political. Perhaps even more than had their medieval counterparts, the kings of the sixteenth century tended to restrict their friends, ministers, and counselors to the aristocracy.[7] Of all the kings of Renaissance France, Francis I was by temperament the most aristocratic; he was quite contemptuous of those men who knew how to handle pen and ink, ledgers, and money-bags. And yet the sharpest increase in bourgeois involvement in French fiscal affairs—the onset of all-out venaltity—came during the reign of Francis I. It is hard to reconcile Francis I's barbarous treatment of Semblançay and his obvious preference for noble advisors with the argument that the chief characteristics of Renaissance fiscal administration can be explained by the growing alliance between the king and the "rising bourgeoisie."

Another explanation of the French fiscal system, and a more satisfying one, can be extracted from the conventional model of early modern political change that can be called "nation building." The picture this concept provides shows a powerful king as the necessary force "for compelling disconnected aggregates of dissimilar men to proceed together at a time in their history when this [cohesion] was a matter of life and death for them." [8] For most nations, and particularly for France, an all-too perceptible gap existed between that which the ruler felt he must accomplish in order to consolidate his régime and the resources he possessed for this task. Political tradition and the examples of other states demonstrated that the king should push back his frontiers, rechannel urban and provincial loyalties toward himself, curb the powers of the magnates (that is, monopolize taxation, justice, police powers, and the armed forces), stamp out heresy, and capture the imagination of his aristocracy through magnificence at home and glorious exploits abroad.

7. J. Russell Major, "The Crown and the Aristocracy," pp. 643–44; H. Lemonnier, in Lavisse 6¹ : 188–89.

8. Roland Mousnier, *Les XVIe et XVIIe siècles* (Paris, 1954), pp. 99–100.

But the obstacles in the path of such goals were so severe, according to the "nation building" view, that impossibly large revenues would have been required to overcome them. This was certainly the case for France, which, unlike England, was not a unitary state where royal agencies had flourished more or less unchallenged for long periods of time. France was put together, over several centuries, out of territories that had quite distinct traditions, laws, dialects, and even languages of their own. As in a mosaic, close scrutiny of the picture was not required to see that individual pieces, in the sixteenth century, still were retaining much of their separate identity. Given the cumbersome transportation and communication then available, futhermore, the sheer number of people in the land, and the vast distances that had to be traversed to distant corners of the kingdom, the administrative techniques of the age were simply not equal to the task of transforming France into a united and obedient polity.

Try as he might, the king could make only limited progress toward a truly centralized and efficient government. The dangers from powerful magnates, from enemies across the borders, and from competing religions were mitigated only to a degree. As vast as they were, royal revenues were barely enough to pay for the great effort required to keep the kingdom from falling to pieces. Therefore every proposal for decreasing the king's tax power carried with it the potential to destroy his entire régime.

To summarize: In explaining why, in spite of all their faults, the main features of the French Renaissance fiscal system changed so little, I have argued that the most important causal lines run from the political needs of the monarchy to the high level of revenues on the one hand and to the overly complex fiscal machine on the other. The explanation of fiscal "absolutism" is to be sought less in the nature of French society and its economy than in its political problems. To use an old joke favored by economic historians: once again we have cut beneath deceptive socioeconomic factors at the surface to find the solid and abiding political realities beneath.

Given the circumstances of the sixteenth century, to maintain the French polity meant to support a strong monarchy and a high level of revenues—but not necessarily a monarchy with an "absolutist" fiscal system. The cost of fiscal "absolutism" should not have been added to the price of national defense and of modernization. It was "absolutism," as well as the level of the revenues themselves, that increased the pressures on the king from the growing horde of needy favorites and courtiers. And it was "absolutism," in part, that inflated the Renaissance tax machine into the awesomely complex and costly apparatus we see by the 1550s.

There is of course no way of measuring how much money fiscal "absolutism" cost the French. But several considerations support the belief that these costs were heavy and that they represented a serious economic loss. The most obvious and most galling of these was all-out venality. As we saw in chapter 4, the sale of redundant and useless offices was one of the ways the king managed to cope with emergency expenses without having to appeal to the Estates-General for subsidies. This resulted in a situation in which the expenses of collection may have amounted to one-fourth or more of the total revenues.[9] And it is logical to suspect that other huge sums were gouged out of the taxpayers by these excess officials. Everything we know about attitudes toward the overabundant fiscal bureaucracy underlines our conviction that if representatives of the French people had participated in the formulation of fiscal policy they would not have tolerated such a gigantic apparatus.

It is also quite possible to imagine that given more popular control, the structure and the geographical (if not the social) incidence of taxes would have been more rational. One good example is the gabelles (see appendix I). If the burghers of north and central France had possessed a voice in the matter, it seems certain they would have forced through some mitigation of the salt tax inequities under which they suffered in comparison with the south and west. This is not to say that consent to taxes would have taken some of the horribly unjust tax burden off the backs of the poor. Almost all European representative assemblies during the Renaissance worked for the interests of the rich and

9. This is my estimate of the total monetary burden around 1600 in salaries, wages, piece-rates, and other expenses of the full-time and part-time officials and others connected with the fiscal system; it was obtained by multiplying the officially designated compensation for each type of fiscal agent by the number of such agents counted (see chap. 4, n. 78). Of course it cannot take into account the profits of the tax farmers and *traitants*. This ratio is slightly above those cited by Mousnier, *Vénalité*, p. 50.

the powerful, and there is no reason to believe France would have been an exception.

Because of "absolutism," the only effective reforming effort in the land had to come from the king. Whereas many of the actual reforms were sincerely aimed at functional improvements or improvements in matters of tax equity, even more of the changes in the tax machine seem to arise from a thinly disguised drive for higher revenues. While there is, of course, no proof that superior reforms would have resulted from a shared responsibility over taxes between parliament and king, it cannot be denied that as matters stood the Renaissance fiscal system became a veritable bastion of corruption and inefficiency (see appendix F).

The most serious cost of fiscal "absolutism," however, is the perversion of entrepreneurial talent it entailed. A large segment of the most enterprising elements in France now concentrated its effort on social climbing, improving its standing in the bureaucratic hierarchy, and obtaining favors from the crown.[10] This meant that its entrepreneurial outlook was conditioned by matters of privilege rather than those of output. In other words, entrepreneurial talent was diverted into redistributing the nation's wealth rather than into increasing wealth through improvements in trade, manufacturing, and finance.

The actual performance of the economy during the Renaissance supports the conjecture that France suffered because of the nature of her fiscal system, as well as from the weight of her taxes. Granted, France's economy grew; but considering her great resources, her relatively large population, and her marvelously favorable location, France's benefits from the world's economic expansion at this time were not as great as could have been anticipated.[11] Of course there were some praiseworthy examples of economic progress; but the lost opportunities seem more striking. France experimented hardly at all with regulated and chartered companies; evidences of the "putting-out" system in manufacturing are puny; and, worst of all, the promising money markets that appeared at Lyons and other centers resulted in no permanent improvement in royal or private credit facilities. It seems clear that the multitude of tolls and

10. Robert Mandrou, *Introduction à la France moderne* (1500–1640) (Paris, 1961), pp. 150–58.

11. Henri Sée, *Histoire économique de la France*, 1 : 100–23, 143.

internal tariffs hindered the flow of goods; that the harsh tax burdens laid on the towns weakened the productive capacity of many merchants and manufacturers; and that venality and tax farming diverted capital into unproductive channels.

For the men of the seventeenth century, the meaning of the fiscal inheritance from the previous era was disguised for a while by the élan with which Sully performed his fiscal housecleaning and by general relief at the end of foreign and civil wars. As we can see from the number and specificity of the demands for lower taxes and for tax reform raised by the Estates-General of 1614, hopes were still high that the fiscal system could be simplified and improved and that the people's representatives could be given some role in fiscal policy.[12]

The timorous and incompetent government of this period, however, reacted to the shocks and uncertainties that came after the assassination of Henry IV by remaining stubborn in its determination to keep the fiscal system as it was and to exploit it as vigorously as possible. There was a faint possibility that substantial reforms could have been instituted when strong government was restored under Richelieu. But as Richelieu freely admitted, he had no competence in matters of public finance and little interest in the details of the fiscal machine—apart from insisting that it produce the enormous revenues he needed to crush internal dissent and to cope with the terrible expenses of the Thirty Years' War.[13]

To say that the tax system of Richelieu's France owed a great deal to Renaissance tax institutions, therefore, would be to make a gross understatement. The significant contrasts that are found between fiscal affairs during the reign of Francis I, on the one hand, and Saint Louis or Charles V, on the other, are not visible when looking in the other direction, that is, to the contrasts between the reigns of Francis I and Louis XIII. Rather than discontinuities, it is the items of stability and continuity that stand out in a point-by-point comparison. The constitutional arrangements of the seventeenth century are almost precisely those of the Renaissance, though it is true that by Louis XIII's

12. Picot, *Etats Généraux*, 4 : 221–29; 5 : 31–51.

13. Orest A. Ranum, *Richelieu and the Councillors of Louis XIII* (Oxford, 1963), pp. 128–29, 136; Mariéjol, in Lavisse 6[2] : 427.

time the prevailing theories are no longer marked by the anachronistic moralizing of the Renaissance. There is no more nonsense about how "the king should live of his own." The burden and structure of Old Régime taxes are likewise carried over from the Renaissance with little change. Aside from the small but intermittently rising general utility subsidies during the era of Louis XIV (roads, canals, public buildings, support for art and letters), the structure of expenditures, too, is the same as during the Renaissance. So far as the main body of Old Régime fiscal officialdom is concerned, it is better described as ossified than unchanging—to the point where it is the source of a flood of despairing hostility toward royal government.[14]

Searching for profit opportunities made available by "absolutism" became virtually a way of life for hundreds of powerful royal favorites and for thousands of fiscal officials, traitants, and tax farmers. Even if he wished, the king could do little to respond to the growing clamor against the tax system without undertaking a fundamental rearrangement of French society.

A few fiscal contrasts with the Renaissance can be found, especially by the time of Colbert. Mercantilism brought with it the notion of a potentially beneficent fisc—a new and fundamental concept in Western thought. Tariffs during the Old Régime were decidedly and avowedly protectionist, unlike those of the Renaissance (see appendix J). Provincial tax administration was taken over by the intendants. And the government, through the General Farmers, supported rather than fought grosses fermes.[15]

In perspective, however, the fiscal reforms of the seventeenth century seem like modifications of the greater and more basic changes wrought during the Renaissance. Historians who study the fiscal institutions of Old Régime France without appreciating how much these owe to the Renaissance era are looking through the wrong end of the telescope.

The chief significance of French Renaissance fiscal history, therefore, is that the institutions and attitudes of the Renaissance system became

14. Jean Meuvret, "Comment les français du XVIIe siècle voyaient l'impôt," in Roland Mousnier et al., Comment les français voyaient la France au XVIIe siècle (Paris, 1955), pp. 59–82.
15. Matthews, General Farms, pp. 46–53.

a deadly burden on following generations in the seventeenth century and, in fact, for most of the eighteenth century. Its ramifications into French society were so deep, its structure so solid, and the high level of revenues it produced so vital to the king that it resisted—apart from a few matters—even the reforming zeal of Turgot. Instead of providing a tool for modernization, the fiscal system turned into the prime agency whereby a moribund autocracy tightened its suffocating grip on a great country.

The Chief Elements of the Tax Machine

A

Provincial Revenue Management
before the Bureaux des Finances

It is traditional to begin a description of the tax system of Renaissance France by explaining that it was divided into two branches—"ordinary" and "extraordinary" finances. These terms refer to a separation between the domaines (royal rents and prerogative revenues) on the one hand, and tailles, aides, traites, and gabelles on the other. The phrase "extraordinary finance," of course, became a sort of grim and long-enduring fiscal joke; there was nothing "extraordinary" about the great national imposts after the mid-fifteenth century, since they were collected every year.[1]

It is true that the middle- and lower-echelon officials who collected the great imposts were a different group from those who managed the domaines revenues; and this separation was maintained, to some degree, all through this era into the Old Régime. However, this does not apply to the upper-echelon officials. Above the district level (élection and bailiwick), the distinction between the two branches began to blur during the later reforms of Francis I, and it disappeared when the bureaux des finances were firmly in place. Furthermore, when we examine fiscal policy formation (see appendix E and chapter 3), we find no such division after the reforms of 1523.

A more rational way to regard the Renaissance fiscal hierarchy is to divide it according to types of functions rather than types of revenues. From this point of view there are four divisions that cut across "ordinary" and "extraordinary" lines. On the bottom level were the numerous persons who had to do the work of separating the taxpayer from his cash and personally collecting the king's rents and dues. Here we find the parish tax gatherers and assessors of tailles and gabelles; the sergents (constables), who had the power to seize and imprison tax delinquents and sell their goods;

---

1. The most widely circulated manual, the Vestige des finances (an appendix to Le Thrésor du nouveau stille et prothocolle), originally printed around 1528, continues to assert in its many editions all through the Renaissance that "there are two branches of finance, to wit, ordinary and extraordinary"; and the Vestige always includes gabelles, tailles, and aides in the second category. Philibert Boyer, in his Instruction pour le faict des finances, p. 9, is still calling the three main imposts "extraordinary taxes" as late as 1583.

the agents of tax farmers, who collected excises and tariffs; and the provosts, castellans, and clerks, who collected the king's rents.

On the second level were the tax farmers. They were not royal officials; the management of aides, traites, and crown rents was an extension of their business activities.

On the third level were the *officiers comptables*, officials who kept accounts because they handled cash from revenues and paid it out to the king's creditors or the king. This group included the *receveurs particuliers* of the élections; the *grenetiers*, who oversaw the salt warehouses; and the various comptrollers who checked accounts. Slightly above these were the *receveurs généraux*, the superior collectors—one to a *généralité*. They received the cash remaining in the hands of the parish and élection collectors. At about the same level were the bailiffs, seneschals, and *maîtres des eaux et forêts* (those responsible for crown timber and forest rights).[2]

The fourth level of the tax machine was dominated by the *élus*, the strong right arm of the king in fiscal matters. In the parlance of the times, élus were supervisory officials, *officiers ordonnateurs*, rather than officiers comptables; élus did not personally take in or pay out cash, and therefore did not keep accounts. The élection district, or the "charge" of an élu, was about the size of a diocese; in fact most élections followed diocesan boundaries. There were some élections based on other jurisdictions: counties, viscounties, *prévôtés*, or *châtelainies*.[3] In the period before the reforms of Francis I there were about eighty-five élections in France. However, they were not to be found in Languedoc, Guyenne, Gascony, or a few minor areas like Rouergue and Quercy. In those territories, where aides were not collected, there were neither élus nor élections, and the chief agents of the crown were royal commissaires. The number of élections increased slowly (through additions to the domain and through subdivision) to slightly more than 100 by the mid-sixteenth century; toward the end of the century, the number rapidly increased to around 150. By the end of the Old Régime there were close to 200 élections in the country.[4]

At one time, historians believed that élus were not to be found in provinces with Estates. But this is an oversimplification, since some provinces with Estates also had élus and élections. This was the case for Normandy

2. A comprehensive list of comptables can be found in the ord. of Paris, Oct. 1554, in Isambert, 13 : 406–10.

3. Maximilien Quantin, *Histoire des impôts du comté et élection d'Auxerre au XVIe siècle*, p. 3, shows that the county and élection in this instance covered precisely the same area.

4. Dupont-Ferrier, *Etudes*, 1 :32 and n. 1.

and a few sections of Burgundy. On the other hand, during certain periods of the Renaissance, Guyenne and some of the fiefs had neither Estates nor élections. A better distinction than that between *pays d'élection* and *pays d'état*, therefore, is one between areas that paid aides and those that paid some sort of substitute, like the *équivalent*. Usually, where there were aides, one found élus.[5]

In the smaller or less important élections, those without at least one medium-sized town, there usually were two élus; in the more important élections there were three or even four. An élection was not a uniform district. The élection of Chartres, for example, covered (in addition to the city) fourteen towns and villages in a relatively large area, while the nearby élection of Dreux had only four minor villages in addition to the city.[6]

The élus acted as the lowest court in tax disputes. When the sum involved was small (less than 50 sous) or the principle of the dispute unimportant, the decision of élus was final. Nobles, however, or persons otherwise "exempts & privilegiez" could take their case to the Cour des aides, no matter how small the amount involved.[7]

There never were enough élus to hear all the cases brought before them. In addition, the distances claimants had to travel were great and the sessions of tax courts were held infrequently. Charles VII tried to ease the judicial burden on élus by allowing other local courts (both royal and seigneurial) some jurisdiction over tax cases. But in the more rural districts local judges knew little of law and taxes; this was particularly true of the seigneurial court judges. Therefore élus were allowed to appoint their own lieutenants, or even clerks, who had the right to hear cases in these "rustic fiefs." [8] As late as 1622 La Barre was urging his fellow élus to hold court at least once a week, in easily accessible towns, preferably on market day.[9]

The élu had to do most of the work that would now be called plugging tax loopholes. For example, he had to check on claims for the exemptions made by nobles and clergy. There were many edicts enjoining élus to

5. Ibid., 1 : 37–38, and 2 : 347.
6. Ibid., vol. 1, frontispiece map.
7. Privilege confirmed by the edict of Paris, May 1575, in Jean Houzé, *Edicts et ordonnances royaux sur l'établissement de la justice de la Cour des aides . . .* , p. 173; see also Boyer, *Instruction,* p. 76.
8. The ordinances of the 1450s recognize that judges in the poor and far-off districts were likely to be "pas bien experts ny cognoissant en telles matieres ançois sont les aucuns simples gens mecaniques." Ords. of Montils-les-Tours, March 23, 1452, and Bois-Sire-Amé, Aug. 26, 1452, in Pierre Charpentier, ed., *Recueil des ordonnances, édicts . . . concernant . . . des éleus,* pp. 14–37.
9. La Barre, *Formulaire,* p. 59.

investigate omissions and suspiciously low rates to be found in the lists of those paying the tailles.[10]

Finally, when the king needed money in a hurry, as he so often did, élus were among the first called upon to advance cash from their own pockets. They were permitted, of course, to compensate themselves from revenues.

One of the most striking features of the élus was that their main function was to safeguard the king's interests. The rights of taxpayers, questions of equity, and even considerations of efficiency were distinctly secondary matters. Again and again the élu was enjoined to "make the strong carry the weak." Again and again he was ordered to survey his districts on horseback personally, checking at least once each year on the zeal and dependability of each subordinate, on the taxpaying abilities of each district, and especially to ascertain whether a district could bear a higher tax the next year.[11] The élu even had the duty of inspecting roads and ferries in his area and checking to see if bridges were passable. This was not in order to facilitate transportation; the aim was to increase the salability of tax farms involving aides and traites, since poor roads hampered merchants who paid such taxes.[12]

The most important characteristic of the part of the tax machine controlling the domaines—the portion of the revenues called "ordinary" before 1523—was that it was tightly enmeshed with other facets of administration. Officials who farmed out the right to collect local rents had important judicial and military functions in their districts. Wardens who sold the king's timber had to thwart poachers and wood thieves. Provosts who gathered in tolls on ferries and roads had to keep these roads reasonably clear of highwaymen.[13] Bailiffs and their subordinates had the duty of supervising the craft guilds and arranging for the pricing of some commodities. They also had to see to the upkeep of the king's public buildings—"the halls where we establish and mete out justice . . . [the] jails and prisons, mills, bake-ovens and [wine] presses. . . ."[14] Bailiffs had the job of keeping the peace at fairs and some of the town markets, and they could

10. E.g., edict of Paris, Feb. 1553, in Houzé, *Edicts et ordonnances*, pp. 469–70.

11. E.g., the ord. of Montreuil, June 30, 1517, in Georges Jacqueton, *Documents relatifs à l'administration financière* . . . , pp. 173–75. This important ordinance, basic for the élus, can also be found in Isambert, 13 : 119–37, and Fontanon, 2 : 910–16.

12. Edict of Paris, Feb. 1553, in Houzé, *Edicts et ordonnances*, p. 467.

13. This admixture of function is best described in Dupont-Ferrier, *Bailliages*, esp. pp. 278 ff.

14. Ord. of St. Germain-en-Laye, Jan. 1562, in Fontanon, 2 : 359–60.

decide to forbid food exports from their districts in years of poor crops. The king's rights to a tenth of the product of all mines was in their keeping.[15] And they supervised the provosts and castellans who had the job of selling royal grain and wine.

The basic unit for the tailles, the élection, was a tax unit. So was the *recette* in areas without élections, and the *grenier* district for the gabelles. The Renaissance bailiwick, on the other hand, the unit for the domaines, was essentially an administrative unit. While the authority of the "extraordinary" tax officials extended into the interior of the remaining fiefs— which also had to pay tailles and aides—the fiscal power of Renaissance bailiffs was limited to royal domain lands.[16] In most of the Midi lands, except Dauphiné, domain units were known as *sénéchausées* (seneschalcies); they were the same in function and importance as the bailiwicks. The west, including Maine and Anjou, also had seneschalcies rather than bailiwicks. Each bailiwick or seneschalcy had a number of subunits called (after the bailiffs' subordinates who were responsible for them) *prévôtés, vicomtés, or vigueries*.

The *receveurs ordinaires* of the domaines were part of a separate collection system from that of the receveurs particuliers who gathered the tailles and aides (and the généralité collectors or receveurs généraux). These receveurs ordinaires were not responsible to the bailiffs, though it is true that they did make certain local payments on order from the bailiffs. Their superiors were the *trésoriers de France;* and for their fiscal accounts the receveurs ordinaires were responsible to the Chambre des comptes—a responsibility they had in common with the comptables of the "extraordinaries."

At the end of the fiscal year, or sooner if so directed by the trésoriers, the cash *restes* from the domaines were sent to Paris to the central receveur of the domaines system, an official who went by the name of *changeur du Trésor.* The *Vestige des finances* refers to him as "a receveur général, who is known as the changeur du Trésor," suggesting he was superior to the receveurs ordinaires. But he was a rather passive official, a sort of court paymaster, no more important than the *argentier* and several others.

The duties and powers of middle- and lower-echelon fiscal officials, whether they were concerned with "ordinary" or "extraordinary" revenues, were far from uniform in Renaissance France. The system described here

---

15. Dupont-Ferrier, *Bailliages*, pp. 283–84, 296–301.
16. This was not the case for some royal forest rights such as *gruerie* and *tiers et danger.*

applies to the bulk of the country; it must be understood that a slightly different picture would have to be drawn for territories where provincial Estates had some role in the tax system. Nor is this account entirely valid for the remaining baronial fiefs still preserving some fiscal autonomy, such as (for various periods) the Bourbonnais, Foix, Armagnac, Alençon, Nevers, and Angoulême.

B

The Bureaux des Finances

In 1542 Francis I gave France a new fiscal map—a system of seventeen *recettes générales* or provincial fiscal districts (see chapter 3).[1] These eventually became the districts of the *bureaux des finances*, agencies which continued throughout the remainder of the Renaissance and the entire span of the Old Régime. The success of the bureaux des finances gave shape and solidity to the *généralité* of the Old Régime, that is, the unit for general provincial administration (judicial, economic, military as well as fiscal). Gaston Zeller calls the bureaux des finances the "masterpiece" of Renaissance tax reforms.[2] Within each recette générale all functions of collection, auditing, supervision, and payment were gradually taken over by these agencies.

The first chief officials for the bureaux des finances were drawn from the ranks of the *trésoriers de France* and the *généraux des finances*. These eight officials had been pushed out of their top-level positions in 1523 and had gradually been reduced to supervising *élection* collectors. In 1551, however, a plan was developed to put these officials to better use by reducing their "charge" to the area of a single recette générale and forcing them to take up residence in the chief towns under their jurisdictions. This reform finally cut the personal connections between the *gens des finances* and the court. Each trésorier and général, by the terms of the edict of Blois in January 1552, was to choose one of the recettes générales as his own, or resign his post. Since there were four trésoriers and four généraux but seventeen recettes générales, nine additional officials were authorized to make up the difference.[3] They were soon given a new title, a fusion of the two old ones: *trésorier de France et général des finances.* Later they were called *trésoriers généraux* and, toward the end of the sixteenth century, simply *trésoriers.*

1. The great reform edict of Moulins (Feb. 1566, in Fontanon, 2 : 666–69) reduced the number of généralités to seven; but by 1570 they were back to seventeen (edict of Paris, Nov. 1570).
2. Zeller, *Institutions*, p. 286.
3. See also the supplementary ord. of Joinville, March 31, 1552. The Isambert edict title of this date is misleading; not seventeen recettes générales but seventeen trésoriers généraux are involved.

The trésoriers généraux were important officials within their diminished area. Like the old trésoriers de France, they watched over crown rights inside the recette générale, overseeing management of rents and dues (which made them superior to the bailiffs) and authorizing repairs of royal and public buildings.[4] Like the old généraux des finances, they also had the duty of checking the *élus* and other élection officials. Some of the more important aides had to be farmed out by the trésoriers généraux directly. In the *pays d'états* they had similar controls over the officials of the local collection bureaus. They had the duty of checking up on the *receveur général* to ascertain whether he had cash that should be sent to Paris. They sat as judges in certain types of fiscal trials, both for domaines revenues and for imposts. Like the old gens des finances, they had to ride through (*chevaucher*) their districts a certain part of each year and send regular reports on their activities directly to the royal council and to the *trésorier de l'Epargne*.

In 1557 the number of trésoriers généraux was doubled, not as *alternatifs* but as two top officials of the recette générale, serving at the same time. The king decreed that one of the trésoriers généraux was to deal primarily with the domaines and the other with the imposts.

Charles IX made the trésoriers généraux "alternating" positions; thus by 1571 there were four in each recette générale.[5] Henry III canceled the distinction between those trésoriers généraux who looked after domaines and those who managed the imposts.[6] All such officials were now to handle both types of revenues "togetherwise and conjunctly."[7]

In 1577 a fifth trésorier général was appointed for each généralité; and all of them were supposed to serve every year, rather than in alternate years. At the same time, the trésoriers généraux and all other fiscal officials at the généralité level were ordered to function in consultation with each other in what was called in the Renaissance a *collège*.[8] At this time, ordinances and treatises refer to all these men collectively—trésoriers généraux, receveurs généraux, and contrôleurs généraux—as a *bureau des finances*, a term that up to now seems to have been reserved for the building or office

4. Hennequin, *Guidon*, p. 141.
5. Edicts of Paris, Nov. 1570, and Blois, 1571.
6. The main summary edict on this matter, Poitiers, July 1577, refers to the change as a "union of charges."
7. Figon, *Discours*, p. 43^v.
8. The great reform ord. issued in 1579 in response to the Estates-General of Blois in 1576 reduced the number of trésoriers généraux to one per généralité (art. 242); but soon afterward the college of five trésoriers généraux per généralité was back in operation.

(*bureau*) in which the généralité tax officials sat to transact their business. The building in which élection officials received payments of tailles and aides, for example, was called a *bureau de recette*.[9] The evolution toward a corps of provincial tax officials in each généralité was now substantially completed.[10]

In 1581 the status of each bureau des finances as a corps was recognized by the appointment of a president for each bureau, plus a sixth trésorier général;[11] in 1586 two more trésoriers généraux were added, along with a vice president. Not that the business of the bureaux was increasing to the point where all these additional officials really were needed. The top-heavy membership of the bureaux, in fact, was one of the great scandals of the later sixteenth century and received special condemnation from the Estates-General of 1588. The astute Dallington reported with astonishment that at the time he was in France (1598) there were ten trésoriers généraux in each bureau des finances, plus three receveurs généraux, three special receveurs for the *taillon*, one for the clerical imposts, and two for the revenues from *eaux et forêts;* "and for every Receiver, so many Controllers generall; two Treasurers generall of the extraordinary of the Warre, for the payment of Garrisons and Souldiers in time of Warre."[12] In Dallington's time, furthermore, the number of recettes générales had risen to twenty-one: the areas of Limoges and Orléans had been turned into separate généralités by Charles IX, Moulins was added by Henry III, and Soissons was made the seat of the twenty-first généralité by Henry IV.

That the country could have operated with fewer subtreasuries seems certain. On the other hand, after 1577 the bureaux des finances performed the tasks expected of them well enough. They now had all responsibility for the proper fiscal functioning of their territory—under the general orders, of course, of the royal council. They undermined the remaining fiscal prerogatives of the provincial Estates that still existed.[13] The bureaux, as groups, were responsible for preparing provisional and definitive budgets for the généralité; they were provided with their own subordinate officials—scribes, ushers, constables, and clerks for the comptrollers. In 1577 they took over the task of supervising municipal finances for all the towns in their jurisdic-

9. Cf. Figon, *Discours*, p. 42ᵛ, who refers to bureaux généraux, obviously to distinguish them from the élection bureaus.
10. Ed. Everat, *Le bureau des finances de Riom, 1551–1789*, pp. 1–3. See also Meynial, "Etudes sur l'histoire financière du XVIe siècle," *Nouvelle Revue Historique de Droit Français et Etranger* 44 (1920) : 480–83.
11. Edict of Blois, Jan. 1581.
12. Dallington, *View of Fraunce*, p. P3.
13. Vannier, *Essai sur le bureau des finances*, pp. 93–95.

tion. They had the right to summon officials at the lower or élection level for conferences, and they could authorize punishment for any subordinate officials they found corrupt or inefficient. They were not necessarily passive agents of the royal will. The bureau in Caen (West Normandy), for example, vigorously protested unfair and higher taxes.[14]

The numerous supervisory officials attached to the généralité (a term that began to replace *recette générale* by the 1570s) absorbed much of the authority of the élus and their assistants in the élection. The élu, therefore, tended to become a less important supervisor. He is hardly ever the subject of more than cursory attention in the fiscal ordinances of the later Renaissance. It is significant that La Barre, in the introduction to his treatise, finds it necessary to defend élus against the charge that their office is "vile ou abiecte." In theory, élus were still responsible for the *assiette* of the taille among the parishes and the grant of farms for the aides; in fact, however, the availability of a bureau des finances in close proximity to any district made it easy enough for peasants and merchants with tax grievances to appeal over the head of the élu to the trésorier général. The personnel of the élection continued to increase; but it is clear these new officials were useful to the king mainly for the purchase price of their offices.[15]

Another fundamental reform of the mid-sixteenth century was the extension to the généralités of middle-echelon comptrollers.

A "contrerooleur" or *contrôleur* originally was a clerk who made "counter rolls," duplicate records that could be used to check reports of revenue agents. "Rolls," of course, were pieces of parchment or tough paper sewn or glued in long strips as they were completed and then rolled up for storage. Unlike modern records, many medieval and Renaissance documents were not kept flat in books of leaves.[16]

Local comptrollers were in existence in large numbers in Renaissance France, even before the reforms of Francis I. Francis I appointed a comptroller for each élection, specifically for the chief imposts. It was also

14. Romier, *Lettres et chevauchées*, pp. 120–21.

15. Each élection, toward the end of the sixteenth century, contained seven élus (a president, a second president, a lieutenant, and four others), and a royal prosecutor, not to mention the many lower-echelon officials.

16. Some legal documents had to be kept this way by government order; thus the edict of Blois, June 1581, in Isambert, 14 : 498, creating additional inspector-recorders of contracts, directs these officials to keep registers of these documents "en parchemin reliez et continuez, et non par feuillets attachez."

their duty to be present at the auction of all élection tax farms. Eventually, they were given the duty of ascertaining whether or not the king was being paid the fines levied by judges or by administrative officials.[17] This was a distinctly minor position, compensated at a piece rate for each budget examined. In fact, élection comptrollers were warned not to aspire to functions reserved for élus, with whom, according to a 1543 edict, some comptrollers were engaging in "grandes contentions, debatz & differentz," partly over questions of "renc." [18]

Two top-level comptrollers were created during the Epargne reforms of Francis I, one attached to the trésorier de l'Epargne and another to the Parties casuelles; the Parties casuelles comptroller, in 1527, was given the duty of following the court to its various châteaux in order to provide the privy council with up-to-date information on available cash reserves.[19] The comptroller assigned to the Epargne had the duty of signing all special expenditure authorizations (*mandements patents* and *rescriptions*), allowing him to check on the trésorier de l'Epargne himself.[20] As the royal council began to rely heavily on their comptroller for fiscal information, his job became the more important one. He too signed expenditure authorizations, those coming directly from a member of the council. He was particularly valuable because of his ability to suggest just where, in the complex fiscal system, needed funds could be obtained. He also had the task of approving all the definitive budgets (*états au vrai*) submitted to the council. The edicts of the period call him the "contrôleur-général de nos finances," a high-sounding title. The contrôleur général, of course, was to become in time one of the chief Old Régime ministers and finally, with the advent of Colbert, the head of the whole finance ministry.

In the sixteenth century, however, the adjective in the title *contrôleur général* refers mainly to comptrollers who operated at the généralité level. That is, the term designates the area covered rather than the amount of authority wielded. Thus we have minor comptrollers called "contrôleur-général du domaine en chaque généralite," [21] and "contrôleur-général du taillon" in each généralité.[22] Figon refers to the "contrerolleur général

17. Edict of Paris, Jan. 24, 1523, in Isambert, 12 : 199–200.
18. Decree of St. Germain-en-Laye, May 17, 1543, in Isambert, 12 : 808–10.
19. See also the duties assigned him in the supplementary edict of Blois, Dec. 11, 1550.
20. Ord. of St. Germain-en-Laye, April 12, 1547, actually prepared during the last days of Francis I. See also Meynial, "Etudes," pp. 474, 496.
21. Edict of Paris, Oct. 1581, in Isambert, 14 : 505.
22. Edict of Paris, Nov. 1576.

provincial des greniers à sel" in each généralité.[23] After 1555 there were at least two chief comptrollers in each généralité, one concerned mainly with collections, the other with expenditures.[24]

Jean Combes had a high opinion of the contribution to the fiscal system made by contrôleurs généraux, comparing them to the ancient ephors; the fact that they had to keep an eye on collectors, he thought, made them the equal of any official at the généralité level.[25] But modern scholars believe they were inferior in status to both the trésoriers généraux and the receveurs généraux.[26]

One function of the comptrollers was to force comptables to record the exact amount and purpose for the expenses they were deducting from receipts; these local worthies were too likely to lump everything together as "wages and expenses." It was up to the comptrollers to require comptables to maintain good records so as to reveal which of the deductions were "superfluous and excessive."[27] Somewhat optimistically, the government required that its comptrollers not have relations with the collectors—blood, business, or otherwise.[28]

If we can believe the edicts on the subject, an even more important function of the généralité comptrollers was to help pry cash out of the tax collectors. The comptrollers were given specific directions on how to encourage local collectors to speed up the flow of the *restes* to the généralité treasuries: they could force local comptables owing the crown more than 200 livres to pay quadruple the amount.[29] In certain cases they could require comptables who had held cash for long periods to pay interest *à denier douze* (8⅓ percent) on these sums.[30] At one time the government experimented with a new officer known as the *solliciteur général des restes;* his duties were to undertake the "poursuites & diligences" against slow

23. *Discours,* p. 61ʳ. See also the edict of Chenonceaux, May 1577, in Isambert, 14 : 326.

24. Edict of Fontainebleau, Feb. 1555, and decl. of St. Germain-en-Laye, Aug. 24, 1555.

25. *Traicté,* pp. 36–37.

26. Zeller, *Institutions,* p. 288.

27. Bodin observes that without good accounting procedure comptables were likely to pay out funds "sans ordonnance, mandatement et acquis." Quoted in Paul Nancey, *Jean Bodin, économiste* (Bordeaux, 1942), p. 271.

28. Ord. of St. Germain-en-Laye, Dec. 1557, item 7. See also Boyer, *Instruction,* p. 125.

29. Ord. of Paris, Feb. 20, 1553.

30. Edict of Vitry-le-Français, Nov. 1573.

comptables, that is, to prepare cases against them for the courts.[31] Figon tells how Catherine de Medici was especially concerned about prompt delivery of the restes because it was these funds that were being used to pay for her palace in "les thuyleries." [32]

At the same time that the provincial bureaux des finances were taking shape, a new institution was being formed by the crown to keep them under a tighter rein. This was the *intendant des finances*, a position that was to grow into one of the most important instruments of seventeenth-century government, when the intendants became the effective governors of provinces. But the origins and development of the intendants des finances in the sixteenth century are not yet clear.[33] Probably the intendants can be traced back to the specialized *maîtres des requêts* of the royal household. These were highly trained and thoroughly respected administrative specialists who heard complaints and submitted reports and recommendations to the royal council on the operation of the royal household. They also acted as agents for the crown out in the provinces.[34] In the 1550s some of them specialized in reporting on and handling complicated fiscal matters, including the construction of the *états de prévision;* [35] and in this capacity they were referred to as intendants des finances.

It was many years, however—not until the period 1580–1600—before intendants des finances acquired a clear and stable position in royal administration. Meanwhile (by whatever authority and title) these élite administrators, highly competent in fiscal matters and enjoying the complete backing of the crown, increased their authority over généralité officials. There were about ten of them, eight for provincial inspection tours, and two for the royal council. Their main job in the provinces seems to have been to see that actual expenditures were in line with the provincial budgets

31. Letters-patent of Offrémont, May 27, 1554; ord. of Romorantin, May 31, 1560. However, comptables could purchase forgiveness from an adverse court decision; see the decl. of St. Germain-en-Laye, Aug. 21, 1559, in Isambert, 14 : 4–5.

32. *Discours*, p. 57ʳ. See also the letters-patent of Paris, April 28, 1578.

33. The subsequent passages follow the somewhat tentatively expressed opinions of Roger Doucet, *Institutions*, vol. 1, chap. 19, and Zeller, *Institutions*, p. 117. For a different view see Meynial, "Etudes," pp. 498–500.

34. For a long time the terms *intendant* and *commissaire* were used interchangeably. It remains to be shown, however, whether intendants were commissaires in the sense that the latter could not hold venal offices; see La Barre, *Formulaire*, p. 56.

35. First clearly in 1547; see Zeller, *Institutions*, pp. 115, 117, 290.

that had been prepared and approved by the royal council.[36] By the 1580s it was common knowledge that the trésoriers généraux and the contrôleurs généraux took orders from the intendants des finances.[37] When working at a bureau des finances, the intendants seem to have possessed definite judicial powers, so that they not only could report directly to the council but also could pass judgments on officials, sometimes arraigning them before local courts, sometimes fining or even dismissing them on their own authority.[38]

Intendants des finances also sat regularly with the royal council—and especially in the weekly meetings of fiscal specialists known as the Conseil des finances. They were developing into what we would call government undersecretaries, specialists who provided needed information and saw to it that policy decisions were carried out. In this capacity they were far more important than the older *secrétaires signant en finances*, who gradually faded from the picture.[39]

36. See Figon, *Discours*, p. 43ʳ; and see the decree of Bar-le-Duc, May 4, 1564.
37. Figon, *Discours*, p. 47ʳ; and Hennequin, *Guidon*, pp. 581–83.
38. An interesting glimpse into the relations between a bureau des finances and the royal council is available in Albert Chamberland, "Remonstrances des trésoriers de France," *Revue Henri IV* 3 (1909–12) : 166–78.
39. "Bref," says Hennequin, "il ne se passe aucune chose dudit Conseil qui lesdits Intendants n'en la Cognoissance, ny qu'ils en donnent leurs avis." *Guidon*, p. 586.

C

Fiscal Courts and Their Functions

There were three main fiscal courts—the Chambre des comptes, the Cour des aides, and the Cour du Trésor. Parlement also had some power over the revenues system, especially where domain lands were concerned.[1] The Chambre des comptes handled most of the cases between the crown and tax officials, especially those officials who were *comptables*. Litigation between taxpayers and tax officials involving tailles, aides, and gabelles had to be settled by the Cour des aides. Most quarrels over rents and dues from the domaines were sent to the Cour du Trésor.

The functions of the three courts can be classified into five main categories. First, they constituted a prime agency for protecting the king's rights over revenue. Fiscal officials sitting in courts at the palace (on the site of the present Palais de Justice) and branches elsewhere were just as significant in extending and defending royal power as were those officials who, so to speak, were "in the field." All the chief fiscal courts had the power of imposing (with no appeal) sentences from a small fine to life imprisonment in the Conciergerie or a provincial dungeon. Sentences of capital punishment by the Cour des aides or the Cour du Trésor, however, had to be reviewed by the Chambre des comptes or by parlement.[2] Cases of prime political importance, such as the trial of Semblançay, or special investigations that could be expected to lead to administrative reforms, usually were handled by specially chosen royal commissions, often judges and lawyers from parlement and from two or three of the fiscal courts.

Second, the fiscal courts were prime sources of information concerning tax affairs. In fact, they were the fiscal archives of the kingdom, by virtue of preserving past ledgers and budgets, with which they could provide the royal council with guides for action.

Third, fiscal jurists acted as wardens to control subordinate officials in each branch of the system, in the sense that they could bring erring officials to trial and punish them.

1. Therefore it is wrong to regard the Chambre des comptes as "the French financial tribunal," as does A. J. Grant, *The French Monarchy, 1483–1789*, 2 vols. (Cambridge, 1900), 1 : 4.

2. Boyer, *Instruction*, p. 71.

Fourth, the fiscal courts provided at least the appearance of a means for taxpayers to obtain redress of grievances. Greedy or cruel tax officers were partly held in check by knowing that those they injured—or rather those who could afford the time and expense of litigation—could haul their oppressors into a court especially designed to punish sticky-fingered or overbearing tax officials.

Finally—in some ways this was a contradiction of other functions—the fiscal courts acted as a check on the king's power to issue ordinances. Each fiscal edict that affected one of the "sovereign" tax courts had to be registered on the rolls of that court; otherwise, the edicts could not be enforced at law. This power of the fiscal courts was protected, paradoxically, by several royal edicts. The edict of Chantilly, May 7, 1554, for example, rules that even royal gifts of privileges, titles of nobility, and exemptions from taxation "will have no standing and produce no effects" if not "viewed, examined, and registered by our said [Chambre des] comptes." [3]

One rationalization of this contradiction was that the power to refuse registration gave the courts the right to protect the king against his own bad judgment. Thus the Chambre des comptes zealously upheld its right to reject alienation decrees involving crown lands.

When courts sent back offending edicts to the king, the action was accompanied by respectful explanations as to why the decree should be withdrawn or changed. At this point it was up to the king and council to decide whether to comply with, or to override, this request. There are several famous cases of resistance to the royal will by parlement (for example, parlement stubbornly refused to register the Edict of Nantes until forced to do so by months of the strongest pressure Henry IV could apply). Less well known is the fact that the Chambre des comptes and, less frequently, the Cour des aides also asserted their rights, sometimes in spite of threats of bodily harm or revocation of the offices of the judges involved. In 1567, for example, at the time when fighting in the Wars of Religion had resumed and the government needed funds desperately, the Cour des aides refused to verify the prolongation of a recent levy on wine and actually stopped this tax from being raised in several provinces. [4]

But these examples of judicial checks on the crown stand out strongly because they are such a contrast to the normal state of affairs. Usually a threat by one of the royal councilors or a formal *lettre de jussion* got the king's bidding done—and promptly. [5]

3. Jean Rousset, *Les ordonnances faictes par le roy . . . sur le faict de sa Chambre des comptes en Bretaigne*, p. 173.

4. Doucet, *L'état des finances de 1567*, p. 12.

5. There is an example of a lettre de jussion in A.N. AD^{IX-2}, dated Villers-

The prestige of the Chambre des comptes was great. Its presidents "deliberate and judge definitively and in a sovereign manner." [6] The anonymous author of *L'auditeur des comptes* called the Chambre des comptes "the sister of parlement." [7] The edict of Blois, December 1520, called it "our court of last resort . . . to be subject to [the king] with no intermediaries. And there may be no appeal from the orders, depositions, and judgments of the said judges of the Comptes. . . ." [8]

At the head of this court were two presidents, who ranked at the top of the privileged magistracy.[9] (The term *noblesse de robe* is Old Régime rather than Renaissance; during the Renaissance the appellation *robe longue* was used for high officials, because of the sweeping robe they wore, as distinguished from the military short skirt, or *robe courte*, of nobles.) One of the presidents of the Chambre des comptes had precedence over the other. This *première présidence* was given to Jean Nicolay in 1506, and it remained in his family from that time until the French Revolution. Some justices of the fiscal courts came from the older aristocracy or even from the church hierarchy.[10] Most of them, however, came from the richer bourgeoisie.

The main business of the Chambre des comptes was carried out by less august officials. There were eight chief accountants, or *maîtres des comptes;* some specialized in trying cases, others in verifying accounts.[11] Further down the ladder were several dozen lesser officials—*correcteurs, auditeurs, greffes* (scribes or archival registrars), and *huissiers* (sergeants-at-arms or ushers). All these officials, from the presidents down to the huissiers, were appointed by the king.

The most important court for the verification of accounts was located

---

Cotterets, Aug. 1552, forcing the Cours des aides of Paris to register an edict granting total exemption to all taxes to the inhabitants of Boulogne, in view of their "fidelité" during the recent fighting.

6. Hennequin, *Guidon,* p. 601.

7. *L'auditeur des comptes* (n.p., n.d.), p. 6. This work has been mistaken for an administrative treatise; but it is a tract against parlement and specifically against the avocat général of parlement, Etienne Pasquier, a famous jurist during the Wars of Religion and a known political moderate.

8. In Isambert, 12 : 183–87.

9. The number of presidents (as well as minor court officials) was vastly increased during the wholesale creation of venal offices by Francis I and Henry II.

10. Gustave Dupont-Ferrier, *Nouvelles études sur les institutions financières de la France à la fin du moyen âge: les origines et le premier siècle de la Chambre ou Cour des aides de Paris,* pp. 12–13.

11. Doucet, *Institutions,* 1 : 190. Maîtres des comptes also could be used "in the field" to check on suspected improprieties involving alienated royal lands and revenues.

in Paris. There was another Chambre des comptes established at Montpellier in 1523 for the Midi, and a third at Rouen in 1580 for Normandy.[12] Later, Dijon (for Burgundy) and Nantes (for Brittany) were given separate branches of the Chambre des comptes. And, temporarily, there was a Chambre des comptes at Moulins, established by Louise of Savoy, the imperious mother of Francis I, who took over the Bourbonnais from the disgraced Constable de Bourbon.[13] The royal inheritance of the Orléans family, which was managed apart from the other domaines revenues, was in the care of a separate Chambre des comptes at Blois.[14]

Before these additional Chambres des comptes were founded, clearing accounts was a troublesome business for the comptables far away from Paris. The comptable (or his assistant) had to bring the ledgers and budgets to the central Chambre des comptes. Usually accounts were cleared every year. Some comptables, however, had the right to appear before a Chambre des comptes once every two years.[15] Certain accounts, no matter where in the country they originated, had to be cleared at Paris; this was the case for the receipts of the clerical tenths,[16] for the revenues from the *ban et arrière-ban*, the town octrois, and the accounts of several revenue officials connected to the armed forces.[17] Copies of all accounts approved at other Chambres des comptes had eventually to be sent to Paris.[18]

When fiscal records appeared before the Chambre des comptes they were, in a sense, on trial. Each account was submitted to the solicitor attached to the Chambre des comptes (*procureur général*) who represented royal interests. The account then was passed on to auditors who compared it to previous accounts for the same district and especially examined it for omission of any items of revenue and in general as to whether it was "bonne, valable, & deuement faicte." Then came the examination "en ligne de compte," made by correcteurs for mistakes in individual items and in arithmetic. Finally the chief auditor prepared "un papier appellé Bordereau" (a

12. The Echiquier of medieval Normandy, or rather the portion of it dealing with finances, had become a Chambre des comptes before Charles VII recovered that province; Charles VII suppressed it in 1451. The other section of the Echiquier became the Norman parlement. Edict of Montilz-sous-Bois, April 1499, in Isambert, 11 : 389–90.

13. Letters-patent of Fontainebleau, June 8, 1529, in Isambert, 12 : 315.

14. Dupont-Ferrier, *Bailliages*, p. 596 and n. 4, pp. 599, 909. See also Devèze, *Forêt française*, 1 : 168–69.

15. Edict of Angers, Feb. 15, 1499, in Rousset, *Ordonnances faictes par le roy*, p. 43; edict of Blois, Nov. 24, 1511, in Isambert, 11 : 614–17.

16. Ord. of Châteaudun, June 15, 1560.

17. Ord. of St. Léger, July 14, 1560.

18. H. Lemoine, "L'incendie du Palais de Justice et le disparition des archives de la Cour des aides," *Bibliothèque de l'Ecole des Chartes* 94 (1933) : 89–94.

memorandum) and passed it over, along with the account and all supporting documents (royal warrants and payees' receipts) to the president or his replacement for the day. The chief auditors then examined the documents again for technical faults or any signs of malfeasance. The maîtres des comptes had the right, at this point, to decide whether to accept or reject the report. If the decision were an adverse one and the comptable refused to accept it, he had the right to demand a hearing before one of the presidents.

If there were no objections to the account, it was returned to the auditors, who prepared a brief summary and submitted it to the royal solicitor; when he was satisfied, the solicitor turned the account over to the archivist (*garde des livres*). The account then became part of the permanent archives and could not be removed from its case or even consulted by outsiders without specific royal permission.[19] The whole process of clearing accounts, in fact, was a royal secret; for example, if a correcteur discovered that a comptable owed more cash to the treasury than reported, this fact was to be made known to no one apart from Chambre des comptes officials.[20] Accounts were in no sense public records. Even delegates to the Estates-General had the greatest difficulty gaining access to them. The king explicitly refused to divulge how much money he was receiving and spending.

The lengthy accounting procedures, reminiscent of the worst sort of medieval red tape, make it easy to understand why auditing occupied most of the time of the Chambre des comptes. By the mid-sixteenth century the Chambre des comptes at Paris was examining about seven hundred accounts in an average year, possibly three every working day. In addition, the Chambre des comptes had to handle cases against erring comptables, hear important claims for exemptions and concessions involving domaines revenues, and supervise transfers of property and rights into and out of the domaines system. This was the court, furthermore, in which all edicts of alienations of domain lands and revenues had to be registered. The Chambre des comptes also received and registered all acts of homage from possessors of royal fiefs and from *engagistes*, that is, persons who held royal lands or revenues in pledge (*en gage*). The Chambre des comptes, finally, had the duty of swearing in all important fiscal officials.[21]

Officials who handled funds and kept accounts had to agree to be tried

19. This description is based on the manual of Philibert Boyer, *Instruction*, pp. 175–79. For earlier procedures see the letters-patent of Meung-sur-Yèvre, Dec. 23, 1454, a general regulatory ordinance for the Chambre des comptes, in Jacqueton, *Documents*, pp. 74–90, and the edict of Blois, Dec. 1511, in Isambert, 11 : 617–28.

20. Edict of Bourges, Nov. 26, 1447, in Fontanon, 2 : 616.

21. Doucet, *Institutions*, 1 : 194.

by this court if they were charged with inefficiency or criminal actions. This applied to all comptables, those connected with "extraordinary" and "ordinary" revenues, the comptables of the royal household, and even special-purpose officials like the army paymasters.[22] Penalties ranged from orders to redo accounts properly to the loss of salary, fines, loss of position, imprisonment, and even death. The Chambre des comptes could also issue its own writs to enforce compliance with its decisions.[23]

In spite of its "sovereignty" and its impressive sounding powers, the Chambre des comptes was mainly a part of the administrative machinery of the royal revenues. With one or two possible exceptions, it did not operate on the policy-making level. However, the court could refuse to register alienations, and it had the right to thwart the royal will by refusing to approve gifts of more than 100 livres.[24] Another policy aspect of its powers was the right to oversee the handling of the municipal octrois of Paris, which gave the court some voice in city affairs.[25] But its main duties, after all, were passive—"le calcul, audition, et closture des comptes." [26]

The Cour des aides possessed a smaller number of high officials than did the Chambre des comptes. There were, at most, four *généraux sur la justice des aides*. This court also had three *conseillers sur la justice des aides* who were the chief assistants to the généraux. They also acted as judges in the absence of a sufficient number of généraux.[27] The presiding official was a president comparable in function to those at the Chambre des comptes. Present also were the inevitable royal solicitor, his assistant, and several clerks, scribes, and sergeants-at-arms.

The area of jurisdiction of the Cour des aides was wide. It included "actions and arguments" between taxpayers and tax officials connected with the whole body of "extraordinary" revenues everywhere in the country. If a commoner claimed exemption from the tailles, if a merchant believed he had been cheated by a tax farmer, if a townsman contested the amount of salt he was supposed to buy—all such cases would go to the Cour des aides. The only exceptions were cases involving small sums of money or those

22. A.N. AD^{IX-470}, dated Jan. 2, 1587.
23. Boyer, *Instruction*, p. 71. See the many commentaries on the status of the Chambre des comptes as well as its procedures in J. Le Grand, *Instruction pour le faict des finances et Chambre des comptes* (Paris, 1582), esp. pp. 2–7.
24. Ord. of Paris, June 24, 1492. See also Rousset, *Les ordonnances faictes par le roy*, p. 173.
25. Henri Sée, *Louis XI et les villes*, p. 121.
26. Boyer, *Instruction*, p. 180.
27. The equal status of conseillers was verified in the edict of St. Germain-en-Laye, Aug. 1550 A.N. Z^{IA-527}, 649 *bis*.

that had been settled first by middle-echelon officials, élus or grenetiers.[28]

In addition to these major areas of jurisdiction, the Cour des aides also controlled the *équivalent* of Languedoc, forced loans, the "free gifts" and tenths of the clergy, and other important revenues.[29] Therefore, the power of the court brought it into areas of France where there were no "aides," properly speaking.

To handle its burden of work, the Cour des aides was split into two autonomous "chambers" at Paris.[30] Languedoc had long had its own Cour des aides, established at the time of the reforms of Charles VII.[31] Additional Cours des aides were set up at Rouen, Blois, Clermont-Ferrand, and Périgueux. In Provence, curiously, the Chambre des comptes sat instead of a Cour des aides.[32]

In the language of the Renaissance, the Cour des aides was a sovereign court "to judge in civil and criminal cases those affairs assigned to it in sovereignty and as a court of last resort." [33] It was jealous of its privileges. As a result, there were many jurisdictional disputes between the Cour des aides and parlement. From the beginning the crown made it clear that only the Cour des aides was to hear cases involving tailles, aides, gabelles, and traites.[34] During the reign of Henry II, new appellate courts (*présidiaux*)

28. Doucet, *Institutions*, 1 : 197. The royal decl. of St. Germain-en-Laye, March 17, 1549, in Isambert, 13 : 75–80, shows the Cour des aides having some authority over cases involving comptables not turning in cash properly. This was a passionately resented encroachment into the area of jurisdiction of the Chambre des comptes.

29. The legal language of the Cour des aides' jurisdiction, as given in Jean Philippe, ed., *Edits et ordonnances du roy concernans l'autorité et jurisdiction des Cours des aides . . .* , pp. 12–13, is worth giving here: it was over "toutes les causes, querelles, débats, rebellions, iniures, outrages, battures, meurtres, exactions, fraudes, & quelsconques excès, crismes, délits, malefices, faussetés, procès, & matières qui viendront, sourdront & procederont de tout le fait des dits Aides, tailles, gabelles, Quatriesmes, Huittiesmes, imposition foraine & autres équivalens à icelle, octroys & compositions en lieu de tailles & aides dons, recompenses assignations, creüs, traittes, quart de sel, fornissemens de greniers à sel & de tous autres aides, dons, octroys & imposts mis sus . . ."

30. Edict of Rheims, March 1552, in Isambert 13 : 264–68.

31. This court was established in Toulouse in 1437, but it was moved to Montpellier in 1467, perhaps to get it away from the Languedoc parlement, which remained at Toulouse. Philippe, *Edits et ordonnances*, pp. 1–3, 7–10. See also the confirmation of the authority and jurisdiction of the Montpellier Cour des aides in the edict of St. Germain-en-Laye, Feb. 3, 1527, in Isambert, 12 : 274.

32. Zeller, *Institutions*, p. 294.

33. B.N. Nouv. acq. fr. 2374, fol. 48ᵛ.

34. Edict of June 1445 in Houzé, *Edicts et ordonnances*, p. 2. Apparently at this time church courts had been claiming jurisdiction over certain types of cases

were given certain limited rights to hear cases appealed from the rulings of the élus; but in the following reign the Cour des aides won back its exclusive right to hear such appealed cases.[35]

An overview of the actual work of the Cour des aides shows that it, like the Chambre des comptes, was primarily a branch of royal administration; it had little significance in determining policy and little "constitutional" standing. In theory it, too, could refuse to register edicts that violated what it considered the legal framework of "extraordinary" taxation. For most of the Renaissance, however, such acts of resistance to the crown were rare compared to those of the Chambre des comptes or of parlement. Both parlement and the Chambre des comptes had the right to issue formal letters of remonstrance against offending royal edicts; but such an action was forbidden to the Cour des aides. During the Wars of Religion, however, and in the era of Sully, the Cour des aides sometimes refused to register grants of large-scale tax farms (*grosses fermes*) when it suspected scandalous profits or collusion between tax farmers and courtiers.[36]

Like the judicial généraux of the Cour des aides, the Cour du Trésor (also called Chambre du Trésor) was originally the *trésoriers* when they were sitting for the "faict & exercise de Iustice" rather than when they were overseeing the "administration, gouvernement & distribution de deniers." [37] One of the reasons for establishing the Cour du Trésor was to provide "ordinary" revenues with the same type of court as that for the "extraordinaries." The Cour du Trésor traces its origins back to the same period as the Cour des aides, and many of the developments in the early history of the two courts are parallel. But the Cour des aides became by far the more important.[38]

---

involving taxes and had forbidden crown officials to interfere on pain of excommunication.

35. Pierre Des-Hayes, *Recueil de plusieurs ordonnances . . . pour le faict des aydes*, p. 55, quoting an edict of Oct. 1569. See also the edict of Blois, Dec. 20, 1559, ruling on a dispute between the Cour des aides and parlement, in Isambert, 14 : 16–17, and many similar edicts in the collection of Philippe, *Edits et ordonnances* (e.g. pp. 54–57).

36. Albert Chamberland, "Jean Chandon et le conflit entre la Cour des aides et le Conseil du roi," *Revue Henri IV* 2, no. 2 (1908) : 124–25.

37. P. Mettayer, *Recueil de plusieurs edicts . . . concernants le pouvoir & iurisdiction de la Chambre du Thrésor*, p. 8a.

38. The Cour du Trésor is barely mentioned and not explained in Jacqueton's famous survey, *Documents*; see esp. p. xxiii. Neither can one find it in Clamageran, *L'impôt*. This is puzzling, since Renaissance treatises devote much time to the Cour

The area of jurisdiction of the Cour du Trésor must have been a lawyer's delight. The Cour du Trésor judged disputes involving rents, *censives*, and the king's seigneurial rights on the royal estates; all royal tolls and some tariffs; income derived from rights over Jews, foreigners, freed serfs, wards, bastards, and treasure trove; feudal income from the vassals and subvassals; and income from the church hierarchy such as the *régale* from vacant bishoprics.[39] Some such matters were trivial and could be decided on the spot by the bailiffs and seneschals. But important cases and cases that were appealed went to the Cour du Trésor. While the total of revenues protected by the Cour du Trésor was tiny compared to those of the Cour des aides, individual cases could involve large amounts. An example is *franc-fief*, the king's rights over noble lands that had come into the hands of commoners; in certain cases this right could bring the king all of the net profits for as long as six years from the estates involved. The Cour du Trésor also had some functions we would call semi-administrative. The court had the duty, for example, of ruling whether tolls for roads and bridges were adequate to pay for proper upkeep of these services.

One significant difference between the Cour du Trésor and the Cour des aides is that there was only one of the former (located in Paris at the Tuileries palace), while by the end of the sixteenth century there usually were seven Cours des aides. The Cour du Trésor had only a relatively small number of officials—the four trésoriers, four powerful assistants known as *conseillers*, a *procureur royal*, and the procureur's assistant, an *avocat royal*. There were no designated "presidents" for this court. Most often only one trésorier, or even one or two conseillers, was sufficient to judge a case. In addition, the court had the usual numerous scribes, ushers, and police. And it had the right to impose penalties up to and including life imprisonment.[40]

The Cour du Trésor worked to offset fraud and corruption—so hard to prevent in these complicated affairs—and to reverse the constant attrition of the royal domaines that came from their being so widespread, complex, and tempting.[41] In the 1450s, when the primary task was the reconstruction

---

du Trésor. See Jean Bacquet, *Trois premiers traictez des droicts du domaine de la couronne de France* (Paris, 1580) and René Choppin, *Trois livres du domaine de la couronne de France*.

39. The forest service, however, had its own superior court called, after the table around which it met, the "Table de Marbre."

40. Gustave Dupont-Ferrier, *Les origines et le premier siècle de la Cour du Trésor* (Paris, 1936), pp. 91–98.

41. That this was a persistent problem can be seen from the pessimistic tone of the royal proclamation of St. Germain-en-Laye, May 9, 1553, in Isambert 13 : 321–23.

of the domaines after the Hundred Years' War, the Cour du Trésor had the important function of ferreting out the innumerable revenues that had disappeared during the confusion of the wars. For generations, property lines between crown lands and others had been neglected, a situation that worked to the advantage of everyone but the king. False charters of grants and immunities were all too plentiful; and too many choice revenues and properties had been alienated by careless or hard-pressed kings.[42] By investigating alienations, grants, and property transfers that appeared to be surreptitious, the Cour du Trésor was able to recover valuable property—which, of course, the kings promptly gave away again.

As this labor of Sisyphus became, year by year, less significant to the total revenues of the crown, the Cour du Trésor became correspondingly less important in the bureaucracy. It was never accorded the prestige of a "sovereign court," as were the Cour des aides and the Chambre des comptes. Parlement could accept appeals of all important cases concerning the domaines from judgments rendered by the Cour du Trésor.[43] In 1533 Francis I made the sovereignty of parlement over cases involving the domaines more formal by authorizing the formation of a special section of the Parlement of Paris, which was to sit regularly to hear appeals concerning the domaines.[44] Before long, the trésoriers themselves were staying away from meetings of the Cour du Trésor, which now were run exclusively by conseillers. In 1544 a fundamental reform, part of the changes that established the bureaux des finances, undercut the Cour du Trésor almost completely, since many of its functions were now absorbed into a single bureau des finances—the one established for the Ile de France.[45]

42. Dupont-Ferrier, *Cour du Trésor*, p. 109.
43. Dupont-Ferrier, *Cour des aides*, p. 167.
44. C. Dareste de la Chavanne, *Histoire de l'administration en France*, 2 vols. (Paris, 1848), 1 : 349–51.
45. Doucet, *Institutions*, 1 : 199.

D

Control and Disbursement of Funds

The Renaissance monarchy, so far as possible, spent its money within the *élection* or bailiwick where funds were raised. By keeping the "porte et voicture" of cash to a minimum, the king saved himself a considerable amount of money, since these shipments were expensive as well as dangerous.

Examples of local expenditures were charitable contributions of all kinds, wages of garrison soldiers, all regular and special wages of the whole corps of local royal officials, the upkeep of royal châteaux and other "public" buildings in the area, and the repair and maintenance of fortresses. All such items and, of course, the expenses of shipment would be "assigned" on the local revenues.

The system of localized expenditures explains why all edicts and Renaissance writings refer to the money that was actually shipped to the king as a residuum—*les restes*. It was "that net [amount] which remains or comes in," or money which comes in as cash (*au clair*, or "free and clear"). This did not mean, of course, that the restes were unimportant—on the contrary. For the government this was the function of the revenue system that mattered most.[1]

A few revenues were shipped directly to the Trésor. Only the expenses of collection and shipment were deducted from such revenues before they went to the king. Examples are the small profits from the royal mints, the sales of wood from the royal forests, and income from *franc-fief*. The same is true of *nouveaux acquêts*, fines to be paid under certain conditions by church bodies acquiring new lands. Profits from the sale of venal offices also were supposed to be exempt from "assignment." The clerical tenths, once they became a regular levy after the Estates-General of Orléans-Pontoise (1560–61), also were supposed to be sent directly to the king.[2]

Shipping money was an expensive undertaking. Hennequin's fiscal manual of 1585 shows that the cash had to be packed in special barrels or money

1. Boyer, *Instruction*, p. 91; see also the edict of Bourges, Nov. 26, 1447, in Fontanon, 2 : 617. Hennequin, *Guidon*, p. 287, shows how complicated was budgetary control over the restes.
2. Hennequin, *Guidon*, pp. 154, 285–87, 317–20.

chests and conveyed either in horse-drawn carts or on the backs of mules, all with suitable armed protection. Each money chest had to carry a standard sum, depending on the type of coins packed in it; thus each *bouge* (casket) of écus had to contain 500 livres in such coins. Not more than one drayman (*un seul chartier*) was to be employed for each four-horse cart; if mules were used, each one had to carry the weight equivalent of at least one hundred pounds. A convoy was to draw pay at the rate of 30 sous per day for each mule or horse, plus 60 sous per day for one "maistre clerc," and 50 sous for one assistant clerk. The convoy was enjoined not to drag out this pay period, but to move along with dispatch—"in summer ten leagues per day, in winter eight." [3]

There always had to be a certain amount of royal cash on the move in France. Money collected in the Paris area that was not spent immediately went directly into the strongboxes of the Trésor, located in the Tuileries (after this palace was finished by Catherine de Medici), the Tour d'Argent in the Conciergerie (near the Chambre des comptes), and the Louvre palace. If the court was not in Paris, some of these surpluses would have to follow along. Other sums had to be sent to the paymasters of the *compagnies d'ordonnance* at their garrisons, to various troops when in the field, and to Switzerland for the annual subsidy that guaranteed the availability of Swiss mercenaries to the French.

In the Musée Carnavalet, the museum of the history of Paris, there is a curious painting labeled "Inconnu—XVIIIe siècle: Incendie de la Chambre des comptes, le 27 octobre 1737." It is a dark impressionistic canvas with vaguely drawn figures struggling down the outside ramp of the Chambre des comptes while dense smoke and flame billows out around them. One of the figures seems to be trying to save some records. That famous and spectacular fire destroyed the greater part of what would have become an enormously wealthy source of documents on medieval and early modern government. The destruction of large batches of royal records during the French Revolution and the Paris Commune of 1871 further decimated the remnants.[4] Despite heroic efforts by French scholars to salvage the remaining scraps and fill in with whatever documents could be recon-

3. Hennequin, *Guidon*, pp. 270–76.
4. Apparently some of the documents that were not in the Chambre des comptes in 1737 were destroyed later—but not before many of them were copied and even published. See Michel Nortier, "Le sort des archives dispersées de la Chambre des comptes de Paris," *Bibliothèque de l'Ecole des Chartes* 123 (1965) : 460–537.

structed from copies in private collections and libraries and from archives outside Paris, there are aspects of the tax history of France that must remain forever uncertain.[5]

The most regrettable loss, of all the categories of documents that went up in smoke that day, is the budget for the whole nation, the *état général*. The most detailed national budget we possess—for the year 1523—is a mine of information about the operation of the fiscal system. Such a document can throw light on many other features of French economic history; for example, Roger Doucet, who transcribed and published the état for 1523, was able to use it to demonstrate the dimensions of the terrible crisis that brought about the fall of Semblançay and the reforms of Francis I.[6]

Most of the documents we do have are estimates for the *following* fiscal year; they are, therefore, provisional budgets (*états de prévision*). In such budgets the government set down what it expected from the various forms of revenue, by *généralités* (for the imposts) and by *recettes* (for the domaines). The Chambre des comptes and (after 1523) the Epargne were supposed to provide information on revenues actually collected in a definitive or "true budget." Most of the budgets we find in our records are provisional rather than "true" budgets, possibly because relatively few of the latter were completed.[7]

At the généralité and local (élection, diocese, city) level, parallel to the national budgets, there was also a double system of accounts. All *comptables* were expected to send to the Chambre des comptes provisional estimates of the amounts they planned to collect each year, "as close to the truth as they can get"; and at the end of the year they were directed to turn in final accounts "with precise figures." [8]

Historians as yet have hardly begun to exploit the existing Renaissance états; but the overall purpose of these instruments seems clear. They were primarily royal affirmations of how much, and in what manner, various districts, towns, officials, and tax farmers were obligated to pay the king.[9] To translate *état* as "budget," therefore, while it is the closest term we have, is something of an anachronism, since to us a budget is primarily an instrument for controlling expenditure by relating it to income. So far as tax-

5. Joseph Petit et al., *Essai de restitution des plus anciens mémoriaux de la Chambre des comptes de Paris.*
6. *L'état des finances de 1523.*
7. Several of the budgets remaining from the later Wars of Religion, however, appear to be *états au vrai*; see chap. 7.
8. Edict of Saumur, Sept. 4, 1443, in Fontanon, 2 : 607 ff.
9. Ed. Meynial, "L'histoire financière," 45 : 475.

payers and collection officials were concerned, Renaissance états were bills presented for payment; so far as the state's administrative officials were concerned, états were primarily aides-mémoire concerning how much the king was owed.[10] Etats also served the secondary purpose of showing from which districts, or which revenues, money would be taken to pay the king's charities, courtiers, soldiers, main officials, and others who had claims against him.

Of one thing we are certain: Renaissance états certainly were not surveys of the entire tax burden of the nation. Sometimes the global figure for individual taxes and total revenues appears nowhere in the état.[11] Even the so-called états généraux do not show all the territories where funds were collected and spent. Scores of specialized accounts were not even reflected in the national budget, including some for military campaigns and for some branches of royal household affairs.[12] The budget-making process, therefore, obviously focused not on what the people had to pay but on what the king expected to receive, not on the national burden but on the royal treasury.

After 1523 and the reforms of Francis I, when the construction of états was taken out of the hands of the *gens des finances*, provisional budgets apparently became even more summary and incomplete; the budget for 1567, for example, consists of only four folio pages.[13] Many payments that had been made locally now were handled by the new centralized treasury, the Epargne. Budgets, therefore, had to carry only the sketchiest information on the assignment of payments. It is also possible that formal budgets became skimpier after 1523 because of the increasing secrecy that characterized royal fiscal affairs after the downfall of Semblançay.[14]

The amount of detail found in any one national état, therefore, varies greatly over the whole span of the Renaissance. Some of the budgets for the later Wars of Religion are quite detailed. But certain features remain the same throughout the Renaissance. General états are always divided into traditional revenues and imposts: the domaines on the one hand and the tailles, aides, gabelles, traites, and emergency taxes on the other. Each large category of revenue is shown in its appropriate fiscal district. Antici-

10. This is true for the seventeenth and eighteenth centuries too, even though Old Régime budgets were technically much better.

11. See chap. 7, under the heading "What Were the Crown's Total Revenues during the Later Wars?"

12. For 1523 Doucet counts no less than 50 of these "annexed" budgets. *L'état des finances de 1523*, pp. 11, 20–27.

13. Doucet, *L'état des finances de 1567*, esp. p. 1 n.

14. Meynial found no national états at all for the period 1524–44. "L'histoire financière," 45 : 496–583.

pated receipts for gabelles, for example, are listed in each area for which gabelles were collected, rather than being carried as a single item for the nation. Another persistent procedure is that immediately after each notation showing anticipated or real receipts come the relevant expenses and deductions and finally the net receipts. The order in which individual items of income and outgo are listed, furthermore, tends to remain the same. Renaissance fiscal experts set great store by "the order which one keeps in setting up accounts." [15]

The purpose of the expenditures section of Renaissance budgets seems to be more a matter of showing proper authorization than of demonstrating whether or not royal funds were being spent as judiciously as possible. Expenditure items were arranged according to a vague set of priorities. First came the sums to be spent for charity and religious foundations, followed by (in order) funds to be spent for the king's household and perhaps those of the queen or other members of the royal family; gifts and pensions for the magnates and courtiers; wages of a select number of high crown officials and heads of the chief courts; *voyages et ambassades*, expenses of those traveling on royal missions. Last came the expenses for the military, forts and town walls, and public buildings.[16] Some états indicate, at this point, how the king's loans were to be repaid; often, however, there is no indication in the national budgets of loans that are known to be outstanding. When revenue shortages appeared, as they did so often, the order of priority indicated who should be paid first. Late in the Renaissance this order was shifted, mainly to put gifts and pensions at the bottom of the list, where public opinion demanded they should go.

Renaissance états display what appears to be a rather naïve concept of tying specific revenues to specific expenses; that is, tailles were supposed to pay the *compagnies d'ordonnance*; aides were set aside for other military expenses; the *taillon* (see appendix G) was supposed to pay for soldiers' rations and quarters; parlement salaries were expected to come from gabelles, and so on.[17] Salaries for the flood of venal offices later in the Renaissance

15. Hennequin, *Guidon*, pp. 276–77; Boyer, *Instruction*, p. 94; and see the order laid down by the *Vestige des finances*, published in Jacqueton, *Documents*, pp. 206 ff.

16. This is the order laid down for the late fifteenth and early sixteenth centuries. For the early Renaissance see the edicts of the 1440s in Fontanon, 2 : 607–17.

17. This was the usual view; however, Combes (*Traicté*, pp. 45–46) felt the domaines should yield enough to pay the compagnies d'ordonnance in peacetime, so that imposts would be needed for payment of troops only during war, and for items such as fortifications and "parties inopinées . . . comme les serviteurs secrets, espions. . . ."

were often linked to specific revenues as well.[18] Expenses of the royal household were supposed to come from the domaines, continuing the medieval notion that "the king should live of his own." Royal charities (*fiefs et aumônes*) were supposed to come from bailiwick chancery fees (*greffes et sceaux*).[19] After Francis I created the office of Parties casuelles to handle the sales of venal offices, receipts from this source were earmarked for the royal household.[20]

The expenses of tax collection—wages and fees for lower-echelon collectors, assessors, constables, and many of the expenses of the tax farmers—had to be borne by the taxpayers. But these expenses did not figure in the national budgets, though together they must have been one of the larger payment items. In other words, the amount entered in a national état for the tailles, for example, was not the total paid by the taxpayers, but rather the amount to be credited to the Epargne or paid to the Epargne in cash; this amount did not include many of the costs of collection and local administration. We can only guess at collection expenses; therefore, the true tax burden of Renaissance France will never be known.[21] Another problem for us is that when certain revenues were sold or given away (a frequent occurrence), they were not always mentioned in the national budgets—presumably because they were not bringing the king any cash.[22]

National budgets served also as guidelines for provincial tax officials, who worked with their superiors to draw up généralité budgets; on the district level *élus* provided information used to draw up local and more detailed

18. Thus when a new *receveur général des deniers communs* (i.e. of municipal revenues) was appointed, he was to be paid one sou for each livre collected from such revenues.

19. Doucet, *L'état des finances de 1523*, p. 32 n. 2; see also Hennequin, *Guidon*, pp. 141–51.

20. Figon, *Discours*, p. 50ʳ.

21. The edict of Paris, May 1575, for example, in Houzé, *Edicts et ordonnances*, p. 174, ordered that wages, travel pay, and other collection expenses for tailles "shall be imposed and established together with the revenue from the ordinary tailles." Sometimes we know specific collection rates; parish tailles collectors, for example, were paid 5 percent (one sou per livre) above the regular assiette. The edict of Compiègne, June 1557, ordered that collectors of décimes and forced loans were to be paid 3 deniers for each livre collected "qui seront levez & imposez oultre le principal." The anonymous *Traitté des finances de France*, p. 397, estimates collection expenses at one-third of the total revenues; but this seems to include wages and expenses of middle- and upper-echelon officials—items that sometimes are indicated in budgets.

22. Doucet, *L'état des finances de 1567*, p. 6. Sometimes, though indicated, a revenue is marked *néant*, because the king drew nothing from it that year.

états.[23] At the beginning of each fiscal year every comptable had to be provided with a duly signed and sealed état that he could display in his office; this constituted his authority to make certain expenditures and his obligation to collect certain sums in revenues.

Expenses of the royal *hôtel* appear in not one but many "annexes" of the general national budget. Besides a special état for the Chambre aux deniers (the most important household budget) there are separate budgets for privy purse expenditures—the "lesser affairs of the royal chamber" and "lesser pleasures of the king." At times there are separate listings for the "collector and functionary for the payment of royal oblation." Finally, after the reign of Francis I, there is a separate état listing the royal pensions.

The list of all those on the pay sheets of the household budget is a long one. No other series of sixteenth-century documents evokes so well the confusion, the gaiety and color, the love of ceremony that marked Renaissance royalty.[24] The king supported, besides his own *hôtel*, that of the queen and sometimes those of his brothers and sisters.[25] The burden of this sort of expense was increased by the new châteaux being constructed—not only expensive in their own right, but giving the court additional excuses to move about the country. *Hôtel* officials constituted a double charge on the treasury since, starting with the time of Charles VII, all commoners who were "ordinaires & commensaux" (that is, sharing the king's food by regular appointment) were exempt from all tailles.[26] Later they were freed of other taxes too, including the aides, the *ban et arrière-ban*, and the *traite*

23. For a transcription of a généralité budget, see Albert Chamberland, "Le budget de la généralité de Châlons en 1602," *Revue Henri IV* 3 (1909–12): 151–65. There is another in Romier, *Lettres et chevauchées*, appendix 2.

24. A very detailed list is available in Doucet, *L'état des finances de 1523*, appendixes F and G.

25. There is a detailed study of these secondary households, unfortunately not for the Renaissance but for the period just before, in Maurice Rey, *Les finances royales, sous Charles VI*, pp. 173–347. We have only scraps of information on *hôtel* expenses during the Renaissance. In the early years of Francis I, these expenses are supposed to have reached about a million livres annually. In his *L'état des finances de 1523*, pp. 10–11, Doucet finds 543,800 livres for the royal households of the king, queen, and royal princes, and 484,850 for pensions. Lemonnier, in Lavisse 5¹ : 209, accepts an impossibly high contemporary estimate that in the later reign of Francis I total court and household expenses were about 1.5 million écus. In his transcription of a retrospective budget for 1580, Dur, "Constitutional Rights," p. 264, shows about 1.7 million livres for the royal households, 1.2 millions for pensions, and 300,000 livres for "Les menuz dons Comprins les présens qu'il fault faire aux estrangers."

26. This was established as early as the edict of Sarry-les-Châlons, June 1445, and verified often during the Renaissance.

foraine, as well as forced loans and quartering of troops; such rights, further-more, were declared inheritable not only by the sons of such officials but also by their widows.

Several more or less secondary household officials were essentially royal paymasters. These included the *grand aumônier*, who was in charge of royal charity; the *maître* in charge of the Chambre aux deniers, whose re-sponsibility was to pay for all the food and drink required by the royal household; and the *argentier*, who handled expenditures for the apparel for the royal family and certain other members of the *hôtel*.[27]

In the preparation and handling of Renaissance budgets, no great techni-cal difficulties were presented by the collection expenses (which were de-ducted before the funds came to the *receveurs*) or by those regularly re-curring expenses which could be "embedded and used in the état"—chari-ties, pensions, pay for soldiers, wages of upper-level officials, and foreseeable purchases. Private individuals, officials, *domestiques* of the royal household, or royal favorites designated in such états had only to present themselves, demand their money, and give a receipt to the paying comptable.

It was in dealing with payments not anticipated in the various budgets that French fiscal procedure was at its weakest. Into this category fell pay-ments to soldiers in the field, new, noncontinuing charitable grants, re-payments of those lending money to the king, and the multitude of cash gifts the king made to those who had won his favor for any reason. Such payments had to be authorized by royal letters signed by the king himself or by one of his secretaries "signant en finances." These royal warrants were called *mandements, mandats,* or *acquits*; sometimes they were called *acquits patents* or *mandements patents*, since they were royal letters-patent and had to bear authorized signatures and seals. I shall use the term *acquit*, the one most often employed.[28]

The basic fault with these complicated arrangements was that there was too much administrative machinery involved in going from the initial de-cision to pay by acquit to the actual payment.[29] After they were written up in proper form and sealed by the chancery, acquits were still subject to a great deal of red tape. The party to whom the acquit was addressed was either the *changeur du Trésor*, in case payment was supposed to be effected

27. For a long list of household paymasters and other comptables see the ord. of Lyons, June 11, 1510.

28. For forms of acquits used later in the Renaissance see Hennequin, *Guidon*, p. 294, and Boyer, *Instruction*, p. 93. Hennequin explains (pp. 713–14) that *acquit* and *mandement* were used interchangeably; but he thinks originally an acquit was payment for services, while a mandement was a gift.

29. See the edict of Blois, Nov. 19, 1498.

by the domaines revenues, or the chief treasurer of the "extraordinary" (impost) revenues, the *receveur général* of a généralité or of a *recette générale*. Except for unusually favored persons, the changeur du Trésor or receveur général, upon receipt of the acquit, responded not with cash but with a *décharge*.[30] This procedure opened the door to one of the most pernicious forms of graft in Renaissance France, the necessity of greasing the palm of a fiscal official to get one's décharge addressed to a comptable who could and would pay.[31]

In chapter 3, we saw that one of the hopes behind the reforms of Francis I was that of ending this grievous traffic. But Renaissance France never solved this problem; and the scandal of décharges continued, though to a diminished extent, during the later Renaissance. A famous incident during the Wars of Religion involved Henri Estienne, the humanist and printer, who received a gift of 1,000 écus from the king for one of his books. When Estienne took his décharge to the collector on whom it was drawn he was offered, rather contemptuously, 600 écus. After trying in vain to peddle the décharge to one comptable after another, Estienne finally had to give up; the vicissitudes of the wars were making it impossible for him, as a suspected Huguenot, to stay near the court any longer, and his décharge was never paid.[32]

It was possible for royal favorites, at least, to bypass this irritating system by obtaining special acquits known as *acquits du roi* or, later, as *rescriptions*. During the reign of Henry III, they were called *acquits de deniers comptant* (hard cash warrants). These were orders to pay cash immediately, without the necessity to issue décharges. The necessary papers for controlling them by auditors and the Chambre des comptes were lacking; and, in fact, now and again a comptable had the unpleasant experience of turning over cash for a forged *mandement portant quittance*.[33]

30. This description follows for the most part the *Vestige des finances*, in Jacqueton, *Documents*, pp. 223 ff.

31. The problem remained just as serious during the seventeenth century until the reforms of Colbert.

32. Pierre de l'Estoile, *Registre-Journal*, vol. 2, part 1, pp. 187–88.

33. See the edict of St. Germain-en-Laye, Dec. 1557, items 30 and 31, instructing the trésorier de l'Epargne to write on the warrant a few words in his own hand so that the comptable to whom it was addressed would recognize it as valid.

E

Policy Control

The role of the royal council in terms of fiscal policy changed from one period to the next. Before 1523, the *gens des finances* had primary responsibility for making policy decisions, though any councilor had the right to advise the king on money matters. Francis I pushed aside the gens des finances and seized personal control over fiscal policy, relying only on his chancellor, Antoine Duprat, and a few trusted advisors. In the last part of Francis I's reign, and during the 1550s and 1560s under Henry II and Charles IX, there begins to be some experimenting with two different arrangements: either making taxes the special responsibility of a regular section of the council (a Conseil des finances) or making one of the councilors effectively minister of finance.

In the fifteenth century the royal council was made up of three groups: princes of the blood and peers of the realm, who were councilors by right; great crown officers, such as the chancellor, the constable, the admiral, and so on; and whomever else the king chose to designate, such as important churchmen, presidents of the sovereign courts, royal favorites, or the gens des finances. Any one of these might become the real master of royal finances. In 1402 Louis d'Orléans, regent for Charles VI, is supposed to have had himself addressed as "président du conseil général des aidés et finances." [1] After 1560 the queen mother, Catherine de Medici, often sat with the council and thus was a direct as well as an indirect participator in formulating fiscal policy.

The form of the royal council itself changed greatly during the Renaissance, often several times during a single reign. The most dramatic of such changes was the appearance, in the late 1520s and 1530s, of a privy council. This small group of councilors (perhaps four to six) met regularly and often with the king, taking responsibility for all major policy decisions, especially those relating to foreign affairs. This is the way Francis I ran his government, especially before 1542. As the sixteenth century wore on, this group became more formalized, and we see references to it in edicts and decrees as, appropriately, the "Conseil étroit" ("narrow council") or "Conseil des affaires." [2]

1. Clamageran, *L'impôt*, 1 : 439.
2. Sutherland, *Secretaries*, pp. 39–40.

The delegation of more responsibility in policy formation to the Conseil des affaires meant that the larger, older council, now confusingly called the "Conseil privé" or "Conseil du roi," was relegated to overseeing high-level but routine royal business. Thus, there was no clear separation of function. The line between the two types of councilors was thin and wavy; individuals often changed over, and the Conseil privé sometimes became involved in financial affairs. In the latter part of the reign of Francis I the small council is sometimes addressed as the "Conseil des affaires et des finances," emphasizing the high (and secret) place assigned by Francis I to fiscal policy.

Another development within the council was the rise in status of the royal secretaries. These *clercs du secret* were on hand during council meetings to provide indispensable clerical functions—keeping records of decisions, providing needed information, and drawing up the required letters, edicts, and warrants that were sent out to officials or private subjects who had to be apprised of council decisions. Their work included writing out the council's orders and attaching the royal seals. Therefore the secretaries were administratively under the royal chancellor, who guarded the seals.

Soon the secretaries became valued (though unofficial) advisors. They acquired the right to sit regularly with the council. Early in the fifteenth century, four of them were designated "secrétaires du Trésor" or, more often, "secrétaires des finances" or "secrétaires signant en finance," since they had the duty of signing all *mandats* or *acquits* which authorized payments not included in the *états de prévision*. In the sixteenth century they were quite independent of the chancellor; as Dallington put it, "The Secretary doeth signe, and the Chancellor doeth seale." The four financial secrétaires were recognized as much higher in status than any other royal secrétaires; around 1547 they were given the title "secrétaires d'Etat." [3] Now they had the important task of preparing and writing up all fiscal ordinances in proper form.

Beginning in the 1530s, there was an erratic but strong trend in the king's council toward specialization. Certain members of the council began to meet regularly, one or two times per week, to consider the nation's finances. By the 1540s this group was referred to as the "Conseil pour le fait des finances"; but it was more like a council committee than a separate institution.[4] On other days the same men could be found sitting in the council in other capacities.[5] At some time during 1544 the group met, ap-

3. Zeller, *Institutions*, p. 118, believes the title was not bestowed until 1559. See Sutherland, *Secretaries*, p. 29.
4. Mariéjol, in Lavisse 6¹ : 220.
5. Meynial, "L'Histoire financière," 44 : 504–08.

parently with the greatest informality, in the private home of the Cardinal de Tournon, Francis I's chief financial advisor.[6]

A more definite Conseil des finances became visible during the reign of Henry II; and in 1563 Charles IX regularized its status in an edict ordering it to meet once a week.[7] The next year, however, Charles IX named Artus de Cossé, baron of Gonnor, as the first *surintendant des finances* to bear that title officially. Whether this official was a sort of chairman of the conciliar finance committee or a real minister of finance is not known.

Henry III could never make up his mind whether he wanted a single executive or a committee at the head of the fiscal system; he stopped the meetings of the special branch of the council in 1574 but revived it the very next year, though only as a function of the privy council, the Conseil d'Etat et des finances. He named two surintendants des finances, Pomponne de Bellièvre in 1575, and François d'O in 1578. Later in his reign, the Conseil des finances again became a regular activity of the privy council. But one should still think of it as an inner council sitting to consider finances rather than as a financial council. In the early part of the reign of Henry IV, just before Sully became a true minister of finance, the government once again went back to a financial committee, a Conseil des finances, though only temporarily. This was the group that was pushed into the background by Sully after 1597.[8]

During the earlier Renaissance those in the royal council most influential in finance were wealthy merchant-bankers like Semblançay, or royal career officials of lower-class origin who, like Duprat, had worked their way up through the ranks. But after the death of Duprat in 1535 the top-level officials making fiscal policy took on a more aristocratic tinge. The next person in the council most responsible for high-level fiscal decisions was the redoubtable Constable de Montmorency himself; in the 1540s it was either Montmorency or Claude d'Annebaut, admiral of France and governor of Normandy. In the 1550s the chief fiscal councilor was Jean de Saint-Marcel, seigneur of Avenson, a favorite of Diane de Poitiers; and in July 1559 it was the Cardinal de Lorraine. Beginning in 1564 the post was held by Artus de Cossé, later marshal of France. Artus de Cossé came from the lower ranks of the older nobility; and the same could be said of François d'O and

6. François, *Tournon*, p. 486.

7. Sutherland, *Secretaries*, p. 42; Doucet, *Institutions*, 1 : 148–52.

8. On the question of Sully's title, see Zeller, *Institutions*, p. 120; but cf. Doucet, *Institutions*, 1 : 150; Meynial, "L'histoire financière," 44 : 513; and Buisseret, *Sully*, pp. 45, 47. On the relations between Sully and the *Conseil des finances* see David Buisseret and Bernard Barbiche, "Sully et la surintendance des finances," *Bibliothèque de l'Ecole des Chartes* 123 (1965).

Sully. Pomponne de Bellièvre's family, on the other hand, were rich, recently ennobled municipal officials of Lyons.

The royal *hôtel* occupies a rather complex place in policy formation. The most important function of the royal household was to provide "domestic" services for the king. This meant food and clothing for his entourage, upkeep of the royal palaces, transportation from one royal residence to another, and maintenance for all the hundreds of royal servants, on all levels, who lived in residence with the king and who were his *commensaux*. Today we would say that the royal hôtel consisted of those who served the person of the king rather than serving the king as chief of the state.

Because Renaissance government was so personal and because the great officers of the hôtel were so close to the king, they could and often did play an important role in fiscal policy even though they were not formally members of the council. It is unrealistic, in fact, to draw lines between the council, the court, and the hôtel in assessing the bases of royal decisions. All three institutions were overlapping; whether the king chose to take guidance from one or the other depended partly on where he found his friends. The chief officers of the hôtel were among the greatest nobles in the realm. A Montmorency and a Guise cherished their places in the hôtel, even though they usually fulfilled the duties involved through a substitute or a subordinate. The great hôtel officials, as such, had an honored place near the king when the army was drawn up in battle array.

In regular government business, however, the royal household of France never became as important as it did in other states, particularly in England. There Tudor kings often bypassed the royal council, which was traditionally the instrument of the English magnates, and ran the country through household institutions, the "chambers." French kings did not have to resort to such drastic institutional shuffling to assert their personal rule, since the hôtel and the council were equally at their command.

F

The French View Their Fiscal Officials

It is the fate of tax collectors not to be loved. But the officials of the French fiscal system during the Renaissance were hated with a special passion, and apparently with good reason.

Part of this hatred undoubtedly came from envy. The upper and middle echelons of the fiscal bureaucracy enjoyed important privileges. They were usually rich men. Their posts were venal and had to be purchased with large sums of cash. It was the mercantile classes who possessed the necessary skills for acting as fiscal agents, that is, the ability to read and write and to handle accounts. Quite understandably, the French made the mistake of thinking these men were rich because they were tax officials rather than the other way around: that "by deceit, fraud, thievery, embezzlement and other evil means" tax officials were "enriching themselves from the public substance" of the land.[1] Bourgoin believed that one needed only to contrast the tax officials' low origins with their "visible and manifest" wealth in their homes, clothes, fine marriage alliances, rich table, and "the nonpareil life they lead" to know they had been stealing.[2]

One grievous practice constantly attacked in the literature of the period was the tendency of fiscal officials to appropriate tax funds and use them in some profitable way rather than keeping them safe in their strongboxes. In an age when the supply of cash was increasing much more slowly than business activity, it was a great temptation for tax officials to put these tax funds to work, albeit illegally. Officials used this cash to buy up other venal offices for themselves or for members of their families.[3] They also bought up fields and buildings; and they even used the cash to buy up grain, which they hoarded until it could be sold at inflated prices during famine years.[4] They conspired to supply each other with tax funds, "so as to make our money travel from one to another, so that they may be able at their leisure

---

1. Ord. of Paris, Feb. 1, 1504, in Rousset, *Les ordonnances faictes par le roy*, p. 50.
2. Bourgoin, *Le pressoir des esponges du roy*, pp. 12–13.
3. Ord. of St. Germain-en-Laye, Dec. 1557.
4. Henri Sée, *Louis XI et les villes*, pp. 388–89.

to long keep the cash in their hands and make deals [*tricoter*] with it . . . and thus to pile up their profits." [5]

Such criminal use of the king's money left the coffers of these officials dangerously low, so that they often had no funds with which to meet proper demands on them made by army paymasters and royal creditors. Therefore they harassed the weaker and more vulnerable peasants in their districts with demands to pay taxes that had been paid already. This last charge against fiscal officials was raised throughout the Renaissance.[6]

A group of tax officials in an excellent position to exploit weaknesses in the system were the *receveurs* who gathered in the funds. These men could line their pockets by a device known as *billonage*. The word means, literally, "alloying" in the sense of debasing; a *billon* coin was made of silver mixed more or less liberally with a base metal. Collectors did not melt down and literally debase coins, of course, but "alloyed" their receipts by holding back full-weight coins and paying out only thin or small coins.

Billonage was made possible by the difference between what we now call "media of exchange" and "moneys of account." The Renaissance *comptables*, like all accountants, kept their books in livres, sous, and deniers (money of account: 1 livre = 20 sous = 240 deniers). But in the Renaissance there were no coined livres; livres were "book money" only. The livre tournois was not a coin but an officially established par value. By a convention going all the way back to Carolingian times, when a livre, or rather 240 silver pennies, actually did weigh a pound (*livre*), 1 livre equaled 20 sous and 1 sou was worth 12 deniers or pennies. Real coins in circulation, the media of exchange, were a host of difference écus, douzains, gros, liards, deniers, and obols, struck by past kings as well as the present one; and of course many of these coins were thin and very worn. Some of them— almost by chance, it seems—were rated at convenient fractions or whole amounts of the money of account—but not for long. Most of the larger coins changed value, usually in an upward direction, over the course of the Renaissance. Thus the chief gold coin, called the écu because of the royal shield emblazoned on its reverse, was rated at 25 sous in 1436, and another écu made of slightly less fine gold in 1456 was rated at 26 sous 6 deniers. On other occasions coins were "cried up" officially without their alloy or their weight being changed; this was the situation of the écu when it was rated at 2 livres in 1519, at 2.5 in 1561, and at 3 in 1575. (See the accompanying table.)

5. Ord. of Châteaubriant, May 16, 1532.
6. See the edict of Paris, Dec. 2, 1620, in Charpentier, *Recueil des ordonnances*, p. 5.

Value of the Chief Coins in Money of Account
(1 livre = 20 sous = 240 deniers)

Mid-sixteenth century	*Value*
Ecu (gold)	45 sous
Henri d'or (gold)	50 sous
Teston (silver)	11 sous
Gros (*billon*, roughly ⅓ silver)	2.5 sous
Blanc (*billon*)	12 deniers
Douzain (*billon*)	12 deniers
Dizain (*billon*)	10 deniers
Hardi ("monnaie noire," i.e. almost all copper)	3 deniers
Liard ("monnaie noire")	3 deniers
Double tournois ("monnaie noire")	2 deniers
Denier tournois ("monnaie noire")	1 denier
Coins added by the reform of 1577	
Franc (silver; equal to ⅓ écu)	20 sous
Quart d'écu (silver)	15 sous
Denier tournois (copper)	1 denier

To complicate matters, goldsmiths and others who used precious metal as a commodity (or to import goods) refused to accept worn thin coins at their official value, though such refusal was illegal. They paid premiums for newly coined, full-weight gold and silver. Thus the "mint ratios"—the coins one could get for turning bullion over to the mint, which had to be the official rates for money of account—could be much less than the "market ratios."

Toward the end of the fifteenth century, when an écu was rated at 1 livre 16 sous 3 deniers, a debt of 18⅛ livres, for example, could be paid off by any proper "face value" combination of actual coins according to the officially established ratios: for example, 10 écus; or 362 douzains plus 6 deniers (1 douzain = 1 sou); or 36 testons, 2 douzains, 6 deniers(1 teston = 10 sous); or 145 gros (1 gros = 30 deniers), and so on. And it did not matter, legally, whether the actual coins used to satisfy this debt were fresh from the mint or thin and eroded.

Of course, the difference between the commodity value of gold and silver coins and their "book money" value *did* matter greatly to bankers, merchants, and goldsmiths; and tax collectors culled their receipts, turning over only the smaller, older, and thinner coins. After seeing that repeated edicts threatening heavy fines for billonage did little good, the crown raised the penalty for this crime to a fine plus loss of office, and finally to death; but the problem remained.[7] This certainly was one of the prime mechanisms by which "bad money drives out good."

Nonfeasance as well as malfeasance was another standard complaint of Renaissance France against its tax officials, who often performed "très petitement leur devoir." Some *élus*, for example, would not even take up residence in their *élection*, purchasing a *lettre de non-résidence* from a higher official and supplying a substitute. Since élus, naturally, paid their substitutes low wages, they could obtain only "petitz & insouffisans" persons for such jobs. Worse, at times greedy élus paid their lieutenants and clerks nothing at all, so that these men had to earn a living by accepting bribes from richer taxpayers and squeezing poor ones.[8] The government often tried to make each élu responsible for the crimes of his subordinates and gave the *généraux* the right to dismiss any élu found treating his post as a sinecure. Invariably, soon after each reform attempt, the same complaints were still being raised.[9]

It was easy for fiscal officials, when challenged, to baffle their critics by retreating behind the complexities of the system or by pleading the need for secrecy. In one edict there is a complaint that only the most gifted and persistent auditors could make sense out of the fiscal accounts. Comptables "put their affairs, figures, and papers in such disorder and confusion the real facts cannot be perceived." [10] Bourgoin accuses fiscal officials of deliberately scheming to achieve such confusion: "To play their game secretly they reduce the management of public finance to such cryptic art that few persons can understand it, unless they are nourished in this cabal; they mock at those who do not comprehend their finesse and call them bad financiers." [11] La Barre admits that "when it comes to public finance there is much finesse, subtlety, dodging, and scheming to snare the unwary penny"; and he groans over the fact that the only way the king knows to

7. Edict of Romorantin, Jan. 26, 1521, in Isambert 12 : 188; edict of Blois, Jan. 1552, in Isambert 13 : 237; and edict of Blois, Nov. 7, 1559, in Isambert, 14 : 8–11. Lapeyre, *Ruiz*, p. 446, suggests tax officials also used their full weight coins after culling to speculate on the margins between gold-silver ratios in France and abroad.

8. Dupont-Ferrier, "Les élections financières en France sous Louis XI et les abus de leurs officiers," in *Mélanges offerts à M. Nicolas Iorga* (Paris, 1933).

9. E.g., only nine years after the reform of 1475 (which was the basis of the essay cited in the previous footnote), the Estates-General of 1484 again were complaining bitterly about do-nothing élus.

10. Edict of Paris, Feb. 1, 1504, in Rousset, *Les ordonnances faictes par le roy*, p. 50.

11. Bourgoin, *Le pressoir*, p. 6.

combat this evil is to multiply punitive edicts and the number of supervisory officials.[12]

"The most cherished parts of any system," a wise but cynical man said, "are that system's abuses." [13] It was only in periods of real emergency that the government could push through important reforms of fiscal administration without encountering impossibly strong opposition from well-entrenched fiscal officials.

The government occasionally tried to counter graft by threatening severe punishments. Particularly corrupt practices were specifically ordered punishable by death.[14] Probably just as ineffective as these ferocious-sounding threats were the sumptuary ordinances directed against tax officials. The reasoning behind such edicts was that tax officials were led to cheat partly because of what we would call "conspicuous consumption." Therefore the king forbade them to dress too magnificently; they were denied the right to wear silk or cloth of gold or of silver; they were limited as to the number of horses and servants they could maintain; and they were forbidden to dower their daughters too munificently.[15] In a similar vein, tax officials were forbidden to indulge in games of dice or cards; if caught gambling they were liable to lose both their positions and their possessions and be banished forever.[16]

Tax officials themselves were not likely to broadcast a defense of their actions. Thus we hear a great deal for the prosecution but little for the defense—perhaps, as La Barre observed, because fiscal bureaucrats were less adept with the pen than with the *jeton* (coin counter).[17] It is rare to find works on taxes by tax officials. La Barre was an exception; he was an élu and a stalwart defender of his colleagues from "enemies hateful toward our kind, and others who denigrate our vocation." But even La Barre repeated the story about Diogenes, who, asked which were the most dangerous beasts, replied "lions and bears in the forests and mountains, tax collectors and contractors in cities and towns." [18]

12. La Barre, *Formulaire*, foreword.

13. Attributed by Joseph Alsop to Paul Reynaud, New York *Herald Tribune*, Paris edition, June 13, 1962.

14. E.g. ord. of Paris, April 4, 1531.

15. Ord. of Châteaubriant, June 8, 1532, in Isambert, 12 : 363 and passim; and see Meynial, "L'histoire financière," 44 : 472; Jean de Beaufort, *Le trésor des trésors de France*, pp. 140–44.

16. The reason given was that "pour les pertes, qui souvent leur adviennt édit jeux [tax officials] sont meuz de malverser, piller et desrober sur nosdites finances, pour eux rembourser." Edict of Châteaubriant, June 14, 1532, in Isambert, 12 : 372.

17. La Barre, *Formulaire*, foreword.

18. Ibid., p. 391.

Renaissance France, therefore, did have standards for its fiscal officials. Royal edicts, fiscal treatises, and declarations by popular assemblies proclaimed, often and vigorously, the virtues and abilities to be expected of such officials.[19] Boyer believed fiscal officials must be not only virtuous, intelligent, and diligent, but also well trained: "One must set to work at training and instruction at a tender age for the management of such affairs." The king should obtain officials for his taxes who are "ydoines" (suitable) as well as "souffisans" (rich), says Boyer, since such men have to be "more careful with public wealth than with their own. . . . For an official represents a public person, not a private and individual one." [20]

Actual installation in fiscal office had some of the flavor of a modern bureaucracy, even during the Renaissance. It was a complicated and solemn affair calculated to impress upon the new officer that he was now in charge of one facet of the public power.

The first step toward procuring an office, of course, was to obtain a proper warrant from the bureau in charge of selling it. This usually was handled by an official attached to the Parties casuelles, this "shop and market for this new merchandise"; but some offices were sold directly by the chancery, by the king, by members of the royal council, or even by royal favorites who received the money from the sale of offices as a royal gift. Once the money was paid and the warrant obtained, a *lettre de provision* was awarded by the chancery, along with the proper seals, ribbons, and signatures that had to be applied to it.

The formal oath of office was administered by the sovereign courts of France: parlement, in the case of positions in justice and administration of domaines lands; the Chambre des comptes for fiscal positions.[21] The candidate swore fealty to the crown and affirmed that he would uphold justice and the laws of the land. In the case of judges and royal lawyers, they swore, in addition, that they had not paid any money for their posts. Since this latter provision was not repealed until 1598, it has been observed that for the whole sixteenth century the justices and royal lawyers began their official careers with an act of perjury.[22]

Before the oath of office was administered, the justices of the court

---

19. See the amusing "Commandements du bon receveur" in Dupont-Ferrier, *Bailliages*, pp. 608–10.

20. Boyer, *Instruction*, p. 5.

21. Forest officials, however, were inducted at the high court of eaux et forêts, the Table du Marbre.

22. Louis Wolff, *La vie des parlementaires provençaux au XVIe siècle* (Paris, 1924), pp. 23–25.

involved had the right to examine the candidate's credentials—that is, both the lettre de provision and his fitness for office. Therefore the "absolute" monarch's power to sell offices was limited not only by the court's right to remonstrate concerning the establishment of a new office but also by its right to examine and accept each candidate for a particular position.

There is no question that courts did reject candidates for venal office. Men were rejected if they were found "ignorants et non lettrez" or if other elements in their background made them incapable or unreliable. Not possessing large enough income or wealth (apart from the salary in question) or possessing too many posts (cumul) also could be grounds for rejection.[23] Candidates could be rejected because they were too young. This was an important provision under the circumstances, since many offices were purchased by wealthy heads of families for sons and nephews. There does not appear to have been a formal ordinance stipulating a minimum age (twenty-five years), however, until the reign of Henry II.[24]

If a candidate for a post as élu demonstrated an alarming ignorance of methods used to raise tailles, he could be rejected. He could also be required to submit his candidacy again after studying the subject. This study could take the form of being tutored by "well-advised persons" or reading and reporting on a manual discussing the subject matter of his field.[25]

This last provision explains the spate of what we would call technical manuals on the practice of public finance during the latter sixteenth century. The standard book of instructions, the Vestige des finances, was reprinted again and again, though it discussed mainly a fiscal system of the late fifteenth rather than of the sixteenth century. But there appeared more up-to-date works such as the Traicté des tailles by Jean Combes, the Instruction pour le faict des finances by Philibert Boyer, and the even better-known Guidon général des finances of Jean Hennequin. There were many other books of the same nature. At least two publishers of such technical manuals were conveniently located near the Paris chancery; presumably after obtaining a lettre de provision a candidate could pick up

23. Verified in the great ord. of Orléans, Jan. 1561, art. 31.

24. Edict of Fontainebleau, Jan. 1549, in A.N. Z^{1A}-527, no. 692.

25. On Dec. 16, 1569, the register of the Cour des aides reports that the court's agents, who had been checking on élus already admitted to their posts but without proper qualifications, found one who, "par timidité ou autrement," was "stupide et froid en ses responses"; but the court decided that since he had qualified friends to instruct him and for "autres considérations," they would allow him to remain in his post. A.N. Z^{1A}-147, fol. 13.

the appropriate manual on his way home to prepare for his examination. When the candidate and his credentials proved acceptable, or when resistance to him was short-circuited by royal interference, the oath was administered. One formality remained. Oaths of office, both venal and nonvenal, required a fee: the *marc d'or*, a flat rate charge for entering upon royal office, was first instituted in the fifteenth century; it was abandoned for a while, then reinstated in 1578.[26]

An office was the possession of its holder, usually for the rest of his life, providing he chose not to resign it or turn it over to somebody else and providing he did not forfeit the post through malfeasance or by acts of disloyalty. This sharply distinguished an *officier* from a *commissaire*, a royal agent whose post could be canceled entirely at the king's discretion.

It was agonizing for would-be reformers of this era when, toward the end of the century, they were forced to realize that royal offices were tending to become the permanent property of the families that possessed them.[27] The hallmark of property rights in offices, and the aspect of such rights that most interested the French, was the right to pass on an office to one's heir and especially to sell it to a successor not in one's family. In theory, the maximum time for which an office was given or sold was the life of an officeholder. When he died the office (like a fief) reverted to the crown; indeed, there were good reasons, fiscal as well as administrative, for the office to revert to the crown, since it could then be sold again. By the reign of Francis I it was common for an official to obtain permission to give his office to a son or nephew. If a transfer of office was proposed while its possessor was still alive, it was labeled a *résignation;* if, according to the terms of a deed the designated new official had to wait until the possessor died, it was a *survivance.*

There was a different principle involved when an officer wanted to "resign" his position to a person not closely related to him. Here the government had to assume the office was being sold rather than given by one of its subjects to another. In such cases of résignation or survivance outside the family, the government insisted on its fiscal rights. During the reign of Francis I at least 10 percent and up to as much as 25 percent of the original sale price was demanded of the new officeholder; and the new official, unlike a blood relative of the old official, always had to go through a procedure of judicial examination and instal-

26. This marc d'or became a heavy charge on upper-echelon officials during the Old Régime; see Marcel Marion, *Dictionnaire des institutions de la France aux XVIIe et XVIIIe siècles* (Paris, 1923), p. 361.
27. See the comments by Pasquier, *Lettres historiques,* p. 261.

lation. The king made it as difficult as he could for officeholders to give, sell, or deed their positions; [28] later, claiming he was powerless to prevent the practice, he announced he was determined to profit from it. The device the government favored to restrict transfers of offices was the "forty-day clause," first practiced in the fifteenth century for royal offices but known earlier in the transferring of ecclesiastical benefices. Where this forty-day clause was in effect, an office had to be deeded to a successor at least forty days before the incumbent died; if he was inconsiderate enough to die before the forty days were up, the office reverted to the Parties casuelles which, of course, would sell it again. In 1534 the king extended this provision to the transfer of all offices, and ordered its strict enforcement.[29]

Henry II also took a hostile stance against transactions in offices among his subjects. In his reign, however, exemptions from the forty-day rule became easier to obtain. The practice developed of sharing the office, and presumably its salary, with one's successor. The excuse provided was that it permitted a sort of apprenticeship and therefore produced a more qualified group of successors.

The reform era after 1559 stemmed the drift toward inheritability; both the great ordinance of Orléans (1561) and the edict of Moulins on alienating the royal domaines (1566) forbade further steps in this direction. But the outbreak of the second War of Religion in 1567 found the state in such desperate financial straits that all expedients had to be tried. The edict of Paris, November 12, 1567, specifically revoked the reforms of Orléans and Moulins on inheritability; it gave royal officers the opportunity of naming any successor to their posts, regardless of whether a blood-relationship was involved and with no need for such successors to submit to a process of examination and installation.[30] The cost was heavy—one-third the original purchase price of the office. It was from the rate of this fee that the expedient acquired the label *tiers denier* (sometimes *tiers partie*).[31] Those who held any "office réputé vénal" and

28. See, e.g., the edict of Argilly, July 8, 1521, in Isambert, 12 : 189–90.

29. The real object of this restriction becomes clear in a later edict, Fontainebleau, Dec. 26, 1541, which forbids transfers of offices except for "ceux qui pour desdits Resignations & Survivances Nous ont fourni & payé aucune Finance."

30. See also the proclamation of Paris, Jan. 22, 1568, specifically on royal offices in the city of Paris. A hint that the king was sensitive to general condemnation of the drift toward inheritability was the royal promise, in the supplementary "tiers denier" edict of Paris, June 1568, to reserve all funds received from this expedient for the urgent needs of war.

31. Hennequin, *Guidon*, p. 86, thought he could trace the practice back to 1422;

who paid the assessment were also to be exempt from the provisions of the forty-day clause; if an official died without naming his successor in time, his family could effect the transfer.

As part of his plan to reduce taxes during the late 1570s, Henry III promised that as redundant offices fell vacant, the right bestowed by tiers denier or other favors notwithstanding, these offices would be canceled. But in the early 1580s the drift toward inheritability was resumed. All venal posts in the royal household were made transferable without the need to pay the tiers denier; all mint offices were made inheritable in 1581, over the opposition of the courts; [32] and all money changers, previously made officials, were also extended the privilege of passing on their offices.[33] In 1583 the same favor was extended to those holding positions in the *eaux et forêts* administration—the royal forest, fishing, and game wardens. Even the new constables authorized in 1586 were granted résignation privileges.[34]

The awarding of venal offices during the worst phases of the Wars of Religion (the late 1580s and early 1590s) became terribly confused, as did all aspects of central administration. Power to grant offices was seized by a score of rebel war lords and grandees and by the Huguenot assemblies in the rebellious provinces. The offices they created and sold constituted one of the problems passed on to the government of Henry IV, which had the task of restoring social order and loyalty to the central government. Henry IV's solution was to confirm almost all of these officials in their posts. In fact, this was one of the prices Henry IV had to pay for restoring royal authority.

This confusion further compounded the problem of survivances and résignations. Officials had taken advantage of the breakdown of central authority to pass on venal offices without regard to the revenue rights of the crown. To return to the system of transfering offices through the Parties casuelles would have stirred up resentment that the government could not afford. Sully, Henry IV's chief minister, chose to take the easy way out. What could not be undone could be taxed. The result was the *paulette*, so called after Paulet, a *secrétaire* in the royal household and a moderately important financier who had been involved in loans to the crown. Paulet advanced his plan for the first time in 1602; the final

---

but this is quite unfounded. Tiers denier was a new and entirely arbitrary fiscal expedient.

32. Edict of St. Maur-les-Fossés, July 1581.
33. Decl. of Paris, Oct. 17, 1581.
34. Edict of Paris, April 1586.

edicts authorizing the new policy of inheritability came in December
1604.[35]

The paulette taxed each official for the right to pass on his office to a
man of his choosing. The rate was one-sixtieth of the official value of the
post, to be paid each year. This tax permitted the office to be given to a
legal heir of the incumbent official. Résignation to a successor not the heir
of the officeholder had to carry an additional fee of one-eighth the office's
value to be paid once, at the time the warrant for résignation was issued.
The forty-day clause was abandoned; if an official died without naming
a successor his family had the right to dispose of the office. All venal offices reverted to Parties casuelles on the death or retirement of the incumbent officer unless the paulette was paid each year.[36]

The transition to making government office into a form of private
property was now complete. Venal offices were now built into the very
structure of French society.[37] Just a few years after the paulette went into
operation Charles Loyseau, a famous political philosopher of the era,
wrote this revealing and bitter account:

> In the beginning of January [1608] I decided, being in Paris, to go one
> evening to the home of the *partisan* [of the paulette] to confer with
> him. . . . But he was too rushed; I had chosen the time badly. I
> found there a great troop of officials jostling and pushing to be the
> first to give him their money: some of them were still booted; coming
> from outdoors, they had not taken the time to take off their boots. I
> noted that the moment they were finished they went straight to the
> place of a nearby notary to hand over their certificates of reversion,
> and they seemed to be walking on ice, mortally afraid of making a
> false step and dying on the way. Then, when night fell, the *partisan*
> shut his register, and I heard a loud protest from those still to be taken
> care of, claiming that their money had been taken but that none
> worried about whether they should die before the night ended. Con-
> templating this state of affairs, I had to say to myself, Merciful God,
> would we were as anxious to save our souls as our offices! [38]

35. Though established first for a limit of nine years, the paulette was renewed
more or less regularly for the remainder of the Renaissance and the Old Régime.

36. Thus the paulette was also called the "droit annuel"; wags also called it the
"widow's edict."

37. Edicts creating new or additional offices carried the notification that the
office was not only "en tiltre d'office formé" (i.e. with full rights), but also "en
tiltre de domaine et hérédité."

38. Charles Loyseau, *Les oeuvres de maistre Charles Loyseau, avocat en Parlement*
(Lyons, 1701), p. 143. This may be the most quoted passage in all the literature
of Renaissance fiscal history. It is enshrined in Marion's *Dictionnaire*, p. 434.

Did venal-inheritable offices weaken royal power? Were such offices "a new form of feudalism" which threatened to bring about "the ruination of royal authority"? [39] Some Renaissance as well as some modern observors argue that an official who could not easily be removed was an administrator who could not be trusted to carry out the king's will. In the short run, at least, venal and inheritable offices strengthened the king's hand. Earlier in the Renaissance, especially before Francis I, and also after the death of Henry II, appointment to offices often had been under the control of a great aristocrat, especially if the office were located in his fief or the province he controlled as governor. Even after peace returned to the country, the passions and provincialisms that had torn it apart were dangerously close to the surface; the grandees still held great power, and they could have been expected to increase their influence by placing their supporters in royal offices. Under the régime of the paulette, security of office, not only for the officeholder but also for his heirs, meant that he was less subject to pressure from these grandees. Henry IV and Sully may have accepted the paulette as a means of ensuring that important families of the lesser nobility and the bourgeoisie had to identify their interests with those of the king.[40]

In any case, the paulette had the virtue of clearing the legal air. Officials knew where they stood regarding their investments. And the state received significantly more income from its traffic in offices. For the officials, however, the paulette represented a loss. Assuming that 8⅓ percent of the purchase price was the average official's salary, the paulette meant a reduction of about 20 percent. But both the French officeholders and the public in general seem to have accepted inheritable venal office as necessary if not admirable. "It is true that if kings could dispense with taking revenues," said La Barre, "they would not have to make [additional] élus, généraux, collectors, or intendants des finances; likewise if we could abstain from drinking or eating we would become quite wealthy, and we would pile up our capital nicely." [41]

39. Mousnier,*Vénalité*, pp. 19, 36. See also Etienne Pasquier's views, *Lettres historiques*, p. 245, and the *Remonstrances* of Rolland du Plessis, p. 32. For the reasons Bellièvre, chancellor at the time, opposed the paulette, see Raymond F. Kierstead, *Pomponne de Bellièvre: A Study of the King's Men in the Age of Henry IV* (Evanston, Ill., 1968), pp. 130–34.

40. But we can only guess as to whether political or fiscal reasons were more important in the government's decision on the paulette. See Mousnier, *Vénalité*. pp. 557–66.

41. *Formulaire*, p. 56.

G

Levying the Tailles

Throughout the Renaissance, the tailles brought in between one-half and two-thirds of all the king's regular revenues. Just after the great reforms of Charles VII, in the 1440s, the tailles amounted to about 1.2 million livres per year. Toward the end of the sixteenth century, tailles were rated at about 15 millions per year. Early in the seventeenth century, Sully reduced them to 10 or 11 millions.

Over the whole course of the Renaissance, then, tailles rose from 1.2 to 11 millions, representing something less than a (nominal) tenfold increase. What of their "real" burden? Perhaps we could say that if recent estimates concerning the tailles are accurate, and if students of price history are correct in their estimates (since general prices are supposed to have increased about fivefold from the 1450s to the 1610s), then the "real" total burden must have doubled.

In the present state of our knowledge, a good estimate of the per capita burden of the tailles is out of the question, since figures for the total French population are not satisfactory.[1] Current guesses range from 14 to 16 million inhabitants in the mid-fifteenth century, and 17 to 20 million around 1600.[2] Taking the midpoints for lack of a better procedure, we can calculate that if during the entire Renaissance French population rose by roughly one-fifth, then the "real" per capita burden of tailles increased by some two-thirds.

An especially irritating feature of the tailles was that they could be increased within the year, by the device known as a *crue*, a term roughly equivalent to our concept of surtax. Surtaxes were used to cope with unforeseen expenses—usually, of course, the onslaught of war or a sharp increase in the cost of a campaign.[3] A crue was a completely arbitrary levy, imposed by decision of the royal council, which was then conveyed to

---

1. *Cambridge Economic History of Europe*, 4 : 32–33.
2. But see Henri Sée, "Peut-on évaluer la population de l'ancienne France?" *Revue d'Economie Politique* 38 (1924).
3. Crues on tailles go back perhaps to 1406. See Rey, *Le domaine du roi*, p. 329. Spont, "La taille en Languedoc," p. 492, shows crues were used in the time of Charles VII. They were used more frequently after the 1520s.

middle-echelon tax officials or to provincial Estates by royal commissions. The surtax was usually calculated as a percentage of a locality's tailles;[4] and the tailles' collection apparatus was the one employed for the collection of the surtax.[5]

Another increase on the tailles (as it worked out) was an important levy known as the *taillon* ("little taille"). First called the *crue de la gendarmerie*, the taillon was levied in 1549 as an earnest of good intentions:[6] the king announced that the purpose of this levy was to spare towns and villages from pillaging by French troops stationed nearby or passing through. The taillon cost the French an additional 720,000 livres a year at first; later it was raised by stages, so that by 1567 it was set at about 1.2 millions.[7] The taillon was "repartitioned" on the same people and according to the same proportions as the tailles.[8] And the same persons exempt from tailles were exempt also from the taillon.[9]

Since we are all cynics as far as taxes are concerned, no one will be surprised to learn that by the 1560s the taillon, though still listed as a separate tax (and though edicts and commentators still referred to it as payment in lieu of troop rations), had become nothing but a permanent surtax on the tailles.

The tailles were *impôts de répartition*, a term used to distinguish them from *impôts de quotité*, that is, taxes based on rates. Modern direct taxes are usually "rate taxes" in the sense that individuals or firms pay set proportions of their income or wealth; the total amount collected, therefore, can vary, depending on whether taxpayers as a group become richer or poorer.[10] But in the Renaissance the tailles were a flat levy, a round sum set by the royal council at the beginning of the fiscal year; this sum, in principle, had to be collected regardless of the state of economic health of the country. Once the council determined the amount that would be needed, the taille was "repartitioned" among the *généralités* and

4. E.g. the edict of Paris, March 1600, in Isambert, 15 : 234–35; after the grande taille was fixed, all its adjuncts were to be collected proportionally at each individual's assiette, "sur le même pied et au sol la livre sans rien changer."

5. Crues were calculated separately for each généralité; thus one province might be called on to bear a proportionately heavier crue than another. See Doucet, *L'état des finances de 1567*, p. 21 and n. 4.

6. Ord. of Paris, Nov. 12, 1549, in Isambert, 13 : 119–33.

7. Doucet, *L'état des finances de 1567*, pp. 5–6; Clamageran, *L'impôt*, 2 : 188.

8. Edict of Paris, Sept. 1576, in Fontanon, 3 : 97.

9. Combes, *Traicté*, pp. 106–07.

10. Poll taxes, too, are not "rate taxes"; but it is an error to think of tailles as poll taxes, as does Norman Hampson, *A Social History of the French Revolution* (London, 1963), p. 14.

élections (for all but a few of the provinces); then the taille for each élection was divided up among the parishes; and finally the amount apportioned to each parish was repartitioned among all the *taillables* of the parish.[11]

For convenience, the term *département* will be used to describe the process of apportionment down to the level of the parishes, and *assiette* for the division of the parish taille among the taillables.[12] Renaissance writers themselves, however, often used the terms interchangeably.

The concept of répartition included the principle that the strong (i.e. wealthy) must carry along the weak. "Le fort portant le faible" meant not only that richer districts (and individuals) had to pay heavier tax portions but also that if one généralité, élection, or parish had to be accorded some tax relief—because of some natural disaster, or devastation by soldiers, or because for some reason the king or his officials wanted to grant that territory a favor—then other areas were supposed to pay higher tailles.[13] The same principle applied to the assiette of the tailles among individuals at the parish level of taxation; thus a village's taille was its collective responsibility.[14]

The way the tailles were levied, therefore, was a matter of burning interest to the country, since each area tried to cut its tax or at least to pay no more than the previous year. Influential town magistrates and nobles interested in the welfare of their villagers argued their case with royal officials at each stage of the département. The same divisions and quotas used for the tailles, furthermore, became the basis for dividing up surtaxes on the tailles, the taillon, and many emergency levies collected as direct taxes.[15]

Once each généralité was assigned its proportion of the tailles, another process of département had to take place—dividing up the tailles for the

11. The sense of this use of *répartition* is conveyed by the term *partisseurs*, sometimes used as a synonym for *asséeurs*.

12. This terminology follows the distinction made in the basic reform edict of Paris, March 1600, in Isambert, 15 : 226 ff.

13. Edicts and writings on this point are perfectly clear; *le fort portant le faible*, however, remains one of the most poorly understood aspects of Renaissance taxation.

14. A village could initiate a legal appeal of its collective taille; but, if such a case were lost, the village had to pay heavy court costs. B.N. Nouv. acq. fr. 2374, fol. 57.

15. Thus the edict of Paris, June 19, 1539, ordered that "la solde & payement de vingt mil hommes de guerre estre assignée & imposée sur les plus riches contribuables manans & habitans . . . le fort portant le foible & comme est accoustumé impose, Tailles & subventions pour le fait de la guerre."

élections. After each élu had received notice of the sum of the tailles in his particular élection—the *commission des tailles*—the élu's main job began. The first step was the département of the total sum among the parishes. The élu was given stern instructions to be fair in making his decisions. He was expected to make the circuit of each parish in order to investigate "the wherewithal of the inhabitants," which probably meant listening to complaints about "misfortunes, losses, and damage," aimed at convincing him the parish should carry a lesser load. One reform edict suggested that he take the amount of "carts and trade" (*charrües & traffic*) into consideration, "together with all the other commodities and incommodities that can render [the parishes] rich or poor." [16] And he was admonished to take "every pain and care to assess and divide up their portion as justly, loyally, and equitably as can be, keeping always to fairness [*égalité*] and let this be so that the rich carry the poor." [17] In practice, if not in the minds of the best thinkers, "le fort portant le faible" was as close as Renaissance France could come to the concept of tax equity.[18]

After the département of the parishes, came the assiette of individuals. Orders showing the parish quota were sent out to all collectors and to each parish, to its "curé or chaplain . . . scrivener or notary." One of these men had the duty of assembling the parishioners, or the majority of them, in village or town, "by ringing church bells or otherwise" so as to establish officially the size of the parish burden for the year; this assembly also had the onerous task of electing *asséeurs* (assessors) and *collecteurs* (tax gatherers).

Assessors had to be taille-payers themselves, that is, neither nobles nor clerics nor otherwise privileged. Theirs was an unpaid service but a compulsory one; if it was not properly performed, the assessors (and others in the town or village itself) were subject to fine and prison. Assessors were enjoined to take into account the "faculties and means" of taxpay-

16. Edict of Paris, March 1600, in Isambert, 15 : 228–31.

17. The same concept was used when requisitions in kind were made; thus an order to commissaires to requisition horses "pour la conduicte de nostre artillerie" directed them to observe this principle; see the ord. of Montreuil, June 30, 1517, in Jacqueton, *Documents*, p. 180.

18. At the Estates-General of Tours (1484), during a crucial debate on the level and département of tailles, "one deputy from Languedoc said that for the last two years he had had to pay a taille of over 350 livres. A Norman replied that this was proof of his prosperity and not evidence that his province had been overtaxed." Major, *Representative Institutions*, p. 103, quoting the contemporary journal of Masselin. See also Clamageran, *L'impôt*, 2 : 57.

ers, to make an honest assessment of a rich merchant's or artisan's presumed income from his "trafic & négociations" as well as his possessions, both his personal property and his real estate. The proper goal for assessors as well as for the élus who supervised them, the government insisted, was a fair tax roll (*compoix*, in some provinces) constantly revised to take into account the altered circumstances of the taillables.[19]

Taxpayers who believed they were assessed too heavily did have the right to appeal informally and in person to the élu, more formally by instituting a case of *surtaux* (overassessment) before a branch of the Cour des aides. But below a certain value of money at issue (in 1561, 5 livres) no appeals concerning tailles were allowed, which effectively ruled out poor persons taking their complaints any higher than the élus.[20]

When the assiette of individuals was ready, it was read aloud in church from the pulpit on three separate Sundays. Meanwhile positions as collecteurs had to be filled—as many as three, depending on the size of the parish.[21] Each tax gatherer kept 12 deniers for each livre he took in, or 5 percent.[22] This was added to each individual's taille, thus becoming an additional burden.[23] The gatherer, like the assessor, had to be a parishioner, and for most of the Renaissance he also had to be taillable. Considering the close personal relationships that existed in villages and towns, it is quite understandable that finding tax gatherers, even considering the pay, could be difficult. Those rare individuals who wanted the pay badly could obtain the post by "negative bidding," that is, by offering to do the job for less than one sou per livre, provided they were able to put up a guarantee pledge equal to one-quarter of the parish quota.[24] After eight days, if nobody came forward, an assembly of the parishioners had to be held to elect the tax gatherers. The parish was to choose gatherers from persons "well-to-do

19. Such a principle, of course, was not always popular. At the Estates-General of Orléans in 1560, for example, complaints were raised that peasants who put up new buildings and made other improvements were penalized by having to pay a heavier taille. Clamageran, *L'impôt*, 2 : 164.

20. Ord. of Orléans, Jan. 1561, in Isambert, 14 : 95. This was confirmed in the edict of Paris, March 1600; but the minimum for appeals was raised at the time to 3 écus (9 livres).

21. Edict of Paris, March 1600, in Isambert, 15 : 230. I have translated *collecteur* as "gatherer" so as not to confuse this official with the one known as *receveur* (for both élections and généralités) to whom money once gathered was turned over.

22. La Barre regarded this as miserably insufficient payment. *Formulaire*, pp. 100–01.

23. Doucet, *Institutions*, 2 : 566.

24. Therefore such bidders are referred to, in various edicts, as "les moins disants."

and solvent"; and they could not refuse to serve at least once every four years.

The whole power of the crown was behind the parish collecteurs; they could use royal constables to force collection, or they could order the seizure and sale of household goods and crops, or even imprison reluctant taillables. But the constables were more of a threat to the gatherers of tailles than to other taillables, since constables often were directed to recover what was owed the king from the purses (or other property) of the gatherers. La Barre lamented the fate of the collecteur who, often through no fault of his own, was placed "at the mercy of the constables, stripped of his goods, and thrown into prison to perish." [25] Before La Barre's treatise was written the government (edict of Paris, March 1600) had ordered that the functions of assessor and gatherer be performed by the same person; but this seems neither to have strengthened the hand of the gatherer nor to have improved his lot.

In the final analysis, then, it was the feared and detested royal constables who provided the force for actually raising the tailles. Royal edicts echoed the bitter charges that were directed against this greedy and heavy-handed crew; but the needs of the royal treasury weighed more with the state than the exactions of the constables employed in collecting tailles. From time to time the king did try to discourage his tax constables from the most blatant misuse of their powers. For example, he ruled that persons whose goods were sold to pay their taxes could buy back those goods by offering the highest price tendered by would-be buyers within four days after the constable's sale.[26] The Cour des aides ordered that no constable be allowed to exercise his office in the same district for more than a year at a time, apparently in an effort to prevent constables from forming permanent alliances with the rich and powerful in their areas at the expense of the poor and weak.[27]

The concept "all commoners pay the tailles," by any definition, includes both townsmen and villagers. It was clearly stated, both in royal edicts and

25. La Barre, *Formulaire*, pp. 47, 100.
26. Edict of Paris, March 1600. But see the decl. of Blois, Oct. 8, 1571, in Isambert, 14 : 239–40, which ruled that peasants in debt could not be deprived of their cattle, furniture, or tools, "excepté toutesfois quand il sera question de noz deniers et affaires," i.e. taxes.
27. Royal decl. of Paris, May 17, 1596, in Claude Monstr'oeil, *Recueil des édicts du roy . . .* , pp. 23–29. See also the edict of Rouen, Jan. 1597, charging élus with moving "lesdits sergens et commissaires, pour d'autant plus obvier auxdites abus, au Soulagement desdites contribuables" from place to place each year. A.N. AD[IX-471], item v.

in the writings of jurists, that peasants and bourgeois alike should pay the tailles. Yet today we know that while the whole peasantry was taillable, this was not true for the bourgeoisie.[28]

The practice of freeing whole towns from tailles goes back at least to the mid-fifteenth century. Charles VII granted exemption from tailles to several towns (including Orléans and Angoulême) that supported him during the Hundred Years' War.[29] At times Charles VII exempted only a selected few in a town; thus in 1447 he freed "from all tailles levied or to be levied the archers, crossbowmen, constables, artillerymen, watchmen, musicians [*ménétriers*] and trumpeters employed in municipal affairs in La Rochelle up to the number of five and fifty." [30] But after he recovered Paris, Charles VII freed its entire citizen body "for all time" from paying tailles partly because of the terrible depopulation it had suffered during the wars, and partly as compensation for a heavier burden of aides he placed on the backs of the Parisians. In this reign, at least, towns seem to be freed from the tailles less as a matter of fiscal policy than as a means of cementing the burghers' loyalty to the crown.[31] Likewise, toward the end of the Renaissance (1590), we find Henry IV exempting Compiègne—one of the few towns near Paris that rallied to him—from the tailles.[32]

Louis XI also freed specific towns when they had suffered a calamity or when he wanted their support; thus he freed Toulouse from the tailles after it had been devastated by fire—but only after carefully stipulating that the rest of the province of Languedoc would have to make up the difference.[33] As we have seen, Louis XI also seems to have had a policy of

28. Some peasant villages near forests, it is true, were exempt from tailles "attendu le dommage que leur causent les bêtes sauvages." Devèze, *Forêt française,* 2 : 316, quoting an edict of Sept. 1604.

29. And in 1396 Charles VI had freed Andelot from tailles "moyennant la redevance annuelle de douze deniers et d'un chapon." ORD, 15 : xx. The exemption for Orléans seems to go back to the famous siege in the days of Joan of Arc; it was regularly confirmed by later kings. Augustin Courbé, *Les privilèges, franchises et libertez . . . d'Orléans . . . ,* pp. 2–3, 7–9, 23. For evidence that in the mid-fifteenth century other towns of central France were paying tailles, see Thomas, *Les états provinciaux,* 1 : 56–57.

30. Edict of Bourges, Nov. 1447, in ORD, 13 : 512–22.

31. See, e.g., the ord. of Razili, May 26, 1449, in ORD, 14 : 52–54; and see ORD, 16 : xxiii. Official documents exempting specific towns invariably indicate that the act is a special favor in return for services rendered. See, e.g., the formulary for such an exemption in *Le Thrésor du nouveau stille,* pp. 87b–88b.

32. Compiègne paid tailles in the 1580s but was exempted in 1590. Baron Bonnault d'Houët, *Compiègne pendant les Guerres de Religion,* p. 309.

33. Sée, *Louis XI,* p. 154.

exempting merchants and artisans from the tailles, perhaps with the idea of encouraging an increase in French trade and manufacturing.

Modern studies on Renaisance France give the impression that this trend toward exempting the towns must have continued to the point where all or almost all towns were free of tailles. Gaston Zeller, for example, in *Les institutions de la France au XVIe siècle*, avoids a definite quantitative statement while giving the impression that exemption from tailles was general. "In Normandy alone," he tells us, "the towns of Rouen, Caen, Harfleur, Dieppe, Cherbourg, Granville, Pont-Audemer, Yvetot, and Le Hâvre were exempt." What he neglects to add is that this does not include towns like Bayeux, St. Lô, Avranches, Evreux, Valognes, Falaise, Aumale, Vexin, Alençon, Coutances, Lisieux, and others—more than those named as exempt—which, until evidence is found to the contrary, must be regarded as paying the tailles.[34]

We have one piece of indirect evidence that at least all the important towns probably were exempt from tailles. This concerns the *soldes*, the special military subsidies specifically designed for paying the troops. The soldes, it seems clear, were raised on *villes closes*, that is, on cities with fortified walls. The king rationalized this tax as a sort of substitute for tailles. As Dallington says, tailles were "onely lyable on the *Plat païs*" (i.e. country villages), all cities being exempt but obliged to compensate by paying the soldes.[35] If this is the case, there seems to be ground for believing that towns paying soldes did not pay tailles.[36]

34. Zeller, *Institutions*, pp. 256–57; speaking of Dauphiné and Normandy, Zeller says "La plupart des villes . . . sont exemptes." It may be that Zeller and others follow Clamageran, *L'impôt*, 1 : xliii. Cf. La Barre, *Formulaire*, p. 97, who says that nobody pays tailles but members of the Third Estate "& habitans des villes & bourgs *non affranchis*" (my italics). Historians are inclined to use phrases such as "most towns were exempt"; see, e.g., Imbart de la Tour, *Les origines de la Réforme*, 1 : 493. Or they may refer to "the tailles imposed on the rural population" as does Doucet, *Lyon*, p. 53. In 1542 the Venetian ambassador reported that "those who live in cities also pay the taille, but not much, and a great part of the cities pay nothing." Albèri, *Relazioni*, ser. 1, 4 : 39.

35. Dallington, *The View of Fraunce*, pp. O3–O4.

36. Documents in the B.N. or the A.N. showing extensive lists of towns obliged to pay soldes are easy to find: e.g., B.N., Dupuy, 500, fol. 20^r–24^r, with 226 towns, dated end of Feb. 1537. But I have located only one list of the other side of this fiscal coin, that is, of towns "free" of tailles. This is B.N., Dupuy, 273, fol. 348^r, entitled "Les villes franches de ce Royaulme." It is undated; but it is later than 1547. It lists only 37 towns. Another and certainly partial list is published as "Etat D" of Doucet's *L'état des finances de 1523*, with only 19 towns, none from Brittany, Burgundy, Dauphiné, or Provence.

The significance of all these exemptions, of course, is that the more there were, the more the rest of the French had to pay. The anonymous author of the *Traitté des finances* said in 1580:

> It seems to many persons that the burdens are badly equalized in France; for one sees that ordinarily great cities push off the [tax] burden on the country villages, and the richer peasants on the poorer . . . and since the wealthy, including those of the church and nobility, push off the burden on the lowest class, that class begins to succumb and collapse, and even to fall under its load.[37]

One flagrant example of evading the tailles was that of rich burghers in "free" towns who purchased farm lands, often far from their towns, and then claimed their exemption applied to their new properties. After much squabbling in the Cour des aides it was decided that exemption in a city did not cover farmlands (*biens ruraux*) elsewhere.[38]

The problem of exemption from tailles for specific persons was undoubtedly one of the most hotly debated issues in Renaissance jurisprudence. Jean Combes, a lawyer, was present at many such judicial disputes and gives us his findings on some interesting problems.[39] For example, is a son living with his parents, but owning property in his own name, taillable for that property?—*No.* Is a man taillable for the income from his wife's dowry?—*No.* Is a "free" burgher taillable for profits made from the revenue farm of another's property?—*Yes.*

Combes also related the case of a poor priest of Limousin who bought a stock of wine for his own use. At the end of the year he had some left, and he sold it; therefore he was declared taillable for all his income. The argument was that such a sale proved he was not "living as a priest" (*clericalement*); clearly, derogation of one's clerical status subjected one to Third Estate taxes. In this case, however, the priest appealed to the Cour des aides; this body ruled he had always lived in a good priestly manner, without "derogation to his presbyterial dignity," and reversed the judgment.[40]

The type of exemption problem that seems to have attracted more attention, however, was that of nobles not "living nobly." Fiscal courts, periodically supported by the royal council, took the position that noble ancestry alone was not enough. One had to live like a seigneur in a manor

---

37. *Traitté des finances,* pp. 382–83.
38. For Lyons, see the letters-patent of Lyons, Oct. 9, 1501, in Philippe, *Edits et ordonnances . . . des cours des aides;* and see Doucet, *Lyon,* p. 61.
39. Combes, *Traicté,* esp. pp. 98–105.
40. Ibid., pp. 72–73.

house and be ready for military service whenever the king called up his levies. From the Cour des aides at Tours we have the case of one Jean Viger, sieur de la Bodinière, who was declared taillable by local élus because he was not making himself available for military service—even though he was sixty years old and had fought for Henry IV before he became king. The court ruled Jean Viger could keep his exemption if he could produce a good patent of nobility and good excuses.[41]

There was such a close connection between noble status and nonpayment of tailles that if a family could prove it had not been taillable this in itself was taken as one element in the proof of its noble standing. Certainly any noble who undertook trade or manufacturing stood to lose his exemption— for all his property and income, not just for his commercial interests.[42]

One of the scandals of the Renaissance—a scandal that lasted through the Old Régime—was that the burden of direct taxes in Provence, Langue-doc, and certain other districts was lighter and more equitably distributed than in the central and northern provinces.[43] This inequity, familiar to every student of early modern France, usually is treated under the heading of the difference between *taille réelle* and *taille personnelle*. It must be said that few historians have grasped the correct significance of this difference.

Broadly speaking, *tailles réelles* fell (in large part) on land rated as *roturier* property, no matter who owned it; tailles personnelles fell (in large part) on land owned by nonprivileged commoners.[44] In those provinces where taille réelle was the practice, lands classified as nonprivileged paid the tailles—whatever might be the status of the person owning that prop-erty. Thus roturier land purchased by a noble or a cleric or a non-taillable

41. In an order appended to a later copy of an edict of March 1577; see B.N. F23610 (379). The letters-patent of Fontainebleau, Oct. 20, 1602, put it this way: "nobles nés et extraits de noble lignée, vivant noblement et suivant les armes ou qui, par vieillesse ou impuissance, ne les peuvent suivre." See also Chamberland, "Le budget de la généralité de Châlons en 1602," p. 147.

42. Doucet, *Institutions*, 2 : 489–90; Combes, *Traicté*, p. 78. La Barre shows how harmful this separation was between nobility and business: "Les foucres [Fug-gers] d'Ausbourg, les plus riches marchands de Chrestieneté, qui ont Marquisats & contez, n'ont jamais voulu quitter le traffic." *Formulaire*, p. 67.

43. Burgundy had no tailles at all; that is why, according to Combes (*Traicté*, p. 119) her Estates were burdened so often with demands for loans and subsidies.

44. This does *not* mean that one can translate *taille personnelle* as "poll tax" (since poll taxes usually are fixed amounts) and *taille réelle* as "land tax" (since more than land was involved in setting the tax), as does R. J. Knecht, *Francis I and Absolute Monarchy*, Historical Association Pamphlet no. 72 (London, 1969), p. 11.

official continued to pay tailles. In provinces which followed the rule of tailles personnelles, on the other hand, it was the status of the person and not the status of his land that mattered. The significance of this distinction was that when privileged persons acquired full possession of land that formerly had paid tailles (in provinces where tailles were *personnelles*) they were not obliged to continue paying.

The privileged groups in *réelle* provinces were at a disadvantage, therefore, compared to their fellows in neighboring provinces; and naturally they worked for the overthrow of "real tailles." Several times the king had to step in and reaffirm the principle of "real tailles" against the incursions of nobles, clerics, and "free" officials. Thus in the royal declaration of Amiens, July 18, 1535, the government took notice of the fact that some privileged groups in Languedoc, having purchased roturier property, were suing for exemption from Languedoc's equivalent of the tailles; but the king, agreeing that taille réelle had been the practice in Languedoc "from time immemorial, and as such there is neither memory of its origins nor of [rulings] to the contrary," ordered such cases thrown out of court.[45]

There are several contemporary references to the terms *réelle* and *personnelle* that imply it was not so much the status of the taxpayers that was being considered as it was the type of wealth being taxed. Combes's *traicté des tailles* (1584), for example, claims that "real tailles" were levied in the Midi but that in other provinces tailles were not *personnelles* but actually *mixtes;* that is, they were calculated on a base of "all the goods and wealth [*fortunes*]of the person indicated. . . ." [46] But this is a semantic confusion, possibly arising from the attempt by Renaissance jurists to read Roman meanings into the traditional distinctions between "real" and "personal" tailles. During the Renaissance *all* tailles were "mixed": buildings, capital, income, and other forms of wealth, including land, were taken into account for the assiette of the tailles in both réelle and personnelle lands.[47] There were not three forms of tailles—personnelles, réelles, mixtes—but only two. Historians have been misled by the attempt in Renaissance treatises to explain that in personnelle lands the tailles fell not only on personal wealth but also on land: hence, "mixed." [48]

In any case, there seems no doubt that réelles tailles were regarded as

45. Isambert, 12 : 407–10.

46. Combes, *Traicté,* pp. 62–69.

47. This problem is cleared up in Edmond Esmonin, *Etudes sur la France des XVIIe et XVIII siècles* (Paris, 1964), pp. 167–73.

48. Among those so misled are Doucet, *Institutions,* 2 : 569–70, and Zeller, *Institutions,* pp. 254–55.

more equitable. Tailles were paid mostly by peasants, and peasants' wealth was largely in their land. When a privileged person in personnelle districts purchased roturier lands, the remaining properties had to bear an increased burden. By the same token, of course, if a commoner in personnelle territory bought lands belonging to a non-taillable, those lands would have to assume a share of the tailles, which presumably would act to lighten the average burden.

While we have no way of estimating the amount by which transfers of land between privileged and nonprivileged persons may have offset each other, it is clear that Renaissance opinion was convinced that the situation in personnelle lands was much more unfair and was deteriorating.[49] This is borne out by the long-drawn-out quarrel over the tailles in Dauphiné. Here, unlike the rest of the Midi, the taille (called, confusingly, the *aide*) was personnelle. The provincial Estates first worked for more equitable taxing by voting to end the exemption of "free" burghers who purchased lands in districts other than that of their home towns. This was supported by royal orders in 1548 and made retroactive to all lands so acquired for the previous thirty years. After Dauphiné became involved in the later Wars of Religion—when Huguenot burghers and nobles ran the province as an antonomous state—the Dauphiné *aide* was made réelle; now nobles and clergy who acquired roturier property had to continue paying its *aide*. This reform was canceled when the Wars of Religion ended. The debate continued, however, through the early decades of the seventeenth century, and it was only in 1639 that the question finally was settled by royal order in favor of a réelle direct tax.[50]

Some taille réelle lands did not pay a taille, but levied some substitute instead. Languedoc's substitute is best known to us.[51] The basis of Languedoc's direct tax obligations to the crown was the tradition (originating in the fourteenth century) that this province should carry one-tenth the total direct tax load for all France. When the global figure for the tailles was set by the royal council, therefore, one-tenth this sum was assigned to Languedoc.

In what seems a ridiculously complicated manner, Languedoc then proceeded to raise this tax in two parts. The first part was fixed at 167,000

49. One can even find this opinion reflected in Adam Smith's remarks on taxes in France; see *Wealth of Nations*, Modern Library ed. (New York, 1937), p. 585. For the Renaissance, see the remonstrances and cahiers in Picot, *Etats Généraux*, e.g. (for the Estates-General of 1614), 5 : 35–36.
50. Zeller, *Institutions*, pp. 257–58.
51. Spont, "La taille en Languedoc"; see also Dognon, "La taille en Languedoc de Charles VII à François Ier," *Annales du Midi* 3 (1891).

livres; this sum came from whatever was raised by the *équivalent*, Langue-doc's substitute for the sort of indirect taxes (aides) levied elsewhere in France, plus the amount needed to raise this équivalent to 167,000 livres. This 167,000 livres was called the *aide*. The second part, the *octroi*, also was labeled with a name that meant something entirely different elsewhere in France. The Languedoc *octroi* amounted to whatever was needed to bring the Languedoc *aide* (167,000 livres) up to one-tenth the global tailles for all France.[52] Obviously the Languedoc *octroi* was the heavier of these two parts; if, for example, we take the round figure for 1550 of 4.6 million livres in tailles for all of France, one-tenth would have amounted to 460,000 livres and the *octroi* would have had to be 293,000 livres.

In Provence a somewhat comparable tax was known as the *fouage*. Brit-tany, too, had its *fouage*; this term, in fact, was the old name for direct taxes in many parts of medieval France. However, the name in the Renais-sance means something different from what one might think. A *feu*, in Brittany, was not a hearth but simply a device for the département of the tax. Each community in the province was assigned a fixed number of *feux* to pay annually; the cost of each feu was determined by vote of the Breton Estates. The number of feux assigned to each district was traditional rather than rational. What was especially irritating to residents of other provinces was that cities in Brittany were exempt from the fouage altogether and paid only a small *aide des villes* in compensation—entirely inadequate compensa-sation, in the minds of contemporaries.[53]

52. Doucet, *Institutions*, 2 : 570–71. In the fifteenth century, however, the figure had been higher: 188,000 livres. Dognon, "La taille en Languedoc," pp. 342–50.

53. Doucet, *Institutions*, 2 : 572.

H

Farming the Aides

"Aides," says La Barre, "are taken on things and not on persons, on produce and merchandise sold at wholesale and at retail. . . ." [1] By the mid-sixteenth century, formidably long lists could be compiled of commodities on which the aides were levied. Such lists would include almost all commodities sold regularly and in important quantities: cheese and lard; cattle, sheep, and poultry; cloth and clothng; wood, stone, and other building materials; wood for heating; even basic needs such as food grains and fish. [2] This list varied from one province to another "according to local custom," says the *Vestige des finances*. The rate of taxation was one sou per livre on merchandise sold either wholesale or retail; once taxed, an item was not subject to additional aides when resold. For wine and other beverages, however, there was a tax imposed on both wholesale and retail sales.

In this kind of taxation there was a cutoff point on sales involving less than 5 sous. In other words, small quantities of the very poorest goods sold at retail, the type of transaction one would expect to find in the villages, did not carry the aides. [3]

Later in the sixteenth century a few taxes appeared that were regarded as aides but actually were production taxes rather than sales taxes. An example is the tax of one sou per livre on the weaving and working of woolen cloth. [4] There were similar levies on producing leather, iron, and pewter goods. Many towns had taxes on manufacturing during the Middle Ages; but the Renaissance levies were the first in France affecting the whole kingdom. These production taxes were minor affairs, neither aggressively enforced nor particularly lucrative.

One of the especially confusing aspects of the category of taxes known as aides (and another reason the list seems to extend indefinitely) was that it included a subcategory of taxes called octrois. These were city taxes on

1. La Barre, *Formulaire*, p. 89.
2. Venison, however—an aristocratic meat—was not subject to aides; nor were spices. Dupont-Ferrier, *Etudes*, 2 : 73.
3. At least this was the intention of the basic law; ord. of Tours, Feb. 28, 1436, in ORD, 13 : 211.
4. Edicts of Paris, Feb. 1582, and Fontainebleau, July 14, 1582.

a wide variety of market activities—sales, production, and even movement of goods. Only part of such taxes were "royal" in the sense that their returns went into the royal treasury; some were local, raised by and for the city concerned.

A favorite type of royal octroi, found in a great many towns, was the levy on livestock, named according to whether it fell primarily on animals for eating, the *pieds fourchés* (forked hoofs—cattle, pigs, sheep, and goats), or on *pieds ronds* (round hoofs—horses, mules, donkeys). As a royal tax this was relatively new, going back perhaps to the reign of Louis XII.[5] Francis I imposed the most important pied fourché tax on Paris.[6] By the terms of this tax, all pied fourché animals brought into Paris or its suburbs, "dead or alive," which were to be sold at wholesale, had to pay 8 sous per ox, 4 per cow, 2 per pig, and 1 per sheep or calf. The same edict also imposed a levy of 8 sous on each *balle* of dyestuff brought into Paris and forbade the merchant drapers to ship their woolen goods out of the city to be dyed elsewhere with the intention of avoiding the new octroi. The first result of this octroi of June 1539 seems to have been not an increase in royal revenues but rather a great expansion of the cattle and meat business in towns outside of Paris.[7]

Taken all together, the aides were the second most important source of royal revenues during the Renaissance. But they were a rather poor second. In the reign of Charles VII the aides had been worth about one-third as much as the tailles, or 400,000 livres as compared to about 1.2 millions for the tailles. Later in the Renaissance the aides usually brought in less than a third of the amount of the tailles. At the very end of the century, when the tailles were valued at around 15 million livres, the aides were reported to be bringing in only about 1.5 million livres.

This is much less of an increase than might have been expected during this time of great economic expansion, especially considering that these taxes were on market activities. Many of the aides were given away by the king—as favors to courtiers, as pensions to worthy servitors, and as necessary support to towns which had to improve and expand their fortifications to accommodate the king's military plans. Renaissance *états* were so slipshod that it is difficult to tell whether or not certain aides, when they were

5. Zeller, *Institutions*, p. 262.

6. Edict of Paris, June 19, 1539, in Pierre Des-Hayes, *Declarations . . . concernans . . . la ferme du bestail . . .* , pp. 4–7.

7. Royal letters-patent issued the very next month complained that the cattle markets of Pontoise, Poissy, and a few others were doing a thriving illegal business. Apparently the housewives of Paris were following their butchers out of town. Des-Hayes, *Declarations*, pp. 13–14.

totally alienated, simply were not reported as revenue. It is possible that many of the revenues from aides that should have appeared on the *états de prévision* were kept off the books; they became secret compensation for the *traitants*. This speculation, of course, amounts to saying that one does not really know what was happening to the revenues from aides; the whole situation, as one authority puts it, is "pleines d'obscurités." [8]

Taxes on the sales of wines so dominated indirect taxing that later in the sixteenth century, when the rates on wines became even heavier, the phrases "aides" and "taxes on wines" were often used interchangeably. By the same token, a Renaissance slang term for greasing the palms of any tax farmer was *vinage*. The production of wine, of course, was one of the great moneymaking activities in France, "one of our gifts from Heaven [*mannes*] . . . [producing] great revenues . . . whether it be drunk in the localities where it grows or is transported." That is why, explained La Barre, "they have heavily weighed it down with imposts." [9] The acreage in France given over to wine production increased substantially during the Renaissance.[10]

There were aides on other commercial drinks besides wine: beer, cider, and perry (*poirée*—the Anjou equivalent of cider, a strong beverage made from pear juice). This last drink seems to have been more highly esteemed in the Renaissance than now.

The rates of 1 sou per livre on sales at wholesale and 1.5 sous on sales at retail—the *vingtième et huitème*—were not levied in addition to the export tariffs on wine; wines paid either the traites or the aides but not both.[11] The vingtième was collected by agents of the tax farmers as the wine arrived at the town gates; the huitième was collected from "hotel-keepers, publicans and cabaret-keepers." [12] During the great reforms of Charles VII the retail aide on wine had been doubled, becoming a *qua-trième*; Louis XI reduced this to a huitième again for Paris and perhaps

8. Doucet, *Institutions*, 2 : 561. A figure of 2.8 million livres is given for aides in the budget of 1588; see Dur, "Constitutional Rights," p. 299. But all budget figures for this year are highly suspect.
9. La Barre, *Formulaire*, p. 93.
10. This is true even though many vineyards of north France that produced inferior grapes were taken out of production. See Roger Dion, *Histoire de la vigne et du vin en France, des origines au XIXe siècle* (Paris, 1959), pp. 417–22, 461 ff.
11. The octrois, on the other hand, were levied in addition to the aides, except in cities that had obtained a royal charter to the contrary. See the letters-patent of Paris, Feb. 7, 1555.
12. Hennequin, *Guidon*, pp. 172–73.

for some other cities.[13] The amount of the retail aide on wine in the six-teenth century for the various regions of France is unfortunately not at all clear.

On the eve of the Wars of Religion, in a period of terrible financial stringency, the Estates-General of 1560–61 accepted a new wholesale tax on wine;[14] this one was specific—so much per cask of a given capacity—rather than ad valorem. The basic rate, at first, was 5 sous for each *muid* of wine, or rather the *muid* of Paris, holding about seventy-one gallons (U.S.A.);[15] other areas, using different capacity barrels, paid equivalent taxes.[16]

The *cinq sols* was to be a wine levy in addition to the older national aides and local octrois—not a substitute for them. This new aide on wine was supposed to be limited to six years, after which it was "to be and remain void, extinct, suppressed, and abolished"; but when the term of the cinq sols was over, the fiscal plight of the monarchy was worse than ever. The Wars of Religion had begun. Therefore the new tax was prolonged in 1568 for another six years; and the same thing happened in 1573, in spite of exceptionally vigorous and widespread protests. Before long, of course, the time limitation on the cinq sols was simply ignored by the king. The tax became a permanent one, collected without any pretense of con-sulting representative bodies and with only the most perfunctory references to its continuation in royal ordinances.

Just as assessors of the tailles had to know their neighbors and the *assiette* each could bear, the farmers of aides had to know the businesses of the merchants, artisans, or landowners from whom they had to collect. The burden of proof, so to speak, was on the government, which had to show that the landowners, artisans, and merchants involved had indeed bought, sold, produced, or moved certain goods in a way that entitled the king to a share. Therefore the government was glad to employ persons who were not merely royal officials but businessmen who could deal with other

13. Clamageran, *L'impôt,* 2 : 5.
14. It is not clear whether the Estates-General of Pontoise voted this tax or if this is simply what the crown later claimed. See J. Russell Major, *The Estates General of 1560,* p. 112; cf. Clamageran, *L'impôt,* 2 : 183; Zeller, *Institutions,* p. 263; and Picot, *États Généraux,* 2 : 390–91.
15. Figuring 268.1 liters to the muid; see Jan Craebyckx, *Un grand commerce d'importation: Les vins de France aux anciens Pays-Bas, XIIIe–XVIe siècles* (Paris, 1958), p. 283.
16. Ord. of St. Germain-en-Laye, Sept. 22, 1561, in Isambert, 14 : 117–22.

businessmen on their own grounds.[17] A further reason the state welcomed tax farmers was that they usually were wealthy men who (once they became entangled in the fiscal system) could be cajoled or forced to lend the king money.[18]

In the *pays d'états* some of the leases were granted by royal commissioners, and some by vote of the provincial Estates themselves. But for the greater part of France it was the *élu*'s responsibility to get the tax farms "raised as dear as possible and knocked down at the top price." [19] He was ordered to publicize, at least one month before the beginning of the fiscal year—by placards and by *cri public*—just which aides were to be offered for lease the following year.

In the Middle Ages nobles and even clerics could and did take tax farms of royal revenues, but this was ended by the mid-fifteenth century.[20] The reason given for ruling out nobles was that when such *grands* were present at auctions they could intimidate the lesser people and so capture the leases at unfairly low prices. For a while the government ruled that even burghers who were royal officials could not bid for tax farms.[21] But in 1540 the restriction was changed so that only nobles, professional soldiers, and the clergy were forbidden to become tax farmers. Royal officials who were commoners could bid for tax farms—but only those serving the king, not those of other sovereigns or of great French nobles.[22]

The auction itself was supposed to be in the evening, when more people would be free to attend; and the adjudication was to be carried on according to the custom of "la chandelle esteinte"—that is, the person who was awarded the lease would be the last bidder to raise the price before a candle on the auctioneer's table went out.

There was always the possibility that only unreasonably low bids would be proffered or that no one at all would bid for the lease. When this happened it was up to the élu and his subordinates to collect the tax themselves (perhaps hiring some additional agents) acting as paid officials of the crown rather than as enterprisers. This put the revenue concerned "en

17. For a valuable discussion of this factor see George T. Matthews, *The Royal General Farms in Eighteenth-Century France*, p. 21.

18. This can be traced back to the Middle Ages. Fryde and Fryde in *The Cambridge Economic History of Europe*, 3 : 437.

19. Jacqueton, *Documents*, p. 66.

20. Joseph R. Strayer, *The Royal Domain in the Bailliage of Rouen* (Princeton, 1936), p. 22; and see the edict of Tours, Feb. 28, 1436, in ORD, 13 : 211–15.

21. Edict of Montreuil, June 30, 1517, in Isambert, 12 : 126–27.

22. Edicts of Aumale, April 4, 1540, and Fontainebleau, Dec. 18, 1540.

régie" rather than "en ferme." Never was this viewed as more than a temporary arrangement. Elus were urged often and strenuously to find adequate bidders for all tax farms; the king obviously felt that the system of tax farming, with all its faults, was on the whole advantageous.

One of the most significant features of Renaissance tax history was the development—toward the very end of this period—of large-scale tax farming. These *grosses fermes* (multiple tax farms) and *fermes générales* (multi-provincial or nationwide monopolies) really belong to the fiscal-financial history of the Old Régime. But they can trace their origins to the later Renaissance.

Much economic activity in the Middle Ages was carried on under charters or licenses that were, in effect, monopolies—the incorporated artisan guilds and the companies of regional merchants, such as the *marchands de l'eau* supplying Paris, are well-known examples. But it is important to realize that these monopolies were only local or regional concerns. There were no nationwide monopolies in the Middle Ages. Medieval governments usually took the stand that large-scale monopolies were infringements of royal power in economic life. The same can be said for royal policy regarding tax farm monopolies before the second half of the sixteenth century. Up to that time, royal policy concerning tax farming can fairly be expressed by the phrase "the smaller the better."

The reasoning behind such an attitude is easily explained. A tax farmer was allowed to keep all he could collect above the agreed lease-price of an aide. If he had no competition from other would-be tax farmers to drive up the price of the lease, he stood to profit enormously. The government, therefore, relied on competition in open auctions to bring the lease prices up to something close to the market value of the tax farms. Grosses fermes, at least until late in the sixteenth century, was a synonym for "bad tax farms" because the king and the public were convinced that such tax farms were obtained only by combines of tax-farm entrepreneurs, who could always conspire to keep the lease price down.

The government first began to reverse its policy regarding grosses fermes during the reign of Henry II. A multiple tax farm was established—temporarily, as it turned out—for the *pays de quart* gabelles of western France in 1548. In 1555 the *trespas de la Loire* went to Jean Meschine for ten years.[23] Beginning in the late 1550s and 1560s the number of grosses fermes of the aides increased. Some of the leases auctioned off in the 1550s did, in fact, go to combines of tax farmers, who had in addition *branchiers des*

23. See Fontanon, 2 : 541.

fermes or subfarmers operating with them. Some of the farms of the wine taxes covered whole généralités or were awarded for several years at a time; thus the wine tax farms for Rouen and Evreux granted in 1567 were contracted out for four years.[24] The term *grosses fermes* began to appear in edicts and even in some commentaries without its older perjorative connotations.

We do have many indications in edicts and Renaissance treatises that the farm of aides, large or small, was at times a risky affair, one that could result not only in a loss to the tax farmer but in his complete ruin. In theory, all tax farmers who could not meet their lease-price contracts had to forfeit their bonds and be thrown in jail for debt. The ruin of a tax farmer could come about through a petty war or uprising that cut short traffic on a trade route; a hard winter could reduce the movement of cattle; a serious drop in the demand for any item, such as the more costly wines, could cut the value of an aide to a fraction of its predicted value. When Christophe Aubry, "merchant burgher of Paris," undertook the farm of the wine octroi for Paris, the conferring lease stipulated the affair was "à ses perils & fortunes." [25]

To judge by royal legislation on the matter, frauds against the aides must have been a standard feature of Renaisance life. Complaints abound against merchants, landlords, tax farmers, and collectors who, through carelessness or worse, forced down the annual value of the aides, with the result that tax farmers felt justified in offering lower bids in succeeding years. Records tell of peasants with mysteriously diminished herds and landlords caught spiriting wine into Paris at night; of burghers who always seemed to have the same number of barrels of wine in their cellars no matter how much they served at the table; of merchants and innkeepers who bought their wine "in the fields" (secretly from peasants rather than at regular markets under the eyes of the tax farmers); of innkeepers who maintained several *caves*, some of which the aides inspectors were never allowed to see; of collusion between élus and tax farmers in order to award the tax farm leases at less than their fair value.[26]

The king gave tax farmers the right to poke and pry into the business affairs of all those liable to pay aides. The result was a perennial struggle

24. Doucet, *L'état des finances de 1567*, p. 19 n. 1.
25. A.N. AD[IX-2], April 24, 1557.
26. Ord. of Paris, Nov. 11, 1508, in Jacqueton, *Documents*, pp. 131–32; edict of Paris, June 15, 1534; royal decl. of St. Germain-en-Laye, Sept. 1553, in Isambert, 13 : 344–49.

among merchants and producers, tax farmers and storekeepers, officials and consumers. Many records present a picture, perhaps exaggerated, of countless agents of the *fermiers* (accompanied by greedy and brutal constables) haunting taverns, toll booths, docks of fishing villages, town markets, fairs, the main crossroads, and the roads leading to river ports—asking accusing questions, forcing nervous housewives to surrender the keys to their cellars, and busily scribbling down outrageous overestimates of the amount and value of the goods they inspected.[27] This sort of commercial spying signalized the belief that it was perfectly natural for anyone who could dodge paying his aide to do so; it also shows that the burden of proof was on the tax farmers and on the fiscal officials.

Almost from the beginning of the royal aides—that is, from the late fourteenth century—farmers of these taxes had the right to *visitation*, entry into a merchant's or producer's premises.[28] At least once a year a tax farmer could request the élu to supply him with an official assistant in order to visit the interiors of all warehouses, wine caves, sheds for drying fish, wine cellars of inns and taverns, and even the homes of all persons in trade; furthermore, the tax farmer—who might be the competitor of a merchant being investigated—had the right to be present at these "visitacions & recherches." [29] River boats carrying wine were not to be unloaded before being "visited" by agents of the tax farmers, since some merchants were trying to unload "at night and at other unseemly hours . . . without paying the said duty and aide." [30] A decline in the amount of visible barrels and bales in a warehouse from one inspection to another was taken as evidence of sale and justification for demanding payment of the aide.[31] At harvesttime the tax farmers had the right to check up on what quantities of grapes were being brought to the wine presses, so as to estimate what their taxes might bring. As a last resort, a tax farmer could even direct the local constables to seize an offender's wares and sell them to cover the tax obligation. An example of what we would call "conflict of interest" is revealed in the order forbidding constables to operate as such in cases where they themselves were the tax farmers.[32]

27. There were *sergents* of aides as well as of tailles; see A.N. Z^{1A-527}, no. 686, letters-patent of Sept. 7, 1549.

28. There are scores of edicts on this point, going back to the 1380s. See Clamageran, *L'impôt*, 1 : 420, 426–28; edicts of Jan. 1383 and July 6, 1388, in ORD, 7 : 764.

29. Jacqueton, Documents. p. 72, See also the royal decl. of Lyons, Aug. 28, 1574.

30. Letters-patent of Paris, Jan. 12, 1585; see also Des-Hayes, *Recueil*, pp. 49–53.

31. Charpentier, *Recueil des ordonnances*, p. 35.

32. Jacqueton, *Documents*, p. 67.

Since the aides fell on commercial transactions, they seemed less harsh. The peasant majority of the population, who produced many of the commodities they consumed, paid the aides only in their capacity as producer-sellers; that is, at the time or just before they delivered their goods for sale. Presumably the incidence of such taxes (as for most indirect taxes) eventually fell not on the peasants but on the final consumer in the form of higher prices. The aides were more equitable, too, in that some of them (not all, by any means) fell on all classes. Nobles and clergy were exempt altogether from the tailles, but they paid at least some of the aides. Specifically, they paid the octrois and—when the laws were properly enforced—the *sou par livre* and the wholesale wine impost on sellers.

For this reason Renaissance writers favored using the aides over other revenues; and they accepted, perhaps too complacently, the idea that the aides were equitable taxes. Combes, for example, saw all men paying the "wine tribute . . . no matter what their estate, quality, and condition." [33] The government, too, often expressed itself as favoring aides because they were equitable taxes. When Charles IX ordered the cinq sols on wine continued for six years, he justified this sort of tax as "the most gracious, equitable, and universal help that we could have from our subjects." [34] And one feature of the "père du peuple" legend glorifying Louis XII was that he forced everyone to pay the vingtième on wine, no matter what his station in life.[35]

One tax privilege involving the aides was the right for nobles and clergy to sell wine at retail without paying the huitième (the quatrième, in some places) if the wine came from their patrimonial lands. The wine had to come from grapes grown on a lord's demesne (*domain prôche*)—not land in his fief worked by peasant or middle-class *censitaires* or tenants, but from personally owned land worked for his benefit by wage or servile labor. Louis XII, a famous enemy of tax inequity, tried to restrict this privilege to wine actually sold by the tankard rather than by the keg (*à pot* rather than *à l'assiette*) and only near the noble's manor or town house. He also made it necessary for nobles who wanted this privilege to obtain a royal

33. Combes, *Traicté*, p. 113. See also Hennequin, *Guidon*, p. 172. Bodin also favored indirect taxes as more equitable; see *République*, pp. 887, 890. But Dallington believed that "the King [of France] hath nothing of his Noblesse, but Sword-service." *The View of Fraunce*, p. B3.

34. Edict of St. Maur-des-Fossés, May 1, 1567. At the beginning of the Renaissance, in justifying the Languedoc équivalent, that province's substitute for the aides, the crown's position was that "Chacun en paye, sans nul excepter, et qui plus despend, plus en paye." Cited in Dognon, *Les institutions politiques*, p. 313.

35. See, e.g., La Barre, *Formulaire*, pp. 90–91.

writ acknowledging it, a document that had to be shown on demand to a wine tax farmer.[36]

The retail wine tax exemption was important, especially for poorer nobles who had little income beyond that from selling their own produce. In 1500 Jean le Prevost, a squire (*écuyer*) whose parents were poor with several children to support, won a case before the Chambre des comptes defending his privileges of exemption from the aides; it seems that "to find means of more uprighteously supporting himself and living," this member of the lowest rank of nobility had taken a post as royal *procureur*, and the case concerned the problem of whether this sort of position carried with it derogation of noble status and therefore an obligation to pay the aides.[37] The retail wine tax exemption for nobles and clerics was important enough to have been the subject of many legal confirmations during the Renaissance.[38]

This privilege did not apply to sales at wholesale; if a noble sold his wine to a wine merchant or to a "hotel-keeper, publican, or cabaret-keeper" he had to pay the vingtième. The basic law of August 16, 1498, on these affairs laid down in strict terms that dealing at wholesale was a "lowly estate and occupation" and not to be allowed to nobles—or for that matter to any privileged group—wanting to enjoy the prerogatives of their group. This applied even to a noble's wine *de son cru* (from his personal lands and production) and to town octrois as well as royal taxes on wine.[39]

Buying wine, however, nobles enjoyed considerable advantages. Wine that was purchased in large quantities—*à l'assiette* rather than *à pot*—for a nobleman's cellars, to be consumed by his household, paid no retail aide. This privilege was enjoyed by all nobles and therefore applied to a larger group than those few who happened to have proprietary vineyards and retail outlets. It meant that wine dealers could sell nobles stocks of wine at a price considerably lower than that paid by unprivileged consumers. The exemption was also enjoyed by clergymen and by members of the king's household and that of other members of the royal family, as well as many of the upper-echelon officials.[40]

As the sixteenth century wore on and the crown began to sell more

36. Edict of Etampes, Aug. 16, 1498, in Des-Hayes, *Recueil*, pp. 97–98.
37. Royal decl. of Melun, Sept. 6, 1500.
38. E.g., the edict of Blois, Sept. 22, 1560.
39. Edict of St. Germain-en-Laye, Dec. 15, 1561; and see Zeller, *Institutions*, p. 50.
40. Whether or not nobles, clergy, and high officials enjoyed similar privileges for other commodities, however, varied so greatly from province to province that no generalization is possible.

royal offices, these were made attractive to investors by including exemption to the wine taxes for commoners who purchased them. By the reign of Henry III the retail purchase exemption was extended down to the level of the middle-echelon élus.[41]

One group of wine tax privileges, resulting in repeated testing before the Cour des aides, was the exemptions for university students—who, of course, were (formally) members of the clergy during the Renaissance as well as the Middle Ages. Too many young men were "working their way through college" by taking advantage of the business opportunities afforded by their temporary clerical status. The government noted that not only relatives of such young men but persons in no way related to them were deeding them extensive vineyards "so that by such means they become and remain free from paying the said aides on home-grown produce [*fruitz croissans*] of the said holdings thus conveyed under cover of privilege of scholarly status. . . ." Tax farmers were allowed to investigate whether a student was really working "to live according to or to serve scholarship" or perhaps was "living largely through commerce." [42] Obviously, in some cases, it did pay to be a scholar in Renaissance France.[43]

In the provinces "où les aides n'ont cours," indirect taxes of some sort were paid. In fact, in all lands where aides were not paid, an internal tariff known as the *imposition foraine* was imposed on all goods coming from the provinces that did pay aides; this impost, not surprisingly, was rated at just one sou per livre (see appendix J). This was in addition to whatever lump sum *composition* such provinces paid. Furthermore, provinces that did not pay the *sou par livre* might have to pay some wine taxes. And each of them had other indirect taxes that were heritages from days when they had been autonomous; Brittany, for example, had taxes on beverages called *devoirs* that were raised by the provincial Estates for the benefit of the royal treasury.

Thanks to the work of Alfred Spont,[44] we know some of the details of how the Languedoc substitute for the sou par livre was handled. In the 1440s Languedoc had established a claim for preferential treatment, partly

41. Edict of Paris, May 1575, in Houzé, *Edicts et ordonnances*, pp. 172–75.
42. Ord. of Bois-Sir-Amé, Aug. 26, 1452, in Jacqueton, *Documents*, pp. 68–69.
43. On the other hand, the University of Paris took the position that many of its students depended on tax exempt sales from their vineyards for their livelihood; and the rector objected when, in Dec. 1555, the government reduced the amount exempted. B.N. Nouv. acq. fr. 2374, fol. 8.
44. "L'équivalent aux aides en Languedoc de 1450 à 1515," *Annales du Midi* 3 (1891). See also Dognon, *Les institutions politiques*, pp. 489–500.

because of its autonomy, partly because of the support given Charles VII during the black years of the 1420s and 1430s. The base of the Languedoc *équivalent* was an annual lump sum payment eventually set at 83,000 livres. The management of the équivalent was to be in the hands of agents (*conservateurs*) of the Languedoc Estates rather than royal officials. These agents farmed out the équivalent in about the same manner as the aides were handled elsewhere in France.[45] At first the Languedociens had tried to obtain permission to raise the équivalent as a direct tax, giving the usual excuse that commerce was damaged by excise taxes. This the king refused to allow; and the équivalent became a tax on sales, principally on meat, fish, and wines. But nobles and clergy could buy household provisions free of this tax.[46]

For a few years the Languedoc équivalent was so haphazardly managed that it produced a good deal less than the agreed annual payment (known as the *préciput*) of 83,000 livres. The Estates had to make up the difference by levying a supplementary tax. Later, however, when the Languedociens became accustomed to it, complaints against the new tax dwindled away and receipts improved. Its base was broadened to include most of the commodities subject to the aides in other provinces.[47] In fact, returns from the équivalent rose to substantially more than the préciput; and the provincial Estates were allowed to keep the remainder for their own expenses.

Other provinces, too, had levies known as équivalents; they were found in Poitou, La Marche, Auvergne, Burgundy, and the northeast districts of Artois and Rethelois. But the only important similarity between these other équivalents and that of Languedoc is that they were substitutes for the aides of north and central France. Invariably, outside of Languedoc they were direct taxes. However, like the équivalent of Languedoc, they were administered by provincial Estates where such existed. These levies were all regarded as conferred privileges; and these privileges often had required an additional outlay to the king at the time they were obtained.[48]

The government evidently regarded the équivalents as bad bargains and tried to cancel them when possible. In 1579–80, during a period of relatively vigorous fiscal reform, the king forced the county of Auxerrois to accept the basic aide, the sou par livre, in place of the équivalent. The county representatives complained; this tax, they pointed out, brought in tax farmers who were harassing local merchants and town authorities. Be-

---

45. See the edict of Vauluisant, end of March 1538, in Isambert, 12 : 554–55.
46. Clamageran, *L'impôt*, 2 : 17–20; Dupont-Ferrier, *Etudes*, 2 : 130–32.
47. Doucet, *Institutions*, 2 : 562.
48. For Auvergne, see Combes, *Traicté*, p. 113.

cause of this, they explained, the new levy was ineffective. Merchants had been driven to meet buyers in secret in their homes or even in the country-side. And in any case, they claimed, the tax could not possibly be worth much; they estimated its revenues as 500 écus and offered the king an équivalent of 800 écus, to be raised as a direct tax using the same mechanism as employed in collecting the tailles.[49]

49. Quantin, *Auxerre*, pp. 44–45.

I

The Salt Taxes

Salt in Renaissance France came almost entirely from salt marshes near the coasts, where the brine was captured with dikes and ditches and allowed to evaporate, or was boiled away in huge vats. A small amount of salt came from salt mines and salt wells and springs in one or two locations in eastern France.[1] A high-quality, high-cost white salt was produced along the Mediterranean. A somewhat grayish salt, called "black," came from the west and from Brittany; small quantities of rather good salt were shipped into the interior from the Normandy salt flats along the Cotentin peninsula and at the mouth of the Touques river (near Honfleur). In these Normandy areas, deposits of salt on the beaches were raked up along with the fine sand the salt clung to; then the sandy brine was boiled off and filtered. Salt not consumed in the provinces where it was produced was shipped into the interior districts of France. Much French salt, also, was shipped to other countries; in fact, it was one of the most important items in French commerce during this era.

The localized production of salt resulted in the formation of syndicates of merchant-purveyors who worked hard to effect monopolies of salt cartage and supply (*tirage*) in their regions. In the late Middle Ages, these companies, by paying local seigneurs and undertaking the expense of maintaining bridges, ferries, and other transportation facilities on their routes, managed to squeeze out competitors. The most succesful among such salt merchant companies was the one that controlled the movement of all salt on the huge Loire river system. Others monopolized the salt trade in the Ile de France, Normandy, Picardy-Champagne, Provence-Dauphiné, and Languedoc.

Early in the Renaissance the kings of France became convinced that they needed larger revenues from the salt trade and that these revenues depended not only on permitting but also on promoting and even enforcing

1. Everyone had the right to evaporate as much salt as he wished; the gabelles applied only to transport and sale. Salt mining, on the other hand, was at least partly controlled by the king, who received a percentage of the profits of all subsoil minerals.

local differences in salt production, transport, and consumption. They began to insist that only traditional transport routes be followed, that each merchant company transporting salt stay out of other companies' territories, and that salt from a given district be warehoused and sold only in a specified area or even shipped to one specific warehouse. The purpose was to maintain an artificial scarcity of salt in certain regions of the country.

The result was surely one of the most thoroughgoing perversions of a developing large-scale market in early modern history. The "black" but cheap and desirable salt of coastal Poitou, for example, was denied entry to neighboring Anjou and Touraine. Poitevin salt could be shipped south to Bordeaux and thence up the Garonne to Angoulême, Périgueux, Limousin, and Quercy; but the same ships could not take such salt north to Nantes, at the mouth of the Loire. The Loire valley was the exclusive preserve of salt from Brittany. Breton salt, in addition, was the sole supply in east Normandy, the whole Ile de France, Picardy, Berry, and Bourbonnais—all the lands, in fact, north of the *pays de petites gabelles* except west Normandy (which produced some of the salt it consumed) and Burgundy. Burgundy and a few neighboring provinces could enjoy the excellent salt from the mines and wells of Franche Comté and Lorraine; but merchant shippers were not allowed to transport this salt down the Seine or to sell it in neighboring Champagne.

The white salt from the salt marshes of the Mediterranean, regarded as the best in France, was produced in such large quantities that undoubtedly it could have supplied a great portion of both western and north-central France. But salt from the Midi was not allowed to penetrate north of a line running roughly from Mâcon southwest to Cahors, and west of a line running south from Cahors to Spain (just west of Toulouse).

The salt trade of the Midi, furthermore, was carefully divided into four territories: (1) Salt from the marshes along the coast near Narbonne was limited to markets in the provinces immediately interior to it, chiefly Toulouse and Carcassonne. (2) The abundant salt of the Peccais marshes in southeast Languedoc had the monopoly of sale in Beaucaire, Rouergue, and the districts of Nîmes and Albi. These salt marshes east of the Rhône were not only limited to specified outlets but had separate administrations. (3) Salt from the western coasts of Provence was given outlets in Gevaudan, Vivarais, Forez, Lyons and its district, and Beaujolais—essentially the right bank of the Rhône. The syndicate of merchant-purveyors serving this group of markets was known as the *tirage à part du royaume* in contrast to the *tirage à part de l'Empire*—that is, Provence. (4) The areas serviced by salt merchants from elsewhere in Provence included all the rest of that land, plus Dauphiné and French Savoy—lands with overlordship claims by the Holy Roman Empire.[2]

There was a blanket prohibition against Frenchmen importing salt. Jean Bodin made a famous attack on this policy, pointing out that encouraging exports and discouraging imports of salt was itself a form of taxation, since it raised the price of salt to French consumers; Bodin remarked that in England, which produced little salt of its own and had to rely on the French, salt cost less than in France, "which is a harmful incongruity in affairs of state and in management." [3]

The most important gabelles region, both in area and in revenues produced, was that of the north and central domain lands as they were constituted at the time of Charles V: Maine, Anjou, Touraine, Orléanais, Berry, Nivernais, Champagne, Paris and the Ile de France, Picardy, and part of Normandy. This is the area where the salt warehouses, the *greniers*, played the most vital role in the taxing of salt, and therefore I shall refer to it as the *"greniers* system." It was about the same area known in the Old Régime as that of the *grandes gabelles*. This system provides our picture of how the salt taxes operated, not only because it was the most important region but also because more is known about its details and because the variations in the other territories are too numerous to be described here.

The best approach to the operation of the salt taxes in greniers-system districts is to visualize it as its contemporaries did: the *présentation* of salt, or its transport to a grenier; the *descente* of salt, which referred to its warehousing and care; and the *vente*, or sale to final customers.

When salt was transported into the greniers-system districts, whether by barges on the rivers or in large carts on the roads, it had to be brought through a designated sequence of royal check points. There, inspectors (*briseurs du sel*) recorded the volume and weight to ensure that some salt was not disappearing into illegal channels. At the grenier, the salt was inspected by the *mesureur* under the eyes of the *grenetier*, the *contrôleur*, and the merchant—all three of them, or at least their respective agents. Using officially approved containers, the mesureur calculated the volume of salt brought in and the contrôleur recorded that amount to the credit of the merchant; meanwhile the contrôleur was checking his records to see that the amount delivered tallied with that originally consigned.

---

2. Salt from this last group of districts also went up the Rhône to the papal enclave of Avignon and Comtat-Venaissin and to western Switzerland. Some of this area's salt also went in the other direction—by sea routes abroad or to centers of the fish-curing industry in Mediterranean France.

3. Quoted in the article on gabelles in Henri Hauser, *Les origines historiques des problèmes économiques* (Paris, 1930), p. 61.

Thus "presented," the salt was ready to "descend." The warehouses themselves, all too often, were actually underground shafts or caves such as those used for storing wine. Since so much salt was "presented" along river routes by barges, many of the underground or ground-level storage places were near rivers in humid locations and subject to real disaster during floods. In the sixteenth century the state became anxious to have its grenetiers provide adequate above-ground facilities for salt, for the reason that one of the most important functions of storing salt was to give it a further drying out period. When salt was "presented" it was usually still damp enough to be cakey. The French had learned that heavy wet salt was a threat to health as well as an injustice to purchasers. Royal edicts decreed that all salt not actually "dry and free pouring" had to be labeled as wet salt and sold only at a heavy discount.[4]

Each particular salt batch, therefore, usually remained in the grenier for two years. Much salt stayed in the warehouses for three years or longer. Once in storage, the salt was locked up with three padlocks and keys, one key for the grenetier, one for the contrôleur, and a third for the merchant whose salt it was. Since each key was different, presumably the salt could not be removed without the assent of all three parties.

The mechanism involved in selling salt was almost as complicated as the présentation and descente. As each batch of salt became sufficiently dry and powdery, the merchant was permitted to apply for permission to sell it. This request took the form of a letter addressed to the *trésorier général* and was countersigned by the grenetier and the contrôleur responsible. When permission was granted, the salt, finally, was ready for sale. The merchant's sale price, the *droit du marchand*, as distinguished from the tax proper, the *droit du roi*, was set by the trésorier général, presumably on the basis of costs of production and especially costs of transport.[5]

To purchase salt, all subjects living inside the greniers-system area were obliged to come to the grenier nearest them, and to that grenier only. In the larger walled cities where a grenier stood (sometimes two or three of them) this was no problem for the burghers; they simply purchased the salt

4. See the restraining order of the Cour des aides against merchants selling salt "non sec ny esgouté," B.N. Nouv. acq. fr. 2374, dated July 23, 1555; and see the ord. of Paris, Nov. 11, 1508, in Jacqueton, *Documents*, pp. 141–42. Cf. the passage in the work by an Englishman, I[ohn] B[rowne], *The Marchant's Avizo* ([1589] reprinted by the Kress Library of Business and Economics, Cambridge, Mass., 1957), p. 24: "*Salt.* Note, that of Salt the brightest and whitest colour is best, & which is cleane without durte or strawes, and that which is old and not new salt. The which if it be new, it is perceaved by the moistness of it, and by sticking of it to your fingers, after hard wringing of it in your hande."

5. S.-C. Gigon, *La révolte de la gabelle en Guyenne, 1548–1549*, appendix, n. A.

at a sales office right on the premises of the grenier. When warehouses were far from one of the smaller cities, the state sometimes provided subgreniers called *chambres à sel*, bureaus provided with some of the officials and the apparatus of greniers and, as the Renaissence wore on, often elevated to the status of greniers. In the smaller towns and in the villages that were too far away from a warehouse for an easy trip, however, additional sales outlets were provided by shopkeepers, known in the greniers-system area as *revendeurs* or *regrattiers*, who traveled to the nearest warehouse and picked up a few sacks of salt. The price they could charge was fixed by the trésorier général himself; it was only a tiny amount above the droit du roi plus the droit du marchand.

Some of the greniers areas were subjected to forced purchases of salt, the practice known as *sel de devoir*. It may have been Charles V, in the later fourteenth century, who was the initiator of sel de devoir.[6] It is not known whether the practice spread gradually during the fifteenth century or remained an exception; but in the general fiscal ordinance of Montreuil, June 30, 1517, it is clearly spelled out: apparently it was the practice, at that time, for a large percentage of the greniers system.[7] Authorities disagree as to how far sel de devoir (also called *sel par impôt* or "taxing salt") spread during the sixteenth century; some believe that it became the rule early in this era, whereas others believe that only a fraction of the greniers areas was forced to take its salt this way.[8]

During most of the Renaissance, it is clear that the sel de devoir was not as obnoxious a burden as it became during the Old Régime. The amount each household had to buy was not large, and supplementary purchases of salt had to be made. As late as August 13, 1579, an ordinance stipulated that in sel de devoir regions each one hundred persons over seven years old had to purchase only one *minot* annually. This amounted to four or five pints per family. Later (1584), Henry III reduced the area of sel de devoir, and in 1588 he abandoned the practice; but Henry IV and Sully returned to it and increased the tax rate sharply, perhaps as much as fourfold.[9] Apparently by this time the sel par impôt required families to buy more than they needed, since there were laws forbidding them to sell, barter, or even give away their excess salt. Sixteen pints of salt per family per year still does

6. Rey, *Le domaine du roi*, p. 190. Cf. Zeller, *Institutions*, pp. 267–71, who believes the practice was started in the reign of Louis XII and that it was first spread by Francis I.

7. Isambert, 12 : 129–37. This basic edict is reproduced in Jacqueton, *Documents*, pp. 170 ff.; see esp. pp. 185–86. See also Fontanon, 2 : 910, 989.

8. Doucet, *Institutions*, 2 : 580; cf. Dupont-Ferrier, *Etudes* 2 : 115–21, 129.

9. Clamageran, *L'impôt*, 2 : 238, 369–71.

not seem too burdensome, however, in an era when many peasant families needed salt for cattle-licks, and when households did some of their own meat preserving and fish curing.

The droit du roi on salt changed so drastically that it is difficult to choose a representative era for estimating the monetary burden of the gabelles. Let us settle on the years around 1530, just about the midpoint of the Renaissance. At this time in the greniers-system area, the tax was set at 30 livres per *muid* (measure of Paris), a huge measure of some 4,600 Renaissance pounds.[10] Even assuming that the 15 or 16 pints of sel de devoir per family per year required in the later Renaissance represented normal consumption, this still works out to a tax of only 24.6 deniers, or little more than 2 sous.[11] Since an artisan around 1530 received about 4 sous for a day's work, this meant he had to work half a day per year for the tax on his salt.

Only a few persons enjoyed exemption from the gabelles. From this point of view, at least, the gabelles were more equitable than the tailles or even than the aides. This appears to be the reason Louis XII favored the gabelles, which his government considered "the simplest, easiest, and lightest subsidy which ever has been levied, because folk from all estates pay it." [12] The rule regarding exemptions to the gabelles was that everybody paid who did not have a specific charter from the crown (verified by the Chambre des comptes) allowing such exemption. This applied to clergy and nobility.[13] Gabelles officials had the right to check through the homes and barns belonging to the upper classes.[14]

The system of salt taxing just described accounts for only one-third to two-fifths of all France during the period of this study. In the west of France, from Poitou to Gascony, including Angoulême and Périgueux, there were no royal greniers at all; gabelles were paid here, it is true (until 1553),

10. Meynial, "Etudes sur la gabelle du sel avant le XVIIe siècle en France," *Revue d'Histoire du Droit* 3 (1922): 126 and n. 6. Salt, of course, was not transported in such huge quantities but rather in sacks or hogsheads of a smaller capacity, often a minot, 48 to the muid. Marion, in his *Dictionnaire des institutions*, p. 375, gives the weight of a minot as between 96 and 100 pounds.

11. This assumes four persons over seven years of age per family.

12. Alfred Spont, "La gabelle du sel en Languedoc," *Annales du Midi* 3 (1891): 435. At the end of the Renaissance, we find Sully, too, favoring gabelles as fair taxes.

13. The French government took the position that the pope had specifically ruled that clergy should pay gabelles. See the edict of Angers, June 28, 1518.

14. Edict Aux Roches, Aug. 25, 1535, in Isambert, 12 : 410–14.

but of an entirely different nature. These lands were known as "lands of the fourth and fifth of salt" (*pays du quart et du quint de sel*). Here the gabelle amounted to a fourth (around Angoulême, a fifth) more than the merchant got for his salt. These gabelles, furthermore, were farmed out even during the early Renaissance; in fact, there was little to distinguish them economically from the aides.[15]

Still more variations could be found in a band of provinces just north of the Midi—Limousin, La Marche, Quercy, lower Auvergne, Rouergue, Forez, the Lyonnais, and Dauphiné. These territories also had no royal greniers. They were known as *pays de petites gabelles*. The state taxed salt (from Languedoc, mainly) only on its way to these provinces—that is, at important way stations (Beaucaire, Tarascon, and others in Languedoc for Midi salt, and Libourne, Bergerac, Bordeaux, and Agen for Poitou-Saintonge salt) rather than after the salt had arrived. It appears, then, that the salt tax in the pays de petites gabelles was really something like a tariff, very similar to the *imposition foraine*. Purchase of salt in these areas, furthermore, was quite free, since it was not limited to royal greniers or licensed retailers as in the central provinces.

The Midi, as we might suspect, also had its own salt tax peculiarities. Unlike the west, the Midi did have royal greniers, but they seem to have had functions somewhat different from those of the central and northern provinces.[16] Here the main purpose of the royal greniers and the royal salt tax officials seems to have been to prevent Languedoc salt from being sent into the other provinces illegally, and especially to prevent the cheaper "black" western salt from penetrating the Midi. The king had a special interest here, since the salt marshes of the Peccais district belonged to him as direct seigneur. The government also attempted to reserve the *petites gabelles* districts north of the Midi for its Peccais salt, especially Quercy, Auvergne, Rouergue, and the Agenais.[17] The greniers were laid out near ports or along the main roads and rivers leading north. Since they did not serve as a base of operations for greniers officials, they seem to have been more like simple warehouses than were the greniers in the other areas.[18]

15. West Normandy, the "quart bouillon" district, also had its gabelles farmed out: see Meynial, "Etudes sur la gabelle," 3 : 140–49; see also Doucet, *L'état des finances de 1523*, p. 142 n. 7. In 1537 rates in west France were increased by one-half, so that the area became known as "pays de quart et demi-quart" (and "quint et demi-quint").

16. There were no greniers, however, in the lands just west of Languedoc proper, in the area of Toulouse and Périgueux.

17. Meynial, "Etudes sur la gabelle," 4 : 131–209.

18. Spont, "La gabelle du sel," pp. 429–30 and passim.

Part of Normandy had other variations from the greniers system. When the English conqueror Henry V had possessed Normandy, he had abandoned the regular greniers system in operation there and had accepted instead a "fourth" (*quart*) above the merchant's price for the whole province. But the change proved too disruptive. His salt revenues fell off so drastically he had to return to the old system for the districts around Rouen. For the western salt-producing areas of Normandy, however, the régime of the *quart* remained in operation.[19]

All of the newer provinces paid lower gabelles than those of the greniers system. But only Brittany paid no gabelles at all. For at least part of this era the Bourbonnais and upper Auvergne also paid no regular gabelles; they paid a special *composition* price instead. Burgundy did have greniers and did pay some salt taxes, but here the salt tax was to some extent under the control of the provincial Estates, which voted gabelles as a grant to the king. But as an economic type the Burgundy gabelles seem to have been mainly tariffs collected on salt coming in from other provinces.[20]

In the districts of the greniers system the cost of salt was extraordinarily unfair, compared to the cost in more favored regions. In Brittany, for example, the final price of salt to the consumer in the mid-sixteenth century was about one-thirtieth the price in adjoining Anjou; and in Poitou the droit du roi was just one-fourth that of neighboring Touraine.[21] Even so, there were only a few outbreaks against the gabelles during the Renaissance, compared to the dozens of such uprisings during the Old Régime. And the most serious Renaissance gabelles revolt, that of 1548, occurred in the west of France, a region where the burden of salt taxes was substantially lower than in the greniers system.

Traditionally, the west was the area of *quart et demi-quart* salt taxes, which meant its salt taxes were perhaps one-third as heavy as those of the central provinces. This part of France was poor, however, and large numbers of people made their living by evaporating salt (and smuggling some of it?) and curing fish. In 1542 they had been upset by an order applying the local gabelles to exported salt and to salt for the fish industry, items previously exempt. A minor revolt against this new gabelle broke out in the Saintonge

19. Clamageran, *L'impôt*, 1 : 467.
20. Meynial, "Etudes sur la gabelle," 3 : 150 ff. Henri Drouot claims that at least during the Wars of Religion Burgundy's salt taxes were heavy. *Notes sur la Bourgogne*, p. 20.
21. Cf. Nef, *Industry and Government*, p. 81, who calculates that toward the end of the Renaissance the French in areas of the greniers system paid "four times as much for their salt as it would have cost them if a free market had existed."

district. In 1543, after the revolt was crushed, the pre-1542 system was reestablished.[22]

Soon afterward, however, it became apparent that the government was planning a much more serious innovation in its western gabelles. These were the years when the king was considering changing over to farming out his salt taxes all over France; and in 1546 orders went out to follow suit in the west. Not only were the tax rates to be raised and tax farms introduced, but something comparable to the entire greniers system of salt tax officials was to be established in the west in order to expedite the business of the gabelles tax farmers. The men of the occupations most concerned with the salt industry complained they simply could not afford the tax increase. And there was a general outcry against the introduction of *gabelous* (catchpolls) in the west. In the hectic last months of Francis I's reign the government was not able to carry out its plan; but in 1548 Henry II ordered the new system into effect. Beginning in Saintonge, complaints turned into violence. The new salt tax officials and some tax farmers were seized and mauled by exasperated mobs. Once the people were committed to revolt they began to attack not only royal officials but agents of local nobles, and soon the movement began to take on the character of a lower-class uprising. It spread to Poitou, the Rochelais, and the city of Bordeaux itself. Montmorency and the duke of Guise, rival favorites of the new king, were sent in with large armies to break the revolt, which they did quickly and, at least in the area controlled by Montmorency, with unnecessary ferocity.[23]

Once the 1548 revolt was thoroughly crushed, however, the king had second thoughts. The sentences imposed on many persons involved in the revolt were lightened, and Bordeaux was forgiven the huge fine levied on it. The government announced that all the lands in the west would be allowed to return to the quart et demi-quart system, in return for a gift to the king of 450,000 livres. In December 1553 the plan to introduce greniers and their officials in the west was abandoned. These provinces were allowed to "redeem" the obligation of paying any droit du roi for a lump sum of 1,194,000 livres. They were now called *provinces rédimés.* This did not mean that they were free of salt tax supervision, of course, since now the government had to make doubly sure the west did not become an important base of supply for salt smugglers.[24]

22. Gigon, *Révolte de la gabelle*, pp. 23–24; see also the edict of Châtellerault, June 1, 1541, verified April 7, 1542.

23. Gigon, *Révolte de la gabelle*, pp. 150–64, 180–85.

24. See the edict of Amboise, Dec. 1551, in Houzé, *Edicts et ordonnances*, pp. 371–75.

During the Old Régime the grim battle to enforce compliance to gabelles seriously aggravated the tensions between the lower classes and the government. Even in the sixteenth century, salt smuggling reached enormous proportions, and Renaissance kings made a great effort to stamp it out or at least to contain it. In addition to surprise search and inspection, salt tax officials had the right to force every householder (including those of ecclesiastical and noble establishments) to take a formal oath as to how much salt he had purchased the previous year.[25] Large numbers of officials and commissioners were required in the fight against the bands of smugglers. In 1581 the government complained that "one-third of the people refuse to come to our greniers to take the salt authorized for them." [26] As early as 1484, deputies to the Estates-General of Tours were complaining that there were at least 500 gangs of contrabandists at work.[27] On the fringes of the salt-producing districts, teams of gabelles constables waged brutal warfare against heavily armed and desperate smugglers, who could be killed on the spot where they were caught. Gabelles constables also ranged through the salt marshes, especially in Brittany and Poitou, swooping down on *faulx saulniers* ("false salters," a term used for both smugglers and those producers who were in league with them). Gabelles constables had the right to stop any merchant, on road or river, and check over his convoy for sacks of illegal salt. The number of gabelles constables seems to have increased by greater proportions than those of any other single fiscal office.[28]

The gabelles constables in north and central France worked under the authority of the généralité fiscal chief, the trésorier général. The grenetiers and contrôleurs attached to the greniers also aided in the enormous task of enforcing the gabelles. But in the privileged provinces there were specialized superior gabelles officials. Poitou and Languedoc had *visiteurs générales* for the gabelles, important officials with crews of assistants. The general reform edict of Châtellerault (June 1, 1541) added another key gabelles official for the western districts—a *conservateur*, who was to coordinate both the payment of the gabelles by merchants and the centralization of these revenues once they had been gathered by special gabelles collectors. During the summer months, when salt making activity was at its peak, the salt marshes were invaded by special watchmen (*gardes*), some of whom actually camped in huts built for them on the premises. The duty of the gabelles gardes was to see that salt being produced did not

25. Edict Aux Roches, Aug. 25, 1535, in Isambert, 12 : 410–14.
26. Edict of Paris, Dec. 1581.
27. Dupont-Ferrier, *Etudes*, 2 : 128.
28. This is true even in periods of fiscal reform when the king was attempting to stem the rising tide of officials. See, e.g., the edict of Paris, May 1578.

mysteriously disappear before the amount produced could be recorded by royal officials. To help the gardes, the salt makers were commanded never to box, sack, or sell a batch of salt until it had reached a certain size; then the salt was measured out into regulation-sized containers and stamped with the gardes' seal.

If illegal salt in transit was discovered by the *gabelous*, they had the right to confiscate not only the salt but also the barges, boats, carts, and mules or horses (together with their equipment) used to convey it. Furthermore, where constables found unusually large amounts of salted pork, they had the right to demand proof that the gabelles had been paid for the salt used. In addition (and this applied also to illegal salt found in homes or taverns), a fine could be levied for the first offense, *punition corporelle* (i.e. a whipping) for the second, and death by hanging for the third. The same punishments would be meted out to the "allies, accomplices, and advisors" of the guilty parties.[29] Those responsible for denouncing and apprehending the criminals would be entitled to one-third the value of the fines or confiscations; and any subject of the king (not only the royal officials), had the right to arrest and denounce violators of the gabelles laws. In fact, the fiscal officials promised immunity to any subjects attacking or even killing persons guilty of "false salting." [30] In the worst years the gabelles officials conducted a virtual reign of terror in some provinces, executing hundreds of persons.[31]

At the beginning of the sixteenth century, after some increases in the gabelles rates by Louis XII, royal income from all the gabelles of all the regions in France was supposed to be only 150,000 livres, or about 4 percent of the total revenues of 3.6 million livres. By 1515, the first year of the reign of Francis I, the gabelles were supposed to be bringing in 284,000 livres out of a total of 4.9 millions, or about 6 percent.[32] In the crisis years of 1522–23 the gabelles increased to about 483,000 livres, or about 10 percent of all revenues.[33] Thereafter the proportion of gabelles to total revenues fell. After the gabelles rebellion of 1548 and the formation of *grosses fermes* for gabelles (that is, amalgamated tax farms), the government seems to have become unwilling to divulge the amount of the lease prices for the

29. Edict of Châtellerault, June 1, 1541, in Isambert, 12 : 749, 755.
30. Dupont-Ferrier, *Etudes*, 2 : 121–25.
31. See François Grimaudet on the barbarous and unfair actions of salt tax officials, *Remonstrance . . . aux estatz d'Anjou . . .* , p. D2ᵛ.
32. Spont, "La taille en Languedoc," p. 369.
33. Clamageran, *L'impôt*, 2 : 125–26.

major salt taxes. All that is definitely known is that at the time of the Estates-General of Blois in 1576, the government admitted collecting about 1 million livres in salt tax revenues, or about 6 percent of the total.[34] During the remainder of the Renaissance the relative as well as the absolute value of the salt taxes was forced up rapidly. At the time of the second Estates-General of Blois in 1588, the gabelles were rated at close to 3.4 million livres; by the end of the Wars of Religion (1598) they were bringing in 3.3 millions; and at the end of the reign of Henry IV they were worth close to 6 millions.[35] At the end of the Renaissance, therefore, the gabelles were bringing in fully one-fourth of total revenues.

At about the same time that Francis I was beginning to raise the rates in the greniers-system districts, there were signs the government was about to turn to tax farming in order to ensure a high revenue from its salt taxes. Before that time, it is true, the petites gabelles and the quart et quint had been farmed out; but Francis I had wanted to keep the management of the most lucrative gabelles of the greniers system in his own hands. Suddenly and without explanation, his government changed its policy and awarded several leases for salt tax farms in the north and central provinces.[36] Three reasons have been suggested for this shift: the king wanted to encourage more merchant-banker capital to enter the country from Italy so that financiers could be tapped for loans; the king was increasingly irritated with the thorny and complex problems the gabelles administration presented; and the government needed to guarantee steady revenues from tax farms on the gabelles in order to float *rentes* on them.[37] Gradually, the tax farms of individual provinces and towns in the greniers system were combined into larger units. In 1559 the government added the taxes on exported salt.[38] The apparatus of the salt tax bureaucracy remained intact; but it functioned now under the management of groups of tax farmers rather than that of the trésoriers généraux.[39] The business of carting salt to the greniers remained outside this new tax farm for most of the remainder of the sixteenth century. Salt transportation continued to be farmed out to associations of merchant-purveyors as it had ever since the

34. Picot, *Etats Généraux*, 3 : 298.
35. Clamageran, *L'impôt*, 2 : 198, 238; Doucet, *Institutions*, 2 : 587; and Nef, *Industry and Government*, p. 83. Cf. *La discouverture des deniers salés* (Paris, 1588), which claims that around 1588 the gabelles were worth almost 4 million livres.
36. Clamageran, *L'impôt*, 2 : 141.
37. Matthews, *The Royal General Farms*, pp. 44–45.
38. Doucet, *Institutions*, 2 : 582.
39. Hennequin, *Guidon*, p. 170.

late Middle Ages.⁴⁰ Finally, in 1598, the business of hauling salt was also lumped together with the taxation of salt in one unified tax farm for the entire greniers-system territory.

40. Edward Hughes, *Studies in Administration and Finance, 1558–1825*, pp. 14–18.

J

Tariffs and Tolls

To equate Renaissance traites with the modern concept of tariffs is an anachronism. In the fifteenth and sixteenth centuries the state did indeed collect taxes at its various frontiers; but these were imposed mainly on goods going *out* of the country. (They were also placed on goods going out of the central regions of France into French provinces that did not pay aides.) The chief tax in the group called traites was the *imposition foraine*; and this definitely was an export tax, falling first on a few staples and on wine, later on many sorts of exports. It is true that France had some minor taxes on spices and luxury cloths coming into the country. But until near the end of the Renaissance, when levies on imports became more significant, the term *traites* has to be understood as export duties plus a heterogeneous group of minor taxes on the movement of goods.[1]

One of the mysteries of Renaissance public finance is the question of how much the traites were worth to the crown. There is virtually no information on this matter, since the traites sometimes do not appear as a separate category in the general *états* of the era; the budgets usually give only a figure for both aides and traites. When references do state the amount of the traites, they seem to be impossibly small.[2] It is true that there was a sharp increase in the reported traites revenues late in the sixteenth century; we have an estimate of 552,000 livres for the period around 1576 and another of 1.1 million livres in 1587, after the great increase in rates imposed by Henry III.[3] These rough estimates suggest that the traites account for only 6 or 7 percent of the total royal revenues during most of the later sixteenth century.[4]

Often, many of the traites were alienated in order to provide gifts for

1. Until late in the Renaissance the term was more often employed as a past participle than as a noun, as in "traités ou menés hors," or "la grant multitude de vins qui sont traiz." See Dupont-Ferrier, *Etudes*, 2 : 144–45. *Imposition foraine*, the chief traite, was often called *traite foraine*, and even *imposition ou traite foraine*.

2. See Doucet, *L'état des finances de 1523*, pp. 10–11 and passim.

3. Clamageran, *L'impôt*, 2 : 198.

4. For comments on the relative unimportance of traites during the late Middle Ages see Edward Miller's essay in the *Cambridge Economic History of Europe*, 3 : 319–20.

favorites and members of the royal family or to pay off royal loans. Much of the *traite domaniale*, an export surtax established in 1577, never reached the Epargne, since its returns were immediately paid over to Swiss mercenaries.[5] The general budget for 1567 shows that the imposition foraine (as well as other traites) was completely alienated; it was carried in the budgets only to show how much had been turned over to royal creditors.[6] Furthermore, some of the officials of the sovereign courts and certain royal household officers were exempt from paying traites.[7] But all these considerations still do not explain the surprisingly low value of the traites in this period of great commercial expansion.

An attempt to improve the returns from the traites came near the end of the Renaissance, around 1584, when the government of Henry III hit on the idea of lumping together some of the more valuable farms of indirect customs taxes in north and central France and auctioning off the lease of these farms all at once. This was the origin of the famous *cinq grosses fermes*—though they were still far from the form in which they were amalgamated by Colbert in the Old Régime tax farm monopolies, the *fermes générales*. In 1584 the cinq grosses fermes included two traites, that is, the imposition foraine and the traite domaniale; the *douane de Lyon* (an octroi administered more or less like a tariff); the *sou par livre* on cloth manufacture (not properly a tariff or toll, but a production tax); and the *cinq sols* on wine. The farm of all these taxes went for 375,000 livres, a real improvement over the total for the bits and pieces of revenues the government had been getting up to then. Even the cinq grosses fermes, however, shifted from farming to *régie* and back again; in 1592 Henry IV took them out of the hands of tax farmers, obviously believing that the lease price was too small. Sully, finally, put the cinq grosses fermes again out to farm and managed to obtain 480,000 livres for them.

All Renaissance commentators agreed that a prince had the right to levy taxes on goods passing out of his domains because export of such goods deprived his subjects of the enjoyment of merchandise. Export duties were advisable, it was argued, because they discouraged foreign merchants from denuding a country of the fruits of its land and labor. In this respect, attitudes toward exports in this period provide the sharpest possible contrast with that of the mercantilist seventeenth and eighteenth centuries, when

5. Edict of Blois, Feb. 1577. See also Dur, "Constitutional Rights," p. 290, budget for 1580.
6. Doucet, *L'état des finances de 1567*, pp. 1, 6, 20, 28.
7. Decree of Fontainebleau, March 18, 1543.

emphasis was laid on exporting more goods than were imported. Renaissance beliefs were closer to those of the Middle Ages, when men suffered from a constant threat of famine. When foodstuffs were allowed to leave France because of especially abundant crops—on the average, once every five or six years—special licenses for exports had to be issued by the king.[8]

Another justification often given for the imposition foraine was that it fell on foreign importers rather than on a prince's own subjects. To the reformers of the later sixteenth century, interested as they were in ways of cutting down on tailles, aides, and gabelles, this was a most important feature of export duties; therefore they argued for a relative increase in this branch of the tax structure. It was well understood by this time that French goods were greatly in demand in other countries.[9] The anonymous 1576 *Traitté* claimed that levies on exports were "founded in equity; for it is thoroughly reasonable that he who wishes to gain from the subjects of another should pay some duty to that prince." [10]

Perhaps one reason the traites did not arouse much controversy during the Renaissance is that they were similar in some respects to the *péages*. Tolls had always been regarded as part of the royal prerogative. In theory, tolls, unlike the traites, were part of the domaines revenues organization; juridically, tolls were the responsibility of the Cour du Trésor and the Chambre des comptes, while the traites were in the area of jurisdiction of the Cour des aides.[11] In practice, however, traites were regarded as the same sort of taxes as the tolls; and they were handled by the same officials who levied the tolls.

Another reason used to justify the imposition foraine—and the most interesting of all—is that such levies were a substitute for the aides in cases where French-produced goods did not pay the aides. The fact that French commodities did not pay French aides when sold to other countries is easy for us to understand; what is more complicated is that when goods from north and central France were sold in Brittany, Burgundy, or the newer provinces in the north, or in the Midi, they, too, did not pay aides. Instead, they paid the foraine. Viewed this way, French goods paid either

8. A. P. Usher, *The History of the Grain Trade in France, 1400–1710* (Cambridge, Mass., 1913).

9. Bodin, *République*, p. 877; cf. Nancey, *Jean Bodin, économiste*, pp. 128–34. And see Louis de Cabans, *Raisons pour montrer que l'édit nouvellement faict sur les monnoies est juste . . .* (Paris, 1609), pp. 114–15: "Car il est très-Certain que la France vend plus de denrées qu'elle n'en achète: de sort que tout le surplus est de necessité payé en argent."

10. *Traitté des finances*, p. 376.

11. In certain cases concerning péages, parlement had final jurisdiction.

the aides or the imposition foraine, even if some of the merchants paying the "foraine" were not "foreigners." "And thus there is no difference between the foraine tax and other aides which are levied in France, if it not be that one originates and is raised from commodities which, from France, are carried elsewhere; and others from the sale of commodities in the kingdom." [12] ("Elsewhere" meant outside of those areas of France where "the aides run.")

This curious fiscal anachronism (discussed in chapter 2) had its origins in the need for Charles VII to deal generously with the inhabitants of Languedoc during the last stages of the Hundred Years' War.[13] When Provence, Brittany, and other areas were absorbed into the realm, they also obtained exemption from the aides; the same privilege was extended to part of the west (the Saintonge-Périgueux area) presumably because it had been under the control of the English during the later Hundred Years' War and so had never given popular consent to the aides. For a host of complicated reasons, similar privileges were extended to Lyons and its district, to parts of Auvergne and Limousin, and to Forez.

The *équivalent*, moreover, which was paid by some of these provinces as a substitute for the aides, did not bring the king what he regarded as a fair share of the value of the aides. Whereas Languedoc and Provence paid the équivalent as the price of their exemption from the aides, Burgundy, Brittany, and Dauphiné paid neither the aides nor the équivalent.[14] Merchants selling in the center and north of the kingdom, therefore, paid higher taxes than those in the provinces without aides. This meant that those in the west and Midi could expect higher profits—a situation that presented a fiscal opportunity to the state.

The result of all these events and traditions was France's famous internal tariff wall, running from just south of Lyons in the east, along a meandering curve through the south-central provinces, and ending just north of Bordeaux in the west. It should be emphasized that this was an internal *export* tariff wall; internal *import* tariff lines were not established in France until the era of the Old Régime.[15] The line between districts paying

12. *Traitté des finances*, p. 365.

13. Charles V, in the 1370s, had first imposed the foraine on territories recently reconquered from the English and not paying aides for the ransom of Jean le Bon. See the edict of Paris, July 14, 1376, in Fontanon, 2 : 447–48; see also Picot, *Etats Généraux*, 1 : 200 and n. 2.

14. Gaston Zeller, "Aux origines de notre système douanier," *Publications de la Faculté de l'Université de Strasbourg*, 1947, pp. 166–67. In 1577 Burgundy was subjected to heavier and highly irritating tariffs, particularly on wines, cloth, and dyestuffs being shipped out of France. See Drouot, *Notes sur la Bourgogne*, p. 122.

15. Zeller, "Aux origines," pp. 165–66.

an internal tariff and those which did not was tortuously complex, a "long and tedious distinction between districts where the aides run and others where [aides] do not run, which the foremost cosmographer of the world could not understand." [16]

The southern internal tariff wall was not the only one. When Brittany was amalgamated into the kingdom of France another tariff line was established inside France: goods entering Brittany from Normandy and the west also had to pay the tax, in this case known as the *traite d'Anjou*.[17] The rate of the traite d'Anjou and the imposition foraine was generally the same as that for the main aides—one sou per livre. Paris merchants shipping goods to Brittany by way of the Seine as far as Rouen, however, had to pay only half.[18]

Given the resources of Renaissance bureaucracy and the complicated nature of the kingdom's tariffs, it is easy to see how difficult it would have been to construct an efficient customs guard system at the tariff borders. In fact, the government, for much of the Renaissance, tried to depend on collecting the imposition foraine before the merchants set out on their journeys. The customhouses themselves were mainly not at the borders of the kingdom but along the highways and rivers where dutiable goods were likely to be shipped.

But this was a clumsy, complicated, and irritating procedure. At the beginning of his journey, each merchant leaving a district where aides were paid was required to go to the office of the nearest tax farmer in charge of the traites. There he had to declare in writing the contents of his shipment and his destination. If the goods were to be shipped outside France or to a French province where aides were not paid, the merchant was expected to pay the imposition foraine then and there, rather than waiting to reach the frontier. If, on the other hand, the merchandise (from anywhere in France) was to be shipped to an area inside the aides territory, the merchant was supposed to pay over a bond to the same tax farmer. In this case he was entitled to be reimbursed by a collector of the aides when the goods were finally sold and he could produce a tax receipt.[19]

Opportunities for fraud were numerous. For example, a merchant could refuse to declare his goods and hope to slip by the check points; or he

16. See the long and amusing introduction to the edict of Paris, Nov. 11, 1551, published by Jean Des Planches, B.N. F46528, p. 3.

17. Edict of St. Germain-en-Laye, Apr. 6, 1519.

18. Dupont-Ferrier, *Etudes*, 2 : 159.

19. This discussion is based primarily on the description set out in the ord. of Poissy, Dec. 18, 1488, in Anthoine Hernault, ed., *Edictz et ordonnances royaux . . . sur le faict des traictes & imposition foraine d'Anjou*, pp. 3–4; and the edict of St. Germain-en-Laye (for the *traite d'Anjou*), April 6, 1519.

could slip his goods out of the aides territory, claim they had been stolen or lost or had spoiled on the way, and thus get his bond back. Insofar as the king was able to enforce the system, it acted as a restraint on long distance internal trade, since merchants had an obvious advantage in selling their goods quickly so as to get back their bond money.[20]

Toward the end of his reign, Francis I launched an ambitious reform of the traites by canceling the requirement that the imposition foraine and certain other taxes would have to be paid at the point of origin of each shipment. The ordinance of Tonnerre, April 20, 1542, ordered that henceforth these imposts were to be collected "at the extremities of the kingdom," in what Hennequin called the *villes limitrophes* ("confining cities"). But the tariff system could not be expected to shift gears easily. For certain provinces, particularly in the East, the government had a good deal of trouble in working out a system to distinguish between goods from central France that were destined for sale, say, in Burgundy and those intended for shipment out of the kingdom. It required the rest of the 1540s to solve these problems; but by the 1550s the new system seemed to be well established in most areas, though complaints were still being raised against it.[21]

At the beginning of the sixteenth century, the rate of the imposition foraine was one sou per livre of the declared value. However, in the mid-fifteenth century it had cost the merchants only 8 deniers, and wine was the chief item tariffed. But by the 1480s wool, cattle, and a few other items were added. Beginning with 1500, more and more exported commodities were required to pay the export tariff: it was applied to leather goods, metals and metal ware, fish, cheeses, salt, paper, and grains. By the 1540s virtually as many goods were paying the imposition foraine as were paying the aides.

Unfortunately for French trade, there were other traites. Two of the most bothersome were the *rêve* and the *haut passage*. These taxes help us understand how complicated commercial life was during the late Middle Ages and the Renaissance. In the reign of Philip the Fair, haut passage appears as a transit tax, intended to fall on goods (especially English wool) shipped across France. The rêve, which first appeared in the 1320s, was a

20. There were repeated and very bitter complaints against this system; see, e.g., the demands of the Estates-General of Tours of 1484, in Picot, *Etats Généraux*, 2 : 97–99.

21. See the general edict on the traites, Amiens, Sept. 1549, in Isambert, 13 : 104–18. But for Languedoc, see the edict of St. Germain-en-Laye, Nov. 1557, suggesting that until this time traites were still being collected in a large number of towns along the Rhône.

schedule of regular export duties intended to replace the earlier system of licensing individual exports. The rêve and the haut passage were canceled, reimposed, combined, separated, and changed in their rates and incidence.[22] During the mid-sixteenth century they cost exporters 11 deniers per livre, so that with the imposition foraine the basic export duty totaled around 2 sous, or 10 percent. Goods from central France coming to French provinces without aides paid the imposition foraine but not the rêve or haut passage, and some goods paid the rêve only. This made it necessary to maintain separate collection records for these two types of tariffs, even though they were levied together and collected by the same persons. Furthermore, the medieval haut passage and rêve were under the jurisdiction of the Chambre des comptes, while cases involving the imposition foraine usually were tried before the Cour des aides.[23]

Perhaps the most revealing bit of history concerning Renaissance tariffs and tolls was the fate of the *domaine forain*—a title given not to a new tax but to a fusion of the rêve and the haut passage. In 1549 the king decided that in the interest of simplicity (especially since these taxes had been handled together) the two old taxes would be canceled and replaced by a uniform domaine forain.[24] The new tax was set at 8 deniers per livre, as compared to the 11 deniers for both rêve and haut passage; but now all merchant exporters were expected to pay it. Those French merchants who had traditionally paid the rêve but not the haut passage, however, objected so strenuously that after a few years (1556) the king went back to the previous system of two separate tariffs.

A third tariff, the traite domaniale, was added in 1577. This was an export surtax on a smaller list of goods, specifically grain, dyestuffs, and wine; each commodity was tariffed separately, and very heavily. Thus the traite domaniale on wheat was 2 écus per *tonneau*. This new tax was collected at the external boundaries of the kingdom and not at the internal tariff walls.[25]

The tolls proper (*péages* or, in the Midi, *leudes* or *leydes*), like the rêve and haut passage, counted as domaines revenues and not as imposts. Usually they were farmed out by order of the bailiffs and seneschals or other important domaines administrative officials. Tolls, of course, were

22. Rey, *Le domaine du roi*, pp. 54–55.

23. On these problems see the treatise of Choppin, *Trois livres du domaine*, pp. 82–86.

24. Zeller, *Institutions*, p. 252, and Doucet, *Institutions*, 2 : 588, state that the domaine forain begins in 1551, that is, with the edict of Rouen, Nov. 14, 1551; but the tax is mentioned in the edict of Amiens, Sept. 1549, in Isambert, 13 : 104.

25. Edict of Blois, Feb. 1577.

levies on the movement of goods within political boundaries, usually across
some well-defined point such as a bridge, a ferry, or past a town gate. Some
péages taxed conveyances, carts, pack animals, or barges; others were fixed
on the value or the bulk of the goods conveyed. Many tolls were levied on
the use of certain main roads. Typically, revenue from tolls was supposed
to equal the cost of maintaining the facilities for which they were charged—
a proper "users' tax." [26] The *barrages*, for example, which were levied at
town gates, were supposed to pay for the maintenance of the chief roads
through the towns.[27] Barrages were just about the same sort of tax as many
of the town octrois (see appendix H). In some areas, tolls and octrois were
regarded as two separate levies, but elsewhere they were lumped together.
Both tolls and octrois were especially equitable since they were not marked
by class exemptions and there were few exemptions for status or function.

The king's tolls were not the only such levies that had to be paid in
France. Still harassing French commerce were the seigneurial tolls, raised
by great and petty lords in every corner of France outside the royal domains. Even inside the royal domains some of the king's vassals still possessed their traditional right to collect certain tolls. Seigneurial tolls, hundreds of them, remained in force all through the Renaissance. Rights to
them were jealously guarded by the poorer lords; all the government could
do, usually, was to forbid the erection of new seigneurial tolls.[28]

The most famous group of French tolls covered the great Loire river system, with its many port towns and its dozens of important tributaries.
During the early Renaissance there were supposed to be no less than 120
major and minor royal and seigneurial tolls on the Loire system alone; and
these were universally held up as a monument to official stupidity for the
way they hampered commerce.[29] Much of this territory was part of the

26. See, e.g., the edict of Fontaine-Française, Sept. 1535, in Isambert, 12 : 414–
16.

27. Zeller, *Institutions*, pp. 230–31.

28. M.-L. Autexier, *Les droits féodaux et les droits seigneuriaux en France de
1559 à 1789*, pp. 247–51. See also the edict of Fontainebleau, March 20, 1548, and
the letters-patent of Lyons (referring to the Rhône-Saône system), April 21, 1503.
See also the royal decl. of Blois, end of Dec. 1559, in Isambert, 14 : 18–21, abolishing all new tolls established on the Loire "since one hundred years ago." There is
a large collection of such edicts published by "La vefue Gilles Hotot," *Recueil des
lettres, tiltres, & contracts des acquisitions faictes par la communauté des marchands fréquentans la rivière de Loire*.

29. A good idea of the complexity of the Loire tolls can be gathered from edicts
listing taxing points and rates; for example, Sept. 27, 1556, in A.N.$^{IX-2}$, carries an
entry "for each hundred lampreys, 3s. 4dt." The merchant company "frequenting
the Loire" sometimes purchased bothersome seigneurial tolls and canceled them.
Contract of June 8, 1492, in the Hotot collection, no. 11.

Orléans inheritance and, as such, was handled rather tenderly by the king after Orléans and Anjou were amalgamated into the royal domain. The guild of merchants working on the Loire was given a good deal of authority by the feudal lords of these lands even in the fifteenth century, and this authority was continued and strengthened by the royal government in the sixteenth century. The merchant guild was authorized to use some of the toll revenues for maintaining the necessary bridges, fords, locks, and dikes, rather than paying them to the seigneurs to whom they were owed.

There is good reason to suppose that the aggregate value of the tolls amounted to much more than the cost of maintaining travel facilities. Royal ordinances and Renaissance writings complain again and again of the damage caused by excessive tolls. Some single tolls amounted to as much as 10 percent of the shipment's value; thus a merchant making a long trip through many such toll gates might have to double the selling price of his commodities. We are told that some goods originating in Burgundy valued at 10 sous had to sell in Lyons for 18 sous and at Aigues-Mortes for 25 sous. It was the task of bailiffs and seneschals to keep an eye on the tolls to see that the rates did not get out of hand.[30] To judge from the great volume of complaints all through the Renaissance, they were not successful.

To a merchant, the complicated multitude of ever-changing rates and regulations concerning the traites and tolls must have looked like a jungle. There was a real need for information that would leave him less at the mercy of the custom guards. To fill this need the Renaissance produced a new sort of publication, a merchant's guide to tariffs and tolls. Beginning in the 1570s there are dozens of such works, usually "pocket book" size; most of them were provided with good indexes and detailed tables of contents for the easy location of fees, regulations, and the established valuations for certain types of goods.[31]

The last category of the traites to develop during the Renaissance were the import duties. These taxes had a more modest beginning and an altogether different rationale than export duties and tolls. In the Middle Ages there had been little comparable to what we think of as tariffs, since entry of goods into states was welcomed; only the entry of goods into towns was tightly controlled, for fear of upsetting local economic interests. In the

30. Dupont-Ferrier, *Bailliages*, pp. 293–94.
31. Some of these are for all France, others for particular provinces and even towns. They are catalogued by Isnard in the Bibliothèque Nationale guide to the *Actes Royaux*.

fourteenth century there were one or two tolls and port duties, like the *coutume de Bordeaux* which, by stretching a point, might be considered import tariffs. Such duties were almost exclusively on foreign luxury items which, it could be argued, caused a serious outflow of gold and silver.

The real *douanes* of France, however, go back no further than Louis XI's attempt to build up Lyons as an important fair town and to encourage the rise of a French silk industry. He established the rule that all Italian silks would have to come into France by way of Lyons and would be forced to pay a 5 percent import tax. Louis XII added a few taxes on the import of spices and alum, but these were soon dropped (1508–14). At this stage it is more accurate to think of these duties as "licenses to import" (that is, devices to obtain the favor of an exemption to customary restrictions) than as general protective or revenue tariffs.[32]

There are one or two indications, however, that even at the beginning of the sixteenth century the levies on silk, and perhaps on one or two other commodities, were beginning to be regarded as means of providing employment for French artisans and profits for French merchants by inhibiting foreign competition. After a few false starts a silk weaving and finishing industry was established in France—in Tours at first, rather than at Lyons; and it became important when the French began to grow mulberry trees successfully, which allowed them to produce their own raw silk. The burghers of Tours and Paris, if not those of Lyons, began to demand special privileges, such as subsidies, monopoly of sales to the royal household, and tariff protection, arguing that these would result in benefits to the kingdom (increased employment, lower prices for luxury cloths, and retention of specie in France). By the reign of Francis I silk manufacturing was fairly well fixed in royal economic policy as an "infant industry" to be encouraged by restricting the entry of Italian silk.

Also significant is the tariff on alum, which apparently was applied when a small amount of this mineral was discovered in the country—an obvious attempt to encourage the search for more alum mines by discriminating in favor of French production. In the case of alum, however, this tariff protection was only temporary, for the growing French cloth and leather industries needed more alum than the national mines could produce. Eventually, the duty on alum was canceled; and in spite of the protests and petitions of the French alum producers, the French king refused to tariff alum, arguing that even with foreign alum imports the price of this essential commodity was absurdly high in France.[33]

32. The following discussion is based primarily on Gaston Zeller, "Aux origines," pp. 171–77.

33. Edict of St. Germain-en-Laye, Jan. 1556.

Gradually, additions were made to the Lyons customs that can be considered as both revenue and protective tariffs. Francis I reconstituted the silk import tariffs that had once been tried under Louis XII; he also added a tariff on cloth of gold and silver threads coming from Italy and Spain.[34] When the Portuguese captured the lion's share of the Far East spice trade and spices began to enter France from Atlantic ports, this new and lucrative trade provided an opportunity for important revenues. In 1544 Francis I established what was called a *gabelle des épiceries*, rated at about 7 percent of the value, on spices coming in from the north, principally through Rouen. At the same time he ordered parallel tariffs on spices to be collected at Lyons.[35] Francis I also reapplied at Lyons the taxes on imported alum first attempted by Louis XII. By the reign of Henry II duties on foreign goods entering Lyons included many luxury cloths (in addition to gold and silver cloth), plus alum and spices.[36]

The *douane de Lyon*, as the whole package of tariffs and tolls was called, was developing into a particularly valuable source of income, especially since Lyons was now entering the period of its greatest commercial and financial boom during the Renaissance. Originally classified as an octroi, this tax package had been given to the city government of Lyons to apply against the forced loans the king raised there. Henry II began to put pressure on the town to yield up the tax; but for years Lyons stubbornly refused. In 1564, however, soon after Lyons was retaken from the Huguenots in the first of the Wars of Religion, the government of Charles IX simply seized the tax; from that time on the douane de Lyon remained a regular part of the royal fiscal system of traites.

The first real signs of a general awareness of the special value of import tariffs appears in the 1570s. It was only then that large numbers of influential Frenchmen began to realize that tariffs were important not only for the royal treasury but also for subsidizing industry and commerce. It was Jean Bodin, perhaps, who first expressed in modern terms the kind of economic nationalism that was a precondition of the mercantilist protective tariffs of the next century.[37] Significant demands for the protection of certain French industries were raised at the Estates-General of Blois in 1576 and Assembly of Notables in St. Germain-en-Laye in 1583–84. At the same time Henry III

34. At the time, Lyons was the staple for all luxury cloth coming into France from the Mediterranean. Ord. of Anet, July 10, 1540, in Isambert, 12 : 687–92.

35. There had been some earlier tariffs on spices brought to southern France from Venice.

36. "Crespes, canetilles, passemens, rubens, centures, franges, pannes, ornemens [et] habillemens," in Hennequin's list. *Guidon*, pp. 217–18. See also the edict of Amiens, Sept. 10, 1549, and the ord. of Paris, Jan. 1564.

37. Zeller, "Aux origines," p. 216.

was forcing through a drastic increase in the rates and scope of all tariffs. As part of these reforms, hundreds of additional commodities were declared dutiable upon their entry into France.[38] Long lists of such commodities were published and posted, together with a standard value and tax for each. Methods of collecting import duties were improved, and the system was strengthened with a special group of new revenue agents who, for the first time, were responsible for import duties only. The heart of this new branch of the fiscal system was a network of douanes offices set up in every important town in the realm.[39] The customs agents in the port towns were increased and organized into *bureaux des douanes*. As might be expected, the new tariff administration was superimposed on the old rather than replacing it; thus the douane de Lyon was retained as a separate collection agency.[40] The retention of these traditional tariffs and tolls meant that the same goods were tariffed at considerably different rates depending on where they entered the country.

38. In the Claude Guyot collection of tariff regulations, *Edicts . . . pour l'establissement des bureaux des traictes foraines . . .* , the list of dutiable commodities stretches on for 74 pages (pp. 60–134).

39. Edict of Blois, May 20, 1581; edicts of St. Maur-des-Fossés, Aug. 1 and Oct. 3, 1581.

40. See the letters-patent of Paris, March 2, 1585.

K

The Domaines Revenues

A working definition of the domaines is any income not classifiable as tailles, aides, gabelles, or traites; or, perhaps, those revenues not under the jurisdiction of the Cour des aides. The domaines revenues were made up of hundreds of separate items, from the most minuscule privilege in a tiny fief amounting (when the noble ruling the fief could not beg exemption) to a few livres a year, to the rather more important rents from the king's inherited and privately owned lands and buildings.[1]

By the end of the Hundred Years' War, the domaines revenues had declined to less than 3 percent of total crown income.[2] Francis I and his son Henry II were so disposed toward giving away domaines revenues (including the income from whole seigneuries and entire taxes) that during their reigns the absolute as well as the relative value of the domaines revenues declined from time to time.[3] In 1523 domaines revenues were worth about 516,000 livres while total Epargne income was about 5 millions; and in 1567 the domaines brought in only about 400,000 livres, while the crown's income was climbing toward the 10 million livres mark.[4] In three-quarters of a century, from about 1500 to about 1576, the relative value of the domaines declined from a sixth to a twenty-fifth of total revenues. At the end of the century, just before the reforms of Sully (who greatly increased the absolute as well as the relative value of domaines revenues), these items were bringing in perhaps 760,000 livres of a total budget of close to 30 millions, or one-fortieth of the whole.[5]

One reason domaines revenues were cherished is that in principle they were the main source of royal largesse. The enormous complexities of royal gift-giving in the Renaissance are well brought out in the 1523 *état*, which carries about 720 items for pensions and gifts, totaling around 800,000

1. Never, so far as we know, did Renaissance kings—or, for that matter, those of the Old Régime—attempt to list and evaluate all their domaines revenues. Dupont-Ferrier, *Bailliages*, pp. 8–9, 52.
2. Petit-Dutaillis, in Lavisse 4[2] : 255–56.
3. In 1519 Francis I alienated the revenues of the entire county of Beaufort for a lump sum payment of 62,000 livres. Doucet, *François Ier*, 1 : 170–71.
4. Based on Doucet, *L'état des finances de 1523* and *L'état des finances de 1567*.
5. Clamageran, *L'impôt*, 2 : 338–39.

livres—a sum far exceeding all the domaines revenues.[6] The king's religious and other charities—the *fiefs et aumônes* appearing in the budgets—were always allocated from the domaines, preferably those farmed out and thus bringing in a fairly regular income.[7] Several large religious communities, as well as chantries, *maladeries* (hospitals), and other charitable services, depended on the royal domaines for their income. Thus the king undertook to supply the bread for the clerics attached to the Sainte-Chapelle of Paris.[8] Sometimes specific domaines revenues were allocated to specific charities; the "poor children of the Holy Trinity of the city of Paris," for example, were supported by chancery fees collected in Paris.[9]

The domaines that were farmed out included some surprising types of revenues. The petty fees collected by the royal and bailiwick chancery clerks, for example—for drawing up and notarizing official certificates and charters and for affixing the appropriate seals—were farmed out.[10] The fines levied by minor officials rather than courts (fines lumped together in royal accounts as "exploitz") also were leased out as farms, though they were so petty and irregular it is difficult to see how tax farmers could have been interested in them. For example, the king's right to charge his own prisoners, in certain royal jails, for their food and other needs (as in the Châtelet of Paris) was farmed out. Another surprising tax farmed out was the *insinuation*, a fee levied on the registration of all important contracts and deeds and all wills.

On the other hand, it seems logical to find tax farmers raising income from the king's crop lands, vineyards, meadows, and rented buildings. This income, carried in the national budgets as *cens et rents*, was the proprietary, steady revenues accruing each year, the sort of business handled by revenue farmers for every important seigneur since the Middle Ages. Renaissance writers labeled this sort of income *immuable*, since it came from "immovable" real estate and since its total sum changed little from year to year.[11] This area of crown income was the particular responsibility of

6. Doucet, *L'état des finances de 1523*, appendixes F and G.

7. Hennequin, *Guidon*, pp. 132–33. Hennequin believed that, in principle, fiefs et aumônes should be paid out of the domaines before domaines were used for other types of expenditures. *Fiefs* is used in the sense of a permanent grant, in contrast to a gift (*don*) which is for a few years or a single year.

8. Doucet, *L'état des finances de 1523*, pp. 48 ff.

9. Letters-patent of Avignon, Dec. 1574.

10. Dupont-Ferrier, *Bailliages*, pp. 547–48.

11. "Cents & rents n'augment & ne diminuent aussi: pour cest cause l'on les appelle domaine immuable." Hennequin, *Guidon*, p. 23. See also Boyer, *Instruction*, p. 9; and Dupont-Ferrier, *Bailliages*, pp. 543–44.

bailiwick officials (acting under the *trésoriers*) whose job it was to see that crown property was kept in good enough condition to command high rentals, as well as to auction off the revenue farms.[12] Even in the mid-sixteenth century, when the relative value of the domaines was small, royal edicts were promulgated every few years sternly commanding the appropriate officials to drain meadows, repair deteriorating buildings, and find occupants for empty cottages in order to build up the attractiveness of such properties to potential revenue farmers.[13] The immuables also included the *dîmes inféodées*—tithes given or sold by the church to the king (and to many other lords)—which were handled as property rights and farmed out. The royal tolls were farmed out, too. Revenue farms could be granted for as much as three years; but they usually were let out for a year and sometimes for less.[14]

An equally large and complex group of domaines was not farmed out but was collected directly by royal officials. There were several reasons, some logical and some arising from tradition, that kept these groups of domaines from being turned into tax farms. Many of the medieval suzerainty rights were simply too small and were applied too infrequently to attract would-be tax farmers. Others were more significant, such as the crown's many rights over transfers of real estate (e.g. *lods et ventes*, a tax on sales of land held of the king in *censive*); the income from certain types of court fines,[15] and confiscation of criminals' property; treasure trove; shipwreck rights (the proceeds of which, logically enough, were shared with the admiral of France);[16] and a host of rights over bastards, waifs and strays, and foreigners dying in the realm (*droit d'aubaine*). Because of the extreme "casual" nature of these revenues one might expect them to have been placed in the authority of the office of Parties casuelles; but, perhaps because they were better handled by local than by central authorities, they remained in the care of the bailiffs and their subordinates in the royal domainial administration.

12. Dupont-Ferrier, *Bailliages*, pp. 550–57.

13. Such improvement in the value of domaines was also recommended most anxiously by writers of contemporary treatises, and by deputies at the Estates-General. It is a major concern in the great reform edict on the domaines of Moulins, Feb. 1566.

14. Doucet, *Institutions*, 2 : 552.

15. Tax delinquency fines arising from gabelles and aides were treated as part of the income from such taxes; and they were handled by receveurs généraux and the Cour des aides. Therefore fines as a whole do not all fit into the domaines category of revenues.

16. For Brittany there were "flotsam and jetsam" rights (*bris de mer*). Edict of Angers, Feb. 15, 1499.

Another group of domaines, some mere feudal tokens but others fairly important, seem to have been denied to tax farmers because they involved important status relationships between the king and his vassals. Examples are the "four feudal aides"; the wardship rights over minors (principally in Normandy); *reliefs* and *rachats* (fines on transfers of noble fiefs to other nobles); *déshérence*, or escheat; and the *régale* over vacant bishroprics and abbacies (apart from those in the Midi, which was exempt). Another important claim on the church was *droit d'amortissement*, a lucrative fee on land "falling into *mainmorte*" at the time such land was transferred to the "dead hand" of an ecclesiastical community. An interesting set of domaines was the *franc-fief*, a fine on commoners buying noble lands, and *nouveaux acquêts*, a similar fine on land acquired by the church bodies or other permanent associations that were excused, for some reason, from the very heavy *amortissement*. These fines, dating back to the High Middle Ages, represented an effort on the part of the nobility and the crown to discourage the passage of lands into nonnoble hands. Franc-fief and nouveaux acquêts were collected only every twenty years or so; but the Chambre des comptes, which zealously oversaw the administration of these fines, was careful not to let forty years go by without imposing them, since prescriptive rights in France gave nonnoble landholders clear title after that length of time.[17]

An especially important example of this sort of revenue was the *ban et arrière-ban*, originally forty days service, exacted whenever the feudal levy was called up and falling on all nobles and commoners holding fiefs, either directly from the crown or from other lords. According to Hennequin, only those "appropriate for carrying arms" actually served, however—which meant, usually, only men in the proper age groups and trained in warfare. Those not "able and adroit" were allowed to provide replacements or to pay a lump sum to the bailiffs. By the 1540s the crown had extended the service to three months (for fighting inside France) and had established a regular monetary scale for this duty, based on the presumed revenue and the size of the fiefs involved.[18] The pay due to possessors of fiefs actually serving as men-at-arms was deducted from their tax obligations. All noble holders of fiefs not fit to fight and most commoners holding fiefs had to pay the full rate. Nobles already serving in the *compagnies d'ordonnance* were exempt from this fee. Nobles possessing more than one fief had to serve (or pay) only for the fief where they customarily lived; commoners, on the other hand, owed ban et arrière-ban for each fief they possessed.

17. Edict of Compiègne, Sept. 2, 1547, in Isambert, 13 : 29–32; and see Autexier, *Les droits féodaux*, p. 9 n. 37.
18. Edict of Fontainebleau, Feb. 9, 1548, in Isambert, 13 : 40–49.

Therefore, in spite of the fact that Renaissance nobles constantly pointed to the ban et arrière-ban, their "blood tax," as justification for their not paying the tailles, the fact is that this fee weighed more heavily on commoners possessing fiefs.[19] When a very large contingent of nobles was called up, their total wages far exceeded royal income from the ban et arrière-ban. How often this sovereign right was employed, therefore, depended partly on how often an especially large army was needed and partly on how often the king was willing to tax the richer lords and the rest of the country in order to pay military wages to poor lords. Henry II called up the ban et arrière-ban every year after 1552; he seems to have used it partly as a method of favoring the poor nobility with royal funds.[20]

Still another group of domaines revenues seems to have escaped being farmed out because proceeds were employed for some aspect of economic administration almost as soon as they were collected. Examples are the fees for use of the crown's weights and measures, which went to police markets and fairs. Others are the *hauban*, a sort of license fee on artisans in large towns. The infamous Old Régime *corvée royale*, however, the obligation of all peasants to work from a week to a month on roads or on carting military supplies, did not exist during the Renaissance.

The right to strike coins, one of the most ancient and most precious attributes of sovereignty, also figured among the domaines revenues. "Nostre domaine des monnoyes" was an unquestioned prerogative right, though there was some discussion as to how much income the king should extract from this right. There is no doubt that there would have been little or no effective resistance if the king had chosen to use his coinage rights as an important source of revenue, as did several English kings during the sixteenth century. But in fact this did not happen. Royal income from coinage was important in the days of the "king of Bourges" (the 1420s and 1430s) but never thereafter until the later reign of Louis XIV. In the late fifteenth and the sixteenth centuries profit from seigniorage, debasements, fees, and other devices declined almost to the vanishing point. Seigniorage charges were deliberately lowered so that they just equaled the minters' wages and other expenses.[21] In the light of the many "absolute" fiscal expedients of the Renaissance kings, their use of restraint in this respect is interesting. The Chambre des monnaies, the court that sat at Paris to super-

19. Dupont-Ferrier, *Bailliages*, pp. 481–82; Clamageran, *L'impôt*, 2 : 195; see also the letters-patent of Paris, Sept. 7, 1568. The budget for 1574, transcribed by Dur, "Constitutional Rights," p. 222, shows 37,500 livres for the ban et arrière-ban.
20. Zeller, *Institutions*, pp. 312–14.
21. Hennequin, *Guidon*, p. 739.

vise the mints, still functioned ostensibly to maximize the crown's resources from coinage rights. The Chambre des monnaies was accorded higher constitutional status in 1552, when it was elevated to the same "sovereign" level as the Chambre des comptes and the Cour des aides. Its personnel was small and its power obviously inferior, however, compared to the older "sovereign" courts, especially regarding checks on the arbitrary power of the king.[22]

One of the great fiscal disappointments of the era was the inability of French mines to produce large revenues for the crown. The crown domaines included the right to one-tenth of the value of all the products of French mines. When a new mine was discovered, no digging could begin without the king's explicit permission, and the work had to be done under the supervision of an agent of the local bailiff or seneschal.[23] But there were only a few sources of gold and silver in France, nothing at all like the great precious metal mines of central Europe. The government encouraged searches for additional mines;[24] but apart from a few mediocre sources of iron, none were discovered. In 1548 the king created a new officer, the *gouverneur et surintendant des mines*; but no mineral "French Peru" was discovered.

The river and forest revenues (*eaux et forêts*) usually amounted to as much as all the other domaines revenues combined, and sometimes more.[25] There were essentially three types of revenues enjoyed by the king and all other owners of forests—the sale of wood; fines and confiscations levied by forest officials; and various fees from pasturing animals (such as *panage*, feeding pigs on acorns and other nuts in the late fall and winter when pigs were left to root more or less for themselves). But the king had another type of forest revenue reserved to himself, more interesting for its constitutional significance than for the revenues it brought in. This was *gruerie*, sometimes referred to as *gruerie et grairie*, and called in Normandy *tiers et danger*. Originally this was a fee vaguely associated with the king's obligation to rid the country of bandits in all French lands, not only in the royal domain; the income was thought of as partial compensation for the forest

22. For a good discussion of coinage administration and the Chambre des monnaies in the late Middle Ages, see Rey, *Le domaine du roi*, pp. 124–41; idem, *Les finances royaux*, pp. 524–31. See also Doucet, *Institutions*, 1 : 200–02.

23. The rates were not actually a tenth for all metals and minerals; it was one-fifth for gold (hence a quint, like that of the king of Spain), one-tenth for silver, and one-fifteenth for copper and lead. Nef, *Industry and Government*, pp. 68–72.

24. Royal decl. of Lyons, Sept. 1548, in Isambert, 13 : 57–60.

25. Devèze, *Forêt française*, 2 : 168–71, 255–64.

officials' wages in helping to keep the peace. As its quaint name indicates, this fee originated in the Middle Ages. In fact Renaissance (as well as modern) scholars were not at all clear as to just what the words mean. Modern scholars, however, have established the reign of Saint Louis as the time at which the fee became a fixed part of domainial revenues.[26] In the sixteenth century it became the king's responsibility to protect the country against deforestation and particularly to protect tall timber (*bois de haut futaie,* i.e. wood for construction). To defray the expenses involved in this responsibility the king had the right to receive one-third (thus, *tiers*) plus one-tenth the sale price of all tall timber coming from ecclesiastical, seigneurial, or town forests.[27] Even when a forest was included in an appanage for a prince, the royal forest administration still operated there and the king still collected his gruerie et grairie.

Each year, as part of the preparation for the provisional budget, the royal council would decide how much revenue it required from the forests. This total would then be parceled out to the regions of France, and provincial officials would have to decide which forests were to be cut. Toward the end of the sixteenth century, revenue from sales of wood plus various fees and fines was stereotyped at around 300,000 livres. But in years of need, the king could order a *coupe extraordinaire,* an emergency sale. Relatively large sums of money were raised this way—378,000 livres in 1575 and 456,000 livres in 1576.[28]

Timber for fuel and construction is abundant everywhere in France. . . . And it is a remarkable fact that with all the forests in France (which cover more than a sixth part of the land) nevertheless wood is twice as dear here as in Venice. It stands thus because almost all the forests belong to the king; and he sells and cuts them as he pleases.[29]

The more the domaines revenues slipped away, the more discussion they aroused. In all the general fiscal treatises of the later sixteenth century, treatment of the domaines comes first. Domaines are also given precedence in government budgets and in general reform edicts. Scores of specific edicts on domaines were promulgated, some on quite niggling points. As late as 1533, for example, the government found it worth while to issue a

26. Strayer, *The Administration of Normandy under Saint Louis,* p. 44.
27. Devèze, *Forêt française,* 1 : 178–79.
28. Ibid., 2 : 170, 217, 256. Many villagers paid for forest usages in kind rather than in cash: one out of each ten animals pastured, for example.
29. Albèri, *Relazioni,* ser. 1, 1 : 221.

national edict clarifying the distinction between *bois-mort* and *mort-bois*, that is, the crown's rights over peasants who gathered up fallen branches as against those who cut down dead trees.[30] There is actually more information about Renaissance attitudes concerning domaines than about any other category of revenue. Domaines were the only branch of the fiscal system to which whole treatises (often exceptionally sophisticated ones) were devoted, such as René Choppin's *Trois livres du domaine de la couronne de France.*

In view of the almost negligible value of the domaines, statements made about them during the Renaissance seem strange and extravagant. Hennequin calls them "the chief fountain of public finance of all states and potentates, the most ancient, honest, legitimate, and sure means princes have for obtaining funds." [31] Similar views were expressed by Bodin and other writers, even in the late Renaissance.[32] In Figon's analysis of French government, the *Discours des estats et offices* (1579), domaines are treated as the constitutional equal of all the main national imposts put together; thus his remarkable illustration, the "Tree of State"—a pictorialized table of organization—shows one "limb" of revenues as domaines, while tailles, aides, and *tribut* are all relegated to another limb.[33]

This anxious attention lavished on the domaines was one facet of a most wide-ranging constitutional problem: what was to prevent the king from taxing away the whole substance of his subject's wealth, now that the Estates were moribund? Everyone understood that the chief taxes were being levied on the king's authority alone. The best minds of the era grappled with the problem of finding some basis for protecting private property from royal tax power. But they came up with rather weak answers, many of which involved the domaines. They seized on the essentially medieval idea that "the king should live of his own" (*doit vivre du sien*).[34] Sidestepping the whole question of the increasing need of the state for high and regular revenues, they insisted, rather unconvincingly, that the

30. Edict of Marseille, Oct. 4, 1533, in Isambert, 12 : 382–84.
31. Hennequin, *Guidon*, p. 1.
32. A large portion of Bodin's chief work on taxes (*République*, bk. 6, chap. 2, 12 pp. of 58) is on the domaines.
33. Figon, *Discours*, p. 38ᵛ.
34. The government made several gestures in support of this principle. Thus in the preamble to the ord. of Paris, May 20, 1563, announcing a forced sale of church wealth in favor of new royal rentes, the excuse is given that the king is imposing this new burden only "after having depleted for these crucial matters that which is our own."

king should find ways of making the domaines adequate both for maintaining the royal household and for paying all public expenses.[35]

Many writers, including Bodin and La Barre, tried their hand at estimating how much revenue would come to the king if only he would hold on to those domaines he possessed and take back or repurchase those he had given away or sold.[36] The inability of the government to take advantage of its domaines was a topic brought up at meetings of every national Estates-General from 1484 to 1614. These same would-be reformers urged the king to display the most rigid self-discipline by reducing gifts and pensions and generally by spending the least possible so as to be able to tax the least possible. Such proposals amounted to telling a Renaissance prince not to behave like one.

The most interesting concept generated by this examination of the domaines was the distinction between "crown domaines" and "king's domaines." These categories represented an attempt to emphasize the difference between the king's personal or patrimonial property rights and those he enjoyed only because he occupied the throne. This was a most vigorously chewed-over question.[37] All writers accepted the idea that there was an important difference between these two sorts of revenue; but there was hardly any agreement at all as to which specific revenues belonged in one class or the other, or indeed what such differences meant in terms of constitutional or practical implications for the fiscal system.[38]

Crown domaines, all writers agreed, "may not be placed on the market." Of course the king might use some of the crown lands to construct an appanage for his younger sons. This was a proper "public" use of crown domaines, a sort of official appeasement of princes who might otherwise be bitter enough to organize dangerous factions and precipitate civil war. He also might sell domaines during a national emergency, or give them to his favorites, or even create entirely new fiefs for vassals. But all such transfers had to be made with the clear understanding that when title to these domaines passed they could only return to the crown, "as rivers and brooks leave from the sea and return to it." [39] In the case of gifts (those not limited by a specified number of years), the death of the grantee meant that the state would reestablish its rights immediately. In the case of a

35. E.g. Hennequin, *Guidon*, p. 2.
36. Bodin, *République*, p. 863; La Barre, *Formulaire*, pp. 410–11.
37. See esp. Hennequin, *Guidon*, pp. 745–47.
38. Choppin, *Trois livres du domaine*, pp. 6, 12.
39. Grimaudet, *Paraphrase*, p. 107.

sale to an *engagiste*, the state could always take back its own by refunding the purchase price. *Domaines du roi*, on the other hand, could be sold, leased out, given away, or split up permanently just as could any piece of private property.[40]

The great edict on domaines issued at Moulins, February 1566, was the Renaissance's principal reform effort on this issue.[41] It was the culmination of the reforms unleashed by the Estates-General of 1560–61 and was helped along by the efforts of the Guises and of the great chancellor Michel l'Hospital. Later edicts always refer to this one as the definitive word on domaines.

Some restrictions on domaines seem to have been enforced. The sales terms of certain domaines were reexamined from time to time, and those that appeared to have brought less than their real value were offered to higher bidders who would then compensate the original engagistes. The Chambre des comptes and parlement worked to ensure that when domaines did go on the block they were sold for only a few years at a time, and that they went only to the highest bidder. And it is true that the king was concerned enough with the scarcity of wood for building that the tall timber forests were not permanently given away. In the less valuable forests, furthermore, the rule was maintained fairly well that no entire forest would be alienated, in the hope that income from the remaining forest revenues could be used one day to buy back the portions sold.[42] Periodically, special commissions were established to go over records concerning alienations of domaines, and these commissions could seize those properties whose users could not establish valid title.[43]

Courts tried to protect crown domaines by ruling that any property or right that had been under the control of the *trésoriers de France* for a period of ten years was to remain crown domaines permanently.[44] If a revenue had been listed in a national budget as crown domaines, this was taken as

40. Therefore Roger Doucet calls the whole principle of inalienability "une simple survivance juridique sans portée pratique." *Institutions*, 2 : 547. But this misses the whole point of the debate over the domaines, since the legal commentators were doing what they could to change inalienability from theory to fact.

41. There were others, e.g. the edict of Paris, June 30, 1539, in Isambert, 12 : 567–70.

42. Edict of Vincennes, May 18, 1574.

43. One such commission in Normandy, during the early reign of Henry III, was headed by Jean Bodin. But this was Jean Bodin de Montguichet, and *not* his famous contemporary Jean Bodin "de Saint-Amand," author of the *République*. Devèze, *Forêt française*, 2 : 212–13.

44. Choppin, *Trois livres du domaine*, p. 47.

proof it could not be sold permanently. This device was supposed to establish a mechanism by which any property or right—those of the king or of others—could be "united and incorporated with the jewels in the crown of France." [45] In theory, then, crown domaines could not fall below a certain minimum, and they could increase indefinitely, presumably to the great advantage of kings trying to lighten the burden of taxes.[46]

Instead of being labeled an anachronism and allowed to fade away during the later Renaissance, the domaines were maintained and even cherished in all their complexities. They constituted a sort of affirmation that the king was indeed attempting to maintain himself and his government without reaching into his subjects' purses more than was necessary. He could claim that tailles and aides were being increased only after he had sold all his own personal and crown property. Apparently this soothing myth was needed by all—king as well as subjects. The doctrine that "the king should live of his own," in other words, was more than a last weak echo of medieval fiscal concepts. It was part of the slow process by which the taxpaying public was brought face to face with the unnerving reality that the expenses of government have to be borne by those being governed.

45. Ibid., p. 18.
46. Ibid., p. 593.

Principal Works Consulted

Albèri, Eugenio, ed. *Le relazioni degli ambasciatori veneti al Senato durante il secolo decimosesto.* 15 vols. Florence, 1839–63.

Anquez, Léonce. *Histoire des assemblées politiques des Réformés de France, 1573–1622.* Paris, 1859.

Armstrong, Edward. *The French Wars of Religion: Their Political Aspects.* London, 1892.

Autexier, M.-L. *Les droits féodaux et les droits seigneuriaux en France de 1559 à 1789.* N.p. [1949].

Bailhache, J. "La monnaie de Toulouse pendant la Ligue (1589–1596)." *Revue Numismatique*, 4th ser. 35 (1932).

Barbiche, Bernard. "Les commissaires députés pour le 'régalement' des tailles en 1598–1599." *Bibliothèque de l'Ecole des Chartes* 118 (1960).

Batiffol, Louis. "Le trésor de la Bastille." *Revue Henri IV* 3 (1909).

Baulant, Micheline, and Meuvret, Jean. *Prix des céréales extraits de la mercuriale de Paris (1520–1698).* 2 vols. Paris, 1960–62.

Beaune, Renaud de. *Première remonstrance faicte au Roy . . . de ce qui est accreu des tailles & impositions depuis les derniers Estats, de Bloys . . . ,* Blois, 1588.

Blanchet, A., and Dieudonné, A. *Manuel de numismatique française.* 4 vols. Paris, 1916–36.

Bodin, Jean. *Method for the Easy Comprehension of History.* Translated by Beatrice Reynolds. New York, 1945.

———. *Relation iournalière de tout ce qui s'est negotié en l'assemblée générale des Estats . . . .* Paris, 1614.

———. *Les six livres de la République.* 3d French ed., Paris, 1580.

Boislisle, Arthur de. "Semblançay et la surintendance des finances." *Annuaire-Bulletin de la Société de l'Histoire de France* 18 (1881).

Bonnault d'Houët, Baron de. *Compiègne pendant les Guerres de Religion et la Ligue.* Compiègne, 1910.

Borrelli de Serres, L. L. *Recherches sur divers services publics du XIIIe au XVIIe siècle.* 3 vols. Paris, 1895–1909.

Boulay de la Meurthe, A. "Histoire des Guerres de Religion à Loches et en Touraine." *Bulletin et Mémoires de la Société Archéologique de Touraine* 45 (1896).

Bourgoin, Jean. *Le pressoir des esponges du roy . . . .* Paris, 1623.

Boyer, Philibert. *Instruction pour le faict des finances.* Paris, 1583.

Brimont, Vicomte de. *Le XVIe siècle et les Guerres de la Réforme à Berry.* 2 vols. Paris, 1905.

Brisson, Barnabé, ed. *Le code du roy Henry III, roy de France et de Pologne,* with the additions of L. Charondas le Caron. 3d ed. Paris, 1609.

Broome, Dorothy M. *The Ransom of John II, King of France, 1360–1370.* Camden Miscellany, vol. 14. London, 1926.

Buisseret, David. *Sully and the Growth of Centralized Government in France, 1598–1610.* London, 1968.

Buisseret, David, and Barbiche, Bernard. "Sully et la surintendance des finances." *Bibliothèque de l'Ecole des Chartes* 123 (1965).

Caillet, Louis. *Etude sur les relations de la commune de Lyon avec Charles VII et Louis XI (1417–1483).* Lyons, 1909.

The Cambridge Economic History of Europe. Vol. 1, M. M. Postan, ed., *The Agrarian Life of the Middle Ages,* 2d ed., Cambridge, 1966 (also first ed. of 1941). Vol. 2, M. M. Postan and E. E. Rich, eds., *Trade and Industry in the Middle Ages,* 1952. Vol. 3, M. M. Postan, E. E. Rich, and Edward Miller, eds., *Economic Organization and Politics in the Middle Ages,* 1963. Vol. 4, E. E. Rich and H. Wilson, eds., *The Economy of Expanding Europe in the Sixteenth and Seventeenth Centuries,* 1967.

Catalogue des actes de François Ier. Académie des Sciences Morales et Politiques. 10 vols. Paris, 1887–1908.

Cauwès, Paul. "Les commencements du crédit public en France: Les rentes sur l'Hôtel de Ville au XVIe siècle." *Revue d'Economie Politique* 9 (1895).

Cavard, Pierre. *La Réforme et les Guerres de Religion à Vienne.* Vienne, 1950.

Chamberland, Albert. "Le budget de l'Epargne en 1607." *Revue Henri IV* 2, no. 5 (1908).

———. "Le budget de la généralité de Châlons en 1602." *Revue Henri IV* 3, nos. 3 and 4 (1909).

———. "Le Conseil des finances en 1596 et 1597 et les *Economies royales.*" *Revue Henri IV,* 2d ed., 1 (1912).

———. "La légende du Conseil de raison," *Revue Henri IV,* 2d ed., 1 (1912).

———. *Un plan de restauration financière en 1596.* Paris, 1904.

———. *Recherches critiques sur les réformes financières en Champagne à l'époque de Henri IV et de Sully.* Rheims, 1902.

———. "La tournée de Sully et de Rybault dans les généralités en 1596." *Revue Henri IV* 3, nos. 3 and 4 (1909).

Charmeil, Jean-Paul. *Les trésoriers de France à l'époque de la Fronde.* Paris, 1964.

Charpentier, Pierre, ed. *Premier livre des privilèges des officiers domestiques & commençaux de la Maison du roy . . . .* Paris, 1655.

—— ed. *Recueil des ordonnances, édicts, déclarations . . . concernant l'origine, progrez, création & restablissement des éleus.* Paris, 1635.

Choppin, René. *Trois livres du domaine de la couronne de France . . . .* Paris, 1613.

Church, William Farr. *Constitutional Thought in Sixteenth Century France.* Cambridge, Mass., 1941.

Clamageran, J.-J. *Histoire de l'impôt en France.* 3 vols. Paris, 1867–76.

Cloulas, Ivan, "Les aliénations du temporel ecclésiastique sous Charles IX et Henri III (1563–1587)." *Revue d'Histoire de l'Eglise de France* 44 (1958).

——. "Un aspect original des relations fiscales entre la royauté et la clergé de France au XVIe siècle." *Revue d'Histoire Ecclésiastique* 4 (1960).

Combes, Jean. *Traicté de tailles & autres charges, & subsides . . . .* 2d. ed. Paris, 1584.

Courbé, Augustin, ed. *Les privilèges, franchises, et libertez des bourgeois et habitans de la ville & faux-bourgs d'Orléans . . . .* Paris, 1636.

Coville, Alfred. *Les Cabochiens et l'ordonnance de 1413.* Paris, 1888.

——. *Les premiers Valois et la Guerre de Cent Ans, 1328–1422.* Lavisse series, vol. 4, part 1. Paris, 1900.

Dallington, Sir Robert. *The View of Fraunce . . . .* London, 1604.

Des-Hayes, Pierre, ed. *Recueil de plusieurs ordonnances, règlemens et arrests, faicts & donnés pour le faict des aydes.* Paris, 1633.

——. *Declarations, arrests & règlemens concernans les droicts des entrées & sol pour livre de la ferme du bestail à pied-fourché de Paris.* Paris, 1630.

Despois, L. *Histoire de l'autorité royale dans le comté de Nivernais.* Paris, 1912.

Devèze, Michel, *La vie de la forêt française au XVIe siècle.* 2 vols. Paris, 1961.

Devic, Dom Cl., and Vaissete, Dom J. *Histoire générale de Languedoc.* New ed. 13 vols. Toulouse, 1872–89.

Dijon, Dom H. *Le bourg et l'abbaye de Saint-Antoine pendant les Guerres de Religion et de la Ligue, 1562–1597.* Grenoble, 1900.

Dognon, Paul. *Les institutions politiques et administratives du pays de Languedoc du XIIIe siècle aux Guerres de Religion.* Toulouse [1895].

——. "La taille en Languedoc de Charles VII à François Ier." *Annales du Midi* 3 (1891).

Doucet, Roger. *L'état des finances de 1523.* Paris, 1923.

——. *L'état des finances de 1567.* Paris, 1929.

——. *Etude sur le gouvernement de François Ier dans ses rapports avec le Parlement de Paris.* 2 vols. Paris, 1921–26.

——. *Finances municipales et crédit public à Lyon au XVIe siècle.* Paris, 1937.

——. "Le Grand Parti de Lyon au XVIe siècle." *Revue Historique* 171, no. 3 (1933); 172, no. 1 (1933).

Doucet, Roger. *Les institutions de la France au XVIe siècle.* 2 vols. Paris, 1948.

Drouot, Henri. *Mayenne et la Bourgogne, 1587–1596.* 2 vols. Paris, 1937.

———. *Notes sur la Bourgogne et son esprit public au début du règne de Henri III, 1574–1579.* Dijon, 1937.

Dupont-Ferrier, Gustave. *Etudes sur les institutions financières de la France à la fin du moyen âge.* 2 vols. Paris, 1930–32.

———. *Nouvelles études sur les institutions financières de la France à la fin du moyen âge: Les origines et le premier siècle de la Chambre ou Cour des aides de Paris.* Paris, 1933.

———. *Les officiers des bailliages et sénéchausées et les institutions monarchiques locales en France à la fin du moyen âge.* Paris, 1902.

———. *Les origines et le premier siècle de la Cour du Trésor.* Paris, 1936.

Dur, Philip. "Constitutional Rights and Taxation in the Reign of Henry III." Ph.D. dissertation, Harvard University, 1941.

Epinac, Pierre d'. *Harangue prononcée devant le roy, séant en ses estats généraulx à Bloys.* Paris, 1577.

Etudes sur l'histoire des assemblées d'états. The French section of the International Commission for the History of Representative and Parliamentary Institutions. Paris, 1966.

Everat, Ed. *Le bureau des finances de Riom, 1551–1790.* Riom, 1900.

Fawtier, Robert, ed. *Comptes du Trésor (1296, 1316, 1384, 1477).* Recueil des Historiens de France, Documents Financiers, vol. 2. Paris, 1930.

Figon, Charles de. *Discours des estats et offices tant du gouvernement que de la iustice & des finances de France . . . .* Paris, 1579.

Fontanon, Antoine, ed. *Les édicts et ordonnances des rois de France traittans en général et particulier du fait de leur domaine & finances . . . .* 2d ed. 3 vols. Paris, 1611.

Forbonnais, F. Véron de. *Recherches et considérations sur les finances de la France depuis l'année 1595 jusqu'à l'année 1721.* 2 vols. Basel, 1758.

François, Michel. "Albisse del Bene, surintendant général des finances françaises en Italie, 1551–1556." *Bibliothèque de l'Ecole des Chartes* 94 (1933).

———. *Le cardinal François de Tournon.* Paris, 1951.

Froumenteau, N. *Le secret des finances de France . . . .* Paris, 1581.

Gandilhon, René. *La politique économique de Louis XI.* Rennes, 1940.

Gay, J.-L., "Fiscalité royale et Etats Généraux de Bourgogne, 1447–1589." In *Etudes sur l'histoire des assemblées d'états.* Paris, 1966.

Gigon, S.-C. *La révolte de la gabelle en Guyenne, 1548–1549.* Paris, 1906.

Grimaudet, François, *Paraphrase du droict des dixmes ecclésiastiques & inféodées . . . .* 2d ed. Lyons, 1574.

———. *Remonstrance . . . aux estatz d'Anjou, assemblez dernièrement . . . .* Lyons, 1561.

Guyot, Claude, ed. *Edicts, lettres patentes, arrests et commissions du roy pour l'establissement des bureaux des traictes foraines . . . .* Dijon, 1618.

Hauser, Henri. "Le crise de 1557–1559 et le bouleversement des fortunes." *Mélanges offerts à M. Abel Lefranc*. Paris, 1936.

———. "The European Financial Crisis of 1559." *Journal of Economic and Business History* 2 (1929–30).

———. *Recherches et documents sur l'histoire des prix en France de 1500 à 1800*. Paris, 1936.

Hennequin, Jean. *Le guidon général des finances* . . . . Paris, 1585.

Hérelle, Georges. *La Réforme et la Ligue en Champagne*. 2 vols. Paris, 1887–92.

Hernault, Anthoine, ed. *Edictz et ordonnances royaux, pancartes arrests & déclarations sur le faict des traictes & impositions foraines d'Anjou*. Angers, 1629.

Hotot, Gilles, publ. *Recueil des lettres, tiltres & contracts des acquisitions faictes par la communauté des marchands fréquentans la rivière de Loire* . . . . Orléans, 1651.

Houzé, Jean, publ. *Edicts et ordonnances royaulx, sur l'établissement de la iustice de la Cour des aides* . . . . Paris, 1597.

Hughes, Edward. *Studies in Administration and Finance, 1558–1825*. Manchester, 1934.

Imbart de la Tour, P. *Les origines de la Réforme*. 2d ed. 3 vols. Melun, 1946–48.

Imberdis, André. *Histoire des guerres religieuses en Auvergne pendant les XVIe et XVIIe siècles*. 2d ed. Riom, 1846.

Isambert, F. A., et al., eds. *Recueil général des anciennes lois françaises, depuis l'an 420, jusqu'à la Révolution de 1789*. 29 vols. Paris, 1822–33.

Isnard, Albert. *Catalogue général des livres imprimés de la Bibliothèque Nationale. Actes Royaux*. Vol. 1, *Depuis l'origine jusqu'à Henri IV*, Paris, 1910.

Jacqueton, Georges. *Documents relatifs à l'administration financière de la France de Charles VII à François Ier, 1443–1523*. Paris, 1891.

———. "Le Trésor de l'Epargne sous François Ier (1523–1547)." *Revue Historique* 55 and 56 (1894).

Karcher, Aline. "L'Assemblée des Notables de Saint-Germain-en-Laye, 1583." *Bibliothèque de l'Ecole des Chartes* 114 (1956).

La Barre, René-Laurent. *Formulaire des esleuz* . . . . Rouen, 1622.

Lafaurie, Jean. *Les monnaies des rois de France: Hugues Capet à Louis XII*. Paris, 1951.

Lafaurie, Jean, and Prieur, Pierre. *Les monnaies des rois de France: François Ier à Henri IV*. Paris, 1956.

Lapeyre, Henri. *Une famille de marchands, les Ruiz*. Paris, 1955.

Laurière, E. J., et al., eds. *Ordonnances des roys de France de la troisième race*. 22 vols. Paris, 1723–1847.

Lavisse, Ernest, ed. *Histoire de France depuis les origines jusqu'à la Révolution*. 9 vols., each in 2 parts. Paris, 1900–11.

Leché, Marin, ed. *Edict du roy, sur le règlement général des tailles.* Paris, 1658.

Leclerc, Joseph. *Toleration and the Reformation.* 2 vols. New York, 1961.

Lemoine, H. "L'incendie du Palais de Justice et le disparition des archives de la Cour des aides." *Bibliothèque de l'Ecole des Chartes* 94 (1933).

Lemonnier, Henry. *Les guerres d'Italie: La France sous Charles VIII, Louis XII, et François Ier.* Lavisse series, vol. 5, part 1. Paris, 1903.

————. *La lutte contre la maison d'Autriche: La France sous Henri II (1519–1559).* Lavisse series, vol. 5, part 2. Paris, 1911.

L'Estoile, Pierre de. *Registre-Journal. Nouvelle Collection des mémoires pour servir à l'histoire de France.* 2d ser., vol. 1, parts 1 and 2. Paris, 1837–38.

Lewis, Ewart. *Medieval Political Ideas.* 2 vols. New York, 1954.

Lewis, P. S. "The Failure of the French Medieval Estates." *Past and Present,* no. 23 (Nov. 1962).

Liautey, André. *La hausse des prix et la lutte contre la cherté en France au XVIe siècle.* Paris, 1921.

Livet, Georges. *Les Guerres de Religion.* Que Sais-Je? Paris, 1966.

Lot, Ferdinand, and Fawtier, Robert. *Histoire des institutions françaises au moyen âge.* Vol. 1, *Institutions seigneuriales.* Vol. 2, *Institutions royales.* Paris, 1958.

————. *Le premier budget de la monarchie française. Le compte générale de 1202–1203.* Paris, 1932.

Luchaire, Achille. *Louis VII à Louis VIII.* Lavisse series, vol. 3, part 1. Paris, 1901.

Lyon, Bryce D. *From Fief to Indenture.* Cambridge, Mass., 1957.

Lyon, Bryce D., and Verhulst, A. E. *Medieval Finance: A Comparison of Financial Institutions in Northwestern Europe.* Providence, R.I., 1967.

Major, J. Russell. "The Crown and the Aristocracy in Renaissance France." *American Historical Review* 69 (April 1964).

————. *The Deputies to the Estates General in Renaissance France.* Madison, Wis., 1960.

————. *The Estates General of 1560.* Princeton, 1951.

————. "French Representative Assemblies: Research Opportunities and Research Published." In *Studies in Medieval and Renaissance History,* vol. 1, ed. Wm. N. Bowsky. Lincoln, Nebr., 1964.

————. "The French Monarchy as Seen through the Estates General." *Studies in the Renaissance* 9 (1962).

————. "Henry IV and Guyenne: A Study Concerning Origins of Royal Absolutism," *French Historical Studies* 4, no. 4 (1966).

————. *Representative Institutions in Renaissance France, 1421–1559.* Madison, Wis., 1960.

Mariéjol, J. H. *La Réforme et la Ligue*. Lavisse series, vol. 6, part 1. Paris, 1904.

———. *Henri IV et Louis XIII*. Lavisse series, vol. 6, part 2. Paris, 1905.

Marion, Marcel. *Dictionnaire des institutions de la France aux XVIIe et XVIIIe siècles*. Paris, 1923.

Matthews, George T. *The Royal General Farms in Eighteenth-Century France*. New York, 1958.

Mettayer, P., ed. *Recueil de plusieurs édicts, lettres patentes, déclarations . . . concernants le pouvoir & iurisdiction de la Chambre du Thrésor*. Paris, 1617.

Meynial, Ed. "Etudes sur l'histoire financière du XVIe siècle." *Nouvelle Revue Historique de Droit Français et Etranger* 44 (1920); 45 (1921).

———. "Etudes sur la gabelle du sel avant le XVIIè siècle en France," *Revue d'Histoire du Droit* 3 (1922); 4 (1923).

Mirot, L. *Les insurrections urbaines au début du règne de Charles VI (1380–1383)*. Paris, 1906.

Miskimin, Harry A. "The Last Act of Charles V: The Economic Background of the Revolts of 1382." *Speculum* 38, no. 3 (1963).

Monstr'oeil, Claude, ed. *Recueil des édicts du roy, et arrests de la Cour des Aydes, concernans le règlement des tailles . . . .* Paris, 1613.

Mousnier, Roland. *La vénalité des offices sous Henri IV et Louis XIII*. Rouen, 1946.

Nef, John U. *Industry and Government in France and England, 1540–1640*. Philadelphia, 1940.

———. "Prices and Industrial Capitalism in France and England," chap. 6 in *The Conquest of the Material World*. Chicago, 1964.

Nortier, Michel. "Le sort des archives dispersées de la Chambre des Comptes de Paris." *Bibliothèque de l'Ecole des Chartes* 123 (1965).

ORD. See Laurière.

Pasquier, Estienne. *Lettres historiques pour les années 1556–1594*. Edited by D. Thickett. Geneva, 1966.

Petit, Joseph; Gavrilovitch, M.; and Gavrilovitch, T. *Essaie de restitution des plus anciens mémoriaux de la Chambre des comptes de Paris*. Paris, 1899.

Petit-Dutaillis, Ch. *Charles VII, Louis XI et les premières années de Charles VIII*. Lavisse series, vol. 4, part 2. Paris, 1902.

Philippe, Jean, ed. *Edits et ordonnances du roy concernans l'autorité et iurisdiction des Cours des aides de France, sous le nom de celle de Montpellier . . . .* Lyons, 1561.

Picot, Georges. *Histoire des Etats Généraux*. 2d ed. 5 vols. Paris, 1888.

Poisson, Abbé H. *Histoire de Bretagne*. 3d ed. Rennes, 1959.

Prentout, Henri. *Les états provinciaux de Normandie*. 2 vols. Caen, 1925–27.

Quantin, Maximilien. *Histoire des impôts aux comté et élection d'Auxerre au XVIe siècle, 1578–1585.* Auxerre, 1874.

Rey, Maurice. *Le domaine du roi et les finances extraordinaires sous Charles VI, 1388–1413.* Paris, 1965.

———. *Les finances royales sous Charles VI: les causes du déficit, 1388–1413.* Paris, 1965.

Rolland du Plessis, Nicholas. *Remonstrances . . . sur les desordres et misères de ce royaume . . . .* Paris, 1588.

Romier, Lucien. *Lettres et chevauchées du bureau des finances de Caen.* Rouen and Paris, 1910.

Rousset, Jean, ed. *Les ordonnances faictes par le roy et ses prédécesseurs sur le faict de sa Chambre des comptes en Bretaigne.* Tours, 1556.

Schnapper, Bernard. *Les rentes au XVIe siècle.* Paris, 1957.

Sée, Henri. *Louis XI et les villes.* Paris, 1890.

Sée, Henri; Rébillon, Armand; and Préclin, Edmond. *Le XVIe siècle.* Clio. Paris, 1950.

Serbat, Louis. *Les assemblées du clergé de France: origines, organisation, développement, 1561–1615,* Paris, 1906.

Spont, Alfred. "L'équivalent aux aides en Languedoc, de 1450 à 1515." *Annales du Midi* 3 (1891).

———. "La gabelle du sel en Languedoc." *Annales du Midi* 3 (1891).

———. *Semblançay (?–1527): La bourgeoisie financière au début du XVIe siècle.* Paris, 1895.

———. "La taille en Languedoc, de 1450 à 1515." *Annales du Midi* 2 (1890).

Spooner, Frank C. *L'économie mondiale et les frappes monétaires en France, 1493–1680.* Paris, 1956.

Stephenson, Carl. *Medieval Institutions: Selected Essays.* Edited by Bryce D. Lyon. Ithaca, N.Y., 1954.

Strayer, Joseph Reese. *The Administration of Normandy under Saint Louis.* Cambridge, Mass., 1932.

Strayer, Joseph Reese, and Taylor, Charles H. *Studies in Early French Taxation.* Cambridge, Mass., 1939.

Sully, *Mémoires des sages et royales oeconomies d'estat . . . . Nouvelle collection des mémoires relatifs à l'histoire de France.* Edited by Michaud and Poujoulat, 2d ser., vols. 2 and 3. Paris, 1837.

Sutherland, N. M. *The French Secretaries of State in the Age of Catherine de Medici.* London, 1962.

Thomas, Antoine. *Les états provinciaux de la France centrale sous Charles VII.* 2 vols. Paris, 1879.

Thompson, James Westfall. *The Wars of Religion in France, 1559–1576.* Chicago, 1909.

———, ed. *The Letters and Documents of Armand de Gontaut, Baron de*

Biron, Marshal of France (1524–1592), Collected by the Late Sidney Hellman Ehrman, 2 vols. Berkeley, 1936.

Le Thrésor du nouveau stille et prothocolle de la Chancellerie de France. Rev. ed. Paris, 1599.

Traitté des finances de France, 1580. In Archives curieuses de l'histoire de France. 1st ser., vol. 9. Paris, 1836.

Vannier, Jean. *Essai sur le bureau des finances de la généralité de Rouen, 1551–1790.* Rouen, 1927.

Le vestige des finances. (An appendix to *Le Thrésor du nouveau stille et prothocolle.* Paris, 1599.) Reprinted in Jacqueton, *Documents,* pp. 205–42.

Vuitry, Ad. *Etudes sur le régime financier de la France avant la Révolution de 1789.* 3 vols. Paris, 1878–83.

———. *L'origine et l'établissement de l'impôt sous les trois premiers Valois (1328–1380).* Paris, 1883.

Wilkinson, Maurice. *A History of the League or Sainte Union, 1576–1595.* Glasgow, 1929.

Wolfe, Martin. "French Views on Wealth and Taxes from the Middle Ages to the Old Régime." *Journal of Economic History* 26, no. 4 (1966).

———. "Jean Bodin on Taxes: The Sovereignty-Taxes Paradox." *Political Science Quarterly* 83, no. 2 (1968).

Zeller, Gaston. "Gouverneurs de provinces au XVIe siècle." *Revue Historique* 185 (1939).

———. *Les institutions de la France au XVIe siècle.* Paris, 1948.

———. "Aux origines de notre système douanier: les premières taxes à l'importation." *Publications de la Faculté des Lettres de Strasbourg,* fasc. 106 (1947).

Index

Where a definition is necessary, and when an entry has more than one page reference, the italicized numbers indicate which reference provides a definition.